BLUEPRINT FOR A NEW AMERICA

Can We Save the World's Most Admired Republic?

Karl Albrecht, Ph.D.

http://KarlAlbrecht.com
http://Blueprint-For-A-New-America.com

D1500005

Foreword:
Major Garrett

GO SANE. Those two words transfixed me as a child. GO SANE was the personalized California license plate of my best friend's father. Because my best friend, Steve Albrecht, was an only child and his parents had divorced, visits from his dad were a big deal. Whatever we did—play catch with a football or baseball, get something to eat or go to the park—I saw those two words as he drove up or drove away.

GO SANE. I first saw those words when I was twelve years old. I have never shaken them, or rather they continue to shake me. All children take cues from authority figures. My best friend's dad certainly was. Plus, he had a Ph.D. and was a member of Mensa. I didn't learn until much later in life what those two distinctions meant. As a child, I just knew my best friend's dad was really, really smart.

GO SANE. It sounded like an order. And a wish. Also a direction. When I was a teen, my father faced enormous mental health difficulties and suddenly GO SANE took on tender, aspirational, and heart-breaking qualities.

Karl Albrecht is my best friend's father. I have known him most of my life. Because of my work I have met presidents and prime ministers, foreign secretaries and finance ministers, scientists and theologians, lawyers and industrialists. Yet I met one of the most brilliant and accomplished people in my life at age eight. He was, and is, Karl Albrecht.

This book is not like others Karl has written. I haven't read all of his books, though I probably should have. But I know Karl's biggest works and they have been devoted to understanding how people think, why things happen and how to make the unsatisfactory satisfactory. Karl studies systems and looks for logical and practical remedies.

But he's not only a practical thinker. By that I mean he is not conventional or constrained. He's imaginative and inquisitive —which means he will ask questions that shatter myths or suggest well-placed disdain for them. Sharp minds can be rude. In journalism the phrase "afflict the comfortable and comfort the afflicted" is now dangerously close to a cliché. For Karl, afflicting the illogical is first and second nature.

This book is a grand thought exercise about the American Republic. It is not in any way ideological, at least as we have come to understand the "left" and "right" axes of contemporary politics. It is not polemical either. Karl attacks neither party nor for any length of time any particular office holder. He actually attacks nothing other than our mindless federal go-about-ism.

I came to Washington in 1990 and started covering Congress and national politics. Over the decades I've noticed that, as the partisan volume has increased, idea generation has decreased. Ask yourself. Can you remember the last time you heard a federal politician of either party suggest a new idea or approach that stopped you in your tracks? I'm guessing not. Even ideas that pass for "big" in this campaign season— Medicare for All, the Green New deal, reciprocal trade, or breaking up Facebook and Google—piggyback on existing programs, seek to revive atrophied regulatory agencies or, reach back to 19th century economic dogmas.

Blueprint for a New America bristles with new questions; new ideas; new constructs and new remedies. It asks, and answers, questions about the fundamentals of this Republic, our concept of liberty and cohesiveness, our purpose for one another, and our example to the world. It also is daringly practical about what isn't working and what fixes we should consider. The chapters on national defense, crime and punishment, immigration and taxation brim with useful data and overflow with edgy ideas about better and more technologically coherent solutions.

I don't endorse these ideas. I endorse their existence. Trust me, Washington's biggest problem isn't corruption. By any historical standard of graft, vote-manipulation, party power-plays or venality, Washington is cleaner than it's ever been. *Washington's most desperate problem is the lack of imagination*; its absolute desert of ideas; its intellectual stasis. Ideologically, Washington is as loud as a chain saw cutting rebar. Intellectually, it is inert.

Blueprint for a New America isn't the first treatise abut what ails our beloved country. But it is the first I have seen of its kind. It is not futuristic as much as it is "Hey, there's a future. Ought we not think about it?" *Thinking* is the key. *Blueprint for a New America* is concentrated originality. For those who disagree with its recommendations, I implore you to produce a second, a third, a fourth and a fifth blueprint.

What paralyzes Washington most now is not the presence of lobbyists but *the absence of radical structural imagination*. *Blueprint for a New America* refreshes as it challenges; invigorates as it punctures; and like America itself it does so with optimism and a brash sense that the future is ours to imagine, shape and improve.

GO SANE. Then as now a way forward. For me. For my best friend. Possibly now for our country.

Major Garrett
Washington, DC
Chief Washington Correspondent, CBS News
Host/Creator of "The Takeout" podcast
Author, *Mr. Trump's Wild Ride*

Preface:
Why I Wrote this Book

Imagine . . .

. . . an old house—one you've lived in for a long time. You grew up there. Your memories, your experiences, your joys, and your sorrows all connect to this comfortable—if slightly dilapidated—old homestead.

And now, you've inherited the old place. While you love it and cherish it, you also realize that it needs some improvements. Years of fixing and patching and painting and scrubbing and scraping have kept it habitable, but you know that the time has come to modernize it. It needs remodeling.

Now you face the very personal question: How can I modernize it and still keep its essential character—the things I love and value about it?

By analogy, that question confronts all Americans as we accept responsibility for the future of the Republic we've inherited. Do we content ourselves with continuing to live in the same old house, and neglect its upkeep? Or do we take seriously our responsibility for its future?

Let's all acknowledge that we live in an *axial age*—a big-time turning point in the life of the great American Republic. We'll get the Republic we deserve, and we'll bequeath whatever remains of it to our children and their children.

This book represents an attempt to set out, in a fairly organized way, the possibilities we can see for the New

America. I've chosen the metaphor of the blueprint, and the related metaphor of remodeling, to emphasize the crucial need to marry the old and the new in an organized, intelligent, and loving way.

We'll sketch the blueprint in terms of *ten key building blocks* that a successful republic needs. In each of these ten remodeling categories, I'll attempt to spell out the need for change and identify some interesting options for improving the way the Republic can meet the challenges.

As a management consultant with a thirty-year career in studying successful leaders and successful enterprises, I assess the main problem we face in rethinking our Republic as a basic and profound *lack of vision and imagination.* Without visionary leadership, I see us as collectively sleepwalking into a very dangerous future.

Our electoral process has given us a long parade of mediocre thinkers—with a few notable exceptions—who have occupied the White House and the Congress. We seem to systematically eliminate the people with the big ideas and bold solutions. We seem to prefer demagogues, charmers, hero figures, populists, and those who pander to our fears, phobias, and selfish interests.

Does my declaration sound a bit extreme? Good. In this book, *I invite you to think extremely.* I want you to look beyond the old thinking and the old cliches, and connect the dots that most others don't even see. George Bernard Shaw declared, "Some men see things as they are and ask, Why? I dream of things that never were and ask, Why not?" In this book, we take the second path.

Would you like a simple and telling example of this woeful lack of imagination in the way we operate our Republic? Try this one: Why, if we claim we want all citizens to vote in national elections, have we always held elections on a weekday—a Tuesday—when most employed people have to work at their jobs? Why don't we hold elections on a Saturday, for example, and make it a national holiday? The reasons might have made sense 100 years ago, but they hardly make sense now. Why haven't we changed this rule? Because, collectively, *we just didn't bother to.*

I only ask that you, the reader, approach this journey with an open mind. As difficult as it can seem at certain times and certain points in this exploration, I ask you to suspend your judgment—*all the way to the end of the reading journey.*

Let's think of this journey into republic-building as a short course in *system thinking.*

As with any system, the various subsystems of the republic must fit together in a special way. Understanding how one solution works can depend on understanding how another one fits together with it. Please get the whole picture before you give in to the temptation to shoot down any one piece of it. Let's judge all of the innovations presented here against the perspective of the overall concept for the new Republic.

You'll discover, as you read, that I like to use our history as a starting point for thinking about our future. I have good company here: the ancient Chinese philosopher Confucius reportedly advised: "If you would divine your future, first study your past." And, brother Mark Twain offered, "History doesn't repeat itself, but it often rhymes."

So, in many cases, I'll offer a short flashback to the relevant stories, episodes, and events that have brought us to our present reality. I hope you'll find some of these little historical brain snacks interesting in their own way, and more importantly that you'll see how they might inform our understanding of the big questions in front of us.

We'll also make it a habit to zero in on the "mega-facts" of each dimension or issue—the defining truths that can help us frame our understanding and think creatively about new possibilities.

Enough talking. Let's roll up our sleeves and get to work.

Table of Contents

Chapter 1.
What Makes a
Successful Republic?

*"If destruction be our lot,
We ourselves must be its
author and finisher."*
—Abraham Lincoln

If we hope to draw up a blueprint for our improved Republic, we first need to agree on what a successful republic looks like. What main parts, or building blocks, does it need and how do they go together to make it work?

How do these all-important building blocks interconnect and interact with one another? What human processes make them come to life?

What makes a successful republic different from, say, a totalitarian dictatorship? A banana republic? A monarchy? A one-party communistic state?

We need a "model house," so to speak, to give us a starting point for our blueprint. Once we have a clear understanding of the building blocks, we can begin to fit them together and discover the possibilities for improving them.

Let's see what a model republic might look like.

Reader Alert: I need to borrow your gray matter for this chapter and also the second one, so we can proceed from a reliable basis of factual and historical evidence as we consider the possibilities for our remodeling venture. I want to refresh your knowledge of some of the very basic, very crucial, and very interesting human events and stories that have brought us to where we now stand.

If you found high-school history deadly boring (as I did), or you now find yourself feeling impatient to skip over the "content" and get to the "how-to" part, I'll forgive you.

For my part I hope to convey some sense of the fascination I've experienced in my adult life as I've purposely delved into the human stories that have had such an impact on the present state of our Republic. If you'll go with me patiently on that journey of discovery and rediscovery, I believe you'll have a much deeper understanding of the creative possibilities we'll explore and a greater confidence in evaluating their potential.

And you might learn some really interesting stuff.

THE TEN BUILDING BLOCKS OF A SUCCESSFUL REPUBLIC

From its very founding, the architects of a successful republic have to get certain things right in order for the new enterprise to survive and thrive. Some things have to come first. In their approximate order of urgency, let's consider solutions to the following challenges. Figure 1-1 illustrates these 10 basic components, or sub-systems, of a thriving republic.

1. **Governance**. What mechanism for control do we need? Who governs, how, and with what kind of authority? What kind of an organization or top-level system shall we create to solve the big problems, make the big decisions, manage resources, and make things work? Which aspects of the republic's life

should government control and which ones should it leave to the citizens?

2. **Defense.** Usually the leaders must immediately tend to the armed defense of the newborn republic, to avoid attack by rival states with opportunistic intentions. The republic needs some kind of defense force, even if it only consists of citizen soldiers with their own weapons.

3. **Law and Order.** Once they've ensured the survival of the new republic against external threats of invasion, the builders must quickly establish the basic elements of a civil society. This requires a set of rules for behavior, a system for enforcing them, punishments for violating the behavior code, and guidelines that determine how individuals must treat one another.

4. **Revenue.** Once the leaders have established an initial state of safety, security, and social stability, they need money to run the republic. This almost invariably requires some form of taxation imposed on the citizens, except perhaps in cases such as ancient Rome, in which foreign wars and ransoms for prisoners funded the republic, or in a few rare cases where the nation-state has control over valuable natural resources it can trade with others. But usually, taxes come next.

5. **Commerce.** Following closely on the heels of Law and Order and Revenue must come some kind of a system of laws governing the way people make use of natural resources and exchange their labor and goods in some kind of collective marketplace.

6. **Public Services.** In any successful republic the citizens expect their governing body to provide a range of services paid for out of the taxes they contribute. In addition to military security and law and order, they often expect things like infrastructure

development, support for commerce, public welfare, and education.

7. **Civil Liberties**. In a democratic republic, "governments are instituted amongst [men], deriving their just powers from the consent of the governed," as the American Declaration of Independence prescribes. Following on from that philosophy, governments must not have the power to deprive citizens of life, liberty, or property without "due process of law." This critical principle requires the existence of an explicit set of laws and standards that specify the rights of individuals and the limited conditions under which governments might have the authority to over-ride them.

8. **Immigration**. Most nation-states have accepted incoming foreigners as visitors, traders, and also as prospective residents. In modern times all major governments have had to evolve rules, policies, practices, and methods for controlling the inflow of outsiders and for assimilating them into the native population.

9. **Foreign Relations**. The founders and leaders of every republic must sooner or later figure out how to get along with the other nation-states in its environment. They need basic policies, practices, and mechanisms for promoting peace, trade, mutual defense, and cooperation. Once the newborn republic comes to life, along come treaties and trade agreements.

10. **Environment**. To head off violent conflicts over land, water, and other natural resources, the founders must establish a system of rights for the use of natural resources. From there they must proceed to develop various shared resources that enable the society to thrive and grow, such as cities and towns, roads, bridges, waterways, forests, and farmlands.

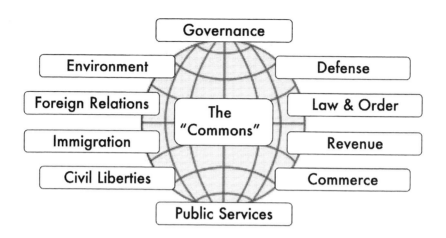

Figure 1-1. The Architecture of a Successful Republic

THE FOUNDERS GOT IT (MOSTLY) RIGHT

The Republic we inherited from the Founders provides for all ten of the key components we've just explored and some more besides. I've often mused that, either they had the benefit of some kind of divine guidance, or they must have had some awesome mental capacities. They managed to create a system and a process that has withstood the challenges and stresses of two centuries of turmoil, as well as the misguided ambitions of more than a handful of bumbling leaders—in the White House, in the Congress, and even the Supreme Court.

It might help us in our thinking about the new American Republic to recap the birth process of our enterprise, in the hands of the statesmen and big thinkers who figured it out. Understanding that process can help us think about the still-basic issues we have to tackle going forward.

First, let's remind ourselves that the American Republic came into existence in several difficult phases. No magic wand or act of one man created it from scratch.

The first challenge dealt with the break-away of the "thirteen original colonies" from the colonial authority of England. Bear in mind that the "United States of America" didn't exist then, except possibly as a figment of the imaginations of a few zealots. No "Americans" existed at that time. Almost all of the colonists held British citizenship. And *many of them had no desire to separate from the mother country*—they just wanted better treatment and respect for their rights as British citizens. Even the legendary George Washington had served as an officer in the British army during the war with the French and Indians.

THE US CONSTITUTION: A MASTERPIECE OF POLITICAL LITERATURE

This proto-republic had no real constitution, no collective laws, no army, no single currency, and no treasury. The nearest approximation to a guiding document, the Articles of Confederation, adopted in 1781, had laid out a basis for cooperation amongst the thirteen separate colonies. They had always governed themselves individually, with the permission and frequent interference of the British crown.

The legendary Declaration of Independence of 1776 didn't refer to them as a single unified republic. It only said that " . . . these united colonies are, and of right ought to be, free and independent states." That meant that, at the beginning, they thought of themselves as somewhat like 13 miniature countries, each with its unique culture, values, and priorities.

A DIFFICULT BIRTH

After the seven-year War for Independence ended in 1781 with the surrender of British forces at Yorktown, Virginia, and the eventual peace treaty in Paris in 1783, it took another four years for the colonies to turn themselves into a real republic. By 1788 they had an actual constitution that bound them together under a single national government. As every American school student forced to memorize the famous Preamble knows, a single elegant sentence laid out the entire concept of the Republic:

"We the People of the United States, in Order to form a more perfect Union, establish Justice, insure domestic Tranquility, provide for the common defence, promote the general Welfare, and secure the Blessings of Liberty to ourselves and our Posterity, do ordain and establish this Constitution for the United States of America."

That one powerful statement just about sums up the design of the Republic we have today and it will help to inform our work ahead as we tackle the challenge of modernizing it.

Let's take a quick recap of our founding document and remind ourselves of the way it evolved.

The original Constitution, adopted in 1787, had a mere seven "articles," each one a brief chapter that defined how some component of the Republic would work.

▸ *Article I* created the Legislative Branch, consisting of the House of Representatives and the Senate.

▸ *Article II* created the Executive Branch, consisting of the presidency and the vice presidency. It prescribed the various departments of government and defined—as well as limited—the authority of the president. Interestingly, the Executive Branch came second on their list, after the Legislative Branch.

▸ *Article III* created the Judicial Branch, consisting of the Supreme Court and the system of federal courts under it.

▸ *Article IV* defined the rights of the individual states in relation to the power of the federal government and confirmed their equal status and obligations to cooperate.

▸ *Article V* defined the process for amending the Constitution, which can originate with either the Congress or the individual states.

- *Article VI* confirmed the Constitution as the "supreme law of the land" as well as the supremacy of all laws originating from it. It also required all federal and state officials to swear an oath recognizing the primacy of the Constitution and promising to uphold it. Curiously, the Constitution spells out the President's oath, word for word: "I do solemnly swear (or affirm) that I will faithfully execute the Office of President of the United States, and will to the best of my Ability, preserve, protect and defend the Constitution of the United States."

- *Article VII* recorded the names of the state representatives who signed the first version of the Constitution.

About a year later, in 1788, nine of the thirteen states—the required two-thirds majority—had ratified the new Constitution. The new government threw the switch to formally begin operating as a republic about a year after that, in 1789. Not until 1790 had all thirteen states formally ratified it, however.

CONSTITUTIONAL AMENDMENTS: HOW THE REPUBLIC EVOLVES

Various states and important political thinkers had different gripes about the first version the Constitution, and some wanted their special concerns added. One particular issue, the lack of an explicit statement about civil liberties, dogged the debates for a long time. Fans of this issue wanted assurance of strict limits on the power of the federal government and the protection of individual rights. Some of them pointed to the long history of abuse by English monarchs and they wanted a modern day *Magna Carta* for the new Republic.

The committee appointed to draft the Constitution had promised to add a series of amendments for that purpose. That commitment helped to motivate the rest of the states to ratify it. In 1791, two years after the kick-off of the new

Republic, they added ten amendments, now famously known as the Bill of Rights. The original shopping list had 12 proposals but two of them didn't survive the ratification process by the states.

As of this writing, the US Constitution has had 27 amendments. After the first 10 amendments—the Bill of Rights, which we'll review shortly—came:

- The *Eleventh Amendment*, ratified in 1795, made the individual states immune from lawsuits filed by individuals or by other states.

- The *Twelfth Amendment*, ratified in 1804, provided for the election of the president and vice president as separate offices. Previously, the Constitution specified that the candidate with the most votes would become president and the runner-up would become vice president. That didn't work very well.

- The *Thirteenth Amendment*, ratified shortly after the end of the great Civil War in 1865, outlawed slavery. It became the first part of the Constitution to govern the actions of individual citizens—slave owners—as well as governments.

- Beginning with the thirteenth, Congress routinely affirmed its right to pass laws to enforce the provisions, by including some variation of the phrase, *"Congress shall have power to enforce this article by appropriate legislation."*

- The *Fourteenth Amendment*, ratified three years after that, jumbled four unrelated directives into one package. It confirmed the right of citizenship for anyone born in the US, including former slaves, and it guaranteed equal protection under the law to all citizens.

- Congress added a clever bargaining chip to the amendment, specifying that no one who had participated in the "Confederate rebellion" could serve in Congress or hold any public office at either a state or federal level. But it specified that Congress could waive that restriction by a two-thirds vote in each house. Congress required all of the Southern states to ratify the thirteenth and fourteenth amendments as a condition of readmission to the Union and representation in Congress. Then they lifted the prohibition.

▸ The *Fifteenth Amendment*, ratified in 1870, specifically prohibited the denial of voting rights "on account of race, color, or previous condition of servitude," but curiously, didn't specify that women could vote. Female voting rights would have to wait for another 50 years, well into the next century.

▸ The *Sixteenth Amendment*, ratified 40 years later in 1913, gave Congress the power to impose a federal income tax.

▸ The *Seventeenth Amendment*, also ratified in 1913, gave citizens the right to vote for their Senators. Before that, surprisingly, state legislatures had always appointed the Senators. The people had always had the right to vote for their representatives in the House but not in the Senate until the amendment passed.

▸ The *Eighteenth Amendment*—the infamous "prohibition" law, ratified in 1920—outlawed the manufacture, sale, and transportation of alcoholic beverages throughout the country.

▸ The *Nineteenth Amendment*, mentioned previously, finally gave women the right to vote. Strangely, the first woman elected to Congress, Jeanette Rankin from Montana, won a seat in the House of Representatives in 1916, four years before women could vote. She could run for Congress but couldn't vote for herself. Rebecca Felton of Georgia became the first woman to serve in the US Senate, in 1922.

▸ The *Twentieth Amendment*, long needed but only ratified in 1933, corrected a strange provision that specified the starting and ending dates of Congressional terms.

▸ The *Twenty-First Amendment* repealed the Eighteenth Amendment. Although Prohibition had quickly and obviously failed, and it led to a massive increase in illicit trafficking in alcohol and organized crime, it hung on for thirteen years—1920 through 1933—before Congress got around to repealing it.

▸ The *Twenty-Second Amendment*, ratified in 1951, set term limits for the presidency. Before that, Franklin D. Roosevelt won four consecutive terms, spanning the great Depression and the Second World War. The amendment dictated that any person elected president, or any person who has held the office of president for more than two years (as in the case of the successor to a president who didn't complete a full term) cannot serve more than one more term. That had the effect of limiting elected presidents to 8 years, and ascended vice presidents to less than 10 years, total, in office.

▸ The *Twenty-Third Amendment*, ratified in 1961, gave Washington, DC three votes in the electoral college and made DC residents formally a part of the process of electing the president. The Constitution has always identified the DC as a special federal district, not a state, having authorized the government to carve it out of land granted by the states of Maryland and Virginia, in 1791. It operates under the direct jurisdiction of the Congress and as of his writing has no representatives in the House or Senate.

▸ The *Twenty-Fourth Amendment*, ratified in 1964, blocked the states from imposing poll taxes, which Southern political factions had used to discourage black people from voting.

▸ The *Twenty-Fifth Amendment*, ratified in 1967, provided a new way for removing a failing president, as an alternative to impeachment. The original Constitution didn't cover a situation where the president might become ill, incapacitated, or mentally incompetent. With this new procedure, the vice president and a majority of cabinet members can notify both houses of Congress that they've determined that the current president can no longer handle the job. Just as with impeachment, the Senate would have to vote as a two-thirds majority to remove the president and make the vice president the head of state.

▸ The *Twenty-Sixth Amendment*, ratified in 1971, reduced the voting age for US citizens to 18 years. During the political turmoil of the Vietnam War the slogan "Old enough to fight, old enough to vote" won popular support for the change.

▸ And the *Twenty-Seventh Amendment*, first proposed by James Madison in 1789 and approved by Congress, languished in political darkness for almost 200 years before ratification in 1971. It prevented the members of Congress from voting themselves pay raises that would take effect during their current terms of office. Any pay increase for an individual member's position cannot become effective until after his or her current elected term has expired.

As of this writing, nearly fifty years have gone by since the last time we amended our founding document. The process of changing the Constitution takes time, patience, and a lot of persuasion. Most of the Founders wanted it that way.

THE BALANCE OF POWERS: THE BRILLIANT CORE CONCEPT

Will Rogers, America's cowboy philosopher, liked to say, "You ought to be glad you're not getting all the government you're paying for." We can take him literally on that point, and maybe the Founders wanted it that way, too.

The ingenious three-part design of the Republic they came up with—the Executive Branch, the Legislative Branch, and the

Judicial Branch—has given us a remarkably stable enterprise, but at the expense of speed, efficiency, a bit of frustration, and, very often, grudging compromise.

In the jargon of today's techno-culture, we can think of it as "a feature, not a bug"—an advantage and not a flaw.

Locking the three branches of the government into a three-way combination of cooperation and conflict made sure that no one branch could out-maneuver the others and dominate the process of governing. I often think of this famous "separation of powers," or "balance of powers," as something like that three-legged race we used to run at picnics as kids. Two kids would run side by side, with their inside legs tied together at the ankles, hobbling comically to the finish line. Imagine that three kids had to hop as a team, with their legs tied together, and you get something like the political dance the Founders bequeathed to, or inflicted upon us.

NO KINGS, PLEASE

The Founders certainly understood the consequences of their design. They had all grown up under the rule of the English crown and they knew all too well the legacy of unbridled monarchical power. England had a long history of bitter and violent conflicts between kings, landowners, and members of Parliament, several times leading to all-out war and once even to the fall of the monarchy.

And they had studied the governing concepts of the other major nations of Europe. In particular, they had watched nervously the turmoil in France, which ultimately led to the bloody revolution there just a few years after the adoption of the US Constitution. After several years of mob rule and a failed attempt at restoring the monarch to the throne, France fell into the hands of Napoleon, who appointed himself Emperor.

The Founders wanted a new model.

They struggled mightily to define the role of the head of state for the new Republic. None of them wanted a European-style king with unchecked power and no job description. Interestingly, a contingent of activists had earlier tried to sell the idea of appointing George Washington as king of the new country. Given his phenomenal popularity after the RevWar, he might have ascended to a new American throne. But Washington himself opposed the idea more vehemently than anyone else.

With the idea of a standard king out the window and yet still wanting a strong head of state, the Founders settled on the idea of a mini-king—a president, elected by the people, and limited to a four-year reign. No divine right, no right of inheritance, no option for violent overthrow by other pretenders to the throne. They reduced the role of the monarch to an executive job.

The Founders also set limits on the length of service by the members of Congress—six years for the Senate and two years for the House of Representatives. They expected each of them to renew their mandate of governance by standing for election again when their terms expired. They wanted to ensure that members of Congress couldn't seize power and hold it indefinitely.

They rejected England's ancient concept of *peerage*, which gave wealthy landowners and favored nobles special status in the Parliament. To this day the British House of Lords holds the status of the "upper house," with the privilege of reviewing, approving, and overturning acts of the "lower house," or the House of Commons as the British know it.

Instead of dividing the American version of Parliament into a chamber for nobles and a chamber for commoners, the Founders opted for a Senate with the same number of seats —two—for each state; and a House of Representatives with the number of seats for each state determined by its population.

HOW THE SUPREME COURT BECAME SUPREME

The third key component of the Republic, the Supreme Court and the system of federal courts under it, also evolved significantly in the early years. As with many other developments in our way of doing things, this one came with a big-time drama.

In the 1800 election, Thomas Jefferson won the presidency, succeeding John Adams. In the interval of a few weeks before leaving office, Adams tried to install as many cronies from his own party into positions of power as he could. He targeted the federal judiciary, hoping that partisan judges would frustrate many of Jefferson's new programs by striking them down when his opponents challenged them in the courts.

Adams' lame-duck Federalist Congress quickly created 16 new "circuit" court judgeships, which Adams quickly filled with his guys. This became one of the first instances of "midnight appointments," which we still see today in some administrations.

Adams believed he had the situation under control but an unforeseen courtroom drama derailed his plans.

One of Adams' cronies, a man named William Marbury, had not received his formal commission as a judge by the time Jefferson took office, and Jefferson blocked his appointment. Marbury petitioned the Supreme Court to issue what legal beagles call a *writ of mandamus*, a directive to force James Madison, Jefferson's Secretary of State, to grant the commission. The case, tagged "Marbury v. Madison" in the lingo of the legal world, became the historical landmark studied by legal scholars ever since.

The Chief Justice of the Supreme Court, a man named John Marshall, spotted an opportunity to fix what he considered a weak point in the Constitution. The text of the Constitution didn't define the Court's responsibility in a very specific way and not everyone agreed that it had the legal authority to overrule laws passed by Congress.

Marshall grabbed the chance to establish the Court's constitutional authority once and for all. He and his justices ruled that Adams' lame-duck Congress had violated the Constitution by passing the law that created the extra judges. They declared the law unconstitutional, making the specific issue of Marbury's job "moot," as legal people like to say.

Marshall didn't care much about Marbury's job one way or the other, but the ruling set in stone the Court's unquestioned authority to evaluate every law of the land—whether passed by Congress, a State, or a local government. The Court could *nullify any law* if they judged that it didn't square with the Founders' intentions as they read them in the Constitution.

By the way, the Constitution doesn't specify the number of Justices on the Supreme Court. These days we take it for granted that the Court should have nine Justices, but the Founders left that up to Congress. The Judiciary Act of 1789, right after the ratification of the new Constitution, set the number of Supreme Court justices at six: one chief justice and five associate justices.

At one time the head count had peaked at 10. Then, in a fierce battle with President Andrew Johnson, an angry Congress passed a law in 1866 cutting it to seven. They did it to prevent Johnson from appointing his cronies to the Court. After his term expired, they reset it to nine, in 1869. It has stayed there ever since.

In a later, despicable episode, President Franklin Roosevelt tried to "pack" the Court by pushing legislation in Congress that would allow him to appoint an almost indefinite number of new Justices. His motivation came from his frustration with having many of his "New Deal" initiatives struck down by the Court he inherited. His plan fizzled in Congress, however, and we've had 9 Justices ever since.

By the early 1800s the Constitution had survived its first shakedown and the balance of powers between the three branches of the Republic had pretty much taken the shape we see them in today.

FEDERAL POWER AND STATES' RIGHTS: TUG OF WAR OR CREATIVE BALANCE?

Once the Founders had figured out how to separate and balance the powers of the three branches of government, they had to tackle another big issue. They had to balance the interests—and the powers—of the thirteen new states with the authority of the national government. That part didn't come easily.

It involved a great deal of debate, political uproar, and animosity amongst the big thinkers who took up the challenge. More than once, the grand constitutional project almost crashed out when compromise seemed out of reach.

Two humongous issues dominated the ongoing conversation and the debates at the meetings, as they tried to frame a constitution for the new Republic: 1) the limits of federal power; and 2) the institution of slavery.

GOVERNMENT BY THE ELITE? OR GOVERNMENT BY THE IGNORANT MOB?

During the run-up to the meetings in Philadelphia to draft the new Constitution, a series of public conversations played out in the newspapers and gazette-style newsletters.

The actors in the constitutional drama soon ganged up into two major factions with opposing ideologies. They called themselves the Federalists and the Anti-Federalists.

The Federalists, led by Alexander Hamilton, James Madison, John Jay, and others wanted a strong central government. They believed that the excesses of the democratic process would lead to civil unrest, regional factionalism, loss of respect for law and order, and populist uprisings devoted to single issues.

They wanted to replace the old Articles of Confederation with a new and much stronger constitution, giving the national government a lot more power. They warned against the risk of making the destiny of the Republic dependent upon "the transient passions of the ignorant mob."

The more extreme Federalists preferred to think of the states as merely departments, so to speak, of the one central government. Federal laws would cascade down to the states, setting up a uniform pattern of government throughout all thirteen states and any new states to join in the future. They strongly favored ratification of the Constitution in its first basic form.

The Anti-Federalists, led by Thomas Jefferson, Patrick Henry, Samuel Adams, George Mason, and others, wanted a limited national government with most of the power in the hands of the various State governments. They wanted the Constitution to include provisions that specifically defined individual civil liberties and guaranteed that the national government could not infringe on them. For the most part, they opposed ratifying the first version unless it restricted national authority to suit their concerns.

The two super-stars of American politics at the time, George Washington and Benjamin Franklin, both preferred the first version but chose not to actively join either of the factions.

The debates raged on in the public media, as well as in private conversations, for nearly two years. The Federalists published a series of 85 essays in New York newspapers under the anonymous pen name "Publius." Each essay argued the merits of some aspect of their design for the new Republic. They eventually published them all in book form, under the title *The Federalist Papers*, which legal scholars study carefully to this very day.

The states finally approved and ratified the new document after a long debate, with two distasteful compromises: civil liberties and slavery. On the first point, the Federalists agreed that they would later amend the Constitution to include a Bill of Rights, satisfying the Anti-Federalists' demand for an explicit limitation on the powers of the national government and the courts.

WHAT TO DO ABOUT SLAVERY?

The second key issue, slavery, had split the Founders along a different fault line. Aside from Federalists and Anti-Federalists, the slave-owning states and non-slave states deadlocked on the treatment of slavery in the founding document. Several states in the North had outlawed slavery by that time but most others had not.

After bitter and rancorous debates the parties came to a crude compromise: the new Constitution would say nothing at all about slavery. This historical fact has caused great anguish to many who concern themselves with civil liberties and social justice. But most reputable historians seem to agree that, without this dishonorable compromise, the process would probably have failed and the new republic might not have had a constitution for decades.

OLD WOUNDS AND UNFINISHED BUSINESS

The slavery compromise, necessary as many have viewed it, served only to paint over a deep fissure in American politics and began a long-term friction between slave-holding states and non-slave states on the national level.

Ironically, England, the mother country, outlawed slavery by a fairly peaceful process in 1833. It would take the American Republic three more decades to do it, and then only at the cost of a devastating civil war that claimed the lives of over 600,000 of its citizens.

Before, during, and after the Civil War, a vast ideological gap separated North and South, as Americans referred to those two cultures and world views. The eventual fall of slavery only aggravated their differences, and a new phase in the relationship brought new patterns of conflict.

THE SOUTHERN "THEORY" OF SLAVERY

As we look back on the situation from our modern point of view, we may tend to simplify and polarize the differences. But historians point out that southern advocates had evolved a "theory" of slavery that they considered not only just and honorable, but morally superior to northern concepts of "free labor." It might help our understanding of the difficult recovery from the Civil War, to consider their carefully constructed justification.

Whereas northern advocates of abolition framed the slavery issue solely as a moral one—no humane society can justify allowing humans to own other humans—southern orators framed it differently. John C. Calhoun, in particular, delivered many passionate and stirring speeches about the benefits of slavery, for blacks as well as their owners.

Mr. Calhoun skillfully positioned slavery as a counter-alternative to the harsh working conditions that factories in England imposed on their workers, in the name of predatory capitalism. Workers there, he reminded his listeners, faced brutal and dehumanizing conditions; dirty and dangerous environments; long hours; starvation wages; and no benefits such as rest breaks, meals, or medical care. When they got too old to work, the factory owners just threw them out. No one had ever heard of a pension, health insurance, or a retirement program. "Free labor," as he characterized that system, didn't have much going for it.

Calhoun's moral position portrayed black people as fundamentally inferior to whites—intellectually, socially, and morally. He and other orators invoked biblical guidance to support that view and pointed out that nowhere in the Good Book does God disapprove of slavery. He argued that, without an institutional environment that gave black people some order and discipline in their lives, they would certainly regress to savage conditions, and they couldn't function successfully in a modern society.

Consequently, he argued, life on the plantation offered them benefits they otherwise could never have. On a humanely managed plantation, he explained, slaves would have a cradle to grave experience of security and social order. They received adequate housing, food, and even medical care.

Children didn't have to work in the fields before a reasonable age. When they got too old to work, they would typically live out their days peacefully, cared for by their masters until they passed away.

Further, Calhoun argued, many slaves received kindly attention from their owners and many reciprocated the feelings of affection. Many of them, he asserted, didn't want to leave the security of the plantation.

Calhoun had succeeded in turning a moral roadblock into a trade-off proposition. By skipping lightly over or around the inhuman practices such as violent capture, brutal punishments for attempting to escape, branding, rape, and selling off members of families to cover expenses, he gave pro-slave white people permission to think of themselves as benevolent saviors rather than selfish oppressors.

THE POSTWAR HANGOVER

After the Civil War, many southerners harbored a deep resentment toward the northern establishment, with three big strands of emotion. First, they felt humiliated by the loss of the war and the surrender of their legendary general Robert E. Lee.

Second, they dreaded a very unpleasant phase in which the victorious Union would impose punishments, sanctions, onerous laws, and harsh restrictions that would make southern life unpleasant.

And third, the Thirteenth Amendment had just freed four million slaves. They feared that the sudden disappearance of slavery and a new socio-economic entitlement for former slaves would disrupt the comfortable fabric of their homogeneous white culture. The labor-intensive cotton industry, which had sustained the southern economy for almost a century, now faced a grim future. Truly, the Old South had gone with the wind.

What would happen when millions of ignorant and uneducated black people got the right to vote; the right to own property; the right to own businesses; the right to go to schools; and even the right to hold public office?

That fear and anger reached its peak in a young actor named John Wilkes Booth, a loyal Virginian and an ardent white supremacist. Enraged by President Abraham Lincoln's re-election in 1864 and General Lee's surrender at Appomattox in March of 1865, he shot the President from behind as he sat watching a play with his wife and guests in Ford's theater.

History fans know that Booth also plotted the simultaneous assassination of Lincoln's vice president Andrew Johnson and his Secretary of State William Seward. Both of his accomplices bungled their missions. Booth escaped into Maryland on horseback and made his way to Virginia. There Union troops tracked him down and killed him in a shoot-out in a tobacco barn.

In the post-war years, two very significant political developments shaped the culture of the South and guaranteed that white racism—and very slow development for black people—would persist for another 100 years.

First, Lincoln's assassination and the takeover of the presidency by his Vice President Andrew Johnson set the nation on a different course. Johnson, an uneducated southerner, a former slave owner, and a pro-slavery former Senator from Tennessee, tried to stall as many of Lincoln's reforms as he could.

Against the advice of his military advisors, he declined to occupy the defeated Confederate states. Military doctrine generally dictates that the prevailing power should impose certain controls and restrictions on the losing coalition, to prevent rearmament and a renewal of the war. Instead, Johnson adopted a hands-off attitude and preferred to let things take their course during the Reconstruction.

Johnson became the first president to face impeachment by Congress, but he managed to beat the rap by a single vote in the Senate.

And second, a broad contingent of anti-Union politicians in the South interpreted Johnson's policies as a license to crack down on black development in all of its forms. Certainly not all southerners favored the total oppression of black people, but the dominant passions of the time left little room for their moral concerns.

The infamous Ku Klux Klan came into existence in late 1865, founded by six former Confederate soldiers in the town of Pulaski, Tennessee. They chose the arcane name for their secret society from the greek word *kyklos* ("circle") and a variation on the English word clan. The Klan spread rapidly throughout the South, where its iconic white robes, pointy hats, and face masks signaled an ominous threat to all African Americans. As of this writing, the Klan still exists in the US, but it has degenerated to an outdated relic of its old self.

Thus began what historians typically refer to as the "Jim Crow" period, which lasted well into the twentieth century. That name came from a character in a minstrel show, a clumsy, dimwitted black man. Fans of segregation resurrected the character as part of their ideology of keeping the Jim Crows of the South from misbehaving.

Across the former Confederacy, state and local laws— sometimes referred to as "black codes"—mandated racial segregation in ever more restrictive ways. Legislators aimed to use laws to freeze African Americans out of the mainstream culture and local economies, keeping them impoverished and politically incapacitated.

Jim Crow laws prevented African Americans from living in the same neighborhoods as whites. They required segregation of public restrooms, building entrances, restaurants, train cars, cemeteries, hospitals, asylums, jails, and residential homes for the elderly and handicapped.

In addition to the Jim Crow laws, social practices also reinforced the wholesale rejection of African Americans in many towns. Town councils often posted signs at the city limits reminding black people of their inferior status and warning them to stay away or expect harsh treatment.

As time went on, the Jim Crow laws became ever more severe, with the objective of completely separating the races and depriving African Americans of a vast range of economic and educational opportunities. In the bigger cities, however —perhaps because of the economic realities of labor and markets—those laws tended to become less restrictive over time. That factor tended to attract more and more African Americans to the cities, leaving rural areas even more white than before. And, of course, better economic and social conditions brought many of them to the big cities of the North.

Illiteracy further compounded the black disadvantage, as slave owners had almost universally prevented them from learning even the most rudimentary skills of reading, writing, and arithmetic. This educational deficit lingered on for many decades, and even in modern times a disproportionate number of African Americans tend to turn away from the educational experience as a strategy for getting out of impoverished environments.

But we should not assume that all black people, either before or after emancipation, helplessly accepted their circumstances. From the early 1700s, black leaders emerged, leading both covert and violent resistance movements against slavery.

Harriet Tubman, having escaped from slavery in Maryland, played a key role in the legendary "underground railroad," a system of routes and safe houses that helped runaway slaves make their way to the North. Frederick Douglass, also an escaped slave and self-educated scholar, writer, and orator, became one of the most prominent voices of the anti-slavery movement, both before and after emancipation.

And, a woman who escaped from slavery in New York and adopted the memorable name of Sojourner Truth, traveled and preached throughout the country. She became one of the most respected abolitionists and advocates of women's rights.

WHITE AMERICA LOOKS THE OTHER WAY

As late as 1896, the Jim Crow laws got a thumbs-up from the US Supreme Court, in a landmark case known to legal beagles as *Plessy v. Ferguson.* The Supremes ruled that segregated facilities didn't necessarily violate human rights, so long as they provided services or experiences of "equal quality." Legal scholars named this the "separate but equal" doctrine. It justified racial segregation for another fifty years, until the Court overturned it in another landmark case known as *Brown v. the Board of Education* in 1954.

In many of the post-Confederate states, violence against blacks ran rampant, often with government officials and prominent white citizens looking the other way. Historians still argue facts and figures, but most agree that lynchings of black people by white mobs numbered in the thousands. Considering that most lynchings involved only one, or a few, victims, we have to recognize it as a widespread cultural pathology, going far beyond a few extreme cases.

An episode that some have called the single worst incident of racial violence in American history took place in Tulsa, Oklahoma in 1921. There, mobs of white residents, many of them deputized and armed by city officials, attacked black residents and businesses during a two-day binge of violence, destruction, and looting, killing or injuring hundreds of them. Not until 1996 did an official inquiry recognize the atrocities —the "Tulsa Massacre"—and order reparations for the survivors and their heirs.

THE CIVIL RIGHTS EVOLUTION

Not until the late 1950s and early 1960s did changing American values, public opinion, and enlightened national leadership begin to roll back the legacy of Jim Crow and its cultural aftershocks. In a landmark test of political wills in

1957, Arkansas Governor Orval Faubus faced off against President Dwight Eisenhower. Faubus had defied a federal court order to desegregate the all-white Central High School in Little Rock. He ordered the state's National Guard to prevent nine African American students from enrolling there.

Eisenhower, a former five-star general, moved decisively, and placed the National Guard under the command of the Army's 101st Airborne Division. Ike's actions sent a clear signal to southern governors and legislators, that the federal government would act decisively and firmly to carry out the Supreme Court's ruling that declared school segregation unconstitutional.

The nine African American students, terrified by an angry mob of white people, managed to enroll and begin their studies. In the face of tremendous intimidation, both by white parents and by local officials, only one of them eventually graduated from Central High. But civil rights leaders and scholars of civil liberties have widely hailed the event as a key turning point in the Republic's relationship with institutionalized racism.

In fact, the Little Rock Incident had such a wide impact that Normal Rockwell, the popular artist of Americana, contributed a painting for the cover of the *Saturday Evening Post*, depicting a tiny black girl walking into school escorted by three big US Marshals.

In a later and similar incident, Alabama Governor George Wallace went nose-to-nose with President John Kennedy in 1963. Wallace had defied a court order to allow black students to attend the University of Alabama at Tuscaloosa. Flanked by state troopers, Wallace personally stood in the doorway of the enrollment office to prevent two students from entering. When he called up the state's National Guard, Kennedy pulled the "Ike" maneuver, federalizing the guard and forcing Wallace to back off.

Let's remember that, in both of those incidents, the state governors had the *overwhelming approval of the white citizens of their states*. And in both cases, the US presidents decided that the Constitution and the Supreme Court's rulings should prevail. Quite possibly their courage and determination helped to shift the attitudes of the American public toward more humanitarian values. And they paved the way for more civil rights legislation, as well as for the generation of civil rights leaders who came thereafter.

In an earlier landmark presidential action, Harry Truman had ordered all armed forces units completely desegregated in 1948, ending the practice of assigning African American soldiers to "black-only" units.

And President Lyndon Johnson, a Texan, pushed through the Civil Rights Act of 1964, which ended segregation in public places and outlawed employment discrimination on the basis of race, color, religion, sex or national origin. That legislation became one of the crowning legislative achievements of the civil rights movement, but Johnson knew he would pay a very high political price for it.

After he signed the bill into law, Johnson reportedly commented to his associates, "We've probably handed the South to the Republicans for a generation, at least." His prophesy did indeed come true.

MARTIN LUTHER KING AND THE RISE OF BLACK CIVIL RIGHTS LEADERS

Through those difficult times, Dr. Martin Luther King, probably the best-known African American leader, scholar, and orator in the modern era, preached a gospel of nonviolent resistance to racial discrimination. King and his close associates did more than any other national figures to raise black consciousness of civil rights, and to encourage a whole generation of black leaders to take up the cause.

King had studied the strategies of nonviolent activists like Mohandas Gandhi in India and Nelson Mandela in South Africa, as well as the more confrontational ideologies swirling around him at the time. His decision to maintain a nonviolent brand of activism probably made much of the civil rights progress possible.

Yet, despite the vast distance between the culture of the pre-1960s and the culture of today, racism remains with us. White Americans slowly—very slowly—gravitate toward a more comfortable experience of multi-ethnicism and social pluralism. We still have a long way to go.

As we proceed with our exploration of the possibilities open to our new Republic, a thoughtful consideration of our differences, our old wounds, and our unfinished business can help us better understand our choices.

MANY AMERICAS IN ONE: THE MELTING POT MYTH

The heart-warming notion of America as a great "melting pot" goes all the way back to the founding of the Republic. In 1908 British writer Israel Zangwill wrote a stage play, the title of which popularized the term that became a metaphor for America itself.

Yet, Americans have certainly not melted together. In many ways, their differences make America a more interesting, dynamic, and vibrant society.

And, in some cases, these differences have torn the country apart. Consider the Civil War, which cost more American lives than all other wars combined, prior to the Vietnam conflict.

Clearly, America remains a very pluralistic society. Any discussion of the future of the Republic must account for the effects of differences as well as similarities. We must ask: how has the melting pot metaphor shaped our thinking about the Republic and how it should operate?

American pluralism takes a number of different forms. Geographic differences, for example, have played a key part in our political history. Racial and ethnic differences have certainly had profound effects. Religious differences have had, and still have, profound effects. In the modern era, we've also become more conscious of other categorical differences, such as age, gender, national origin, and economic status. We have more "categories" than ever before.

THE TEN MINIATURE AMERICAS

With regard to geographic differences, for example, one might think of the United States as divided—very approximately—into about ten socio-political regions, as illustrated in Figure 1-2.

These ten "miniature Americas," as we might view them, persist as:

> **New England**—Maine, New Hampshire, Vermont, Rhode Island, Massachusetts, and Connecticut. Many New Englanders like to think of themselves as "original Americans," with a deep commitment to historical values and traditions.

> **The Mid-Atlantic Zone**—New York, Pennsylvania, New Jersey, Delaware, and Maryland, plus Washington, DC. With much of the national government and many of the financial institutions concentrated there, Mid-Atlantic people tend to focus to some extent on modernism, materialist values and political engagement.

> **The "Old South"**—Virginia, West Virginia, Kentucky, North Carolina, South Carolina, Georgia, Florida, Alabama, Mississippi, and Tennessee. The prevailing Old South culture, although it has gradually evolved toward a multicultural pattern, tends to place a high priority on history and heritage, local cohesion, white-European values, and Christian identity.

> **The "Land of Lakes"**—Michigan, Ohio, Indiana, Wisconsin, Illinois, and Minnesota. Somewhat removed from the customary centers of power and commerce, and experiencing generally colder weather than other areas of the US, the "Lakes" culture tends to combine urban, suburban, and rural identities.

- **The Heartland**—Iowa, Missouri, Arkansas, Oklahoma, Kansas, and Nebraska. Largely rural, sparsely populated, primarily white, socially pragmatic, and culturally traditional, the heartland culture seems to prefer a live-and-let-live experience, comfortably out of the national limelight.

- **The "Frontier" States**—Texas, Colorado, New Mexico, Arizona, Utah, and Nevada. With the exception of Utah, a historically white Protestant culture, the Frontier states tend to have significant hispanic populations, and have a long history of commercial orientation toward Mexico. People in the Frontier states tend to prioritize their individual state identities and have their own particular economic development agendas.

- **"Cowboy Country"**—Montana, Idaho, Wyoming, North Dakota, and South Dakota. Sparsely populated, ethnically uniform (mostly white), mostly rural and suburban, people of the Cowboy states tend to value their relationship to the land and private property, and prefer a live-and-let-live social pattern.

- **The "Left Coast"**—Washington, Oregon, and California. The Left Coast states, especially California, tend to have the greatest extremes of ethnic and cultural diversity. People there tend to think of themselves as socially conscious, politically liberal, economically progressive, and generally open to experimentation.

- **"Polynesia"**—Hawaii. Hawaii stands unique due to its remote location in the mid-Pacific, the effects of its warm tropical climate, its history of ethnic diversity, and its relatively small population of 1.4 million.

- **The "Far North"**—Alaska. Alaska also stands unique, due to its remote location in the Northwest, its extreme temperatures, and the absence of large urban centers. Although blessed with oil reserves, its tourist industry and ecological regions typically shut down during the most severe parts of the winter. Socially and politically, it tends to resemble the Cowboy states, but its relative isolation puts it in a separate category.

Figure 1-2. Many Americas in One

THE "MISCELLANEOUS" AMERICANS

Beyond these familiar subdivisions, the US has a collection of "miscellaneous" territories, which most Americans don't think about very often and some don't even know about. These include American Samoa, Guam, the Northern Mariana Islands, Puerto Rico, and the US Virgin Islands. Leftovers from the quasi-colonial days, these unincorporated territories—not incorporated into the body of the Republic—exist in a kind of political limbo.

The political status of people in those territories evolved out of an eccentric colonialist ideology that continues its peculiar patterns to this day.

For example, despite American Samoa's status as a US territory, people born there don't hold US citizenship, but people born in Puerto Rico, Guam, the Northern Mariana

Islands, and US Virgin Islands do. Samoans have special passports that define them as US nationals but not US citizens. They need visas to travel to any of the states in the US. They can, however, serve in the armed forces.

People born in Puerto Rico, Guam, Northern Mariana Islands, and US Virgin Islands do have US citizenship, and they can travel around the US without restrictions. Like Samoans, they can vote in primary elections, but they can't vote in presidential elections. They have no seats in Congress and no electoral votes. Curiously, a native of one of those territories who moves to one of the mainland states gets to vote for president while residing there.

Civil rights activists have struggled for decades against a massive inertial indifference, to have the Constitution and national laws grant full citizenship privileges for all territorial peoples. Advocates have proposed statehood for Washington, DC, as well as Puerto Rico.

Before we leave the subject of American subcultures, let's not overlook the status of Native Americans—Indians and Alaskan natives such as Eskimos, Aleuts, and Inuit—who continue to live in the political twilight of historical marginalization. Their numbers have dwindled radically, and they've become almost politically invisible and mostly unheard in the national conversation.

The need for this attention to the cultural and attitudinal differences across the American population goes to the impact of those differences in running the Republic. Politically, for example, a presidential candidate supposedly needs to understand the key differences and to craft a message—or a variety of messages—based on those key cultural drivers. In recent times, neither of the two major political parties in the US has demonstrated a real understanding of these differences, or at the very least, a willingness to engage with them.

Second, the voices of the many interest groups don't carry equal weight, although social activists seek to increase the attention given to them and the impact they can have. American Indians, for example, have declined in numbers radically over a century or more and their isolation on remote reservations tends to put them out of the mainstream of the national conversation.

Going forward, all of us co-architects of the New America have a responsibility to honor the existence of people of all identities.

AMERICA AS A WORLD POWER: DOES MIGHT MAKE RIGHT?

By the late 1890s, America had started looking like a real country. Its population had grown from about four million to about 75 million, driven by new states joining the union, immigration, high birth rates, and improving health conditions. The growing Republic had expanded from the original thirteen colonies to a collection of 45 states. Its leaders had pushed its boundaries all the way to the Pacific Ocean, northward to Canada, and southward to the Rio Grande.

They had bought the entire Northwest from Napoleon; bought Alaska from Russia; kicked the Spanish out of Florida, California, and the territories of the far west; and had pried the western "frontier" states out of the hands of the Mexican government. The Spanish empire, once one of the most powerful in the world, had seen its day. It had lost control of Mexico and virtually all of the Spanish-speaking South American and Caribbean countries.

A MANDATE FROM GOD

The more aggressive political figures had talked for many years about a "manifest destiny," a mandate from God that recognized the fundamental superiority of Americans over other inhabitants of the planet. They saw as foreordained the role of America as the leader of the world and the unquestioned entitlement of the emerging Republic to populate the entire landmass from Atlantic to Pacific.

As far back as 1823, President James Monroe declared that the US would not tolerate any further colonization of the western hemisphere by European powers, nor would it allow them to install puppet dictators who would favor their interests. This "Monroe doctrine" held sway in American politics for a century or more and some advocates of "American exceptionalism" still invoke it today.

The time had come, many of America's political leaders began to say, for the country to come of age—to take its place amongst the great powers of the world.

Theodore—"Teddy"—Roosevelt agreed. Some historians see "TR" as the axial figure in America's rise to world power status.

Long before his well-known career phase as the elected President, TR had distinguished himself as a nationalist and a get-things-done kind of guy. He had made a name for himself by reforming New York City's notoriously corrupt police force and he masterminded the reform of the national government's bureaucratic civil service system.

When he became the Assistant Secretary of the Navy, TR began to think seriously about the world-power issue. He concluded that, for America to gain serious recognition as a first-power nation, two things had to happen. First, it had to build a formidable deep-water navy that could project American military power anywhere in the world. Second, it had to fight a war with some other country and win. He set out to make both of those ventures happen.

He pursued the first of his agenda items aggressively in his role of Assistant Secretary of the Navy, taking advantage of the ill health and weak leadership of his boss the Secretary. He commissioned the construction of a growing fleet of modern warships and their supporting craft.

For his second agenda item, he had to look no further than 90 miles south of Miami to the island of Cuba, occupied precariously by the fading empire of Spain. A war with Spain met all the specifications: a battle with a—formerly—great power, an easy win, and a relatively small operation.

He had sent the Navy's battleship USS *Maine* to Cuba and parked it provocatively in Havana harbor. Under mysterious circumstances, still debated by historians, a massive explosion sank it, killing over 250 sailors onboard. The US newspapers had already begun a campaign of disparaging Spain, and condemning its violent occupation of Cuba. The sinking of the *Maine* set off the spark for a national sense of outrage. Newspapers across the US began calling for war.

Sensing his moment in history, TR resigned his position as Assistant Secretary and formed an *ad hoc* military unit—the "Rough Riders"—with himself as its commander. In the bar of the old Menger Hotel in San Antonio, Texas, he organized a motley force of about 500 cavalry-style fighters, equipped them with uniforms, rifles, and horses, and set off for Cuba.

Most Americans, having only a vague recollection of the stories they heard in high school history class, seem to think that Roosevelt's Rough Riders won the war almost single-handedly. The famous "charge up San Juan hill," glamorized by the news reporters and photographers he took to Cuba with him, became the defining icon of the event.

But, as it often happens, the truth bears little similarity to the fantasy. The invading force consisted of over 17,000 US troops, from the Army's Fifth Corps. Teddy's Rough Riders made up a tiny contingent of the entire force, but they enjoyed the indulgence of an admiring press corps who wanted drama and glory.

Lack of space on the transport ship meant that they couldn't take their horses with them. Roosevelt took two of his own horses, one of which died during the landing in Cuba. Some versions suggest he rode up San Juan Hill, but his Rough Riders certainly didn't. This legendary cavalry force fought all of its skirmishes on foot. They suffered a 37 percent casualty rate, the highest of any American regiment during the operation.

THE US CLAIMS THE WESTERN HEMISPHERE

After a fairly easy victory, the weak Spanish military forces surrendered and the Spanish government sued for peace. In the ensuing negotiations, the Spanish government agreed to pull out of Cuba entirely, leaving it under the protection of the United States.

As part of the agreement, the Spanish government also gave up all claims to the Philippines, Guam, and Puerto Rico, and pulled out its forces without firing another shot. That spelled the end of the Spanish empire in the Western hemisphere, and indeed pretty much around the world.

It also spelled the rise of the United States to world power status.

By the way, Teddy's military superiors recommended him for the Medal of Honor, but the War Department nixed it. A century later, President Bill Clinton made the posthumous award in 2001, a few days before his second term expired.

NEXT: THE "CANAL CAPER"

A few years after the Cuban invasion, having parlayed his war-hero status into a successful run for the presidency, Roosevelt mounted several other naked power plays, most notoriously the takeover of the Panama canal. That adventure more or less normalized the use-of-force doctrine, which a long succession of presidents has continued.

To briefly summarize the "canal caper": the government of France had given up on trying to build a grand canal across a neck of land in the northern part of Colombia. France's canal expert, Ferdinand de Lesseps, had made his name building the Suez canal through Egypt, a fairly simple operation that only involved carving a big ditch across a desert plain.

He hugely underestimated the difficulty of building a canal across Colombia, with its mountainous terrain, rainforests, wet weather, and unstable soil. After nine years, several billion dollars in costs, and 20,000 lives lost to accidents and diseases like malaria and yellow fever, the French threw in the towel.

Roosevelt recognized the tremendous economic payoff that could come with the completion of a canal that would cut thousands of miles and weeks of travel off of the movement of goods between the Atlantic and Pacific oceans, and he believed the US Army Corps of Engineers could do it.

However, when he approached the government of Colombia with a proposal for a deal, they wanted none of it. For various reasons—possibly economic and political fatigue, possible technological doubts, and possible concern about the repeat of thousands of deaths during the construction—they turned him down.

But, enjoying his new status as president of a world power, TR decided he would have his canal. He stationed a small Navy fleet off the coast of Colombia and made a deal with a band of Colombian exiles for a quick and decisive invasion of the northern region where the canal would go. With the well-supported invasion on one side and the threat of bombardment from the US Navy on the other, the Colombian government quickly capitulated, yielding the territory to the *insurrectos*.

The victorious invaders declared the region independent of Colombia and named it Panama. Shortly thereafter they struck a deal with TR for the construction of the canal, giving the US control of its operation—and most of its revenues—under a 99-year lease.

For some historians, Roosevelt gave birth to an overt mentality, which prevails to this day, known as the "might makes right" doctrine. This worldview held that a powerful country like the US could justify using force and the threat of force in its relationships with other countries, to protect or advance its status as a primary power. He considered the overthrow of foreign governments by violent or covert means as reasonable and proper actions to fulfill its strategic aims. He liked to advise his political counterparts, "Speak softly, and carry a big stick."

To treat Teddy fairly, the doctrine of might-makes-right got started a long time before he came along. He just continued a controversial tradition established in the early 1800s. Amongst the political luminaries of those days, some opposed it and some advocated it. The opponents wanted the American Republic to serve as a model for all democracies, hoping that the principles and practices would serve as examples for other nations to follow.

The canal story and others deserve our attention because they frame a very basic question of American values: does might really make right? Do we accept the justifications offered by our leaders for invading countries that won't give us what we want; for "annexing" territories that serve our strategic advantage; for toppling unfriendly foreign governments by covert military operations; for assassinating heads of state that we don't like? Do the ends achieved always justify the means used?

These questions will trail along behind us all the way through the journey of reflection we make with this book.

THE COMING AMERICAN TWILIGHT: CAN—OR SHOULD —AMERICA LEAD THE WORLD?

Most Americans and most of their political leaders seem to have a deeply ingrained conviction about America's permanent and unassailable position as the alpha-nation in the global tribe of states. And one can well understand how they've come to this fundamental view of themselves and their Republic.

THE AMERICAN HEAD START

Contrast America's long and almost uninterrupted rise in economic prosperity; industrial capacity; technological capacity; education; business innovation; political innovation; social, literary, and artistic innovation; and military capacity, with the ups and downs of almost all of her contemporaries on the world stage.

Two world wars had left most of the stalwart economies of Europe, Asia, and the Soviet Union nearly in tatters while the US had prospered. America's Great Depression induced an equally powerful contraction in most of the major economies of the world but the US pulled out of it more quickly then they did (although, in fairness, the US's role as the supplier of war materiel to the Allied nations played a large role in that recovery).

The economies of Germany and Japan crashed out as a result of their devastating war losses and their occupation by the Allied nations. China sank into a 25-year Dark Age of social and economic stagnation after its civil war brought Mao Tze-Tung and his Marxist ideology to power.

Meanwhile, America, with relatively few lives lost and almost no damage to its infrastructure, sailed into the post-war recovery period with a huge head start—one that it never really lost.

But now, a century after Teddy Roosevelt's big-stick leadership brought the US to a new role in the community of nations, we can see the beginning of certain tectonic changes in social, economic, and military power politics that may well change that role.

America's gold-plated image on the world stage seemed to fade a bit with the humiliating pullout of its forces from Vietnam in 1975. A small, underdeveloped, poorly equipped Asian country had withstood a decade-long pounding by the world's most powerful military machine and finally saw them retreat in disarray.

Japan made a truly astonishing comeback in the 1980s with its "quality miracle," which placed it in the top tier of exporters of consumer products. By 1990 it had become the world's second largest economy, after the US.

China made an equally astonishing comeback after the death of Mao Tze-Tung in 1976. Under the leadership of Deng Xiao-ping and a succession of reformers, it displaced Japan as the number-two economy by 2010.

Meanwhile, the Soviet Union had crashed out politically and economically by 1991. With the sudden and humiliating loss of its fearful threat posture toward the West and the enthusiastic migration of its former client states into the European Union, Europe began evolving toward a new consciousness.

While some American political figures portrayed this new world as having only one superpower—the US—others saw it as an economic and political see-saw with the US as one key player and the EU collectively as the other.

Various theorists in international politics began to view the "new world order" as drifting away from its traditional American dominance in all things, toward a multi-polar and multi-national state of shared influence. China, for example, while not yet a world military power, began to play a bigger role in international commerce. Its leaders, particularly under Xi Jinping, who took over in 2013, launched a large-scale economic outreach, working out deals with developing countries the US had shown little interest in.

Germany emerged as the strongest of the EU economies and its leader Angela Merkel took a strong hand in the management of continental affairs. From 2005 onward, she preached a philosophy of a partnership of equals between the EU and the US. This new view implied that many national leaders no longer wanted to dance to the American music.

Meanwhile, America's might-makes-right doctrine continued to look increasingly ill-suited to the modern world. Under President George W. Bush, Jr., the US invasion of Afghanistan, launched in 2001, dragged on without achieving its supposed goal of capturing the notorious terrorist Usama bin Laden. As of this writing, the 19 year-old Afghan operation remains America's longest-running military venture, having cost thousands of lives and over 1 trillion dollars with little or nothing to show for it.

Also on Bush's watch, the morally and strategically questionable invasion of Iraq in 2003 had turned into a public relations disaster. In the process of overthrowing Iraq's despotic Saddam Hussein, the US occupation destroyed the country's military structure, aggravated a long-running wave of intra-Muslim conflict, and nearly brought its economy to stone-age levels.

Little wonder, then, that many world leaders have begun to rethink their relationships with the US and to arrange the pieces on the international game board in new ways.

Some theorists have begun referring to this new evolutionary phase as a coming "American Twilight." The term implies a phase in which America loses its alpha-nation status and becomes just one of several players in a multi-polar arrangement of nations and regions. Each power-nation or power-bloc will have its own patterns of influence, with all of them becoming increasingly interdependent for economic development and for maintaining peace and stability.

They describe this evolving situation, not so much as an actual decline in America's power, but as an increasing degree of confidence and self-determination on the part of many of the other nations.

A CONSTELLATION OF PEERS

If this new multi-polar arrangement becomes the accepted state of affairs, many Americans and many of their leaders will face a very difficult psychological adjustment. Can

Americans and American politicians come to peace with the idea of a partnership of equals? Can we view our relationship with China, for example, as a relationship between equals and not one between a powerful first-world country and a backward developing country? Can we accept the economic success of other countries as cooperative with our interests, and not necessarily competitive?

As we think about the evolution of our Republic in the coming years, we must think about the necessary evolution in our own attitudes, opinions, and expectations. That evolution might present us with the toughest remodeling task of all: remodeling our own thinking.

Chapter 2.
Do We Deserve the Republic
We've Inherited?

"Ask not, what your country can do for you.
Ask what you can do for your country."
—John F. Kennedy, US President

Let's begin our journey by asking ourselves a big question: if we hope to have a new and better America, will we need to become new and better Americans? Can we, as the heirs and stewards of this grand Republic, handle the job of protecting it and caring for it?

The Founders bequeathed us something more than just a place on the map, more than a country. They gave us an idea —a way of thinking about the welfare of the people, a set of values, and a mechanism for making it all work. With all of our fumbles and stumbles, our historical blunders, our irrational conflicts, and our cultural stresses, America still has the admiration of most of the world, but we must recognize our warts as well as our dimples.

So, what about the next 200 years—or the next twenty? Do we just hang on for the ride and hope for the best? Or will our evolving Republic need more from us?

THE TALENT DROUGHT: WHY DO WE GET SUCH MEDIOCRE LEADERS?

Surely we Americans get the leaders we deserve. We know it and we don't like it, but we can't seem to bring ourselves to change it. After every big election, we raise the familiar lament: "With all the talented people we have in this country, how did we end up with this bunch in charge?"

This perplexing question does have answers. The process we've evolved for choosing our president and our congressional leaders just about guarantees mediocrity, and political disaster in some cases.

WHAT KIND OF PRESIDENT DO WE WANT?

We don't have—and don't seem to want—a set of "specs" for the national office. We've never agreed on even a few basic skills that a president needs to run the country well. Instead, we conduct our elections like beauty contests—who can impress, charm, and inspire us the most?

We don't choose presidents—we choose personalities.

Any corporate board of directors seeking to hire a new CEO would hire a search firm, and before interviewing anybody the searchers would first ask, "What particular skills do you want in your leader? What qualifications count the most—technical know-how; knowledge of the industry; financial expertise; strategic vision; ability to build and lead a team?"

And yet, we Americans—the "board of directors" of the Republic—haven't a clue about the skills we need in the CEO for our enterprise. We accept the ID tags hung on the various contenders by the popular news media. We see Person X as a "Wall Street billionaire." Person Y gets tagged as a "green" candidate. Person Z stands accused of running on his or her Hispanic identity.

The second reason why we get mediocre leaders has to do with the comical—and tragic—selection process we use. Winning the election requires an entirely different set of skills from those needed to govern the country. When the winner of our national beauty contest walks into the White House, we may have no clue as to his or her leadership talents.

In the US as with most other elective democracies, candidates must tap into the selfish interests, prejudices, fears, and phobias of enough people to become their hero figure. At the same time the candidate—or his or her campaign operatives —must tag the opposing candidates with negative ID codes. "Soft on crime." "Weak on defense." "In the pocket of big business." "Ivory tower liberal." "Socialist." Veiled references to racial or ethnic differences can arouse a certain part of the population. And, of course, exposing disreputable aspects of the opponent's history and personal life usually helps the process.

This two-part method—arousing emotion and demonizing the opponent—has become the *de facto* standard process for political campaigns. Campaign slogans, carefully designed to suspend critical thinking and arouse emotions, become the trademarks of the various competing campaigns.

Meanwhile, our electronic media simplify, polarize, and amplify the discourse, in order to create drama that holds attention—and brings in advertising dollars.

We can do better. In Chapter 4 (Governance) I'll describe a fascinating research study that asked international leadership experts to describe the skills they considered most relevant and important for a US president. The findings of that study could make a radical difference in the way we hire the leader of our Republic.

We'll also consider the merits of a *mandatory voting law* that can revolutionize our election process.

OUR NATIONAL CONVERSATION: HEALTHY DISCOURSE OR SHOUTING MATCH?

Beginning with the year 2000, the marker for a new millennium, we officially entered the Age of Bullshit. Please indulge me this rare bit of blunt vulgarity as we take an honest look at how Americans and their leaders talk to one another.

Let's use the term *national conversation* to describe the collective thought process of the culture, told out loud. Every modern culture has one.

Unless you've chosen to live a life isolated from the rest of society, you probably experience the national conversation every day, during much of your waking time. Your conversations with your family; your significant other; your neighbors; your close friends; your colleagues, co-workers, or fellow students; your casual acquaintances; the people in the shops you patronize—all influence the way you think about the Republic that you co-own and co-inhabit. And, of course, your mental model of the Republic can influence their mental models through the everyday conversations you have with them.

In addition to our own personal microcosm of relationships, we modern citizens live our lives deeply and unavoidably embedded in an information environment. Let's pause for a moment to think about this all-pervasive field of ideas and influences. What can we observe about the never-ending tide of messages swirling around us? How does it affect us? And, do we have the power—and the means—to influence it?

We can make a few key observations about the national conversation:

▸ It consists of a vast collection of simultaneous overlapping and competing narratives—sales pitches, so to speak—for various ideas, ideologies, agendas, and special interests.

- Not all narratives get the same amount of attention, respect, and acceptance. The voices of the privileged and powerful tend to dominate.

- The narrative of the dominant socio-political coalition —currently, in the US, the white, male, European, Protestant, upper-middle class cohort—gets the most traction.

- In recent years, with the phenomenal proliferation of online media—the electronic culture—the national conversation has become more crowded, chaotic, adversarial, intolerant, amplified, strident, uncivil, vulgar, dramatized, and—unfortunately—dishonest and manipulative.

- Socio-political factions emerge and die out, tribalizing around their own specialized agendas and narratives. Every new faction adds another narrative to the conversation, however faintly heard.

- Commercial news producers control a very large part of the content of the national conversation. The businesses that operate this media ecosystem wage a relentless, never-ending battle for our attention, selecting stories for their drama value and amplifying the dramatic elements to maximize advertising revenue.

- The entertainment industry—TV, movies, and popular music—plays a dominant role in the national conversation, with a pervasive influence on factors like language; gender, ethnic, and generational stereotypes; attitudes toward civility, authority, and national identity; and contemporary socio-political values.

- No one individual can experience all of the national conversation at any moment in time. Each of us has only his or her own narrow window on a very small part of it. We all have our individual interests and biases, which determine the parts of the message environment we pay attention to.

Throughout this journey, we'll see again and again how the national conversation plays a crucial role in decisions about the design of our Republic, the way it operates, the way we deal with the choices facing us at various turning points, and the very untidy process of deciding what comes next.

HAS HOLLYWOOD SHAPED OUR REALITY?

Allen Ginsberg, the 1960s "beat poet" and new age philosopher, warned about the rising influence of the powerful media companies on the American popular culture. He said,

> *"We're in science fiction now, man. Whoever controls the images—the media—controls the culture."*

America's entertainment industry dwarfs the entertainment industries of all other countries by far. In movies, TV, music, sports, amusement parks—American products have influenced the rest of the world more than those of any other culture.

You can go to just about any developed country in the world and hear American popular music, played in shopping malls, hotels, bars, radios in taxi cabs, and in elevators. American films and TV shows have spread across the globe, influencing film-making in other countries, including, over the past couple of decades, India.

Much of what people in other countries know—or think they know—about Americans and their culture comes from the entertainment media they've experienced. I've met people in my travels who think all Americans have lots of money; that everyone in Chicago carries a gun; that most people in Texas ride horses; or that just about everyone in California knows a movie star.

And here in America many people get their impression of their own culture from images they see on screens. Our media constantly ply us with images, stories, and stereotypes from a synthetic reality, which they create to entertain and amuse us.

Perhaps we should ask: how does the media environment, with its "Hollywood" values, shape Americans' world-views, perspectives, values, and biases? And how do those perceptions shape their consciousness as citizens and owners of the Republic?

"THIRTY LIES PER SECOND"

Somewhere in the history of the US film industry, the expression "twenty-four lies per second" arose, as a recognition that the sequence of pictures the film maker strings together into a story doesn't match reality as anyone could actually experience it. In modern media parlance, "thirty lies per second" recognizes the same defining feature of video footage.

Think about it: before the invention of moving pictures, no other human communication device or process could rearrange reality so profoundly. Paintings and still photos, such as the clever images of the Dutch artist M.C. Escher, could present visual illusions—things no one would see in normal reality. But none of those media could create an immersive, synthetic reality that could never have happened.

MEDIA AWARENESS: A MODERN SURVIVAL SKILL

As media consumers, we've become conditioned to accept a series of fragmented images and episodes as a legitimate version of reality that might not even follow the usual movement of time. When one scene cuts or fades to another, we instantly interpret the change as signaling the passage of time. When the scene jumps from one camera's view to that of another, we willingly interpret the change as equivalent to turning our heads to look at one of the actors or another. When the camera zooms in or out, we sense the change as shifting our attention more closely to the subject on screen or back out to the setting in which the action unfolds.

This "willing suspension of disbelief," as some psychologists have described it, allows the film maker to play with our perceptions in a very fluid way. We don't notice the switch from one camera angle to another, just before the action hero dives through a window. During the actual filming, the cameras stop, the highly paid star actor steps aside, the cameras start up again, and a similar-looking stunt double dives through the window. On the other side of the window, the actor replaces the stunt double, the cameras start rolling again and our hero shoots it out with the bad guys.

THE HOLLYWOOD LEGACY

Hollywood—a generic handle for a place, an industry, and an ideology—has contributed richly to the life of the Republic and has helped to shape our society in a number of ways.

In its Golden Age, from the 1930s through the 1950s, it gave us some of the classics in film making. Some film fans, myself included, consider the great iconic movies of that time a valuable artistic legacy of a newly awakening society.

Black-and-white masterpieces like "Citizen Kane" in 1941, "Casablanca" in 1942, and "It's a Wonderful Life" in 1946 still stand as towering artistic—and commercial—achievements. Even the late 1950s and early 1960s, well after color films had become the norm, saw the release of "Twelve Angry Men" in 1957, and "To Kill a Mockingbird" in 1960, two of the outstanding examples of black-and-white cinematography.

A second Hollywood contribution took the form of an ever-improving technology for image making. Anyone who has seen some of the jerky, flickering, grainy silent films from the 1920s and early 1930s, with the quaint subtitles in those old-fashioned fonts, can love them for themselves and can also appreciate the enormous advances we've seen since then. Those technologies have spread to other sectors like business, education, and corporate settings.

THE DARK SIDE OF ENTERTAINMENT

But a third legacy of Hollywood's commercial success has troubled many thoughtful Americans and students of the Republic. That legacy, which we could probably best describe as "Hollywood values," has seeped into the national consciousness and has shaped the national conversation in ways we barely understand.

Broadcast television had become a commercially viable industry in the US by the late 1950s. Less than a decade after it appeared it had reached nearly 95 percent of American households. No other commercial or cultural phenomenon has spread so far and so fast—not even the Internet.

People born after 1960 have very little concept of the daily experience of life before TV. The big Hollywood movies brought drama into American lives but most families could only afford to go to the theater about once or twice a month.

Before TV, the newspaper delivery boy pedaled by on his bicycle every morning and flung the daily edition up on the roof. Popular magazines like *Life, Look*, and the *Saturday Evening Post* enjoyed wide circulation, again mostly via home delivery. And in small towns, people went to church meetings, bake sales, and Independence Day celebrations to mix with their neighbors.

With the arrival of the television era, the social habits of Americans, as well as their information diets, began to shift. The TV dinner, kept in the freezer and heated in a matter of minutes, became one of the defining icons of middle class life. It displaced the traditional family dinner-table conversation with the shared experience of "watching TV."

In the early days, TV watching filled more and more of the family's discretionary time, but didn't displace moviegoing or magazine reading to any great extent. The broadcast industry at that time consisted of the Big Three networks—American Broadcasting Company (ABC), the Columbia Broadcasting Company (CBS), and the National Broadcasting Company (NBC). In a typical evening of three or four hours of TV watching, most people found plenty to amuse themselves.

When white middle-class Americans looked at TV shows, they mostly saw themselves. Dramas, comedies, variety shows, talk shows, and game shows almost invariably featured white actors, with people of color usually relegated to stock characters or stereotyped support roles. Males played nearly all of the lead roles and the feminist consciousness had not yet come to life in a big way. The family sitcom "Father Knows Best" probably best exemplified the sanitized white middle-America content of popular broadcasting. Gay characters seldom played any positive roles if they appeared at all.

Then came the 1980s, cable TV, junk food, and—for urban dwellers—pizza delivered to the front door. With the proliferation of cable channels and the non-stop flow of news shows, TV watching became a round-the-clock experience. It began to replace social interaction with the passive viewing of a synthetic reality. Some families even allowed teen-agers to have their own TVs in their bedrooms.

More recently, the social media epidemic—launched by the ubiquitous smart phone—has flooded the national conversation. It has generated a wave of digital pollution with personalized pornography; inane text messages; narcissistic "selfie" photos; celebrity cat fights; misbehavior of sports stars; malicious lies, rumors, and fabricated news stories; vicious personal attacks on public figures—and even death threats.

AMUSING OURSELVES TO DEATH?

The late Professor Neil Postman, who founded a department of media ecology at New York University, predicted many of the current effects on individuals and societies of the "information swamp" in his landmark book *Amusing Ourselves to Death*.[1] Postman viewed the modern electronic society as incurably addicted to amusements of all kinds. He predicted that all forms of commercial media must inevitably drift toward a consumer experience of arousal, amusement, and entertainment in order to capture attention. In this strange new world, a second of someone's attention has become the new unit of currency.

Postman passed away before the Internet phase had exploded, but he would certainly have seen the current state of media addiction as supporting his thesis.

Along with the media revolution, other trends such as urban migration, mass use of automobiles, shopping malls, and convenience foods contributed to the near disappearance of the small-town idea of American culture. Sprawling suburban developments made anonymous neighbors of people who hadn't known one another to begin with. The town square, the church meeting hall, the general store, the barber shop, and the café began to disappear.

The ever-increasing saturation of the media environment forced film makers, TV producers, and news companies to resort to extreme measures to try to capture and hold—and monetize—viewer attention. Many of them met that challenge with a progressive vulgarization of the content, with ever more violent, sexualized, fearful, and bizarre footage. The charming flirtations and coded language of sexual attraction in the films of the 1950s gave way to explicit scenes, vulgar language, and the portrayal of sex as a sport rather than a subtle component of human relationships.

The particular Hollywood values—implied in the stories and behavior of many on-screen characters—which many commentators find worrisome, include *hyper-masculinism*; relegation of women to stand-by girl friend status; marginalization of people of color; disrespect for established authority; a preference for violence over cooperation; vulgarization of the language; preoccupation with firearms; and a sanitized depiction of injury and death that trivializes and commoditizes its human meaning.

This discussion, of course, raises more questions than it settles. I have no comprehensive "fix" to recommend. At best, it can make us more acutely aware of the role of information in general, and the media environment in particular, in our lives and habits. As we press on with our journey to understand and rethink our Republic, this understanding can play a big part in our approach to some of the big issues.

HAVE WE BECOME A NATION OF SHEEP?

America's legendary homespun humorist and philosophical curmudgeon Mark Twain declared,

> "We are discreet sheep; we wait to see how the drove is going, and then we go with the drove. We have two opinions: one private, which we are afraid to express; and another one—the one we use—which we force ourselves to wear to please Mrs. Grundy, until habit makes us comfortable in it, and the custom of defending it presently makes us love it, adore it, and forget how pitifully we come by it."

That seems a bit harsh, but still . . .

Anthropologists classify human beings as *herd animals*, which means that we imitate one another. We behave according to learned patterns that emerge and evolve amongst us over time. But unlike most other herding species, we also behave as *pack animals*—banding together in smaller units like families, clans, tribes, and affinity groups.

We constantly react, often unconsciously, to many of the signals in our social and physical environment. For example, statistical studies show that suicide rates typically rise by ten percent or more in the days and weeks following a celebrity suicide. Popularity ratings of US presidents invariably rise by five percentage points or more right after a State of the Union address. A single positive mention of a book by a popular TV star like Oprah Winfrey can turn an author into a millionaire.

PLEASE, HERD US—SOMEWHERE, ANYWHERE

Those who understand our herding and pack-joining instincts can amuse us, sell stuff to us, terrify us, anger us, polarize us, and even lead us into war. Of course, we consider ourselves thinking animals, so we need to give ourselves good reasons to do what we do. Those who can supply us with reasons, ones that fit with our sense of self-approval, can usually take us where they want us to go.

We love to believe that we think for ourselves, and yet abundant evidence shows that we pick up the majority of our beliefs, convictions, and opinions from our environments—what we see and hear in the media; the advertising messages that swirl around us; and the people we come into contact with every day. We live in a *pervasive media environment*, and its crafted messages constantly soak into our brains.

Those who seek to manipulate our attention count on two truths: one, that we all want to believe we think independently; and two, that our brains run on "autopilot" mode most of the time.

The legendary inventor Thomas Edison declared,

> *"Five percent of people think.*
> *Another ten percent think they think,*
> *and the other 85 percent would sooner die than think."*

If you get your news from Internet sites, ask yourself: how often have I clicked on some "cute" item—a cat story; a list of "ten things your dog wishes you knew"; "ten foods you should never eat"; a racy account of some celebrity's misbehavior; or the story of the crazy old lady with the hundred cats? Website operators refer to those items as "click-bait"—morsels that entice the wandering mind to linger a while longer and absorb the advertising messages.

WHO DECIDES WHAT YOU KNOW?

Have you wondered who chooses the stories that appear on the web pages you see; how they decide what to offer; and how long they stay up? Most news sites now deliver "dynamically curated" stories, which means that the stories that have the most prominent position and those that stay the longest stay there because they get the most clicks. The software that creates the web page you see also tracks the choices you and other viewers make with your clicks, the time you spend viewing each item you select, and your total viewing time at the site.

The item that gets more clicks stays up longer and it might move to a more prominent position. One that gets very few clicks will get bumped off the page by the next candidate on the list. News value? Journalistic importance? Forget it. No one sits there and chooses the "best" stories for their literary significance. The expression goes, "If it clicks, it sticks."

So, please relieve yourself of the naïve fictional belief that you "keep up with what's current events." And you might also want to let go of its companion, the idea that the website offers you "the news." Keep reminding yourself that the news "content," as web techies like to call it, comes about as a byproduct of the advertising content.

AMERICAN VALUES: IMAGINED, REAL, AND POSSIBLE

Please consider the following question: Under what circumstances, if any, would you consider it acceptable for the President of the United States to lie, knowingly and deliberately, to the American people?

That question could have more implications than we first realize. Let's consider a real example from our history and ask ourselves how our shared values come into play.

On May 1, 1960, a Soviet missile battery shot down an American spy plane, the fabled U-2, over Soviet territory. Flying at 70,000 feet altitude and operated by a pilot working for the CIA, the U-2 took photographs of Soviet military facilities, with particular interest in their nuclear weapons.

The US had run these high-altitude missions for several years, above the combat ceiling of Russian fighter aircraft, and—military experts thought—above the reach of their surface-to-air missiles. Soviet premier Nikita Khrushchev had known about the flights for some time but kept the information secret. He hoped to reach an arms reduction agreement in the upcoming Four Powers Summit talks in Paris with the US, UK, and France.

When the Russians broke the story, President Dwight Eisenhower stood before news cameras and described the mission as a weather research flight for NASA, the US space agency. He explained that it had drifted off course, probably as a result of an oxygen malfunction that rendered the pilot unconscious. In truth, he had overseen the U-2 spy program since its inception and personally approved every flight.

He mistakenly believed that the pilot, Francis Gary Powers, had died in the crash. To the contrary, Powers had miraculously survived the missile encounter and parachuted unharmed. Russian forces captured him—he had not used the cyanide pill he carried—and held him in a secret location.

Khrushchev demanded that Eisenhower admit that the U-2 had spied on Russian territory, and apologize to the Russian government and the world community. By custom, most nations generally consider unauthorized penetration of their airspace by military planes as an act of war. Khrushchev didn't let on that they had Powers in custody.

Still believing that Powers had died in the crash, Eisenhower refused, and doubled down on his weather plane story. He even had NASA put out a bogus news release about a research plane that had "gone missing," together with photographs of a U-2 painted with NASA markings.

Khrushchev had set a trap for Ike. When Ike refused to come clean, he released the full news story, complete with photos of Powers and his plane, as well as his confession. The Soviet delegation walked out of the Paris meeting, and the bitter acrimony of the Cold War continued.

Backed into a corner, Ike had no choice but to admit the existence of the U-2 flights, but claimed justification for them because of the USSR's hostile conduct.

Ike had kept Congress completely in the dark about the U-2 operation. When House and Senate leaders discovered the story, they demanded a full explanation of the program. In an unprecedented move, House Appropriations Chair Clarence

Cannon revealed the details of the incident and the main features of the program in a public session of the House.

Eisenhower found himself in an embarrassing position. Either he had known about the program for four years and had lied about it to the Congress and the American people; or he didn't know about it, which implied that he couldn't control the CIA and other covert actors in his administration.

COVERT MILITARY OPERATIONS: A NECESSARY EVIL?

As you assess this historical episode, how do you evaluate Eisenhower's actions? Would you say that he did the right thing(s), considering the circumstances, and that you have no moral concerns about it?

Or, would you endorse his actions—albeit reluctantly—because you believe that serving the nation's interests sometimes calls for distasteful but necessary methods?

Or, would you say that he betrayed a higher principle—honesty—for political convenience?

At the extreme, would you say he should not have authorized the U-2 flights at all?

To make this question of American values even more complicated: if you believe Ike did the right thing in covering up the U-2 flights and the crash of the Powers mission, how do you feel about the congressional committee's public disclosure of a sensitive classified program? Do two wrongs make a right; or do two rights make a wrong?

If we posed these questions to a roomful of Americans, I doubt we would get one single answer, and maybe not even a close consensus. Questions about values often seem simple at first glance and yet they almost inevitably get complicated as we start to unpack them.

Let's consider a few other examples of value dilemmas that confront us as members and keepers of the Republic.

REGIME CHANGE, ANYONE?

As a citizen, would you approve of, condone, or tolerate a covert mission by the CIA—or a third party operative sponsored by the CIA—to overthrow the government of a foreign country?

Arguments persist about how many countries US presidents and CIA operatives have overthrown or tried to overthrow. Political historians tend to agree, however, on at least seven successful coups engineered by Washington since WW2: Brazil, Chile, Congo, the Dominican Republic, Guatemala, Iran, and South Vietnam.

In earlier times, less-covert operations included sponsoring the overthrow of the last Hawaiian queen, Lili'uo'kalani, by a group of American missionaries turned merchants in 1893. Another involved sponsoring a targeted invasion by an exiled guerrilla group from Colombia, who seized the northern neck of land that became the Panama Canal.

Many reputable historians assert that none of the overthrow operations just named have any realistic justification in the defense of the US against credible foreign threats. All of them grew out of the raw expression of naked power, ideological fervor, or the influence of corporate special interests seeking to secure access to resources like land, oil or mineral rights, or favored status as traders in the target countries.

As owners and developers of the Republic, we face a sobering question: how can we condemn other nations for doing the same things our leaders have done for over a century? Can we rationalize, morally or practically, a double standard of behavior for our government? Manifest destiny? Might makes right? Necessary evil? If we accept that our leaders have the moral authority to bring down the elected governments of countries who don't share our purposes, then perhaps we should at least own up to it.

HOW ABOUT ASSASSINATIONS?

Next question: would you approve of, condone, or tolerate a covert mission by a unit of the CIA—or by a third party operative sponsored by the CIA—to assassinate the head of a foreign government?

Well, in 1975 a Congressional committee led by Senator Frank Church published a report that detailed US government sponsorship of attempts to assassinate President Patrice Lamumba of the Democratic Republic of Congo; President Rafael Trujillo of the Dominican Republic; President Rene Schneider of Chile; President Ngo Dinh Diem of South Vietnam; and none other than Fidel Castro, President of Cuba.

Spanning across four presidential administrations— Eisenhower's, Kennedy's, Johnson's, and Nixon's—the CIA reportedly made a series of comically inept attempts to kill Fidel Castro. His biographers claim that, over several decades, America's famed spooks tried hundreds of times to knock him off.

They employed methods that ranged all the way from poisoning his cigars, to hiring a call girl to assassinate him, to making a deal with the American Mafia's operatives in Cuba for a contract hit. All of their creative ventures aborted, fizzled, or failed. One can almost picture the CIA as the coyote and Castro as the roadrunner in Warner Brothers' popular cartoon series.

The ever-elusive Castro continued to rule Cuba for over 50 years, dying of natural causes in 2016 at the age of 90.

Again the question confronts us: can we rationalize this kind of behavior on the part of our elected leaders? Do we consider this a part of the mandate we give them when we elect them to office?

As we pursue this exploration of the new Republic, we'll need to engage other questions of values. We'll need to think them through, dissect them, and make informed judgments about the kinds of solutions they might call for.

DOES AMERICA NEED A NEW "BIG IDEA?"

> *"To make a great dream come true,*
> *you must first have a great dream."*
> —Dr. Hans Selye, researcher and
> pioneer of the medical theory of stress

On July 20, 1969, astronaut Neil Armstrong stepped down from the Lunar Landing Module and became the first human being to walk on the moon. Millions of Americans sat in front of their televisions, mesmerized by an event many had thought would never happen in their lifetimes.

The Apollo 11 landing marked the culmination of nearly a decade of research and development, design, testing, and simulation that set a new world standard in science and engineering.

Less than ten years earlier, on May 21, 1961, US President John F. Kennedy had set forth a grand vision for America. Before a joint session of Congress, he declared,

> *"I believe that this nation should commit itself to achieving the goal, before this decade is out, of landing a man on the Moon and returning him safely to Earth."*

That vision launched the $23 billion Apollo project and made NASA—our space agency—a new part of the American consciousness. It also made Americans proud again, a feeling they hadn't had for a long time.

American scientists actually came from behind in the space race. The USSR surprised the Eisenhower administration in October 1957 with its stunning launch of the *Sputnik* (Russian for "traveler") satellite, a basketball-sized device that circled the Earth and transmitted a tracking signal.

Two years later, well before Kennedy's declaration, they launched the first moon mission, crash-landing an unmanned craft into the moon's surface. By 1961 they had sent the first *cosmonaut* into Earth orbit. Through the early 1960s, their scientists repeatedly one-upped their American counterparts with the testing of powerful launch rockets.

By the mid-to-late 1960s, however, their momentum began to wane and the Americans pulled ahead. After the triumphant landing and safe return of the Apollo 11 craft in 1969, plus another five successful American landings and moon walks, the Soviets more or less threw in the towel.

America had officially won the space race.

After the last landing in 1972, however, NASA ended the moon missions and turned its attention to a broad research agenda, based partly on orbital platforms like the Space Shuttle and the Hubble Telescope, and partly on deep-space probes. For all of its stunning engineering achievements in the decades since, the space agency has never again held the awe and admiration of Americans that it had during that golden age of Apollo.

As of this writing, more than four decades after the last moon landings, America has not had another great cause, a grand vision, a new "big idea"—something to sign up for.

The unpopular Vietnam War dragged on for over 10 years, bitterly divided the American public, and ended with the ignominious withdrawal of US forces in 1975. It certainly didn't qualify as a great dream or a noble cause.

A series of economic booms and recessions; Wall Street scandals; an ill-advised misadventure in Afghanistan; and the misguided invasion of Iraq all have left Americans with little to believe in and not much to feel proud of.

As we venture on in our journey of discovery, insight, and renewal, let's keep that possibility alive in our mental incubators. Do we need—and can we find or invent—a new Big Idea that will bring Americans together again?

Chapter 3.
The Concept of The "Commons": Who Owns the River?

"Civilization is more and more a race between education and catastrophe."
—H.G. Wells, British author

I magine that you operate a factory that sits along the bank of a river.

The river can play an important part in your business operations. You can draw water from the river and use it in your manufacturing processes. You might also use the river's water for cooling, if your machinery generates excess heat. You might even bring your raw materials in and ship out your finished products on boats or barges.

Taking advantage of your river location can save you a lot of money. It might even make the difference between a profitable business and one that can't make it.

And, of course, you can also dispose of your waste products by dumping them into the river and letting them float away. No harm done—your little factory couldn't harm that great big river—at least not very much.

Of course, a few fish might die or have mutated offspring from the abnormally warm wastewater. And maybe a few farm animals downstream might get sick from drinking the contaminated water. But you can't worry about those "hypotheticals." You have a business to run; you have customers who want cheap products; and you have shareholders who demand profits.

THE ILLUSION OF THE INFINITE ENVIRONMENT

Now we come to a major, big-time, blockbuster question: Who owns the river?

This question brings us to an elegant—and profoundly important—philosophical concept: the idea of the "Commons." We can define the Commons as the whole of the natural environment that surrounds us, *plus* all of the human-made infrastructure we've emplaced within it.

The term and the concept have bubbled up now and then in the ecological literature. It deserves first-class status in the vocabulary of our remarkable Republic.

Who owns the Commons? Some would say, "Nobody." Others would say, "Everybody." We can take both answers as true, but neither one helps our thinking process very much. Maybe we should think of ourselves, not as owners, but as guests of the Commons.

The "mill on the river" example can serve as a powerful metaphor—a shorthand expression for the problem facing all of us who hope to evolve a newer, better, and stronger Republic. How do we balance, or re-balance, the rights and interests of all stakeholders in the Republic?

Reverence for the Commons, respect for its organic and evolving nature, and awareness of the impact of humans on the "Common-wealth" varies widely from one collection of humans to another. Conquering Europeans have, for centuries, thought of the Commons as infinite, or nearly so.

Localized conflicts over land rights, water rights, access to game animals, and thoroughfares for travel typically get settled locally, often by violence. Somebody wins and somebody loses. The winners usually leave the larger questions of the health of the Commons for a later day.

Peoples whom the conquering Europeans like to think of as primitive tribes often take a more naturalistic view of the Earth-Mother as a living, nurturing, almost sentient presence, deserving of gratitude, awe, and profound respect.

A famous speech attributed to Chief Seattle of the Suquamish tribe in Washington, in 1854 or thereabouts, stands as an historical masterpiece of ecological consciousness as well as poetic language[2]:

> "The President in Washington sends word that he wishes to buy our land. But how can you buy or sell the sky? The land? The idea is strange to us. If we do not own the freshness of the air and the sparkle of the water, how can you buy them?

> "Every part of the Earth is sacred to my people. Every shining pine needle, every sandy shore, every mist in the dark woods, every meadow, every humming insect. All are holy in the memory and experience of my people.

> "We know the sap that courses through the trees as we know the blood that courses through our veins. We are part of the Earth and it is part of us. The perfumed flowers are our sisters. The bear, the deer, the great eagle, these are our brothers. The rocky crests, the dew in the meadow, the body heat of the pony, and man all belong to the same family.

> "The shining water that moves in the streams and rivers is not just water, but the blood of our ancestors. If we sell you our land, you must remember that it is sacred. Each glossy reflection in the clear waters of the lakes tells of events and memories in the life of my people. The water's murmur is the voice of my father's father.

> "The rivers are our brothers. They quench our thirst. They carry our canoes and feed our children. So, you must

give the rivers the kindness that you would give any brother.

"If we sell you our land, remember that the air is precious to us, that the air shares its spirit with all the life that it supports. The wind that gave our grandfather his first breath also received his last sigh. The wind also gives our children the spirit of life. So, if we sell you our land, you must keep it apart and sacred, as a place where man can go to taste the wind that is sweetened by the meadow flowers.

"Will you teach your children what we have taught our children? That the Earth is our mother? What befalls the Earth befalls all the sons of the earth.

"This we know: the Earth does not belong to man; man belongs to the Earth. All things are connected like the blood that unites us all. Man did not weave the web of life; he is merely a strand in it. Whatever he does to the web, he does to himself.

"One thing we know: our God is also your God. The Earth is precious to him and to harm the Earth is to heap contempt on its Creator.

"Your destiny is a mystery to us. What will happen when the buffalo are all slaughtered? The wild horses tamed? What will happen when the secret corners of the forest are heavy with the scent of many men and the view of the ripe hills is blotted with talking wires? Where will the thicket be? Gone! Where will the eagle be? Gone! And what is it to say goodbye to the swift pony and the hunt? The end of living and the beginning of survival.

"When the last red man has vanished with this wilderness and his memory is only the shadow of a cloud moving across the prairie, will these shores and forests still be here? Will there be any of the spirit of my people left?

"We love this Earth as a newborn loves its mother's heartbeat. So, if we sell you our land, love it as we have loved it. Care for it, as we have cared for it. Hold in your mind the memory of the land as it is when you receive it. Preserve the land for all children, and love it, as God loves us.

"As we are part of the land, you too are part of the land. This Earth is precious to us. It is also precious to you.

"One thing we know—there is only one God. No man, be he Red man or White man, can be apart. We are brothers after all."

THE NATURAL ENVIRONMENT AND THE "BUILT" ENVIRONMENT

We can understand the Commons as consisting of two dimensions: the natural environment and the "built" environment. The built environment includes all of the physical modifications we humans have made to the natural environment: cities, buildings, roads, rivers, bridges, harbors, railroads, farms, mines, factories, oil wells, power plants, refineries, dams, canals, reservoirs, parks, the pyramids, the Great Wall of China, cars, trucks, trains, ships, airports, airplanes, shopping malls, schools, colleges, military bases, orbiting satellites, and lots more.

The concept of the Commons has a long and distinguished history as an intellectual proposition, but it has never played a very big role in the national conversation. Political debates and emotional rivalries have customarily degenerated to differences around the notion of the "environment."

"Protecting the environment" seems to imply some kind of preoccupation with the plants and animals, or possibly keeping the air clean. And maybe keeping the water clean, too. But the concept of the Commons goes beyond the physical environment as we think of it, to include both natural and man-made resources, as we'll see later.

Figure 3-1 illustrates the crucial relationship between the people, the corporations, and the government, as they try to live, survive, and thrive as neighbors in the Commons.

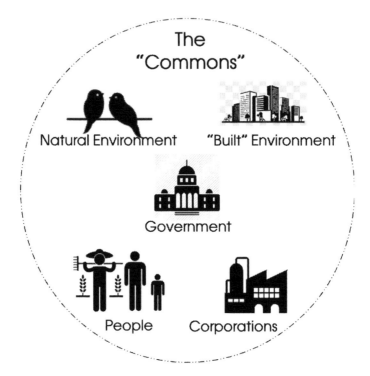

Figure 3-1. The Concept of the Commons

We've usually taken for granted that any reference to the Environment, an ecosystem or subsystem, or the Commons deals with what happens on the Earth's surface. A responsible approach to our environmental challenges, however, now has to include the natural and built environments of space, at least near-Earth space.

The zone above the Earth that scientists call "orbital space" has an estimated 20,000 man-made objects, moving at very high speeds. Many of them now qualify as space junk: old, dead satellites; burned out rockets; debris ejected from space missions; and remnants of explosions or collisions. They range in size from a few centimeters to bus-sized carcasses.

Moving around—rather dangerously—through that sea of

technological flotsam, we have, at latest count, over 2,500 live and functioning satellites. They whiz around in just about all directions, at altitudes ranging from 110 miles to 22,300 miles. The US owns about half of them, with China and Russia a distant second and third.

The orbital junk problem has become a much more significant concern in recent years. The Union of Concerned Scientists maintains a database of all detected space objects, and continually analyzes collision risk.

Platforms like the International Space Station have to adjust their orbital paths to avoid collision with the smallest piece of debris, which could cause catastrophic damage at those high velocities. Some experts have forwarded the idea of "janitor" satellites, which would collect orbital junk and eject it back towards earth, leaving it to burn up on the way down.

Recent to this writing, several American commercial firms have begun launching their own satellites, mostly for handling dedicated Internet traffic. Astronomers have begun expressing concern about the obstruction of their fields of view caused by transiting satellites, and by "visual pollution" in the form of reflected light from the satellites, which poses a problem for viewing faint objects at great distance.

I know of no laws in the US, as of this writing, that attempt to govern or regulate the activities of commercial corporations in the orbital ecosystem.

Another troubling aspect of the orbital ecosystem relates to the prospect of military operations there. All major nations use spy satellites routinely, but the more extreme prospect of satellites attacking other satellites, or missiles launched from orbital platforms looms, looms as yet another phase in the pathological competition for military superiority.

Soon we'll also have to think realistically about a further extension to our concept of the Commons, namely *planetary space*. As NASA and the space industry focus more and more on returning to the moon, we'll have to devote more attention to what goes on in our solar system. We don't even have a conceptual structure for thinking about that yet, and we ignore those implications at our peril.

THE AMERICAN PIE: WHO GETS THE BIGGEST PIECE?

In modern industrialized societies, social activists argue, the extremely lopsided control of wealth—denominated in dollars and in things—has resulted from two centuries of free use of the Commons by corporations and their owners, with no particular obligation to pay anything back. We'll devote close attention to this critical issue—the "corporate exemption"—as we explore the need to rethink the roles of corporations in the life of the Republic.

Some advocates of unrestrained corporate growth like to conjure up scenarios that pit the economic value of a dam or pipeline against the survival of some biologically obscure bird or fish. Some eco-fanatics, on the other hand, seek to demonize corporations in a topdog-underdog scenario that pictures them as heroic crusaders against the evil empire.

Both factions miss the point, I believe. As I see it, both have mis-framed the issue by not thinking big enough. We need to enlarge our perspective from a focus on the physical environment to a focus on the Commons.

This concept of sharing the fruits of the Commons and a balanced co-existence will play a critically important role as we proceed through our journey of discovery and rethinking. It will radically reshape our options with respect to revenue; taxes; regulation; economic cooperation; the pressing issue of infrastructure renewal; and the looming issue of the climate crisis.

THE CORPORATE EXEMPTION: OUR GREATEST HISTORICAL BLUNDER

The Founders missed one colossally important judgment call as they went about setting up the mechanisms of revenue, taxation, and commerce. That missed call had to do with the roles and responsibilities of corporations in the Republic.

In their defense, they couldn't possibly have known that things would turn out the way they did.

Four prospective developments that apparently didn't appear in their crystal balls have had an enormous influence in shaping the Republic as it stands today:

1. They had no clear grasp of the concept of the Commons (and, we should note, neither do most of our citizens and political leaders, even today). They all understood the value of land and natural resources and the need to conserve Nature's offerings, in a general way at least. But looking out at the vast expanse of uninhabited territory, the abundance of fertile land, and the vast waterways, they understandably tended to think of the natural environment as practically infinite.

2. They had no real experience or understanding of corporations as economic machines, at least not the kinds we generally know today. The vast mega-corporations we see in modern times, with tens of thousands of employees and many billions of dollars of capital, didn't exist yet. Thomas Jefferson, for one, did take notice of the early corporate empires in the making and warned that large and powerful corporations would one day threaten the power of the central government. But in general, even knowing what they knew, the Founders made no mention of corporations in the Constitution, and seldom emphasized it in their public discourse.

3. They especially didn't anticipate the capacity of the corporation, as an economic entity, to concentrate ever-increasing wealth in the hands of its owners. The legendary robber barons—John D. Rockefeller, Andrew Carnegie, and J. P. Morgan—wouldn't come on the scene for another 50 years or so. Mergers, acquisitions, cartels, and interlocking trusts developed later, during the so-called Gilded Age. Also,

the commercial banking industry had not grown to the point where corporations could borrow enormous sums of money to fund grand capital projects that could generate mind-boggling profits. They also had only a vague inkling of the political influence that corporations would eventually wield by using their money to shape the laws in their favor.

4. They could only see the faint glimmerings of the developing Industrial Revolution, which would eventually compromise the natural environment on a grand scale. Air and water pollution, mass deforestation, habitant destruction, and extinction of species had not become noticeable yet. The ecological side-effects of the Industrial Revolution had begun to show up in England in a big way, but they hadn't yet migrated to the New World in full force.

The net result of the Founders' innocent and understandable ignorance of these four driving influences brings us to the problematic role of the corporation in the Republic of today, and an unfortunate political polarization between detractors and advocates of capitalism.

What might the Founders have done differently, if they had known 200 years ago what we know now?

CAPITALISM, AMERICAN STYLE

From the very early days of the Republic, corporate leaders, bankers, and the legislators who served their interests had begun to preach a doctrine known as "laissez-faire" capitalism. The French term means, approximately, "allow to do," or in plainer language, "leave us alone." Laissez-faire doctrine promoted the belief that unimpeded capitalism would create the greatest benefit for all. Its fans argued that government interference, including taxes, tariffs, trade laws, or close regulation, would ultimately cause more harm than good by promoting or protecting inefficiency.

Laissez-faire fans liked to claim support from the theories of Adam Smith, a Scottish economist who wrote the landmark book known as *The Wealth of Nations,* in 1776[3]. Smith offered a metaphor that quickly became famous, the idea of the "invisible hand." He argued that a free market economy would tend to evolve to greater and greater levels of efficiency as individuals pursued their own selfish financial interests. He likened this ever-improving allocation of resources to the influence of some invisible hand, as if guided by an imaginary supra-intelligent consciousness. He argued that government attempts to control or change this dynamic allocation process would only interfere with the wisdom of the invisible hand, and would inhibit economic evolution.

The laissez-faire guys took Smith's principles to extremes, developing a political ideology that called for the absolute minimum government interference in the processes of capitalism. Smith, however, never advocated a complete hands-off approach and in fact he cautioned emphatically against concentrating economic power in the hands of a few.

By the mid-to-late 1800s the Industrial Revolution had begun to kick in with greater and greater impact, and an increasing number of talented capitalists began building large factories, mills, mines, railroads, oil refineries, and other production facilities. Adam Smith's enlightened version of capitalism quickly morphed into a cynical form of predatory capitalism. In this profit-above-all world, factory owners took advantage of the influx of desperate workers from the impoverished countryside, offering them grueling labor for long hours, in inhumane working conditions, and near-starvation wages.

Ecological consciousness, as we know it today, barely existed in those days of unbridled capitalist power. The owners of textile mills in New England thought nothing of dumping their waste products into the Charles River—typically after midnight, so they'd have floated far downstream by dawn. Steel mills vented coal fumes into the air, although they used tall smokestacks to make sure the particulate matter floated above the landscape and drifted far away before it settled.

Massive slaughterhouses in urban centers like Chicago emitted foul-smelling odors that wafted across the residential areas of the city.

Predatory capitalists also used their accumulated economic power to exterminate their smaller or weaker competitors. John D. Rockefeller, the founder of the Standard Oil empire, used his buying power with the railroads to bring oil to his refineries and ship the refined kerosene (and later, gasoline and other derivatives) to markets. He offered to buy a guaranteed amount of their shipping capacity at high rates, if they agreed not to ship the products of his competitors. After crippling his competitors with those kinds of deals, he acquired them at bargain prices as they sank into bankruptcy.

And, of course, the robber barons and their cohorts gave us a long and distinguished legacy of buying influence in Congress and the state legislatures. Bribery had become just another cost of doing business.

Rockefeller, the steel baron Andrew Carnegie, and the financial kingpin J. P. Morgan, as well as other members of the new capitalist nobility accumulated massive fortunes. Rockefeller, for his part, had become one of the richest men in history. During the period that Mark Twain christened the Gilded Age, the *nouveau riche* built fabulous mansions, bought yachts, collected artwork, and entertained lavishly.

This corporate excess eventually attracted the attention of more and more political leaders—notably Teddy Roosevelt. He introduced legislation to limit or break up the gigantic "trusts," or interlocking combinations of corporations that owned one another's stock and had the same people on all of their boards. This "trust-busting" phase peaked with the act of Congress that broke up Standard Oil in 1911.

A KINDER, GENTLER CAPITALISM?

By the early 1900s, governments had become fed up with the extremes of laissez-faire capitalism, and a series of presidents supported legislation that would rein in some of the worst excesses of corporations. In the 1930s, the federal government officially recognized the legitimacy of trade unions, and forced corporations to allow union recruitment, and to bargain in good faith if their employees adopted unions to represent them.

But laissez-faire capitalism never really died, and in modern times we still have corporate leaders and political pundits who adamantly defend the ideology. A patchwork of miscellaneous laws has accumulated over decades, aimed at getting corporations to behave themselves as willing partners in the Republic. We would have to judge the results as mixed, at best.

Willful pollution and environmental destruction still prevail, especially in some particular industries. Unfair employment practices, with discrimination against women, people of color, and people of nontraditional gender orientations haven't gone out of style. Cynical lobbying and campaign financing have turned the Capitol into the national whorehouse. Clearly, we still have a long way to go.

The Environmental Protection Agency, for example, only came into existence in 1970, during the Nixon administration. EPA has the responsibility of conducting research, monitoring various environmental processes, setting quality standards for air, water, and other resources; and for enforcing standards of corporate behavior. In its modern incarnation, the EPA plays only a weak hand in the process of managing and protecting the Commons, and a series of presidential administrations has done little to empower it as a real player in the ecological mission.

Considering the long history of corporate behavior, some of it noble and some of it ignoble, the business-as-usual approach —regulation and watchdog enforcement—doesn't seem to work very well. If we continue thinking about commerce in the same old ways, we can only look forward to a continuing stalemate, with anti-corporate sentiment reflexively opposed by the political influence of wealthy corporate owners and political donors.

In the exploration that follows, we'll consider a fundamentally new way of thinking about the role of the corporation in the modern Republic, and a new set of relationships between the corporation, the people, and the government.

WHAT WOULD THE FOUNDERS THINK?

Let's climb into our imaginary time machine, set the date for 1787, and pay a visit to the Founders. We'll land in Philadelphia, on the steps of the stately Independence Hall on Chestnut Street. We'll walk in through the entrance beneath the majestic clock tower and present ourselves at the Assembly Room, where we'll ask for permission to address the busy working session. We arrive just as the representatives from the various colonies roll up their sleeves and get ready for the difficult task ahead.

We'll report to the distinguished gathering of the Founders about how their blueprint for the original Republic has worked out, as of the early decades of the twenty-first century. What shall we tell them that might help them think about the role of the corporation in the new Republic?

We'll report that:

1. One the one hand, corporations have had a phenomenal impact on the economic development of the Republic and on the material standard of living of its citizens, making possible grand ventures such as the Hoover Dam, the moon landing, and Disneyland.

2. On the other hand, uncontrolled corporate growth has wreaked havoc on the natural environment, and has brought us to a critical point with regard to global climate change. It has raised fundamental existential questions about the survival of the Republic as we know it.

3. Political parties and activist groups have degenerated into a stalemated conflict about what to do with corporations: how to tax them, how to regulate them, and how to charge them for their share of the repairs to the Commons—if, hopefully, we haven't passed the point of no return. One extreme faction sees the corporation as the savior of the American Way of Life. The other extreme faction sees it as an evil empire, controlled by self-interested kleptomaniacs who can never satisfy their greed. The two factions will probably never reconcile their world views.

After listening to our sober assessment of the legacy of the "corporate exemption"—the benign neglect of the unanticipated issues associated with the activities of corporations—the Founders solicit our advice and opinions.

AMENDING THE BLUEPRINT

Let's suppose we advise them to do the following:

1. Declare and define the corporation as a constitutionally recognized—and regulated—component of the Republic.

2. Declare that every legitimate corporation exists by permission of the Republic, and by extension the permission of society at large. It exists to contribute value for *all participants* in the life of the Republic; to preserve the integrity of the Commons in the normal course of its operation; and to enable its sponsors and owners to enjoy the profits it earns through the use of their ingenuity and their capital.

3. Assert the doctrine that, because every corporation takes advantage of the resources of the Commons— the fruits of the natural environment, and the facilities of the built environment—the Republic (as keeper of the Commons) claims entitlement as a figurative shareholder in each enterprise.

4. Explain that the Republic grants to every legitimate corporation a figurative *license* to use the abundant resources of the Commons. In addition to the natural resources, the Republic provides for national security; a system of laws and law enforcement; public transport; public safety and public health services; emergency and disaster relief services; postal services; clean air; clean water; electrical power; a national highway system; an educated workforce; and many other "valuable considerations."

5. Affirm that the Republic has the right and responsibility to collect a figurative "license fee" from every corporation, in view of the benefits it enjoys from the Commons. We recommend that this license fee take the form, not of an "income" tax (a misguided fix that we'll take up later in this book), but as an ongoing dividend measured in *shares of the corporation*.

Later in our journey of rethinking the Republic, we'll consider a radical new concept for the Revenue component—a new system of taxes and other collections that provides the national government with the money needed to deliver all of the services it owes to the people. We'll see how completely eliminating the problematic and outdated income tax can give way to a much simpler, fairer, and streamlined system of taxes that will eliminate the ideological conflicts about the corporation's "fair share" of the costs of the Republic.

Stay tuned . . .

Chapter 4.
Let's Rethink Governance:
Fixing the Top of the Pyramid

*"No one with a weak stomach
should watch sausage—or the law—being made."*
—Oliver Wendell Holmes
US Supreme Court Justice

The "balance of powers" mechanism given to us by the Founders—the three-way combination of the Legislative, Executive, and Judicial branches—sometimes seems like a mixed blessing.

When it works best, the members of each branch respect the rights and responsibilities of the others. Cooperation and compromise become necessary to doing business. Then the Republic benefits.

But when the players become so divided ideologically or they become so obsessed with factional identities that they no longer want to compromise, the relationships can become antagonistic and even toxic. Then the Republic suffers.

As of this writing, the dominant narratives in the American national conversation all seem to revolve around *conflict.* Everywhere Americans look they see battles going on.

The leaders of the two political parties that control Congress have become deadlocked in a toxic relationship of mutual contempt, attack and counterattack, and payback politics. Combative, vindictive, self-serving behavior on both sides has nearly paralyzed the entire legislative process.

WHERE HAVE ALL OUR LEADERS GONE?

More and more Americans have started asking, "Does anybody in politics really care about the country any more? What happened to the statesmen, the thought leaders, the compromisers, the dealmakers?" Public opinion polls consistently show that Americans no longer respect or trust their political leaders. A recent poll showed Congress with an approval rating of just 18 percent.

Meanwhile, the news industry, with its addiction to conflict as the standard model for framing the big stories, now relentlessly simplifies, personalizes, and amplifies the differences that divide the various factions.

The practical effect of this paralyzing conflict and deadlock in so many aspects of the political process means that *we don't get the big things done.* And without the respect and approval of the public, how can we mobilize energy and commitment for the big challenges we face?

Meanwhile, antagonistic foreign governments enjoy watching us acting like our own worst enemies.

In this chapter we analyze the root causes of the paralysis at the top of the national pyramid and identify specific measures that might possibly change the motivational forces acting on the key players.

LET'S CHOOSE OUR PRESIDENTS MORE INTELLIGENTLY: CHARACTER AND COMPETENCE

Every four years, Americans go through a comical spasm of collective emotional incontinence, euphemistically referred to as "electing the President." Then they have four years to discover the consequences of their visceral decisions.

Picking a president has become just another of the many channels of entertainment that help Americans avoid the strenuous use of their gray matter. The theatrical production that passes for the presidential election process has become so addictive to all participants—the news industry, the promoters of the candidates, and most of the citizens of the country—that rational thought and discourse seem strangely alien, an unwanted distraction from our amusement.

WHAT KINDS OF PRESIDENTS TO WE LIKE?

Looking back at the line-up of 45 presidents, we can try to detect some common characteristics that might reflect our collective historical preferences. A few patterns seem obvious, but not necessarily enlightening.

As of this writing, we've had no female presidents; one African-American; no Asians; no Hispanics; no Jews or Muslims; one Catholic; one gay (by speculation); 26 who served in the military; one-third with considerable personal wealth, and another third with near-zero net worth.

Strangely, nearly a third of our presidents—14—have belonged to the order of Freemasons. Most had college degrees, but some (Lincoln) had almost no formal schooling.

We've never had a president with a name we couldn't pronounce or spell (Washington, Adams, Jefferson, Madison, Monroe—Kennedy, Johnson, Clinton, etc.). Beginning with Lincoln in 1860, all but two of the next 12 presidents had beards or mustaches. Facial hair went out of presidential style with William H. Taft in 1913; since then, no president in over 100 years has had it.

CAN WE FIND A BETTER WAY?

In the run-up to the 2008 elections, I decided to tap into some of the best minds on the planet to discover a *presidential leadership model*—a set of meaningful evaluation criteria that could help thoughtful people compare candidates and choose the leader they want.

I planned to interview some of the world's top thinkers and experts on leadership and pin down maybe six to eight key criteria: What *high-level skills* does a US President need to lead the nation effectively?

I had percolated the idea for a long time. Many years before, I proposed it to one of my editors. We would create a voter's handbook, a sort of journal that people could use to rate the candidates on some reasonably meaningful criteria other than personality, hairdo, or an attractive wife.

My editor chuckled and said, "That's a great idea. I'll bet I can sell at least 10 copies—counting the ones your Mom buys." I suppose he had it right then, but I never gave up on the idea.

CHARACTER AND COMPETENCE—A PRESIDENT NEEDS BOTH

Never having given up on my quixotic idea of picking a president based on the capacity to actually lead, I took up the question again. I combed all the books in my library dealing with high-level leadership, looking for key competencies. I contacted a number of prominent academic experts I knew and asked them to identify key competencies. I considered my own experience of over thirty years consulting to top executives and tried to recall the things they'd told me.

I solicited the inputs of a group of professional consultants in an international online community focused on leadership. Of the 1500 members, about 100 decided to play.

First, I presented them with an alphabetical list of about 75 commonly known character traits and asked them to choose the top ten they considered most critical for a President.

The following list shows the percentage of the experts who scored each trait in their top ten.

Key Presidential Character Traits

(Expert ratings of top ten traits, 86 responses)

Trait	% Rating as Critical
5. Trustworthy	77.01 %
6. Intelligent	59.77 %
7. Visionary	58.62 %
8. Collaborative	49.43 %
9. Courageous	49.43 %
10.Authentic	43.68 %
11.Open Minded	43.68 %
12.Compassionate	40.23 %
13. Wise	40.23 %
14. Articulate	39.08 %

Next, I went back to the experts and asked them to describe as many *key competencies* as they could think of—in any form, any terminology, any degree of generality or specificity. Of about 450 competency terms they submitted, about 50 seemed relevant and useful. I combined those potential competencies with the others I'd collected from interviews and finally managed to boil down the list to nine, arranged in an order that seemed to make sense conceptually.

The following list shows the top nine presidential competencies that made the final cut.

Key Presidential Competencies

(Synthesized from over 400 contributions)

1. Strategic Thinking
2. Promoting A Grand Vision For The Country
3. Leading Public Opinion
4. Leading The Executive Team

5. Practical Politics (Getting Others On Board)

6. Political Autonomy (Freedom from Partisan Obligations)

7. Building Coalitions

8. Advocating America's Highest Values

9. Representing America To The World

Then I put up a website, *pickingapresident.com,* and provided an online evaluation form that visitors could use to score any or all of the candidates running at the time, on the top nine competencies and the top ten character traits.

When I looked at the scoring data provided by the website visitors, I could see only one clear conclusion: my editor probably called it right.

To say that people didn't exactly stampede to my website might qualify as the understatement of the decade. I counted less than 100 visitors who rated any of the candidates. Probably no more than 1000 people even visited the site.

Worse, almost all of the ratings skewed heavily in favor of one candidate or another, and heavily against his competitors —typically all 5's or all 1's. Apparently most of the respondents took the exercise as simply a chance to cheer for the candidate they already liked. The data proved useless for my research purposes.

My conclusion after all that research: Americans like the election process they have. They don't want to over-think it.

LET'S GIVE THE VICE PRESIDENT A REAL JOB

Reading the Constitution, one might get the impression that the Founders thought of the Vice President as sort of a spare tire, with no other purpose than to wait around in case a main tire goes flat. They prescribed no duties or responsibilities for the Vice President other than casting a deciding vote in the Senate in case of a tie.

Will Rogers, America's cowboy philosopher, declared,

"The man with the best job in the country is the Vice President. All he has to do is get up every morning and say, 'How's the President?'"

Through most of our history, vice presidents have hovered in the background, occasionally seen and seldom heard. The candidate for President usually chooses a running mate who rounds out the ticket, broadening the appeal to the widest possible population of voters.

John F. Kennedy chose a Texan, Lyndon Johnson, as his running mate, to offer voters in the Old South and Heartland states a balance between his aristocratic, old-money New England image, and a savvy politician familiar to them.

In other cases, presidential candidates have chosen running mates specifically for their blandness, to avoid contaminating the chief's brand image with someone of a more complex or controversial identity.

NO PLACE TO CALL HOME

Before the opening of the White House in 1800, presidents and vice presidents commuted from their estates to Philadelphia—and later to the District of Columbia—to take care of government business. But for more than a century after the White House became the official residence of presidents, vice presidents had no official residence.

Surprisingly, not until 1974 did Congress designate an old mansion, built on the grounds of the US Naval Observatory two miles across town, as the Vice President's residence.

"NOT WORTH A BUCKET OF WARM ..."

The spare-tire concept of the Vice President has had some big political consequences. Vice Presidents tended to become ever more bland and ineffectual as they dutifully remained in the shadows behind their presidents.

John Nance Garner, who served as Franklin Delano

Roosevelt's VP during his first two terms, said,

"Worst damn-fool mistake I ever made was letting myself be elected Vice President of the United States. Should have stuck with my old chores as Speaker of the House. I gave up the second most important job in the Government for one that didn't amount to a hill of beans. I spent eight long years as Mr. Roosevelt's spare tire. I might still be Speaker if I didn't let them elect me Vice-President."

More pointedly, Garner described the Vice President's job as "not worth a bucket of warm piss." The often-quoted version got sanitized as "not worth a bucket of warm spit."

But of all the unusual and intriguing stories about vice presidents, none can match the strange episode of Harry S. Truman's rise to the presidency. Truman came to Washington in 1935 under the political patronage of a Missouri political boss who saw him as a colorless, compliant amateur, easily manipulated by those who put him there. He served as a Senator, quietly and obediently, until the election year of 1944, when Franklin Delano Roosevelt ran for an unprecedented fourth term.

According to most historical narratives, Truman and FDR barely knew each other at the time when FDR's political machine kicked into gear for his fourth presidential run. When the architects of his campaign deadlocked on the choice of his running mate, several insiders suggested Truman as a safe and non-controversial choice. After a brief phone conversation FDR accepted Truman as his VP.

Roosevelt died of a massive stroke on April 12, 1945—just as the WW2 conflict in Europe came to a close—making Truman the President after only 82 days in the VP role. By that point Truman had only met FDR a few times.

FDR apparently saw little value in having a second in command and Truman seldom attended cabinet meetings or other significant events.

His first big shock as President came when his staff told him about the massive Manhattan Project, the now-legendary effort to build the atomic bombs the US dropped on Japan. To this day it remains an astonishing fact of political life that Truman knew nothing about the most important military undertaking in the history of the Republic, even though it had begun five years earlier, employed some 120,000 workers at several locations, and burned through $2 billion in expenses.

Most historians agree that Truman made a remarkable personal transition from the role of an ignorant bystander to an effective head of state. He had the awesome responsibility of approving the completion of the Manhattan Project and of deploying a new and fearsome weapon of astonishing power. Few of his minders and contemporaries would have predicted his success in guiding the country though the Great War and into a new era of Cold War.

FROM SPARE TIRE TO REAL EXECUTIVE

This brief historical flashback brings us to a big question for the American Republic of the future: shouldn't the Vice President contribute more effectively to the leadership and operation of the government? Should the VP have a real job?

The President's workload of non-executive activities— developing policy, sparring with House and Senate leaders, receiving foreign dignitaries, participating in international meetings, and making public appearances, makes it impossible for him or her to manage the Executive Branch in a manner typical of a corporate CEO. As a result, the many cabinet departments tend to go off in their own directions, following their own internal compasses and often not coordinating their activities very well.

An intriguing possibility for the VP role seems worthy of careful consideration. It involves placing all cabinet departments under the direct management of the Vice President, while allowing all cabinet heads to maintain direct personal access to the President whenever they want it.

Making the vice presidency a true executive job could give us a much more effective White House operation, one that could enable the various cabinet departments to cooperate much more effectively. Of course, if we want a Vice President who can lead and manage, we'll have to change the emphasis on selecting candidates for the office.

LET'S SET TERM LIMITS: THE TRIPLE-SIX FORMULA

The Constitution currently dictates that US presidents can serve a maximum of two four-year terms. Senators serve for six-year terms, with no restrictions on getting re-elected. Members of the House serve for two-year terms, also with unlimited re-elections if they can keep winning.

As of this writing, we have five senators past the age of 80, with the oldest at 86. Another 18 have reached their 70s. The average age for all currently serving Senators stands at 57 years. Members of the House average 61 years. Those averages make it the oldest Congress in US history. The average (median) age of the general US population stands at 38, making a difference of nearly a whole generation between the members and the people they represent.

The longest serving member of Congress, John Dingell of Michigan, occupied a seat in the House of Representatives for 59 years. In the Senate, Strom Thurmond of North Carolina served for 48 years. We have to wonder whether a member of Congress who's occupied the seat for 20 years or more still has the vision, ambition, and energy to do big things.

SIX YEARS AND OUT

The largest collection of US presidents ever living at one time included Gerald Ford, Jimmy Carter, Ronald Reagan, George H.W. Bush, Bill Clinton & George W. Bush, Jr. All of them discussed and advocated the idea of changing the period of the presidency to *a single six-year term*.

This idea has received relatively little attention so far, but it deserves serious consideration.

Jimmy Carter and other advocates of the idea pointed out

that a single six-year term would liberate the President from the ugly process of election politics and would allow him or her to devote full attention to the affairs of state. He or she wouldn't have to pander to factions, kingmakers, news pundits, wealthy donors, and political operators from the first day of office, out of a need to get re-elected.

ONE AND DONE—BACK TO THE FARM

The same kind of thinking applies to the terms of the elected Senators and House members. The short two-year term of office for members of the House means that daily life for them becomes a non-stop campaign for the next election.

That two-year limit probably has its origins in the attitudes of the Founders, who wanted a government controlled by the elite members of the society—read "elite" as meaning men of means who owned land. That tended to mimic the pattern of the British Parliament, with its House of Lords occupied by the titled nobility—the "upper house," as they called it—and the House of Commons—the "lower house"—populated by commoners. In the British system, to this day, the House of Lords can override any measure passed by the Commons.

A similar set-up in the US Congress gave greater influence to a Senate—a small body of elite citizens—who would serve for a longer term of six years. The US Senate has the power to "advise and consent" on the appointment of cabinet members and senior officers of the government. Only the Senate can remove a sitting president after impeachment. Only the Senate can declare war.

By setting the term of office for the lower chamber at a very short two years, the Founders may have hoped to keep a steady turnover in the House membership, thereby preventing the rise of seasoned politicians and powerful coalitions who might vie with the Senate for power.

It didn't work out that way. The well-known incumbent advantage means that any new candidate for either chamber faces an uphill battle against the entrenched office holder.

Actually, the Founders never intended for a seat in the Legislature to become a career. Most of the elected members enjoyed at least moderate degrees of wealth. Most wanted to contribute their talents to the process occasionally and then get back to their privileged lives. The Founders didn't provide for salaries, benefits, or pensions. They decreed only that senators and House members receive a *per diem* payment—a daily expense allowance of six dollars each—only for the days they actually convened in legislative sessions.

Over time, the payments grew—as they voted raises for themselves—the legislative process became more ponderous, and the career politician gradually evolved. Annual salaries for members of Congress passed the six-figure mark in 1991. As of this writing, a Congressional salary stands at $174,000. Considering all the other benefits that come with the job, such as free medical care, free travel, and retirement plans, one might say that serving the country has become a rather cushy job.

The time has come for a Constitutional amendment. Let's change the President's office and the VP's, to *a single six-year term.* Let's make the House and Senate terms equal, also at six years, with no re-elections.

Let's refer to this approach as the Triple-Six formula.

It would mean that every election for President, VP, the House, and the Senate would involve a contest between two completely new candidates. No incumbent advantage.

Interestingly, our cowboy philosopher Will Rogers proposed the single six-year term limit for presidents years ago, saying,

> *"The President should hold office six years with no re-election. Stop this thing of a President having to lower his dignity and go trooping around asking for votes to keep him another term. Six years gives him time to do something. Then pay the man when he goes out one-half of his salary for life."*

Will would have made a great consultant.

LET'S SET TERM LIMITS FOR JUDGES

As we consider term limits for the President, Vice President, and members of Congress, let's go ahead and set limits on the length of service for Supreme Court justices, as well as for all other life-appointed federal judges throughout the system.

Why impose these limits now? Wouldn't the Founders have set those limits if they considered them important? Well, for one thing, the Founders lived in an era with an average lifespan of less than fifty years. Physical senility and dementia presented very few risks because most people died from infectious diseases and accidents long before those disorders could possibly set in.

Second, as a general principle, a certain amount of turnover can help to bring new energies and new perspectives, and can average out political biases over the long run.

And everything we can say about term limits for the High Court, we can also say about the various federal courts under its jurisdiction.

Some would argue that an institution like the High Court should operate on a longer time line and that its doctrines should outlast the short-term variations in the political process. If that proposition makes sense, let's consider setting the term of service for the Supremes at twice the time we allocate for the Executive and Legislative branches, making it a total of 12 years. We might consider an option for a single extension, subject to Senate reconfirmation.

LET'S ADOPT MANDATORY VOTING

At the time of this writing, 22 countries have compulsory voting requirements, although only 10 of them strictly enforce it. The concept has received relatively little attention in the US but it deserves serious consideration.

WE CAN LEARN FROM THE AUSSIES

Australia's voting system has received considerable praise

over the years. Scholars have analyzed the effects of the higher turnout on elections and on public policy.

Since the country introduced compulsory voting in 1924, turnout has ranged as high as 96 percent in some elections and has never fallen below 90 percent. About 96 percent of eligible citizens there have registered to vote.

By comparison, turnout rates in US elections have typically averaged about 50% of registered voters, peaking at 55 to 58 percent in the most recent elections. Turnouts typically drop much further during mid-term elections, when only Congressional seats and local offices come into play.

One has to read even those numbers carefully, however. Turnout rates indicate the percentage of *people registered to vote*, not the percentage of all citizens. Several national studies indicate that about 20 percent of Americans across the board typically don't register to vote and therefore can't participate. So, if 50 percent of the 80 percent who have registered show up to vote, we have an actual turnout of about 40 percent of the whole population.

How can we describe the American Republic as a representative democracy when less than half of the people choose its leaders?

WE'VE MADE VOTING A CHORE—LET'S MAKE IT FUN

The way we schedule our elections surely has an impact on the relatively low turnout. Way back in the 1800s, Congress set the dates for the national election and the President's inauguration. By some peculiar reasoning process they ended up with the election always occurring on a Tuesday. In those days, when most people lived and worked on farms, it didn't matter much. Today, when a majority of employed people work the standard 5-day work week, it matters a lot.

Many people find it inconvenient to leave work or close their shops or juggle a visit to the polls with picking up their children. By moving election day to the last Saturday in November, two days after the traditional Thanksgiving celebration, we can make a four-day national holiday out of it. Imagine having voting parties and election-watching parties at clubs, pubs, churches, and homes—a four-day food and drink festival that rivals the Fourth of July.

A mandatory voting system could become one of our most effective mechanisms for modernizing the political process, and we might also find it one of the easiest ones to adopt. No longer could political candidates get elected by pandering to key factions with special interests and selfish demands.

I've had some personal experience with this system. I spent a few days with friends in Australia a few years ago, during their election. As I walked with them down to the neighborhood polling place, I asked how they felt about the compulsory aspect of voting and whether they ever considered not voting and risking a fine (failing to show up at a voting place incurs a relatively small penalty, in the form of a $20 fine—about US $14 at the recent exchange rate).

The typical answer I got went something like, "We've done it so long that it's just a habit now. It's no big hardship to go and vote, and it's good for the country. Nobody thinks about the fine. We just vote because we've always voted."

One potential push-back that can arise in a conversation about mandatory voting asks, "What about individual rights? Suppose I just don't *want* to vote? Suppose I don't like any of the candidates?" The answer, according to my Aussie friends, makes it simple: you don't have to vote—you just have to turn up at the polling place. You can drop in a blank ballot or you can write in Mickey Mouse or anybody you like.

The obvious advantage of the mandatory voting system becomes clear: the national vote provides a *statistically valid statement* by the entire population of the Republic, not just a fraction of the people who choose to show up for their own idiosyncratic reasons. It represents the will of the people because it *includes* all the people—or almost all of them.

LET'S ABOLISH THE OBSOLETE ELECTORAL COLLEGE

As of this writing, 45 men have moved into the White House and assumed control of the presidency.

Five of those men—more than ten percent—became presidents even though a majority of the voters chose someone else. This category of accidental Presidents includes John Quincy Adams in 1824, Rutherford Hayes in 1876, Benjamin Harrison in 1888, George W. Bush, Jr., in 2000, and Donald Trump in 2016.

How did this happen? How could a candidate ascend to the White House against the wishes of the majority of the voters?

The answer lies in a dusty old relic of the early Republic: the Electoral College, which survived as a hand-me-down from the old European politics dominated by the aristocracy.

Debates have raged ever since the first incident, about whether to keep or abolish it. After every election the same old debate heats up again and shortly thereafter the discussion always dies. We came close to getting rid of it in 1970, when the House passed a Constitutional amendment, but the measure died in the Senate in a filibuster.

For the record: you won't find a place or a building called the Electoral College. It exists—and persists—as a political process, not a physical thing. The Constitution defines it and gives a few brief directions about how it should work.

Each state gets a number of *electoral votes* equal to the number of seats it has in the Congress. That means two electoral votes corresponding to its two Senators, and one vote for each of its seats in the House of Representatives. That number depends on the size of its population.

The least populous state, Wyoming, with about 575,000 residents, gets 3 electoral votes (the same as the six other smallest states). California, with the most people, gets 55. Washington, DC gets three—although it has no seats in Congress. To win the presidential election, a candidate must capture more than half of the national total of 538 electoral votes, or 270.

The most contentious feature of the process specifies that the candidate who receives the most citizen votes for any particular state gets *all of the electoral votes* allocated to that state, even if he or she only wins in that state by a single vote. As of this writing, two states—Maine and Nebraska—allocate their electoral votes in proportion to the popular votes. All the others use the winner-takes-it-all method.

People who want to abolish the EC point to the sense of anger and injustice that arises when a candidate ascends to the White House after having lost the majority of the popular vote. It happened five times and will probably happen again.

The all-or-nothing rule has the effect of statistically nullifying the votes of a huge number of citizens, as if they had never voted at all. Conceivably, a single vote in a single state could swing the whole election one way or the other, even if one candidate had a clear majority overall.

Defenders of the EC claim that it somehow gives the small states some degree of extra clout against the political desires of the biggest ones. But that claim doesn't hold up logically. Only in an exceedingly rare circumstance would North Dakota's 3 electoral votes tip an election.

Let's make it simple: in most elections, where a popular majority causes a decisive win in electoral votes, the Electoral College procedure becomes a meaningless exercise, so why even have it? On the other hand, in the case of a very close election, the procedure could cause an illegitimate outcome, as we've seen five times so far. In either case the Electoral College system does not serve the Republic well.

The solution: a Constitutional amendment that abolishes the Electoral College and reverts to the natural process of accumulating all votes at the national level. In cases of close ties—say a margin of 0.5 percent—a run-off election between the two top candidates would settle it. In case of 3 or more candidates, if none scored at least 50 percent of the vote, a run-off election between the top two would settle it.

LET'S REIN IN PRESIDENTIAL MISCONDUCT

We Americans love to hear our pundits declare, "No one is above the law, not even the President." But this charming affirmation doesn't necessarily hold true. A president certainly can place himself above the law if those legendary checks and balances we learned about in high school don't actually check and balance.

It often seems that we have one set of rules for John and Jane Citizen and a different set for the people in public office.

The Founders of the Republic displayed remarkable insight— and foresight—as they worked out the basic design for governance. But a few weaknesses in the arrangement they gave us have surfaced repeatedly over the years, and particularly during the past several decades. Both leave the Republic vulnerable to misbehaving presidents.

The Founders might have believed or hoped that presidents, chosen by a rigorous process of scrutiny by the citizens, would invariably keep faith with the higher values of the Republic and would always place their sworn constitutional responsibilities above their own self-interest. And, thankfully, most of them have. But in the unusual case of a corrupt or destructive chief executive, the system can fall apart.

PINOCCHIO FOR PRESIDENT?

More than one US president has deliberately misled the American people or outright lied to them about matters of national importance. Most of them have paid no significant price for it. Let's review the big cases.

> ‣ President Dwight Eisenhower, as previously recounted, knowingly and willfully lied to the American people, Congress, and the world about the infamous U-2 spy flights over Russia in 1960. Yet Ike remains a revered soldier-president in the American cultural memory.

> ‣ President John Kennedy reluctantly authorized the secret CIA-led Bay of Pigs invasion of Cuba in 1961,

which he had inherited from the Eisenhower administration. The botched attempt to overthrow the communist government of Fidel Castro caused a political crisis for JFK when he and his senior military leaders could no longer conceal the disastrous outcome. Aside from that, his extra-marital affairs with actress Marilyn Monroe and several other women only came to light after his death. Yet Kennedy also remains an admired and beloved president, martyred by an assassin's bullet before completing his first term.

▸ President Lyndon Johnson knowingly promoted a false report that claimed North Vietnamese patrol boats attacked two US warships in the infamous Gulf of Tonkin incident in 1964. He used the story to justify escalating the war and the aerial bombing of North Vietnam. The news story eventually blew over and LBJ won a full term as President in a landslide election.

▸ President Richard Nixon denied all knowledge of the botched Watergate burglary, carried out by rogue operatives who broke into the offices of the Democratic Party's headquarters, hoping to copy sensitive documents and plant listening devices. He stonewalled the investigation by Congress and ordered the firing of the Justice Department's appointed special prosecutor.

Yet, during the height of the scandal Americans re-elected him in one of the biggest landslides in presidential history. Only later did the infamous Nixon tapes reveal the depth of the corruption. Nearly a dozen of his co-conspirators went to prison, but Nixon avoided prosecution by resigning, knowing that his Vice President and successor Gerald Ford would pardon him.

▸ President Ronald Reagan professed ignorance of the infamous Iran-Contra affair, in which White House insiders funneled money to an insurgent group in Nicaragua, defying an act of Congress that specifically forbid it. They got the money secretly by selling US military equipment to the government of Iran, with the Israeli government acting as go-between.

A Congressional investigation couldn't prove Reagan knew about the operation, but many observers believe he did. All of the key actors, although convicted and given prison sentences, escaped justice after Reagan left office. His Vice President and successor, George H. W. Bush, pardoned all of them. Reagan remains one of America's most admired and beloved presidents.

▸ President Bill Clinton stood in front of news cameras and lied to the American people, and later to a grand jury, about his sexual relationship with a young White House intern. He survived an impeachment for perjury and obstruction of justice and finished his second term with an approval rating of 65%, higher than every president since Harry Truman.

▸ President George Bush, Jr., sold the American people on the disastrous and costly invasion of Iraq, the overthrow of its despotic ruler Saddam Hussein, and the disruption of the power balance in the Middle East. He and his Vice President Dick Cheney conflated various questionable intelligence sources into a claim that Saddam had sponsored the horrific "9-11" attacks on New York City and the Pentagon.

They preached the story so relentlessly that, even today, nearly 40 percent of Americans believe Saddam supported the attacks. As the occupation dragged on, claiming more and more lives and huge military expenditures, Bush won a second term by a landslide.

These case studies and others raise several very provocative questions, related to the issue of presidential honesty we explored in Chapter 2: will Americans condone lying by their presidents, either explicitly or implicitly? Have they perhaps accepted the premise of national politics as dirty business? Do they just accept that the ugly realities of conflict with other nations require doing things they might consider immoral but a necessary evil? Will they look the other way when a president engages in unethical or immoral behavior, so long as it doesn't jeopardize their own personal interests? These questions remain before us.

FAKE NEWS AND THE POST-FACTUAL AGE

Yes, all modern presidents have played fast and loose with the truth. But all of those prevaricating presidents, put together, couldn't hold a candle to the modern P.T. Barnum of politics—one Donald J. Trump. As of this writing, he holds a place unique among presidents in his dedication to the role of the showman-president—a government of one.

Donald Trump burst on the American political scene in the national election of 2016, winning the presidency in a once-in-a-century combination of accidents just as amazing to himself as to the other players in the political drama. Unique among modern presidents for never having held an elected office or served in the military, he parlayed his notoriety as a TV reality show host into a radically new species of politician.

A combination of masterful populist campaigning; image management; favorable coverage by a Republican-leaning news network; statistical voting quirks in several swing states; and covert social media campaigns run by operatives of the Russian government propelled Donald Trump to the White House with a majority of electoral votes, even though his opponent Hillary Clinton won nearly 3 million more popular votes than he got.

As his adversaries in the Democratic party watched in shock and horror, Trump brought his larger-than-life persona to the business of running a government. Volatile, profane, aggressive, confrontational, anti-intellectual, willfully ignorant, and clinically narcissistic, he loomed over the federal establishment like a Colossus. He dominated the national news cycle almost every single day.

Going into the election scramble, Trump had discovered the Twitter short-message platform and quickly understood its power as a tool that could give him daily contact with a fan club that eventually grew to more than 80 million tweeters.

He also became a uniquely effective political actor in another way, a brand new one. Much earlier in his career as a commercial property developer, and later as a TV reality show host, he intuited, discovered, or decided that, in the media free-for-all that serves as modern political theater, truth and factuality had lost their sacred status. Half-truths; misleading claims; unsupported assertions and accusations; sarcasm; innuendo; and outright fabrications, he believed, had become the preferred tools for a new age of politics.

By the time he arrived at the White House, he had already used this new realization to fashion for himself a larger-than-life public persona unlike any president ever had, with the possible exception of Teddy Roosevelt.

Displaying an uncanny grasp of the dynamics of the American media culture, he confronted critical reporters by simply shouting them down. "Fake news!" he declared, whenever they barraged him with unwanted questions or accusations. He used his White House Twitter account to broadcast a daily stream of insults, accusations, and outright falsehoods to discredit any and all who dared oppose him.

Fact-checkers employed by news platforms couldn't keep up with his unrestrained declarations of his version of the truth. They began to count and record his whoppers, giving each one a "Pinocchio" score for the degree to which it stretched—or murdered—the truth. By the middle of his presidential term, his total score had exceeded *10,000 disproven assertions*, either casual falsehoods or outright official lies.

Meanwhile, his strongly committed fan club—a demographic cohort composed mostly of middle-aged, white, non-urban males without college degrees, plus a dedicated Christian evangelical contingent—saw him as their "man for the times." They typically acknowledged his less than perfect character and his mercurial personality, convinced that he had the solutions the country needed.

His political adversaries seethed with outrage at every unpresidential act or statement, and tried in just about every way they could think of to hold him to account. They discovered, to their profound frustration, that no part of the Constitution and no national law has anything to say about sanctions against presidents who lie, even in their official capacity. The Founders, apparently, didn't see it coming.

Political historians, philosophers, and commentators will surely study the Donald Trump presidency for decades. No president has scrambled the accepted norms, habits, customs, and assumptions of the American political culture as he has. The insights and conclusions of that analysis will surely shape the Republic in a multitude of ways.

SLEEPY GUARD DOGS WITH WEAK TEETH

The Founders did build a mechanism into the Constitution for removing delinquent officials from office for serious offenses: *impeachment*. Unfortunately, it has never worked.

Article II, Section 4 specifies that Congress can remove the President, Vice President, and "all civil Officers after Impeachment for, and Conviction of, Treason, Bribery, or other high Crimes and Misdemeanors." Note the two separate terms, impeachment and conviction.

Removing someone from office by impeachment takes two steps. First the House conducts an investigation and the members vote on whether to impeach the accused. If the vote fails, nothing else happens. If a majority of members vote in favor, the accused person stands impeached, a permanent historical status. The House leaders then send a set of formal charges to the Senate.

Then the Senate conducts a trial and either convicts or acquits the accused. The impeachment ruling remains a part of the accused's rap sheet for all time, regardless of whether they survive the Senate vote.

In simple terms, only the House can impeach and only the Senate can convict. The Constitution specifies that, if the

House impeaches the President, the Chief Justice of the Supreme Court will provide over the trial in the Senate.

We've had a number of misbehaving presidents and vice presidents over the years, and some outright crooks, but Congress has only ever impeached three of them. None of them lost their jobs in the subsequent Senate trial.

  ‣ The House impeached Andrew Johnson in 1868, for dismissing Lincoln's leftover Secretary of War Edwin M. Stanton without Congressional approval. Johnson, an exceptionally unpopular president, survived his trial in the Senate by a single vote.

  ‣ The House impeached Bill Clinton in 1998 as previously described, for charges of lying under oath about a sexual relationship with a White House intern, as well as lying to a grand jury. Clinton, too, survived his ordeal in the Senate. Only 50 senators voted to remove him for the charge of obstructing justice, well under the required two-thirds minimum of 67. No Senator from his own party voted to convict him.

  ‣ The House impeached Donald Trump in 2019, accusing him of trying to coerce the President of Ukraine to incriminate his political rival in a commercial scandal, thereby helping his chances for re-election. Predictably, the Democrat-controlled House readily impeached him and the Republican-controlled Senate just as readily dismissed the charge.

It appears that none of the conventional remedies for presidential misconduct left to us by the Founders has worked very well. We'll need to tighten our definitions of official misconduct, create a system for real accountability, and associate meaningful consequences to them. Later in this discussion we'll consider some new and stronger options.

LET'S CRIMINALIZE NON-JUDICIAL PERJURY

Reader alert: Now comes another of those conceptual curveballs I promised I'd occasionally throw at you: let's make *ex officio* lying by public officials a criminal offense.

Why do we tolerate deliberate, calculated lying on the part of our public officials? Have we granted them the privilege of telling us anything they think we want to hear, to pacify us and distract us from their failures of leadership?

Typically, when a senior official—the President; the Vice President; the President's press secretary; a Cabinet member; a senior advisor; or a spokesperson for a federal agency—appears in public and lies to the press or the public, or knowingly misleads them with questionable information, they pay no price. If the press exposes the lie, a minor storm ensues in the public conversation, lots of people shake their heads and cluck their tongues, and life goes on.

I propose a new federal law that defines the felony crime of *non-judicial perjury* on the part of the President, Vice President, and all "civil officers" of government. Non-judicial perjury means knowingly and deliberately lying in any public statement, made orally or in writing, in their official capacity. That includes all messages on social media.

This law would rest on the idea that, when a person takes the oath of office for any appointed position, he or she *remains under oath*, every day, 24/7, for the duration of the assignment. Just as a person who testifies in a legal proceeding or an appearance before Congress faces punishment for lying under oath, the same conditions should apply to someone who swears an oath when they accept a position of public trust. The oath should include, in addition to upholding the Constitution, a promise never to lie to the press or the public when speaking in one's official capacity.

LET'S RETHINK THE POWER OF THE PARDON

Executive clemency, a power granted to the President by the Constitution, echoes an ancient ritual privilege long associated with kings, queens, and tribal chieftains in almost all cultures—the power to forgive. Presidential pardons have become increasingly controversial in recent years.

The Constitution imposes very few limits on that power:

- ▸ The President's powers of clemency apply only to cases involving federal crimes.

- ▸ A *full pardon* absolves a person from specified crimes and prevents, stops, or nullifies all forms of federal prosecution. A pardoned offender has no criminal record, and retains all rights of citizenship.

- ▸ *Commutation* of a sentence mitigates or terminates court-imposed penalties and releases the offender from imprisonment if incarcerated. It does not, however, overturn the conviction.

- ▸ A *reprieve* interrupts the imposition of the punishment, sometimes temporarily, such as in death penalty cases.

Federal statutes provide a process by which a person requesting a pardon can plead his or her case to the President. The public record shows the name of the offender, the offense, and the disposition of the case.

The last several presidents have used the powers of clemency in very different ways. Bill Clinton issued over 450 orders of clemency, including 140 of them on his last day of office.

George W. Bush, Jr., pardoned or commuted sentences for about 200 people in his 8-year presidency.

Barack Obama granted clemency to almost 2,000 individuals, more than his 13 predecessors combined. He issued over 300 orders of clemency on his last day in office. Obama cited special circumstances, in that most of his actions overrode sentences he considered overly harsh for non-violent crimes.

Donald Trump racked up the smallest number, less than 50 for his term. Unlike his predecessors, Trump frequently bypassed the Justice Department's Office of the Pardon Attorney and issued a pardon without request, particularly in cases involving his business associates or close friends.

Recent to this writing, Trump announced his intention to pardon a historical figure, the famous suffragist Susan B.

Anthony, nullifying her conviction of 1872 for voting. Within hours the Susan B. Anthony Museum vigorously rejected the pardon on her behalf (US law requires that the person pardoned either requests it or agrees to it). They wanted her crime and her conviction to stand in the history books as an act of citizen defiance against an unjust law.

As of this writing, we have no checks or balances on the presidential power to pardon. A president can pardon anyone for any reason without having to justify the action. No third party can contest a presidential pardon, no matter how egregious, suspicious, or self-serving it might seem.

Some presidential pardons have stirred up considerable controversy and public outrage. Two that we've studied stand out. In the first case, the ascended Vice President Gerald Ford pardoned Richard Nixon after Nixon resigned in the infamous Watergate scandal. Ford allowed a half-dozen of Nixon's conspirators to go to prison, however.

In the aftermath of the infamous Iran-Contra scandal, George H.W. Bush pardoned all of Ronald Reagan's convicted operatives after he succeeded Reagan to the presidency.

Those two cases of lopsided clemency have continued to stir debate, and in particular the call for some form of checks or restraints on presidential pardon power. In the following discussion I propose a mechanism that could rein in the most egregious misuses of presidential clemency, while still allowing the President wide latitude of discretion.

LET'S MODERNIZE THE SUPREME COURT

Reader alert: here comes another of those conceptual curveballs. We can eliminate the conditions that make it possible—and tempting—for presidents to corrupt or politicize the democratic processes of the Republic, by *modifying the mission of the Supreme Court*. This might qualify as one of the most mind-stretching of all the recommendations in this book, so please suspend your automatic reactions as you read the following proposition.

We've always talked about three co-equal branches of government, and yet we've restricted the Court's participation to a single narrow function: reviewing laws for Constitutional compliance, and even then only for cases appealed against rulings by lower courts.

The Constitution doesn't have much to say about the Court. It doesn't even say how many justices it should have. It would take an act of Congress or possibly a Constitutional amendment to broaden its mission.

Why should we do it? Why mess around with the role of one our most respected and least politically contaminated institutions of governance?

BOSSES BEHAVING BADLY

We have three main governmental mechanisms for discovering criminal behavior by high-ranking appointed officials and bringing them to justice, as we'll discuss shortly. All three mechanisms, however, have failed us time and again.

Impeachment? Meh.

As we've seen, the first mechanism—the impeachment process—has never removed an offending president from office, and Congress has seldom tried to impeach anybody else. The Constitution permits Congress to impeach any "officer of government," which includes Cabinet members, Supreme Court justices, and many people who get their jobs by presidential nomination and Senate confirmation.

Impeachment remains, fundamentally, a political process. It serves as a political weapon in some cases and a political shield in others, depending on which of the political parties gets to call the shots.

The Special Counsel: Hired and Fired

The second method, the "special counsel," has kicked in on several occasions when a president has faced accusations of criminal behavior. Here we see a fatal flaw in the rules of the game. The Department of Justice, the government's law firm, has the responsibility for investigating federal crimes, mainly by deploying the Federal Bureau of Investigation—the legendary FBI. The Attorney General and the Director of the FBI, however, both work as employees under the President.

How can the employees of a department, whose careers depend on the whim of the big boss, investigate him or her in an impartial, unbiased, and uninhibited way? They can't.

In the three most infamous cases—the Nixon Watergate investigation, the Clinton impeachment, and the Donald Trump impeachment—the Justice Department tried to minimize the obvious conflict of interest by hiring out the investigation to a private individual, typically a highly respected legal expert.

But in two of the three cases, the president acted to thwart the special counsel investigation.

In a Constitutional showdown known as the "Saturday Night Massacre," Richard Nixon ordered his Attorney General Elliot Richardson to fire the Special Prosecutor, a distinguished professor of law named Archibald Cox. Richardson refused and resigned on the spot. Nixon then ordered Deputy Attorney General William Ruckelshaus to do it. He also refused and resigned. Nixon then ordered the third most senior official at the Justice Department, Solicitor General Robert Bork, to do it. Bork complied.

In the drama leading to the Trump impeachment, Donald Trump fired FBI Director James Comey for refusing to cancel an ongoing investigation of one of Trump's friends. Other ongoing FBI investigations into Trump's pre-election campaign activities raised a new outcry that forced the appointment of a special counsel, the esteemed ex-FBI director Robert Mueller. Trump's Attorney General, Jeffrey Sessions, recused himself from the investigation, having played a part in Trump's campaign operation. Trump fired Sessions, and several times hinted at firing Mueller.

The Inspector General: Don't Make the Boss Look Bad

The third method for protecting the Republic and its democracy from dishonest officers of state has a long and distinguished history. The inspector general concept, long used in military organizations and widely used in federal government departments, empowers a special department— the "IG"—to investigate any and all of the organization's activities and to bring forward findings of misconduct. In recent years, the "whistle blower" law has invited front-line workers in all departments to report misconduct, fraud, or corruption to the IG in secret and without fear of retaliation.

But the IG mechanism suffers from the same fatal flaw as the Justice Department investigation: investigating your boss can end your career. Recent to this writing, a number of IGs have lost their jobs by scrutinizing the chiefs of the Cabinet departments they served.

We have a fourth ethical malfunction, which we can solve in the process of fixing the three just mentioned. That consists of the systematic "packing" of the federal court system—the courts and judges scattered across America—by a partisan Senate in cahoots with a same-party president. Recent to this writing, Senate leaders have unapologetically declared their intention to appoint only judges whose records show a clear political bias in their direction.

A New and Better Supreme Court

Now we come to the solution for the "bosses behaving badly" syndrome. Lets expand the Supreme Court's operation to include two additional functions: *government oversight* and *judicial oversight*.

With this plan the Court will get two new divisions, enlarging it from one function—Constitutional review—to three. The expanded organization will have three co-chief-justices, one with the traditional role of reviewing lower-court decisions as to constitutionality; one that oversees the investigation and prosecution of misconduct by members of the Executive and Legislative branches; and one that oversees the federal court system and all of the appointed federal judges.

We'll have a new method for selecting justices to fill vacancies. The Court itself will identify candidates for new appointments—as well as candidates for federal judgeships —and will present them to the President for selection and subsequent confirmation by the Senate.

We'll move the entire federal court system—all courts and judges—out from under the Justice Department and put it under the Supreme Court. The judges should not work for the prosecutors.

We'll also move the entire IG system—the inspectors general who reside in the various departments of government—out of the Executive Branch and put it under the Supreme Court.

Thinking back to the problem of unconstrained pardon power in presidential hands, let's change the law to require that the division of the Court responsible for government oversight must sign off on all pardons.

Leadership will rotate amongst the three Joint Chief Justices on an annual basis, much the same as with the Defense Department's Joint Chiefs of Staff. The Court will, of course, take on an additional administrative structure for managing the full range of oversight responsibilities.

Expanding the Supreme Court's mission with greater oversight and more meaningful checks against presidential overreach can take us a long way toward the more just and equitable institutions that we—and the Republic—deserve.

LET'S HAVE A SMARTER GOVERNMENT: FIXING THE "ORG CHART"

We start this part of the conversation with a bold assertion: *our federal government badly needs reorganizing.* The boxes on the org chart don't make sense. Let's see why.

Currently, the Executive Branch—the collection of government departments and agencies that fall under the

President's control—consists of at least 17 separate organizations. Each one has an executive who serves *ex officio* as a member of the President's cabinet.

TOO MANY MOVING PARTS

Over many years, these Cabinet departments have proliferated into a chaotic assortment of bureaucracies with overlaps in their activities and silo-like boundaries.

In alphabetical order, we have:

1. Agriculture Department
2. Commerce Department
3. Defense Department
4. Education Department
5. Energy Department
6. Environmental Protection Agency
7. Health & Human Services Department
8. Homeland Security Department
9. Housing & Urban Development Department
10. Interior Department
11. Justice Department
12. Labor Department
13. National Intelligence
14. State Department
15. Transportation Department
16. Treasury Department
17. Veterans Administration

TWO RULES FOR ORGANIZING A GOVERNMENT

Management experts generally agree on at least two basic rules for arranging the boxes on the org chart. The first calls for a sensible and logical *subdivision* of the various responsibilities into manageable units. At every level of the monkey bars, from top to bottom, each unit, department, division, or agency should have a clear and unified mission.

The second rule calls for an appropriate *span of control*—the number of agencies, sub-departments, or workers that fall under the jurisdiction of any one department executive, manager, or supervisor. A workable span of control usually involves a minimum of 3 sub-units, and a maximum of 5 or so —7 at the very most.

Our national government falls short in both categories. The 17 cabinet departments represent a hodge-podge of big and small; narrow and broad; and specialized as well as general missions. And, with a span of control of 17, the Executive Branch can't possibly operate effectively.

Browse the list of cabinet departments above and you'll see that their titles imply lots of overlap. Some of them seem more narrowly specialized than others. And, in general, they don't all seem to fit together in any consistent way.

For example, two separate departments—the Interior Department and the Agriculture Department—both deal with the natural environment, which we know as the Commons. The Environmental Protection Agency does as well. Yet they operate as three separate organizations. A fourth department—Transportation—deals with the physical infrastructure—the *built environment*, as we've called it.

Consider another peculiar case. The Bureau of Alcohol, Tobacco, and Firearms—a strange mix of responsibilities— formerly operated under the Treasury Department. Then Congress moved it to the Department of Justice. Then it got the extra responsibility of regulating explosives. It currently goes by the peculiar title of the Bureau of Alcohol, Tobacco, Firearms, and Explosives (admittedly a rather deadly combination in the hands of certain citizens).

Without careful coordination, these separate agencies might pursue conflicting objectives or implement programs that don't play well with one another. We can bring them all together under a single parent department.

We can bring a measure of sanity and focus to the government's operation by realigning all of these building blocks in a more logical arrangement with a smaller span of control, based on our ten-part model of the modern republic.

This issue deserves a more thorough and detailed analysis than we can give it here, but the Fix-it List at the end of this chapter offers a general concept for realigning the federal org chart. The plan calls for a special blue-ribbon study commission, composed of noted management experts, who will examine the entire federal organization from top to bottom and recommend a modernized arrangement.

THE WHITE HOUSE: DYSFUNCTION JUNCTION?

Physically, the White House serves as the headquarters of the presidency. Politically, it sits at the center of a figurative hurricane, with a mob of staffers trying to manage a very complex set of programs, processes, and relationships. And psychologically, it symbolizes the desire of Americans for a government that truly serves the Republic.

Of the 1,800 or so civil service appointees employed by the Executive Office of the President, about 350-400 of them typically work in the West Wing.

As a management consultant, I tend to view the current White House operation as somewhat of a menagerie of disparate activities. At first glance, I see an outfit with more than 20 seemingly disjointed functions and a haphazard organizational structure. As previously explained, this wide span of control makes coordination of disparate activities nearly impossible.

At second glance, an impressive mishmash of high-sounding job titles suggests some really important goings-on. Titles like "Assistant to the President and Principal Deputy Chief of Staff"; "Deputy Assistant to the President and Chief of Staff to the Senior Counselor"; and "Deputy Assistant to the

President and Advisor to the Senior Advisor" (even advisors need advisors) makes one wonder what they actually do.

As a general recommendation, I'd say the White House needs a comprehensive review of the organization and its operations, carried out by an independent panel of experts. This blue-ribbon review commission forms one of the key items on our Fix-It List, at the conclusion of this chapter.

LET'S MODERNIZE THE CONGRESS

While many people don't tend to think of the Congress as an organization, in the same way they might think of businesses or government agencies, it has become a very large bureaucracy over the years. It deserves a thorough, objective, and impartial review by outside experts just as the White House does.

At least four dysfunctional syndromes have plagued the US Congress since the early days of the Republic: 1) hyperpartisanism—polarization along party lines so extreme as to make it almost impossible to accomplish any major goals; 2) subservience to private special interests—people or groups willing to give them money in exchange for legislative favors; 3) procedural paralysis—using obscure and archaic rules of procedure to block initiatives by political rivals; and 4) busy work—dealing with a seemingly endless stream of routine measures, especially in the Senate, that waste far more time and resources than they deserve.

HYPERPARTISANISM ERODES PUBLIC TRUST

As of this writing, the polarization of the two major parties in Congress exceeds almost all historical precedents. While we have no magic cure for selfish party politics, term limits can go a long way to limiting its negative effects. The recommended blue-ribbon review commission can at least spotlight the problem and bring it forward for consideration.

As just one example of partisan deadlock, the Senate's infamous *filibuster* probably stands as one of the most offensive gimmicks for delaying a vote in the Senate. The rule dictates that, once a Senator rises to deliver a dissertation, he or she can hold the floor indefinitely. In an absurd twist, if the filibustering Senator sits down, or leaves the chamber for any reason—including a biological break—he or she loses the floor and the filibuster fails.

PROCEDURES CAN PARALYZE INSTEAD OF STREAMLINE

An even more egregious rule allows the floor leader—the Speaker of the House, or the Senate Majority Leader—to decide which measures get voted on. That excessive authority enables them to kill a measure passed by the House, by making sure it never comes up for a vote.

In a notorious hardball incident, the Senate Majority Leader refused to bring Democrat President Barack Obama's Supreme Court nominee to a vote for confirmation. He kept the Court seat vacant for over a year, until his party won the White House in the next election. Then they confirmed the candidate nominated by his successor in near-record time.

BUSY WORK: POISED TO DO NOTHING

A study by the Congressional Research Service estimated that approximately 1200-1400 federal government positions require Senate confirmation. Even with routine approvals, just imagine how much time that process consumes—time they could use to take up the really big issues. Reducing the list of critical positions to 100 at most would make a huge difference in the Senate's productivity. The government's Office of Personnel Management could manage the selection and approval of the other candidates much more effectively.

Another huge time-waster, which slows the legislative process to a crawl, involves the tedious process of reconciling bills between the House and the Senate. Typically, one chamber—most often the House—passes a bill dealing with some supposedly important matter. The other chamber cooks up its own bill. Then, committee members from both chambers have to develop a third version that meets the demands of both sides. Common sense suggests that a joint committee could work out a single draft of the bill, take it to their respective bodies for review, and revise it as necessary.

The proposed blue-ribbon review commission will highlight these petty and destructive practices, and propose more ethical alternatives.

LET'S GET DIRTY MONEY OUT OF POLITICS

The issue of financing election campaigns has long plagued members of Congress and inflamed a whole menagerie of political activists. For all the energy and adrenalin expended so far, we still don't have an effective solution.

Congress passed a few laws in the early days, limiting corporate influence in campaigns, but only in 1907, with the Tillman Act, did they attempt anything like comprehensive reform. The Act banned corporations from paying for election campaigns. In 1947 Congress extended it to include labor unions. In 1971, they passed a measure that required disclosure of campaign contributions and set certain limits.

But a lack of an effective enforcement mechanism and a series of pro-corporate Supreme Court decisions had weakened the restrictions on corporate funding and paved the way for the creation of the infamous *political action committees*, or "PACs." Corporations could not fund campaigns directly from their treasuries, but they could set up PACs to accomplish the same purposes.

Over the next few decades, enforcement remained lax and mostly ineffectual. Corporations and wealthy individuals diligently searched for new ways to evade the restrictions. Big money still played a key part in getting people elected.

CITIZENS UNITED? WHAT CITIZENS?

In 2010, the Supreme Court rendered a cataclysmic decision that essentially struck down all significant restrictions on corporate campaigning. In the now-legendary case of *Citizens United v. FEC*, a corporate financing operation argued that any laws that prevented corporations and unions from using their funds for independent political advertising violated the First Amendment's guarantee of freedom of speech.

Citizens United argued, and the Court essentially agreed, that a corporate entity should have the same status as a citizen with respect to First Amendment rights. CU claimed that giving money or running advertising for a candidate amounted to a protected expression of political opinion.

The Court's knife-edge 5-4 ruling set off a firestorm of political debate, outrage on the part of some observers, and rejoicing by others. The Citizens United ruling came at the midpoint of the four-year election cycle, and by the start of the presidential campaign season for the 2012 election, corporate money came gushing in to the many PACs that had formed on behalf of various candidates. The contest of 2012 became the first billion-dollar election in US history.

This turbulent period also gave birth to the "super-PAC," a mechanism for collecting funds from many contributors and distributing them to a number of candidates. Whereas the original PAC usually served as a vehicle to fund one candidate's election run, the super-PAC could fund many at one time. The previous per-person limit of $5,000 per year given to any one candidate or PAC became a casualty of the Court's landmark decision. The super-PAC could now transfer unlimited sums to either of the political parties as a whole, allowing them to allocate funds to those candidates they considered critical to party power.

The US Chamber of Commerce became, in a sense, one of the most powerful super-PACs. With its member companies now free to contribute unlimited amounts and its directors free to allocate the donations as they saw fit, the Chamber became a *de facto* money laundering operation. In the words of the venerable journalist and political commentator Bill Moyers,

> *"The US Chamber of Commerce is the new red light district of American politics."[4]*

Even worse, Moyers asserted, the Citizens United decision gave birth to a new political party in America, one that has no name, no face, no logo, no headquarters, and no appointed leader or spokesperson, but a very clear and focused shared agenda. The thought leaders and engineers of this new political party—a "virtual" party, perhaps we should call it—have become skilled at arousing and shaping public opinion via the use of political "sock puppets," in the form of people, factions, and movements whom they activate and fund in order to attract (or distract) press attention and dramatize opposition to policies and laws that contradict their agenda.

The covert counterpart of the sock puppets—a swarm of shadow organizations like "policy research" firms, targeted political action groups, and sham consulting firms—funnels money to elected officials and their spouses. That supports the usual process of carrying bags of cash into the national whorehouse (a.k.a. the Congress) and buying laws.

As of this writing, a large number of activist groups have committed to overturning the Citizens United decision and the doctrine that supports it. Polls indicate that a significant majority of Americans who know anything about the issue want to see it overturned.

Reversing Citizens United would probably require bringing another case before the Court and asking it to overturn its previous ruling and uphold a century of law and custom.

Alternatively, Congress might figure out how to craft a law that offsets the provisions of Citizens United, and restores the previous state of affairs. Such a law might sustain a Court challenge, or it might provide an opportunity for the Supremes to rethink their position on corporate citizenship.

A third avenue, outside of formal government influence, would promote the acceptance by corporate boards of the socially conscious New Model Corporation charter, as described in Chapter 8 (Commerce). That model commits corporate leaders to a set of key principles that align with the values of fairness, responsibility, and sustainability. It forbids the use of corporate funds to support or promote any political candidate, cause, or organization.

THE FIX-IT LIST: GOVERNANCE

So, how can we improve this component of our Republic—Governance? Let's start with these actions.

1. *Let's Set Term Limits.* Congress will pass, and the states will ratify, an amendment to the Constitution that sets new term limits for the President, Vice President, members of Congress, and federal judges. The President and Vice President will each serve for one six-year term with no possibility of re-election.

   Members of the House and Senate will each serve a single six-year term with no possibility of re-election.

   Supreme Court Justices will serve a 12-year term with the possibility of extension for an additional 12 years by Senate reconfirmation.

2. *Let's Adopt Mandatory Voting.* Congress will pass a law establishing mandatory voting in national elections for all US citizens. The law will prescribe a modest but meaningful fine for eligible and able-bodied citizens who don't vote. A National ID Card (described in Chapter 6) will serve to verify eligibility, prevent multiple voting, and identify those who don't vote.

   And let's make voting fun. Congress will pass a law that changes voting day to the last Saturday in November and makes it a national holiday. Coming two days after the Thanksgiving celebration, this would give some workers a 4-day holiday.

3. *Let's Get Rid of the Electoral College.* Congress will pass, and the states will ratify, an amendment to the Constitution that abolishes the Electoral College. The amendment will specify that the national total of all

votes—the popular vote—will decide which candidate wins the presidency. In an election with more than two candidates, if no one gets more than 50 percent of the votes cast, a run-off election between the two highest-scoring candidates will determine the winner.

4. *Let's Define Criminal Misconduct by Government Officials.* Congress will pass a law that defines a code of specific violations of oath by government officials, including the President, Vice President, and members of Congress. The measure will define more specifically the constitutional terms like "high crimes and misdemeanors" and "emoluments" and will prescribe methods for prosecution and associated penalties. It will also define specific criteria and penalties for conflicts of interest on the part of all government officers—defined as those nominated by the President and confirmed by the Senate.

5. *Let's Outlaw Non-Judicial Perjury.* Congress will pass a law defining the federal crime of *non-judicial perjury* on the part of the President, Vice President, and all sworn government officials. Non-judicial perjury means knowingly and deliberately lying in any public statement, made orally or in writing, in an official role or capacity. The Office of Government Ethics, under the jurisdiction of the Supreme Court, will have the authority to bring cases to trial in federal court.

6. *Let's Modernize the Supreme Court.* Congress will pass a law that expands the operation of the Supreme Court to three oversight functions, as described in this chapter. The Court will oversee judicial proceedings in terms of constitutionality (its traditional mission); government ethics, through the Office of Government Ethics (which will move to the Supreme Court's operations); and the operation of the federal courts (which will move from the Justice Department to the Supreme Court's operations).

7. *Let's Schedule the Executive Branch for a "Full Physical."* Congress will appropriate funds for a special blue-ribbon task force, which will make a comprehensive review of the organization of the Executive Branch. The task force will recommend changes and realignment of the organizational structure that can enable the Executive Branch to operate more effectively.

8. *Let's Schedule the Congress for a "Full Physical."* Congress will appropriate funds for a special blue-ribbon task force that will make a comprehensive review of the Congress itself. The task force will recommend changes in operating rules and administrative practices of both chambers, to enable the Congress to operate more effectively.

9. *Let's Get Dirty Money Out of Politics.* Congress will pass a law limiting donations to the election campaigns of candidates for public office at federal, state, and local levels, and contributions to PACs and other cash aggregators. The law will restore the restriction on contributions by individuals or corporations.

The law will declare, as public policy, that *corporations do not have the same constitutional rights as persons*, and that money paid by corporations to candidates does not qualify for the free speech protections of the First Amendment.

The law will *prohibit all direct contributions by corporations* to candidates or political campaigns, of money or equivalent forms of value, and will prohibit corporations from advertising or otherwise using shareholder resources to influence public elections. It will also prohibit executives from trying to coerce or persuade employees to donate to candidates or engage in other political activities.

Chapter 5.
Let's Rethink National Defense: War Department or Peace Department?

"Every gun that is made, every warship launched,
every rocket fired signifies, in the final sense,
a theft from those who hunger and are not fed,
those who are cold and are not clothed.
This world in arms is not spending money alone.
It is spending the sweat of its laborers,
the genius of its scientists, the hopes of its children."
—Dwight Eisenhower
Five-Star General, US President

Let's begin our rethink of this component of the Republic with a mega-factual perspective on the military state of the planet. Then we'll proceed to explore some of the mega-issues and mega-opportunities.

▸ The Pentagon, the largest building in the world, serves as the headquarters for the entire US military establishment. The iconic five-sided building, built during WW2, has five concentric rings of offices arranged around a central courtyard. With seven floors and over 6 million square feet of work space, it houses more than 25,000 workers. It has all of the functions, activities, and logistical systems of a small city.

- About two million active duty personnel and some 700,000 civilian employees make up the Defense Department's work force.

- As of this writing, the US operates about 800 military "sites" in 70 countries. They range from tiny outposts to giant bases the size of complete cities.

At home, all 50 US states, special territories, and protectorates have multiple military bases of various sizes and for various purposes.

Overseas, we have some 40 so-called named bases with significant operations.

We have about 50,000 active-duty military personnel stationed at more than a dozen bases in Japan, along with about 40,000 family members and about 5,000 American civilian employees.

We have about 30,000 military personnel in South Korea, at more than a dozen bases, with equivalent numbers of dependents and civilian workers.

As of this writing, we still operate bases in Iraq. Military operations in Afghanistan continue—after 19 years— with several thousand combat troops there.

We also operate a Navy and Marine base on the southeastern tip of the island of Cuba—Guantanamo Bay—a peculiar legacy of the Spanish-American War. The US took control of "Gitmo" and established a naval base and coaling station there in 1898 as part of the peace agreement that ended the Spanish-American war.

The UK, France, Russia, China, and various small military powers have a total of about 40 overseas bases.

- Recent figures put the number of military aircraft owned and operated by the US at about 13,000. Russia has an estimated 2,000–3,000 planes. China has roughly the same.

- Similar estimates indicate that the US Navy has about 300 ships of all kinds, including carriers, destroyers, specialized support ships, and submarines, with about 100 more in development or planning stages. China has more ships than the US, while the Russian navy has a much smaller fleet.

- The Defense Department operates a system of universities that train military officers. The four service academies—the Army's Academy at West Point, New York; the Naval Academy at Annapolis, Maryland; the Air Force Academy at Colorado Springs, Colorado; and the Coast Guard Academy at New London, Connecticut —operate as fully accredited colleges, granting degrees while preparing future officers for their careers.

MONEY MAKES THE WAR GO AROUND: THE TWO-PERCENT ADDICTION

In the brief summary above, we've looked at the physical dimensions of warfare. But to understand the current strategic situation, we need to shift the focus of our thinking, especially about both Russia and China, from the military dimension to the economic dimension.

Every war ultimately comes down to a contest between two economies. One side might have smarter commanders, and luck often plays its part, but in the long run the stronger economy usually prevails.

In the US Civil War, for example, the southern Confederacy just couldn't match the resources controlled by the established government—the Union. The South's fragile economy, based mostly on cotton and tobacco, stood against a stronger, more broadly based Northern economy and a military machine that took advantage of better weapons, a more extensive railroad system, and the new technology of the telegraph.

In the early days of the two World Wars, the attackers— Germany and the Ottoman Empire in WW1; and Germany,

Italy, and Japan in WW2—seemed to have seized the permanent advantage. But as the war dragged on, the combined resources of the Allies finally overpowered them.

If we want to rethink the role of military operations in the future of the Republic, we can analyze the various options and their costs in the cold, hard logic of *return on investment.* We face two questions: 1) how much peace of mind can we buy for any given level of military investment; and 2) how much will we consider enough?

BASKETBALL, SOCCER, OR PING PONG?

To get a handle on the various scenarios we might face, let's look at the relative sizes of the economies of America's most likely adversaries compared to the US.

Recent figures put America's Gross Domestic Product, or GDP, at about 20 trillion dollars. China comes in second at about 14 trillion. Russia comes in at eleventh with about 1.7 trillion.

In terms of ratios, that puts the US economy at nearly *12 times the size of Russia's.* China's economy stands at 8 times bigger than Russia's, with continuing rapid growth. For perspective: the state of California alone outpaces the Russian economy by more than 1 trillion dollars.

To visualize the sheer magnitude of these differences, imagine the US economy as about the size of a basketball and China's economy as about the size of a soccer ball. In proportion, that would make Russia's economy smaller than a ping pong ball, or slightly bigger than a child's marble. Figure 5-1 gives a sense of these proportions.

But even GDP comparisons don't tell the full story. When we compare countries on the basis of *GDP per capita*—the generally accepted measure of standard of living—we see that Russia ranks even further down the list from the US. Based on recent figures, Americans enjoy a unit-GDP of just over $60,000. Russia scores at about $12,000—a stunning *one-fifth of the American standard of living.* China clocks in at a slightly higher level. Obviously, a country with a much higher standard of living could sustain a war with far less damage to its economy and less suffering by its people than the one with a much lower standard.

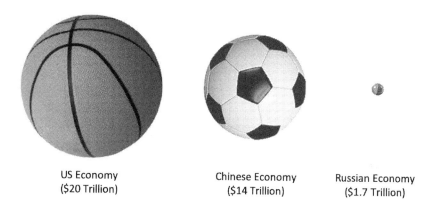

US Economy
($20 Trillion)

Chinese Economy
($14 Trillion)

Russian Economy
($1.7 Trillion)

Figure 5-1. Comparing Economies: US, China, Russia

And finally, let's keep in mind the mega-fact that these comparisons, both economic and military, only include the United States, before we even add in the combined economic and military power of over 30 allied countries, including those in the European Union and NATO.

Does any sensible person really imagine that Russia's leaders, even in their most manic nationalistic fervor, might think they could survive a war with the Western coalition? Or America alone?

Then, why do we still hear the steady, ominous drumbeat of threats and counter-threats between the two sides? Why does the apocalyptic narrative still dominate the thinking and emotions of American leaders? Why do both sides continue to spend vast resources on exotic state-of-the-art weapons they'll never use? Let's consider some possible explanations:

1. *Ignorance of the economic reality.* News pundits, members of Congress, nationalistic think tanks, some of our military planners, and many ill-informed Americans continue to recite the outdated slogans of the old Cold War. That reality no longer exists.

Remember the analogy of the basketball and the ping pong ball.

2. *Russia's leaders fear and distrust America's leaders.* For decades, they've harbored a paranoid fear of invasion from the West, and for good reason. How else would a reasonable person interpret 50 years of relentless spending on military bases and equipment, plus constant development of new weapons designed to secure a permanent military advantage? The NATO alliance, currently with 29 nations, has always had only one purpose: to provide a credible military threat to Russian territorial ambitions.

3. *Males run most of the governments on the planet, and almost all of the military forces.* Hyper-masculinized values of aggression and dominance have formed the discourse about safety, security, and self-defense of sovereign nations for centuries. Masculine mindsets don't change easily or quickly. Influential advisors to US presidents have often preached a doomsday scenario that would surely come about if they didn't approve astronomical defense budgets.

4. *Special interests always have a thumb on the scale.* In his last address in 1961, President Dwight Eisenhower—one of the most respected military leaders of the modern age—warned against the rising influence of those who have a selfish stake in war. He said, "In the councils of government, we must guard against the acquisition of unwarranted influence, whether sought or unsought, by the *military-industrial complex.* The potential for the disastrous rise of misplaced power exists and will persist." US arms manufacturers have become very skillful in recruiting members of Congress to the cause of "preparedness." Money talks, and it says, "Spend more money on defense—especially in my state." Figure 5-2 shows the vast interlocking network of commercial and political relationships Ike considered problematic.

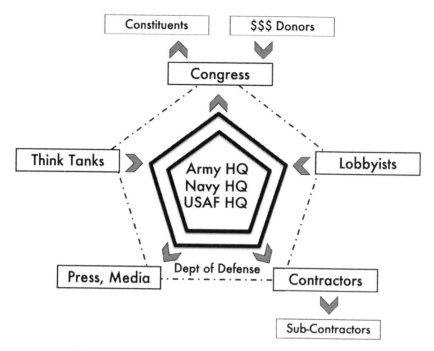

Figure 5-2. The Military-Industrial Complex

THE TWO-PERCENT ADDICTION

NATO has had a long standing policy that expects member states to spend at least two percent of their respective GDPs every year on military forces. While the US outspends its target level, most of the other members fall short.

On the global level, the 29 members of NATO spend an average of about 1.6 percent of their respective GDPs on military readiness. The US accounts for just over 50 percent of the total GDP, but accounts for slightly more than 70 percent of the military outlay for all countries in the alliance. That amounts to about 3.4 percent of US GDP.

In comparison, Russia allocates about 4 percent of its GDP to its military. China allocates about 2.1 percent.

None of those percentages makes any sense.

Several US presidents have made an issue out of these shortfalls, complaining that the partners don't pay their "fair share." The perverse logic dictates that, as an economy grows, the more of its wealth should go to military spending.

No one knows the right amount to spend on war preparation, but if the two-percent rule ever made any strategic sense, it makes very little sense now. Even a figure like one percent for the US would still far exceed the spending of most other nations.

THE CORNPONE PRINCIPLE

We'll probably always have highly vocal military advocates taking part in the national conversation. We can probably expect the senior leaders of the Army, Navy, Air Force, and Marines to advocate for virtually unlimited spending on our military capacity. Members of Congress whose states and districts benefit economically from military bases and weapons companies doing business there will probably not favor changes that threaten those benefits. Executives of weapons firms and defense-oriented think-tanks also have skin in the game.

America's beloved novelist, humorist, and cultural critic Mark Twain offered a commentary on personal biases and political advocacy in general. He quoted his childhood companion Jerry, a young enslaved boy who seemed possessed of a wisdom well beyond his years. Jerry commented,

> *"You tell me where a man gets his cornpone, and I'll tell you what his opinions is."*

People who remain emotionally attached to the win-lose doctrine of the old Cold War and those who get their cornpone from it will preach that, all of the economic mumbo-jumbo aside, we still need to outgun the Russians for the Armageddon scenario, even if it never comes. And we'll eventually have to deal with China in the same way.

Some of the more extreme Armageddon fans tend to deride those who disagree with them as soft, naïve, unrealistic, and even unpatriotic.

Thesis: if we Americans, and our leaders, can have the courage of our common sense, and we can leave behind the mindless win-lose posturing that we've clung to for decades, perhaps we can find a new and more intelligent strategy for steering both Russia and China toward recognizing their own best interests. If we acknowledge their right to exist in the modern world, and we understand the needs of their peoples for international legitimacy—a *come-back* on the part of Russia, and a *coming of age* by China—we can maintain a credible military threat and still redeploy an enormous amount of money, talent, and time to deal with the big new issues that threaten us all.

Albert Einstein admonished us,

> *"No problem can be solved from the same consciousness that created it. We must learn to see the world anew."*

KINETIC WARFARE HAS BECOME OBSOLETE: LET'S STOP BUYING WEAPONS WE'LL NEVER USE

Discussions and debates these days about the future of warfare tend toward the use of non-traditional weapons and operations such as information technology, with traditional massive use-of-force scenarios becoming less probable.

It might help our understanding to take a quick flashback view of the way warfare has evolved, and the radical changes that now present us with a very different future than the one we might have expected.

THE STAGES OF WARFARE

Warfare, since the early days of the Greeks and Romans, has evolved through three technological stages:

1. *Hand-to-hand Combat:* for many centuries, war mostly involved mobs of young males hacking one another to death with edged weapons, with bows and arrows occasionally adding interest to the drama.

2. *Gun Fights:* gunpowder, imported from China in the 1500s, changed the scale of warfare radically, as rifles and cannon turned land battles into mass homicides.

3. *Mechanized Warfare:* massive investments in permanent armies introduced tanks, planes, ships, submarines, big bombs, and missiles capable of wholesale destruction.

Military historians sometimes refer to the early style of warfare as the Napoleonic model—the *Grande Armée* concept —with massive land armies colliding on large fields. That remained the primary style of doing war up through WW2 and even into the Korean conflict, but it began to give way to more diversified and less monolithic types of operations.

Beginning especially with Vietnam, American military thinkers found themselves perplexed by the unpredictable and seemingly irrational behavior of an enemy that wouldn't stand and fight. The Napoleonic model and the military machine didn't seem to work very well. Vietcong forces operating in South Vietnam developed a style of fighting suited to what military theorists began to call unconventional, or *asymmetric* warfare—a hit-and-run method of fighting a more powerful enemy by avoiding its strengths and exploiting its weaknesses.

I don't mean to imply that asymmetric warfare started with Vietnam. It had a long and impressive history, going at least as far back as the American colonists using unconventional weapons and tactics to frustrate the rigid and inflexible style of fighting by the British occupiers. But American forces hadn't often found themselves in the top-dog role, facing ragtag bands of delinquents who wouldn't "fight fair."

As the lessons of Vietnam began to soak in, a new model of micro-operations began to take shape, with more focused mission objectives, rapid-deployment forces, and tailored *force packages—ad hoc* units with a special combination of soldiers, weapon systems, and support resources.

But despite the lessons offered by Vietnam and various

micro-wars, both the US and the Soviet Union carried on their maniacal competition to develop ever more advanced and sophisticated weapons systems, designed mainly for use against each other in an imagined Armageddon.

Even after the long-running Cold War had finally bankrupted the over-extended Soviet Union and led to its humiliating collapse in 1991, American leaders kept pouring billions of dollars into constantly increasing its total military advantage.

American sea power eventually eclipsed that of every other nation on the planet, by far. As of this writing, the US has 11 nuclear-powered aircraft carriers, each with the capacity to launch 60 fighter airplanes. The world's other navies operate a total inventory of 33 carriers. Russia has one carrier—an ancient, oil-powered rust bucket with no catapult.

Supersonic fighters, nearly useless in asymmetrical or micro-warfare situations, became faster and more maneuverable in aerial combat, armed with missiles of incredible range and accuracy, and incredibly expensive. Long-range supersonic bombers with radar-avoiding stealth designs—completely irrelevant for small-scale warfare—soaked up huge portions of the national budgets of both countries.

Drones now come in an ever-growing variety of forms, from high-altitude surveillance platforms, to bombers and missile platforms, to anti-drone drones, all the way to small and cheap anti-personnel drones. Drones of all sizes, shapes, and purposes will surely play a prominent role in our lives as citizens, and certainly a crucial role in military operations.

The hundreds of billions of dollars worth of ultra-fighter airplanes now in inventory and in development will soon become obsolete as remote control technology produces drone fighters capable of out-maneuvering human-piloted aircraft. Without the life-support systems, displays, and controls required for human operation, they'll become smaller and more lethal—although probably not cheaper.

AND NEXT COMES . . .

Post-Kinetic Warfare. Kinetic warfare, in mil-speak, refers to the standard methods of physical violence—the use of *kinetic energy*, which, you'll remember from your high school science class, means the energy of things in motion: soldiers, bullets, artillery shells, missiles, trucks, tanks, aircraft, submarines, and ships—to kill people and break things.

The evolution of warfare, technology, and strategy we've just reviewed has brought US military thinkers to a crossroads. Down one fork in this figurative road lies the never-ending and vastly expensive continuation of "Star Wars" weapons development. Down the other fork lies a calculated gamble—a new approach to leveraging military resources with three emerging new warfare options: *economic warfare, political warfare*, and *cyber-warfare*, which we'll explore shortly.

THE NUCLEAR PARADOX, ARMAGEDDON, AND THE TRIAD

Consider a question: what gives a few dozen men on the planet the right to gamble with the lives of hundreds of millions of human beings? Other questions follow: why have the citizens of the nuclear-armed countries allowed their leaders to dice with their lives? Why has opposition to the insane proposition of all-out nuclear war never gained the place it deserves in the national conversation?

When thinking about the nuclear weapons issue, I often flash back to the words of a 1960s song by Ed Ames, a dark meditation on purpose and meaning titled, "Who Will Answer?" The song muses:

'Neath the spreading mushroom tree,
The world revolves in apathy.
As overhead, a row of specks
Roars on, drowned out by discotheques;
And if a secret button's pressed
Because one man has been outguessed,

Who will answer?
If the soul is darkened
By a fear it cannot name;
If the mind is baffled
When the rules don't fit the game;
Who will answer? Who will answer? Who will answer?

How shall we approach the fearful issue of nuclear weapons? What course of action, what revision to the way we think about the security of our Republic, could we consider both sane and safe?

LET'S FACE THE FACTS AND FIGMENTS

As usual, let's begin with a brief historical snapshot of the issue, a look at the mega-facts, and a quick assessment of the current state of affairs.

Two atomic bombs brought an end to the Pacific war with Japan in August of 1945. Since then—a span of over 70 years —no nation has ever fired a nuclear weapon in anger. For a weapon used only once, under such rare and extreme circumstances, a surprising number of nations have invested mind-boggling amounts of money, time, talent, and human adrenalin in making them ever more lethal, more accurate, more mobile, and more numerous. Why?

The concept of the *nuclear triad* has dominated American and Russian military thinking for over 50 years. The triad consists of three nuclear weapons delivery platforms: 1) long range bombers; 2) ICBM missile silos; and 3) nuclear-armed submarines. According to the triad doctrine, even with a massive nuclear strike by an enemy regime, this diversified delivery system would virtually assure the destruction or incapacitation of the attacking regime.

The "nuclear club," or the "nuclear nine" as some analysts refer to it, currently has nine nation-states as its members. Recent estimates of their *deployed warheads* show:[5]

US	1750
Russia	1600
France	300
China	280
UK	215
Pakistan	150
India	140
Israel	80
North Korea	20

As a result of various treaties and attempts to reduce nuclear arsenals, the US and Russia both have large stockpiles of mothballed warheads, as well as others on standby. Both countries began reducing their active inventories as a result of talks between US President Richard Nixon and Soviet Premier Leonid Brezhnev in 1969 and onward. Known as the Strategic Arms Limitation Talks (SALT), the negotiations and the following treaty began to reduce the nuclear tension somewhat. Ronald Reagan and Mikhail Gorbachev continued the dialogue and both advocated further reduction.

But historical alliances and animosities amongst the various countries in the nuclear club have created an intricate pattern of threats and counter-threats. For instance, the US and Russia have mostly stood at sword points ever since the end of WW2. The UK and France, through NATO, have aligned with the US against Russia.

China has typically positioned its nuclear arsenal against the US, originally because of its early alliance with the former Soviet Union, and continuing though the Cold War period. Even after China's entry into the United Nations in 1971 and its improving trade relations with the US, their leaders still seem keen on having a nuclear footprint across Asia.

India's leaders have long feared the increasing nuclear power of China. But then Pakistan got ahold of nukes and used them to balance the perceived threat from India. That put India into an intricate triangular pattern of animosity with both China and Pakistan.

Israel, by contrast, became a separate and unique case, using its nukes to persuade its Arab neighbors that they themselves might suffer more than Israel if they attacked. Israel acquired its weapons-grade uranium by mysterious means. Some experts claim a shipment of processed uranium that went missing from an American arsenal ended up in Israeli hands and gave that country a head start over its Arab neighbors.

And North Korea, widely considered a rogue state, has in recent years built a modest arsenal of its own. As of this writing, its mercurial leader Kim Jong-Un has aroused international concerns with threats to bomb South Korea as well as Japan, and to launch ICBMs supposedly capable of striking the continental US.

NUCLEAR PSYCHOLOGY: THE STAND-OFF

Let's return to our first question under this discussion: how shall we understand nuclear weapons and their unique, frightening, and controversial role in national security? How shall we frame the discussion of their role and their potential future in the life of our Republic? I propose that we frame our understanding in psychological terms. We need to think of a nuclear warhead as fundamentally *a psychological weapon.* The value of a nuclear warhead—even one—lies in its capacity to induce fear in the leaders of an adversarial state. Quite aside from its mode of delivery, its accuracy, or its yield, it exists to scare the hell out of people.

Nuclear nations try to establish superiority—or, least, nuclear parity—with their adversaries in order to achieve a state of *reciprocal fear.* Each side would like to have complete superiority, which would terrify the other side; but it usually turns out that both players have to settle for a fear-stand-off.

This bizarre logic of fear makes sense in a perverse sort of way.

Think of a nuclear weapon, or an arsenal, as setting up either of two possible conditions, one stable and one unstable. In the stable scenario, two adversarial nations both have nukes. When their inventories grow to a certain number of warheads, they arrive at what strategic planners call a state of *mutual assured destruction*—the MAD threshold, which we'll explore shortly.

Oddly, in the stable or *symmetrical scenario*, the nukes probably serve to *prevent* war. When both sides can essentially annihilate one another, neither side would benefit by launching first. That might even prevent a conventional war from developing, because the awful option of escalating to total destruction always hangs over their heads. They might well have incentives to limit the scope of a localized skirmish, for fear that it might escalate to a level where the nuclear temptation sets in.

The unstable or *asymmetrical scenario*, on the other hand, presents a much greater risk because of the underdog factor. If one country or a group of countries faces a much stronger adversary, the leaders of the underdog side might elect to acquire nuclear weapons as a way to present a big-time counter-threat. The existence of the nukes creates a psychological offset to the unbalanced power relationship. The underdog side will almost certainly never fire a nuclear weapon, but the mere fact that it could changes the psychological calculus completely.

The MAD concept, and its bizarre lingo, sprang from the fertile mind of a colorless technocrat named Donald Brennan, one of the intellectuals working at the prominent Hudson Institute, a defense policy think tank founded by mega-thinker Hermann Kahn. He and his followers seemed to like to strip away the human meaning from the language of warfare with terms like "megadeaths," "overkill," and "nuclear winter." Never mind that tens of millions of people in the non-aligned countries might also die in a nuclear exchange—an effect known as "collateral damage." That would just go with the territory, as they say.

By an impersonal sort of logic, MAD advocates reasoned that aiming all the missiles at the other side's military bases and missile launchers would have less effect than simply targeting their major population centers. Accepting the impossibility of defending all of their own missile sites in a MAD scenario, they would just make sure the other side could no longer function as a country.

Try this macabre thinking exercise: how many nuclear warheads—ICBMs launched from land silos or submarine platforms, or delivered by long-range bombers—do you think it would take to completely incapacitate the United States?

Suppose we define incapacitated as something like a condition in which all major population centers and their infrastructures sustain irreparable damage. Overwhelmed emergency systems fail to cope with widespread death, injury, and disease; death rates and refugee counts climb so high as to cause a breakdown in the customary social order; public transport systems, including airports, shut down or operate at minimal capacity; stock exchanges collapse and the entire financial system fails; credit mechanisms no longer work; money becomes worthless; food shortages quickly set in; people resort to looting, hoarding and fighting over food, water, and fuel; bands of wandering refugees battle with one another to seize resources from farms and factories; and law enforcement agencies cannot cope with widespread disorder.

As input for your estimates, consider that the bomb dropped on Hiroshima had an explosive force, or *yield*, equivalent to 14,000 tons (kilotons) of TNT. Detonated 1,800 feet above the city, it killed 70,000 people instantly and flattened over 70 percent of the structures. A typical modern warhead has an explosive force of 20 *million* tons (megatons) of TNT— equal to a thousand Hiroshima bombs.

How did you arrive at your estimate of the MAD threshold? Would you base it on the 25 biggest cities in the country? Or 50? Would one warhead per major city do the job? Would you allocate a few extra for the big dams, harbors, and airports? A few more to allow for duds and misfires?

Whatever number of missiles you came up with, you can think of it as your estimate of the MAD threshold—the number of missiles in the inventory beyond which any additional quantity, however large, has *zero strategic value.*

It seems to me that about 100 missiles per side, at absolute most, would pretty well guarantee mutual destruction in an Armageddon exchange. So, by even the most perverse, inhumane logic, how can anyone make a case for stockpiling thousands of them?

By all logic, the next immediate goal for arms reduction should aim for a nuclear inventory of just enough warheads to meet the MAD threshold on both sides. An international treaty between the nine currently nuclear-armed nations could dictate no more than 100 warheads per side—total.

From that point, the parties might begin the process of reducing inventories further. The only reasonable target, eventually, would call for zero weapons.

Would, or could, the current belligerent nations ever agree to de-nuclearize? Maybe, maybe not.

PROTECTING THE INTERNET—THE GLOBAL NERVOUS SYSTEM

One other very important point deserves attention before we move on to other related topics. Cyber-war practices have developed rapidly over the past 5 to 10 years, becoming increasingly sophisticated and increasingly destructive. People unfamiliar with those kinds of methods might not realize their destructive potential and how critical it has become to defend against cyber-attacks as well as use them.

Let's consider just one frightening possibility, which so far has received very little attention in the national conversation: *attacking the Internet.*

While developed countries have a strong commitment to

keeping the Internet and a vast array of online resources intact, less developed rogue states might have more destructive motivations. The leaders of a backward country like North Korea would suffer very little from a mass take-down of worldwide Internet traffic, but it could inflict incalculable damage on its first-world adversaries.

Would it surprise you to know that *nearly 99 percent of the world's international Internet traffic—messages between countries—runs through undersea cables*? Over the past 20 years or so, governments and private companies have laid more than 300 cables spanning several hundred thousand miles, most of it fiber optic.

One might think of satellite links as the favored option, but telecom engineers see certain big advantages in cables. They provide much higher message capacity—*bandwidth*, as the geeks call it—and shorter signal delays—*latency*, in geek-speak—than satellite links.

From the big-nation perspective, US intelligence agencies and others regularly wire-tap undersea cables, at points where they pass through accessible coastal waters.

Imagine the havoc that a rogue state might cause with a fleet of specially configured small submarines, for example, sent out to find and sever these Internet cables.

Another possible form of cyber-warfare, seldom discussed so far, would include attacks by a rogue state on the orbiting satellites of a modern one. This would involve deploying high-altitude missiles or killer satellites to attack, disable, or de-orbit satellites of rival countries.

The Global Positioning System (GPS), on which all modern economies now depend, relies on a system of satellites that transmit synchronized signals to all points on earth. Damage to that system could have catastrophic economic effects.

We've come a long way from our preoccupation with the kinetic threat of the now-obsolete nuclear triad, to a post-Napoleonic world in which ideas, information, and small customized force packages have become the weapons. The global nuclear threat remains a high risk, even though it has become obsolete, but the real action has moved from the physical domain to the information domain.

LET'S STOP PLAYING THE WALMART OF WEAPONS FOR THE WORLD

The national flag of Mozambique displays a silhouette of an AK-47 assault rifle.

One has to wonder what kind of message that sends to the other nations of the world community. Does a rifle with the dubious reputation as the weapon of choice for mass murder deserve a place of honor on a nation's primary symbol of its identity?

The AK-47 probably deserves its reputation as the weapon of choice in the mad underworld of sectarian violence. Current estimates put the number of them at something like 75 million worldwide. It has become the very symbol of clan warfare, revenge, and rebellion.

Its inventor, a retired Soviet Army general named Mikhail Kalashnikov, had studied the advantages and shortcomings of the various small-arms options available to the military forces participating in WW2. He decided to create a next-generation weapon for the ground soldier—one that would combine the reliability and automatic reloading capability of the 8-round American M-1 *Garand*, which had out-performed the 5-round bolt-action German *Mauser* rifle, with a high-capacity magazine and the high rate of fire. His creation eventually became the most famous and widely used firearm around the world.

The AK-47's rugged simplicity made it easy for arms manufacturers around the world to copy and mass-reproduce it. Dozens of gun factories around the world churn out their own AK-clones. No self-respecting "freedom fighter" would want to leave home without one. This weapon, more than any other, has contributed to a world-wide epidemic of sectarian violence, terrorism, and civil war. A widespread network of arms dealers handles the buying and selling of small arms of every imaginable type.

The Stockholm International Peace Research Institute (SIPRI) estimates the worldwide stock of small arms at 875 million, produced by more than 1,000 companies from nearly 100 countries.[6]

In the US, the ArmaLite Rifle—a.k.a. the AR-15—a commercial replica of the military M-14 and M-16 assault rifles, has become wildly popular with gun fans, and enjoys the dubious distinction as the weapon of choice for mass shootings.

But beyond the easy availability of high-powered murder weapons, we have a huge market in more advanced military weapons, ranging from machine guns, mortars, landmines, and explosives all the way to missiles, bombs, and fighter aircraft. Weapons manufacturers in a dozen or more countries, once they've satisfied the demands of their national governments, typically feel free to market the same weapons to the governments of other countries.

As of this writing, the five leading arms exporting countries include the US, Russia, China, Germany, and France. The five leading importers typically include India, Saudi Arabia, China, the United Arab Emirates, and Pakistan.[7]

If we remember Eisenhower's caution about the military-industrial complex as he left public life, we have to ask ourselves: if America's leaders truly want world peace and a general reduction in hostilities between nations and factions, then why do they allow, condone, or sponsor the flooding of the world market with cheaply available weapon systems? Why, if they favor reducing the antagonism between nations, do they sell sophisticated new weapon systems to all parties?

Has the time come for America to stop playing the role of weapons supplier to the world? Should we prohibit US weapons makers from selling their products outside the US, and to no other buyers than the Department of Defense?

Could we prevail upon the other arms-exporting nations to do the same? Could we confine—or at least limit—arms production to satisfy internal demand only? Could we crack down on opportunistic gun-runners who buy weapons illegally and sell them into third-world conflict zones?

LET'S ELIMINATE WEAPONS THAT KILL INNOCENT PEOPLE

Throughout most of human history, military commanders and fighters seem to have operated on the assumption that their immediate objectives outweigh everything else in importance, and they have the right to resort to any means necessary to prevail. That way of thinking has produced the most destructive weapons and methods imaginable.

Consider the following scenario. An invading force sets fire to a town, aiming to drive out the defenders holed up in the homes and shops and barns. The defenders respond with machine gun fire. The attackers throw grenades. Both sides seem to feel free to destroy the property the unfortunate residents of the town have worked their whole lives to build.

A defender fires a machine gun from the bell tower of the 200 year-old church, so the attackers fire artillery shells that blast away the tower. Farm animals die in a hail of bullets. Their rotting carcasses will eventually spread disease.

Before the operation even began, the defenders planted dozens of anti-personnel (AP) mines along the roads and fields leading into the town. They don't have time to record the locations of the mines, so by the time the battle ends, neither side can make use of the dangerous terrain. Then they move on to other battles, leaving the town in smoking ruins and many of the inhabitants dead. The survivors may discover, to their unhappy surprise, that their farms and fields no longer belong to them. After several farm animals— and possibly some children—die in sudden explosions, they understand these weapons on a very personal basis.

Landmines probably represent the most cruel and

destructive "collateral damage" weapons, and in modern times more and more social activists have adopted the cause of eliminating them altogether.

The International Campaign to Ban Landmines, launched in 1992, brought together representatives from over 100 countries, plus a number of advocacy groups. It played a key part in creating the Mine Ban Treaty, ratified in 1997, also known as the Ottawa Convention.[8]

According to ICBL's website, only a few countries still keep landmines in inventory, and most of them have more or less accepted the long-term objective of eliminating them. Russia announced in 2010 that it had destroyed ten million mines. China reportedly reduced its stockpile of landmines from over 100 million down to about five million in 2014.

While those figures offer some encouragement, one has to ask, why in the world would any country want or need to produce millions of antipersonnel mines? Who can imagine a military operation so vast as to employ even a fraction of that number? So, when Russia and China announce big reductions in their stockpiles, let's not forget that they still retain an ungodly number of them.

Does the US government endorse the Mine Ban Treaty? Well, sort of. President Obama endorsed the ban, but hedged his bet on one count. US and South Korean forces have planted AP mines in the Demilitarized Zone (DMZ)—the no man's land that separates the two countries at the 38th parallel—for many years. The peculiar rationale holds that South Korea, not a member of the treaty coalition, keeps several million mines in its stockpile, and because the joint-defense agreement might someday place South Korean forces under the command of an American general in an emergency, the policies of the two countries would come into conflict.

Consequently, the US hasn't formally signed the treaty, but aside from the Korean exception fully supports it. ICBL estimates that US stockpiles of AP mines have come down from more than 10 million to about 2-3 million. Now that laws in the US and other major nations prohibit the export of landmines, international trade has fallen close to zero.

As of this writing, ICBL estimates that about a dozen countries still maintain the capacity to manufacture AP mines and four—South Korea, India, Pakistan, and Myanmar—actively do. Its estimate of worldwide stockpiles still stands at about 50 million.

But reducing the manufacture, storage, and use of landmines only gets at part of the problem. ICBL estimates that over 60 countries still have significant areas of land contaminated by unknown thousands of emplaced mines. Over 8,000 people die or get injured in a typical year. That equates to nearly one human life lost or ruined every hour of every day.

Quite aside from the appalling numbers of ghastly injuries and deaths, consider the economic impact on farmers and rural people who cannot safely use the land to grow food, raise cattle, or even allow their children to play safely.

The action item here needs very little argument. How can any thinking American condone the use of landmines or accept that many thousands of them remain in place? Let's make sure the US government stays behind the Mine Ban Treaty, presses all other nations to join and to destroy their stockpiles, and contributes significantly to the de-mining of contaminated areas and the care of people who suffer the disastrous consequences.

LET'S START BRINGING THE TROOPS HOME

How many military bases, in how many countries, do we need to keep us safe from our potential enemies? Let's approach that question by thinking about the role of overseas bases in today's changing strategic environment.

Many years ago, as the great empires expanded their global military influence, they all recognized the need for a permanent presence in those parts of the world they wanted to dominate. Imagine trying to fight a war against an enemy nation by sending out expeditions of soldiers—either by land or by ship—equipped with only the weapons, food, and supplies they could carry with them. After a few battles they'd have to turn around and go home, as the next contingent passed by on the way to the war. The concept of military *logistics*, and the forward military base—fort, fortress, or outpost—became a key part of military practice.

Home-country bases, of course, existed to provide protection against foreign attacks (e.g., with coastal fortresses); and to muster and train soldiers for possible expeditions to war zones. These days, most of the imposing coastal fortresses have become historical stops for tourists.

We operate two kinds of bases: land bases and floating bases. Think of a naval fleet with an aircraft carrier and a collection of special-mission ships sailing with it as very similar—conceptually, at least—to a fixed base on land. It can host a big inventory of planes, thousands of troops, weapons and ammunition, supplies, and all of the support facilities that a regular land base would have. It has food service facilities, laundries, hospitals, movie theaters, a morgue, and a jail. A carrier task force works like a floating airport that can move all around the world.

Foreign bases have evolved to serve a variety of national purposes: 1) to control conquered territory and govern conquered peoples; 2) to establish military footholds outside the home territory; 3) to threaten the governments of geopolitical rivals or prospective adversaries with the prospect of attack, as a potent factor in negotiating for land, resources, and trade; 4) to pre-position military equipment and supplies for possible use if war breaks out in a particular region; 5) to refuel and resupply naval fleets so they can patrol the oceans for long periods without having to return home; 6) to assist allied countries that face existential threats from rivals in their geographic spheres of influence; and 7) to support commerce and colonization.

We need to evaluate each of our bases against these potential objectives, to see whether we might want to locate a particular base in a particular country. We should ask: if we didn't have this base at this location today, would we want one here? Does every base fulfill the purpose we had in mind for it when we created it—possibly many years ago?

As a good case example, let's consider the controversial naval and marine base at Guantanamo Bay, on the southeastern tip of the island of Cuba. That example raises an important new consideration in thinking about bases: namely, what side-effects or unanticipated consequences, if any, might arise as a result of occupying the base? At the very least, it raises the question: do the government and people of the host country really want the base there?

Clearly, Cuban governments (beginning with Fidel Castro, at least) and most of the Cuban people have resented the US presence at Guantanamo for decades. The occupation continues solely under the might-makes-right doctrine. Presidents since Eisenhower have asserted America's right to occupy the base, and clearly the Cuban government couldn't hope to oust the world's most powerful military by force.

Another controversial basing question involves the tiny island of Okinawa in the south of Japan. About half of all US forces stationed in Japan operate out of several bases there. Ever since Japan's ten-year transition from a defeated, occupied country after WW2 to a sovereign modern nation, the status of US forces there has caused controversy.

While most Japanese citizens express gratitude for the military protection provided by the US after the war (Japan's post-war constitution prohibited it from having any military force at all), many of them feel the scale of the operation far exceeds any necessary level. Many Okinawans also feel strongly that the presence of thousands of young male soldiers has disrupted their culture, brought increased crime, and created friction between them and the locals.

US military planners tend to argue for a formidable presence in that part of Asia, not only to deter any hostile ambitions on the part of North Korea's rogue government, but also to contain China's aspirations for dominance of the region.

Taking the broad view, it seems clear that we have more overseas bases with more troops at the ready than all other modern nations combined, and far more than we can realistically justify in terms of our strategic needs.

The Department of Defense has had an ongoing review of overseas basing for quite some time and has closed a number of unneeded ones, as well as some state-side ones. Now the DoD should accelerate and intensify that review and set a higher standard for retaining any particular base.

LET'S TURN SOME SWORDS INTO PLOWSHARES

The US can easily maintain a robust defense capability, unmatched by any other country in the world, as we also re-orient our vast military expenditures for non-destructive purposes. The time has come for us to rethink the colossally wasteful blank-check spending spree that has done more to increase the risk of war than it has to reduce it. We must have the courage of our common sense and we must change our priorities. America, as the mightiest military power on the planet, also has the special opportunity to take the initiative in bringing the world back from the brink of destruction.

One intriguing possibility involves converting some of our carrier fleets, some of our overseas bases, and some state-side bases to multi-purpose roles. We already have a history of experience with the use of military resources for humanitarian purposes, going back many years. For example, when the small Pacific island nation of East Timor went through a near collapse in 1999 and onward, with sectarian violence and widespread economic crisis compounded by massive destruction from a tsunami, a number of nations teamed up to stabilize the situation. Led by Australia, military forces from the contributing countries, including the US, quelled the riots and disarmed renegade militia groups, and provided humanitarian aid to rebuild the country.

With a large fleet stationed just offshore, they began

supplying water, food, medical supplies and treatments, and other emergency resources. They followed up by repairing damaged infrastructure and building schools and hospitals.

US military forces have often played a key role in early response to national disasters such as hurricanes, floods, and earthquakes. The US Army's Corps of Engineers has a distinguished reputation for large scale facilities construction —they masterminded the construction of the Panama Canal. The Corps also played a key role in reconstructing flood control resources in New Orleans after hurricane Katrina devastated the area. US soldiers and National Guard members have often mobilized to fight forest fires.

The relative balance of those two seemingly contradictory missions, military and humanitarian, could vary widely depending on circumstances. In the process of patrolling the seas and demonstrating America's military might on land—if that still takes priority—our forces can take a simultaneous proactive role in building the capacity for peace.

In Chapter 12 (Foreign Relations), we'll see how a more enlightened view of military investment can support a more cooperative relationship with friendly nations, and how it can actually offer advantages in the long-running chess game with belligerent foreign governments.

THE FIX-IT LIST: NATIONAL DEFENSE

So, how can we improve this component of our Republic— Defense? Let's start with these actions.

1. *Let's Begin to Rationalize Military Spending.* The US Congress will pass a law permanently restricting defense spending (not to include Homeland Security spending) to 2 percent of expected GDP for 3 successive years. For the next 5 years the allocation will decrease by 0.1 percent per year, to a permanent maximum of 1.5 percent. Any change to this defense ratio will require a majority vote of a joint session of Congress and will expire after 12 months.

2. *Let's Defuse Nuclear Tensions.* The US government will unilaterally reconfirm its commitment to a "no first strike" policy of using nuclear weapons. It will invite all other nuclear states to do the same.

The US Congress will pass a law that prevents any sitting president from launching a first-strike nuclear attack, including the use of low-yield tactical nuclear weapons. The new law will limit and clarify the President's authority and responsibility with regard to the launch of nuclear weapons and the associated duties and responsibilities of the Secretary of Defense and other senior government officials.

The US government will invite the governments of all nuclear-armed nations to de-manufacture all nuclear-armed missiles in excess of 100 units. The US government will begin that process regardless of whether the other governments agree.

3. *Let's Start Turning Swords Into Plowshares.* The US Congress will broaden the mission of the US aircraft carrier fleets, to specifically incorporate humanitarian assistance and logistical support to nations in need, to the extent that those components don't compromise the primary mission of military readiness. The US Navy will equip designated carriers with equipment, facilities, supplies, and specially trained personnel to provide immediate assistance in natural disasters, refugee rescue and transport, and the support of infrastructure development in needy countries.

Congress will broaden the mission of certain overseas bases to specifically incorporate local economic development and peacekeeping efforts in support of developing governments. These bases will maintain necessary levels of military readiness while serving the broader civil support component of the mission. As part of base realignment, the Defense Department will negotiate support arrangements with local governments and will assign staff and materiel resources for civil support activities.

4. *Let's Get Rid of Inhumane Weapons and Practices.* By act of Congress and presidential order, the US government will formally reject and outlaw the use of coercive interrogation methods, commonly regarded as torture by reputable psychologists.

The US government will formally declare that it will not use military weapons, materials, or methods that endanger the lives or health of innocent civilians, or make large areas of land uninhabitable, under any circumstances. These include chemical weapons such as tear gas and related toxic gases; napalm; and Agent Orange (a defoliant) and its derivatives.

The US will destroy or de-manufacture all such weapons now in inventory. We'll invite all other nations to do the same.

5. Congress will unequivocally commit to US acceptance of the Mine Ban Treaty, and will allocate funds to support international cooperation for demining, restoration, and reparations to victims, with the goal of eliminating 95 percent of all landmine contamination within 5 years.

Chapter 6.
Let's Rethink Law and Order:
Building a Civil Society

"The hungry judges soon the sentence sign,
and wretches hang that jurymen may dine."
—Alexander Pope
British Essayist, Philosopher

As societies grow beyond their primitive stages and become more complex and diversified, the problem of defining and maintaining law and order becomes ever more complex. We must understand—and sometimes rethink—the relationship between the individual and the society, and the expectations they can reasonably have of each other.

LET'S ADOPT A NATIONAL ID CARD

We begin this investigation from a seemingly peculiar angle: the idea of a nationwide system that *uniquely identifies* every single human being within the borders of the Republic. We'll see how that system can help revolutionize the component of Law and Order, as well as contribute to just about every other key component of a successful republic.

The concept of a national ID card has bounced around for a decade or more and now its time may have come. I've placed it here mostly for topical convenience but it could easily support a number of other topics. We'll revisit it several times in the following chapters as we take up the various other components in more depth.

Admittedly, in the current climate of bewildering technological change, Americans have real concerns about loss of privacy and the dangers of a "Big Brother" state that might take advantage of such a system. Privacy activists point to the Chinese government's appalling efforts to impose 100 percent surveillance on its citizens, for example, as a worst-case lesson in police-state use of technology.

In this chapter we'll examine the benefits of a National Citizen Identification System (NCIDS) for the Law and Order component of the Republic and take up the privacy concerns again more fully in Chapter 10 (Civil Liberties).

WHAT WOULD AN NCID SYSTEM LOOK LIKE?

Wikipedia lists over 100 countries that have universal ID systems, including Argentina, Belgium, Brazil, China, Germany, Greece, Hong Kong, Indonesia, Iran, Israel, the Netherlands, Russia, Saudi Arabia, Singapore, and Taiwan.

In some countries, laws require possession of an ID card at all times, but not all countries punish failure to carry it. Some do impose strict penalties. As we might expect, the most totalitarian governments have imposed the strictest requirements on citizen identification. But few, if any, modern governments have fully integrated digital identity into the systems that support civil rights such as voting; national security requirements such as immigration and law enforcement; and administrative systems such as driving licenses and car registration.

The tiny Baltic republic of Estonia, when freed from the Russian orbit after the collapse of the Soviet Union, immediately began moving to become a full digital society. Most Estonians register online to vote, file and pay their taxes online, and do most of their banking and other personal transactions online. An ID card entitles the 1.3 million Estonians to free use of a wide array of public and online services. The government in Tallinn seldom enforces the requirement for carrying the card, partly because almost all citizens have their online identities and the requirement for physical possession has become moot.

Introduced in 2002, the Estonian system has become a model that other governments have begun to copy. In 2015, Japan's finance minister visited Estonia to study their system. As a result, the government announced a similar program, aiming to become a "one-card society," as Estonia has.

The US probably comes closer to having such a system than many people realize, but not all of the parts of the system fit together. We currently have a vast multitude of special-purpose databases, most of which don't talk to one another. The geeks call it "interoperability," and we don't have it yet.

The system would need only two main components: a simple plastic ID card with the citizen's photo and fingerprint; and a single national database containing every citizen's basic data package. No personal data would go on the card—only a serial number that would serve as the citizen's unique identifying number, plus a PIN number for verification.

Let's consider some of the most interesting applications— and presumed benefits—of this one-card system.

FRAUD MIGHT DECLINE

This new system could go a long way to reducing fraud and identity theft.

Most types of ID cards used today—driving licenses, military ID cards, student cards, social security cards, welfare eligibility cards, alien work permits, and lots of others—all have the same fatal flaw: crooks can easily counterfeit them.

Most of the identification systems commonly used in the US today depend on static ID devices—simple plastic or cardboard credentials that don't connect to any online systems. That makes it dirt simple for crooks to copy or counterfeit them.

With the card-and-database system just described, however, crooks and counterfeiters face a big challenge. If they try to invent a citizen serial number that doesn't exist, the system will reject it as invalid. But if they try one already in the database, they'll get nowhere online without the password, which the actual owner controls. And anyone trying to use a stolen ID card at a point of sale would have to look a lot like the actual owner, have a fingerprint that matches his or hers exactly, and know the PIN or password for online access.

LAW ENFORCEMENT WILL GET SMARTER

A second fatal flaw in the vast majority of our identity-based data systems—driving licenses, credit cards, medical plans, arrest records, tax rolls, jury lists, and lots of others—lies in the way we keep track of them: by the names of the people. That method almost guarantees duplicates, spelling errors, and falsification by aliases. If your name happens to match one of those on the government's no-fly list, for example, you might have a very unpleasant experience at the airport.

The NCID system would nearly eliminate false matches and the costs and hardships they impose on law-abiding citizens.

Just as the system would thwart some incursions on individual rights, it would also prevent people who break the law from disappearing and avoiding legal consequences.

For example, consider the obvious case of a divorcee under court order to pay child support to his former spouse. By pulling up stakes, relocating, and assuming a fictitious name, he might escape his legal obligations—unless they can find him. This remains a significant unsolved problem in the US.

Coordination between state-level law enforcement agencies varies from fragmentary to nonexistent. Typically the deprived spouse has to pay a private investigator to do what an intelligent data system could do in a split-second. With a national ID system, a flag on the divorcee's record would alert the proper authorities, including tax authorities, of his obligation and possible delinquency.

Many of these linking and integration mechanisms might lead to a streamlining of law enforcement and much greater coordination across all jurisdictions nationwide. When police officers stop a suspect, they typically search the local database for their jurisdiction—typically a city or county—for arrest warrants. But in cases of multiple false identities, they might not get a match. And, of course, outstanding warrants in other jurisdictions typically don't come up. With a national ID system a flag in the individual's central record would cue them to contact the previous arresting agency.

A similar problem arises with registered sex offenders. If an offender relocates and chooses not to register in the next city, his presence—or absence—typically does not get detected automatically. Many US states require landlords to check their "hot" lists when considering prospective tenants, but many of those systems have wrong or obsolete records, inadequate updating, and sloppy list maintenance.

With a national system, the citizen ID number would point to the new address whenever he signed a rental agreement, set up mail service, or applied for a state driver's license.

The same possibilities apply to keeping track of felons on probation, bail jumpers, people with unpaid traffic fines or expired driving licenses, and those under restraining orders.

Welfare fraud might go down. A person deemed eligible for social services would have his or her record flagged in the national database during the period of eligibility. Because all eligibility records would link to the unique citizen ID number, no one could register for public assistance more than once by setting up multiple accounts under fictitious names.

At the time of death—just another data point for the NCID system—the system would flag the citizen's record as deceased. "Dead people," to paraphrase the pirates of old, "commit no fraud."

Voter registration fraud would become harder with a national ID system. Although most experts assess the degree of voter fraud in the US as very small, those who still worry about the problem might find it quickly solved. A national ID system would register eligible voters automatically and routinely purge fictitious names. No "imaginary" citizens.

Once a person pulled the lever in the voting booth, the system would flag his or her record as having voted, so no one could use the ID number to vote more than once. Death codes in the database would make the practice of registering names from graveyards as live voters impossible. Online voting would become feasible, with each citizen having a one-time access password for the procedure.

THE NCID SYSTEM COULD SAVE A LOT OF MONEY

A single master database could save the federal government millions of dollars in computer system costs and lots of errors, with the use of a proven technology known to geeks as *relational databases.*

Instead of keeping multiple copies of a person's primary dataset—name, gender, date of birth, address, citizen status, preferred email address, and others—scattered through a multitude of separate databases, the key information only has to reside in one place—the master database. Other databases, such as those for driving licenses, social security, veteran status, Medicare benefits, voter registration, IRS tax records, law enforcement, gun registration, and many others, would only need a slot for the individual's unique ID number.

Whenever a computer system accesses a person's record in one of those specialty databases, it merely picks up his or her ID number in that database and then finds the one record in the main database with the matching ID. It fetches the key data from that record and uses it for its processing task.

Any time the information in the master database changes, such as when a person moves to a different address, the updated information becomes instantly available to all of the other systems that need it, just as if the person had gone to each of the agencies involved and updated each of the accounts one by one. Each citizen would only need to keep his or her record current in a single database.

Consider, for a moment, the phenomenal improvement in cost and efficiency such a system might bring.

For one thing, it would eliminate a huge number of errors in the data, because correcting a record in the master database automatically corrects it everywhere else. It would also reduce the labor required to enter data into those databases.

So far, we've only looked at the national database as a tool for citizen data—information related to a person's relationship to the Republic and its government. But how about the thousands of businesses that use the same information to provide services to their customers?

Consider the simple case of magazine subscriptions. When a person moves to a new address, he or she has to notify all of the magazine publishers of the change. Association memberships, banks, and credit card companies all need the same maintenance. The US Postal Service estimates that mail forwarding costs almost $300 million a year and returning undeliverable mail to senders costs another $800 million.

At the national level, we can rethink the census. Every 10 years, on the "zero" year, going back to 1790, the federal government has conducted a count of Americans—or, more accurately, American homes. Mailed-out census forms and door-to-door census workers gather an enormous mountain of data, which the Census Bureau processes into a report that describes Americans in statistical terms. A comprehensive national database would make the traditional census process unnecessary, because it gets updated every day.

THE KILLER APP: IMMIGRATION

In Chapter 11 (Immigration), we'll explore the role of a national ID card system further. For the moment, let's settle for a brief overview of the key features of an immigration policy based on universal and unique identities.

First, we can scrap the emotionally loaded terms like "illegal aliens," "migrants," "immigrants," "refugees," and "undocumented workers," and recognize only two categories of people: *citizens* and *visitors*.

A universal visitor card, similar to the citizen card, would work much like a gift card or store card. For tourists and short-term visitors, a cheap and disposable product, possibly made of sturdy card stock, would have a serial number on a magnetic card stripe. For longer-term visitors such as students, authorized workers, asylum grantees, and citizenship candidates, it might include a photo and fingerprint just as the citizen card would.

A single database for visitors of all categories would provide up-to-the-minute eligibility status of every card holder, as designated by the issuing agency. A simple swipe through a card reader would immediately show the cardholder's name, unique ID number and identifying data, and the status of his or her eligibility. Approved changes in status, such as permission to work, extension of expiration, change in category, or grant of citizenship, could go into effect instantly.

LET'S RETHINK CRIME AND PUNISHMENT— COMPLETELY

Reader alert: you might find the ideas and proposals offered for this next component of the Republic so contradictory to your acquired beliefs and opinions about how things should work that you might instinctively reject them as unrealistic.

I can only ask, as with previous proposals, that you try to suspend judgment until you fully understand this alternative view. For this journey, we need to put on our thinking caps and take a big-system view of the challenge of keeping order.

LET'S FACE THE FACTS AND FIGMENTS

As a Republic, we spend a large share of our resources on trying to catch and punish people who misbehave. At city, county, state, and national levels, we've evolved a haphazard conglomeration of "correctional" operations—courts, jails, holding facilities, juvenile detention centers, and prisons. No one seems to know what or how they correct.

- Recent to this writing, the total number of people behind bars in the US—the *incarcerated population*—stands at 2.3 million, or about 0.7 percent of the population. With 3.6 million offenders out on probation and 840,000 on parole, the "correctional population" numbers about 6.6 million, or about 2 percent.

- The US, with 5 percent of the world's population, now holds almost *25 percent of the world's prisoners*—the highest incarceration rate in the world. We lock up 5 to 10 times as many people as other modern democracies.

- On any given day, about 750,000 people sit in local jails around the country and about 13 million pass through the jails in a typical year. By analogy to hotel rooms, a typical jail cell "turns over" about 17 times per year.

- The largest jail in the US, operated by Los Angeles County, holds almost 18,000 people. Louisiana State Penitentiary, the largest maximum security prison in the country and known as the Alcatraz of the South, houses 5,000 inmates. It has a reputation for chronic violence and inmate abuse.[9]

Something, it seems, has gone wrong. Either Americans misbehave more often and more seriously than their counterparts in other countries, or our criminal justice system doesn't make sense. We seem to over-punish and over-incarcerate, compared to other modern societies.

"THREE STRIKES": DID WE GET TOUGH ON CRIME OR JUST GET CONFUSED?

We haven't always had the distinction of imprisoning more people than any other country. During the period from 1920 through 1980, our incarcerated population grew at just about the same rate as the general population, holding steady at about 0.25 percent, even as the overall population doubled.

Starting in about 1980, things went crazy. A combination of rising crime rates, populist trends at the political level, and changing ideologies among law enforcement and corrections officials, triggered an unprecedented tough-on-crime phase.

The American public had become increasingly concerned about drug abuse, particularly very dangerous drugs like crack cocaine. The "War on Drugs," launched during the Reagan administration and publicized energetically by First Lady Nancy Reagan, promised to drive down drug abuse, addiction, and drug-related crimes. It didn't.

The drug problem, plus demands by political figures for more severe penalties for all crimes; longer sentences; mandatory sentencing requirements; and the closure of public treatment facilities for the mentally ill caused a huge rise in the number of candidates for prison.

During the years from 1980 through 2016, as the US general population grew by about 40 percent, the prison population *quadrupled*, as shown in Figure 6-1. The "lock 'em up" mentality took over in a big way. The American Psychological Association estimated that closing mental health treatment facilities pushed as many as 40,000 to 70,000 people with disorders into prisons instead of clinics.[10]

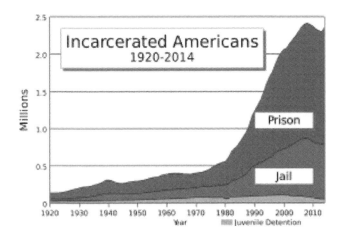

Figure 6-1. Incarcerated Americans

California's legislators raised the stakes even higher in 1994, with the state's notorious "three strikes" sentencing law, aimed at keeping repeat-offending felons behind bars. The law required judges to sentence offenders with prior felony convictions—"one-strikers"—to a period of incarceration equal to twice the usual sentence. Two-strikers, with two previous felony convictions, faced a mandatory prison term of at least 25 years to life for a third-strike offense.

Over the next decade, about 30 other states and the federal government passed their own versions of three-strike laws.

By 2011, California's three strikes law had created a capacity crisis in that state's prisons. The legislature had continually refused to vote enough funds to build new prisons or expand existing ones, while the tide of new inmates kept on growing. The prisons became jammed, overcrowded to as much as twice their intended capacity. Reports began to hit the news: inmates living in filthy conditions, 3 or 4 to a cell; shortages of bunks; inadequate food; dangerously inadequate medical care; inmate violence; and abuse by staff.

Lawsuits against the state, charging intolerable and life-threatening conditions in the prisons, brought the issue to a crisis. A special three-judge federal court ordered the state to reduce its prison population substantially. The state appealed to the US Supreme Court and lost. Under the court order, corrections officials resorted to measures like freeing inmates approaching their release dates, increasing good-behavior time allowances, and shifting them to local jails.

After seeing the huge tide of inmates, the costs of the prison-building boom, rising operating costs, and catastrophic overcrowding, California voters passed a measure in 2012 that restricted the use of the 25-to-life sentence to cases involving very serious or violent felonies. Many other states, experiencing California's same political drama—or knowing they soon would—began moving in the same direction. Federal and state courts now give judges more discretion, especially on the third strike option.

As of this writing, prison overcrowding remains a serious issue for at least half of the 50 states. As prison building becomes ever more expensive and less popular and the costs of incarcerating inmates continues to rise, more and more political leaders now question the logic of our penal system.

In particular, the three-strikes policy clogged the prisons with non-violent offenders, serving life sentences for crimes like drug possession or dealing, theft, or fraud. Some experts argue that the policy will accumulate a geriatric prison population for decades into the future with ever rising costs —particularly medical treatments—for elderly inmates. People who study those things estimate the annual cost of keeping a young, healthy, fit male in prison at about $30,000, while elderly prisoners can cost nearly twice that amount.

Further, they argue, older inmates present a much lower risk of violence or continued crime, whether incarcerated or not. Young males between the ages of 15 and 24 commit the vast majority of crimes. Males over 60 account for about one percent of all serious crimes.

Some experts advocate releasing well-behaved, non-violent inmates after age 60, arguing that they should bear the costs of their own retirement and medical care in their later years. That option might not sit well with Old Testament law-and-order advocates, but it does have a certain pragmatic appeal.

SIN, SUFFER, AND REPENT: WHY DO WE IMPRISON PEOPLE?

It might seem obvious, but it deserves saying: *We've built our entire approach to law and order on the concept of vengeance.* Society, we believe, has a natural right to retaliate—to exact revenge, to inflict suffering—on those who violate its norms.

Nowhere does this preoccupation with vengeance become more emotionalized, more stressful, more contentious—and more confusing—than when the question of capital punishment arises: *the death penalty.* We'll explore that issue more carefully later in this chapter.

A broader question: if we imprison someone for a victimless crime such as evading taxes or setting a fire in a national park, how does society benefit from his or her suffering? What debt has he or she actually paid?

LET'S SUBSTITUTE RESTITUTION FOR RETRIBUTION

The principle of *restitution,* or *restorative justice,* makes a lot more sense for our concept of law and order but we typically haven't given it more than occasional lip service. Let's start by requiring all offenders to pay their debts back to the victim, either directly by court-ordered restitution, or more generally by having to provide their labor to a pool used to make victims whole to the greatest extent possible.

Can we trade in our outdated medieval preoccupation with *vengeance*—punishment, suffering, humiliation, and estrangement from society—for a more enlightened approach based on *restitution, atonement,* and *re-integration?*

We already have a good start on a national policy for restitution. All 50 states, plus the federal government, have victim compensation programs. The 1984 Victims of Crime Act created a national Office of Victim Services and set up a Crime Victims Fund. Special assessments imposed on offenders convicted of certain crimes go into this national pool, along with various specific fines and penalties, plus money from forfeited bail bonds. The operation redistributes billions of dollars back to the states to compensate victims for financial loss, property damage, medical expenses, loss of wages, pain and suffering.

We can use restitution much more extensively by making it an essential part of every sentence, regardless of the offense.

Now, let's take some of these unconventional ideas and build a system with them.

We need an entirely new architecture for the Law and Order component of our Republic, based on four key principles:

1. Uniform national standards and practices.
2. Matching penalties to the offender.
3. Restitution.
4. Rehabilitation and re-entry into society.

In our new concept and system we'll still need high-security incarceration facilities, but far fewer of them. By separating violent and dangerous offenders from non-violent ones, we can reduce the costs of incarceration. Most of our opportunities and our need for rethinking come with this strategy of separation.

We'll still take away or restrict a non-violent offender's right to move about freely, for three reasons:

1. To require a formal *experience of penance* associated with the offense and suited to the offender's circumstances.

2. To put the offender into a *developmental environment* that can help him or her reform and return to society as a normal citizen.

3. To make use of his or her labor and productive energy to generate funds for victim compensation and restitution.

LET'S DEFINE NATIONAL STANDARDS AND PRACTICES

Sentencing practices, and indeed the very definitions of crimes, vary wildly from state to state and between states and the national level.

One young person who sells drugs might spend time in a juvenile detention facility while another might go to prison for several years—*within the same state.* An offense classified as a misdemeanor in one jurisdiction might constitute a felony in another. Some states try offenders under the age of 16 as adults and some don't. Consider a few examples:

- According to recent news reports, a court in Texas sentenced a woman to 5 years in prison for the offense of voting illegally in the 2016 election. She claimed she didn't know that, as a felon out of prison on parole, she had no right to vote in that state. The judge rejected her request for leniency.

- A New Jersey judge decided a 16 year-old high school student who raped a 16 year-old girl—and video-recorded the experience—deserved a lenient sentence because "He came from a good family, he went to a good school, he got good grades, he was an Eagle Scout, and it could be devastating to his career to be tried as an adult and convicted of a crime as serious as rape."

- In Florida, a wealthy sexual predator who used his money to build an international harem of underage women got caught trying to recruit one of his young victims into prostitution. The court sentenced him to 13 months in a minimum security facility, with unlimited visiting privileges—including members of his harem— and freedom to leave the facility during daylight hours.

- Alabama's supreme court rejected the appeal filed by attorneys for an inmate who spent 30 years on death row, most of it in solitary confinement. By the time his execution date approached, the 68 year-old black man had experienced several strokes, significant loss of brain function, loss of sight, impaired speech, loss of motor and bowel control, and dementia. On the findings of psychologists who examined him, the judges agreed that he had no comprehension of his crime—murdering a police officer—but still decided he had to die.

The case went to the US Supreme Court. The state's attorney argued that, "Alabama still has a strong interest in *seeking retribution* for a horrible crime." However, the Supremes overruled the state court and sent the case back for re-sentencing.

We need a national *standard set of definitions* for all crimes, great and small. Let's consider a useful analogy. Psychiatrists, psychologists, and licensed therapists use a standard "catalog" of psychological disorders published by the American Psychiatric Association, known as the Diagnostic and Statistical Manual of Mental Disorders, or the "DSM."

Currently in its fifth version, the DSM-5, it defines all named disorders recognized by the mental health profession, with explicit guidelines for diagnosing each one. (In case you find those things interesting, the DSM-5 lists the five most often diagnosed disorders as depression, anxiety, eating disorders, substance abuse, and attention deficit disorder.)

A DSM-like system for crimes and punishments, established at the national level, will help to classify all criminal offenses more precisely. It will also serve as a basis for associating standard consequences—and the inevitable situational variations—with those offenses.

LET'S MATCH THE PENALTIES TO THE OFFENDER

With our new system, we'll *stop sending people to jail or prison for non-violent offenses*. We'll use conventional prisons only for violent, disturbed, or dangerous people or those who chronically violate the law, such as sexual predators or malicious computer hackers.

We'll also stop using jails, such as New York's infamous Rikers Island or LA's massive county jail, to lock up people accused of crimes before trial. In a typical year, thousands of Americans who can't afford to pay bail money spend days or weeks in jail but get acquitted at trial or have the charges dropped. In most cases, they receive no compensation for the suspension of their liberty and violation of their civil rights.

We'll operate two kinds of actual prisons:

1. Level 1: high-security prisons for the most violent, dangerous or uncontrollable offenders, deemed too

difficult to manage.

2. Level 2: medium-security prisons for short-term detention of less dangerous offenders, whom we can manage by less severe incarceration practices.

A variation on the second type of incarceration facility, which we've used in the past but largely abandoned in the 1980s, consists of a *psychiatric detention center.* These residential facilities can house and treat people with significant mental disorders who pose a potential threat of violence against others or harm to themselves. Highly qualified mental health professionals will manage their residential experience and in some cases help with their transition to less restricted treatment facilities. For some of them, treatment might require long term incarceration, possibly for life.

LET'S THINK REMEDIATION

The third and most extensively used corrective option, for people who've committed garden variety non-violent offenses, will include a large number of *remedial detention centers* (RDCs). Reminiscent of the long-abandoned "reform school" model of the late 1800s and the 1900s but using modern methods, these low-security facilities will combine:

‣ A developmental environment that supports individual growth, responsibility, and social maturity.

‣ Education and learning of occupational skills.

‣ Revenue-generating work activities that contribute restitution for their offense.

‣ Job readiness and placement for re-entry to general society after they've completed service.

With a minimal form of physical security, RDC residents in good standing can obtain permission to leave the premises for personal activities that don't interfere with their scheduled obligations.

In order to fulfill the terms of their court orders and regain normal citizen status, residents will have to follow rules, maintain work and study schedules, and meet certain standards of achievement. Failure to comply with the requirements will nullify their time served, put them back into the jurisdiction of the court, and subject them to more severe penalties.

Some offenders will almost surely continue their self-defeating behaviors and flunk out, but we could hope that the great majority of them might accept the experience as a valuable opportunity to reorient their lives.

These remedial centers might look a bit like austere college campuses, trade schools, or commercial businesses with the residents providing the labor. They'll operate on a quarterly program schedule. New residents will arrive on designated dates so as to begin their development experiences as members of peer groups. Each center might focus on a particular type of population, such as young offenders, adult offenders, addiction and substance abuse victims, people with developmental disabilities, and special-needs females. Each will evolve its own unique set of programs.

LET'S GET SERIOUS ABOUT RAPE AND SEXUAL MISCONDUCT

The crime of *forcible rape* should have its own unique set of consequences. Forcible rape stands alone as a personal, physical, and psychological violation of a person's very humanness. With our vague and inconsistent legal doctrines and haphazard practices of prosecution and punishment, we've allowed the practice of rape to continue when we should have eliminated it long ago.

Cases of sexual assault, which include forcible rape, vary widely in both the severity of the charge and the standard of proof. We must carefully balance the presumption of innocence on the part of the accused with consideration of the suffering of the victim in cases of proven misconduct.

The national standard catalog of crimes should include four

distinct levels of sexual misconduct, each with its appropriate punishment:

1. Provable harassment, verbal threats, intimidation, or other sexual behavior deemed by law enforcement as likely to cause emotional distress to the victim or concern for her personal safety.

2. Provable inappropriate or unwanted physical contact of a sexual nature, likely to cause similar distress.

3. Provable, persistent physical contact that physically restrains, entraps, or otherwise subjects the victim to unwanted sexual contact.

4. Provable, forceful attempts at penetration, whether achieved or not.

Penalties associated with the various degrees of violence should range from fines, to confinement in an RDC for various periods, to prison terms in extreme cases. A conviction for sexual assault will entitle the victim to bring a lawsuit against the perpetrator for the distress and possible physical harm suffered. Courts will award paid compensation from the national Crime Victims Compensation Fund, aligned with the degree of severity of the assault and matched by a payment-to-victim assessment imposed on the perpetrator.

Courts should carefully assess the veracity and severity of alleged assaults based on available evidence. False or fraudulent accusations of sexual assault will incur prosecution under separate criminal standards.

RE-ENTRY: THE MOST IMPORTANT—AND NEGLECTED—PHASE OF ALL

We've long given lip service to the problem of re-entry, or re-assimilation, but in fact we've never approached it on a scale and with the resources that it needs. This component might have more impact and more economic leverage on crime than all of the other things we do.

Parole and probation officers can presumably help offenders

with the challenges of returning to normal life, but in most cases they can do little more than keep tabs on their assigned population, making sure they meet the terms of their conditional release. One-to-one follow-up and support requires time and talent, which don't come cheap.

But we do have vast resources we can bring to bear, which often cost little or nothing: *community volunteer agencies.*

Nonprofit organizations such as Goodwill Industries specialize in raising funds to help returning inmates with job readiness and placement. Well-known service clubs provide volunteer resources and funds for charitable purposes— Rotary, Lions Clubs, Optimists and Soroptimists, Shriners, Masons, Knights of Columbus—just to name a few. Add in well over 100,000 churches, synagogues, and mosques, and non-denominational groups, and we have more potential volunteer labor than we could ever use. We only have to activate it. Chapter 9 (Public Services) offers an approach to organizing volunteer services on a national scale.

Every Level 2 prison and every Remedial Detention Center will have an outreach program that creates a bridge between the needs of its residents and volunteers in the community. By activating and funding local volunteer groups and individuals, we can match every non-violent offender who becomes eligible for release with supportive people who can help him or her return to a normal life as a well-behaved, fully integrated citizen.

GETTING IT ALL DONE: THE NATIONAL SOLUTION

So, how shall we get all of this done? What steps do we need to take to rearrange the system?

A simple, streamlined, and effective solution would *transfer jurisdiction over all residential confinement facilities, of all kinds, to the federal level,* except for an adequate number of small local jails. All state prisons would become federally operated institutions and all RDCs would become branches of a common, nationally managed network. Local governments and courts will become the clients, so to speak, of the RDCs they choose when placing non-violent offenders.

That solution can relieve state and local governments of a huge burden for the costs of incarceration and it would bring long-needed standardization of methods and practices to the whole system. Placing offenders in facilities close to the communities where they've offended will allow local authorities to maintain legal jurisdiction. It will also allow family members and local service providers to maintain supportive contact with them and ease the process of re-entry with job readiness programs and placement services.

We've wasted too many years, too much money, and too many lives with our scrambled system of Law and Order. We can do so much better. We can reduce crime rates; protect society against the most dangerous violent criminals; change our insane practices of over-sentencing and excessive incarceration; provide meaningful restitution for crime victims; suit the penalties to the offenders; and provide rehabilitation, developmental experiences, and paths back to normal citizenship for the vast majority of offenders.

LET'S RETHINK GUN VIOLENCE: CIVIL RIGHTS ISSUE OR PUBLIC HEALTH ISSUE?

Few issues have polarized the national conversation more than the problem of gun violence. This intensely emotional conflict pits the interests of gun owners and the gun industry against the interests of a less well-organized cohort of people concerned about the steady proliferation of firearms and the deaths associated with them.

Many gun owners have tribalized around the goal of virtually unrestricted entitlement to own and carry firearms, especially handguns. The opposing faction has tribalized around their concerns about the astonishing levels of gun violence in America and the appalling number of gun deaths —averaging over 100 per day.

Let's begin our investigation of this issue from a mega-factual perspective.[11]

Who Gets Killed by Guns?

‣ *America outranks all other countries in gun homicides.* United Nations figures show Australia at 1.4 killings per million people. Switzerland comes in second to the US at 7.7. The US figure stands at 29.7. Americans shoot one another four times as often as Italians, six times as often as Canadians, and 16 times as often as Germans.

‣ Latest available records show the number of gun homicides in Japan during 2015, a typical year, as—one.

‣ According to recent figures, total American deaths due to firearms—accidents, suicides, murders, and killings incidental to other crimes—average almost 40,000 per year. That means about 400,000 Americans have lost their lives to bullets in the decade just past.

‣ The US government's Center for Disease control reports that about half of all gun deaths—20,000—involve suicides. Suicide rates for men run 3 to 4 times higher than for women. Over 50 percent of men who kill themselves use guns; 30 percent of women use guns.

‣ If we separate out gun accidents and gun suicides— about 5,000 and 20,000 per year respectively—we end up with about 15,000 homicides—deliberate killings— in a typical year. About 75 percent of murders involve firearms.

‣ *Every 30 minutes, 24/7, someone deliberately shoots an American to death.* Every 16 hours a woman dies by the hand of her current or former partner.

‣ Over the past seven years, to the time of this writing, American schools; churches, synagogues, and mosques; bars; parties; and community gatherings have witnessed over 1600 mass shootings—about one episode per day. The people who study these matters define a mass shooting as an episode in which four or more people get shot or shot at.

▸ America has less than 5 percent of the world's population, but *one-third of the mass shootings* happen here. Mental health experts lament that news stories only cover the most appalling episodes of mass shooting, a practice which—ironically—distracts attention from the thousands of every-day gun deaths.

▸ Urban emergency rooms typically get a spike in gunshot injuries after midnight on Friday and Saturday nights. Trauma surgeons joke grimly about the "Friday Night Knife and Gun Club," made inevitable by the combination of firearms and free-flowing alcohol.

Who Owns the Guns?

▸ *Americans own more guns than citizens of every other country.* Estimates vary, but most reputable sources report that Americans, with 5 percent of the world's population, own about 40 percent of the world's guns. The US has twice as many guns per 100,000 people as its nearest first-world comparator, at this time the tiny country of Switzerland. We have three times as many as Canada and eight times as many as Spain.

▸ With a current population of about 325 million people and an estimated 300 million guns in their possession, one might infer that just about every citizen has a gun. However, it appears that *a small percentage of gun owners, perhaps 3-5 percent, own a large fraction of the guns, perhaps as much as 50 percent.*

▸ An estimated 36 percent of US households now contain guns, a big decline from 50 percent in 1980. The rate of new household formations has exceeded the rate of gun purchases. However, if we count only one individual per household as the real gun owner (excluding children, for example), we might estimate the percentage of gun-owning individuals as much smaller than the percentage of gun-containing households, possibly about 15-20 percent. That means *non-owners probably outnumber gun owners by about five to one.*

Do More Guns Mean More Deaths?

Statistical research has shown, for a decade or more, that countries with high rates of gun ownership have higher than average rates of gun-related deaths. One of the most reliable studies, published in *The American Journal of Medicine,* compared those two variables for 27 modern countries.

A sampling of scores, normalized to population size, shows the unmistakable pattern: [12]

Country:	Guns/100	Gun Deaths/100,000
Australia	15.0	1.04
Canada	30.8	2.44
Finland	45.3	3.54
Japan	0.60	0.06
Netherlands	3.90	0.46
Switzerland	45.7	3.84
United Kingdom	6.20	0.25
United States	88.8	10.2

Despite the of statistics thrown about by gun advocates in the US, the evidence from state-by-state comparisons tells the same story: *states with more guns have more gun deaths.* More homicides, more suicides, more accidents.

‣ Delaware has the lowest percentage of gun-owning citizens, estimated at about 5 percent. Alaska has the most, at about 62 percent. Arizona and Kansas stand in the middle with about 32 percent.

‣ *States with tighter gun control laws have fewer gun-related deaths.* Factors such as urban density, stressful living patterns, size of immigrant populations, and rates of mental illness don't fully explain the variance. A review of laws in 10 countries found that new legal restrictions on buying and owning guns correlated fairly closely with a drop in gun violence. In this case, science clearly validates common sense.

▸ Australia's gun buyback program, begun in 1996, reduced the number of firearms there by about 20 percent. They saw a ten-year decline in both homicides and suicides, by 50 percent and 74 percent respectively. New Zealand's police recently bought over 60,000 assault rifles, a remarkable number for a small nation.

▸ When the Israeli Defense Force stopped allowing soldiers to take their guns home with them they saw a 40 percent drop in their suicide rates.

▸ *More police officers get killed on duty in states that have high numbers of guns.* Researchers suggest that the perception that American cops shoot more citizens than their counterparts in other developed countries relates to the fact that they encounter more armed perpetrators. They also probably expect more life-threatening encounters, and may draw their weapons more often when they engage problem situations.

▸ *Public support for gun control laws has sagged over the past two decades.* The number of people polled who considered it more important to control gun ownership than to allow citizens to freely own guns declined from about 65 percent in 2000 to about 50 percent by 2017. Some researchers attribute much of this decline to aggressive and well-funded lobbying by the National Rifle Association. The NRA claims nearly 5 million members—less than 10 percent of estimated owners—but doesn't disclose membership data.

Why Do People Own Guns?

Before we consider the points of view and the key arguments of the two opposing factions in the gun violence issue, let's recognize the differences amongst people who want to own guns. They fall into some very distinct categories:

1. Law enforcement personnel who need to carry firearms as a necessary part of the jobs they do, both on duty and off duty. This also includes off-duty police and some commercial security personnel.

2. Private citizens who just want to have a gun at home for protection of self, family, and premises. They might not actually shoot a gun, or even want to, for years.

3. People who actually like to shoot at things, like targets at firing ranges; and those who like to shoot for outdoor sports—target shooting or skeet shooting at managed ranges, trying new or exotic weapons, or hunting wild animals. This category also includes farmers and ranchers who want to have guns handy for varmint shooting and occasional hunting.

4. Gun collectors, who like to own lots of them, for various personal reasons. Not all of them necessarily do a lot of shooting. Many serious gun collectors cherish their rare and valuable antique firearms, some of which date back to and before the Civil War.

5. People who want to carry guns, usually concealed, for their own protection. They claim the right to shoot back in a public place if threatened or if a berserker starts shooting people.

6. Self-appointed vigilantes and proto-patriots, who believe the government intends to take away their guns—and their civil rights—and who want to fight back when the black helicopters start flying overhead.

7. Criminals or aspiring criminals, who want to use guns to rob people, murder people, or kill other criminals they consider their enemies. This category also

includes the lone shooter—the alienated, typically suicidal, sociopath who feels the need to act out his grievances against society or some group of people he believes has wronged him.

These differences count for a lot in our understanding of gun violence and they bear heavily on potential solutions.

CONCEALED CARRY: SELF-DEFENSE OR COWBOY FANTASY?

As of this writing, all 50 states and the DC allow citizens to carry concealed weapons in public places. Laws vary, but most require permits for concealed carry. Twelve don't. Current estimates put the number of people with concealed carry permits at about 15 million. Most permits don't specify the particular gun or guns the holder can carry.

A number of states have repealed restrictions on concealed carry recently and several Supreme Court rulings have struck down restrictive state laws. Some states don't restrict "open carry," allowing individuals to display firearms openly.

Gun control advocates consider the act of carrying a firearm in a public space an unacceptable threat to the safety of the people inhabiting the space and an incursion on their basic right to move about safely. So far, however, they can't seem to prove a strong correlation between concealed carry practices and gun deaths in general.

While the very idea of concealed carry makes many gun control advocates nervous, it might not actually pose a significant threat to their personal safety. Carrying around a bulky, three-pound handgun every day turns into a nuisance pretty quickly. It won't fit comfortably in most pants pockets or in a jacket pocket. A serious owner would typically use a waistband holster or an ankle holster—a shoulder holster doesn't serve well on a hot day because it reveals rather than conceals the gun.

Standing or walking around with a gun strapped to one ankle for 16 hours or more every day can make the gun owner reconsider his personal commitment to the "right to bear arms." Sooner or later he has to weigh the nuisance factor against the exceedingly small probability of having to defend himself in a gunfight.

We don't have reliable estimates but we can probably guess that not all owners actually "pack heat" all or most of the time. As a practical matter, with 5 percent of citizens holding permits and not all of them armed at all times, the chances of finding an armed citizen at a shopping mall or a sports stadium don't seem very high.

OWNED GUNS AND ORPHAN GUNS

Looking at the various categories of gun owners brings us to an obvious and very important distinction: the difference between "owned" guns and "orphan" guns. The kinds of people in the first six categories listed above typically own their guns legally and typically keep them in their possession.

The category of orphan guns, on the other hand, includes a rather large supply of stolen guns circulating amongst the criminal population. This includes cheap, illegally imported guns of all types and "Saturday night specials," which the members of the lawless subculture buy, sell, trade, and steal.

Clearly, the greatest threat to public health and safety comes, not from owned guns, but from orphan guns. Legitimate gun owners do, of course, occasionally shoot other people and sometimes themselves. But the criminal population, with ready access to orphan guns, poses the biggest threat.

POINTS AND COUNTERPOINTS: ASSESSING THE ARGUMENTS

Let's look at the claims and arguments offered by both of the factions that have polarized the gun violence issue.

Point: the more vocal gun advocates cite the US Constitution's Second Amendment as the foundation for their claim that governments should not restrict gun ownership in any way. They customarily quote the phrase

". . . the right of citizens to keep and bear arms shall not be infringed," as a near-biblical justification for their cause. They claim it justifies the ownership and use of firearms for at least three purposes: 1) to protect home and family; 2) to defend against assault or robbery in public places; and 3) to resist the incursions of a diabolical government bent on taking away their guns and their civil rights.

Counterpoint: Constitutional law experts make it clear that *all civil liberties must have boundaries*. Supreme Court Justice Oliver Wendell Holmes famously declared, "The most stringent protection of free speech would not protect a man in falsely shouting 'fire' in a theater and causing a panic." Freedom to practice religion in America, for example, does not include polygamy or barbaric practices such as female genital mutilation, which violate American laws. Just as the First Amendment right to free speech has its boundaries, so does the Second Amendment right to use firearms. It certainly doesn't imply the right to shoot it out in the street with other citizens. That went out with the Old West.

To refresh our memories, the exact text reads:

"A well-regulated Militia, being necessary to the security of a free State, the right of the people to keep and bear Arms, shall not be infringed."

Almost all reputable historians and constitutional scholars agree that the Founders intended the Second Amendment to provide for *state militias*—organized military units employed by their respective State governments and composed of citizen soldiers, at a time when the young Republic had no standing national army.

In times of war—as in the Revolutionary War and the War of 1812—the government would hire them for duty, expecting them to bring their own rifles. The idea of self-appointed vigilantes arming themselves for the prospect of shooting it out with police or government soldiers coming to take away their guns represents a complete perversion of the Founders' intent. No amount of flag waving or conspiracy theories can justify vigilantism.

Point: NRA leaders, vocal gun advocates, and some state legislators oppose restrictions on ownership of semiautomatic rifles such as the highly popular AR-15 and its various imitations. They argue that governments should not have the power to restrict sales of auxiliary products that make those weapons more lethal, such as high capacity magazines. They contend that such restrictions limit the legitimate use of their firearms for activities such as sport shooting and hunting.

Counterpoint: the highly lethal AR-15 and similar weapons belong in a special category. They pose special dangers and risks to public safety when in the hands of unskilled non-military people. The claim that rapid-fire rifles such as the AR-15 have any legitimate role in hunting makes no sense. No rational concept of hunting as a sport can include a military style assault rifle.

The AR-15 doesn't qualify as a suitable weapon for home defense either. Its rapid-fire spray of high-velocity bullets can easily pass through the walls of houses and kill innocent people on the street or in neighboring homes.

And the argument for having many rounds of ammunition to protect home and family simply falls of its own weight. A shoot-out with an intruder would likely last no more than a few seconds and would certainly not require hundreds of rounds.

Point: the NRA aggressively promotes the claim that laws and police departments cannot prevent or cope with mass shootings in public places and they call for arming and training schoolteachers and others working in vulnerable environments so they can shoot back.

They repeat the slogan, *"The only thing that stops a bad guy with a gun is a good guy with a gun."* Several state legislators have taken up this mantra and some have even introduced bills to fund programs to issue guns to teachers and train them to shoot.

Counterpoint: this stunningly obtuse proposition would hardly deserve consideration if some political figures hadn't taken it seriously. It reveals a profound ignorance of the realities of a spontaneous episode of gun violence. Shooting episodes in public places don't unfold neatly like the Hollywood movie with the high-noon gunfight on main street, between the good-guy sheriff and the bad-guy delinquent and a two-camera setup that shows our man calmly dispatching the crook with a single shot.

Studies of police shoot-outs with armed criminals show that even highly trained police officers, reacting in states of extreme arousal and stress, typically miss their targets as often as they hit them. In chaotic situations, they sometimes shoot one another or innocent bystanders.

Further, when police officers approach a threat situation they must consider the possibility that a missed shot could kill someone behind the assailant, in a house across the street or in a passing car or bus. We could hardly expect a minimally trained amateur, suddenly thrown into a life-and-death shooting scenario, to do any better.

Further yet, police officers responding to a chaotic shooting situation have no way of knowing the intentions of any person on the scene who brandishes a gun. With two or more people exchanging fire, they have to consider all participants potential threats to the officers' safety.

BALANCING RIGHTS: GUNS, CARS, AND CIGARETTES

The problem of gun violence in America cries out for a full-scale *national solution.* The insane patchwork of confused, inconsistent, and conflicting laws across 50 different states has gotten us nowhere.

A national firearms policy, supported by a uniform national law, can serve at least four purposes:

1. It can affirm and preserve the rights of qualified

individuals to buy, keep, and use their guns for legitimate purposes, such as home defense; target shooting and hunting in legally approved environments; and collecting them for aesthetic purposes. It should also allow individuals to buy, sell, or give guns to one another, provided they manage the transactions so as to preserve the identities of the guns and the associations with their owners, and to keep them out of the hands of disqualified individuals.

2. It can drastically reduce and minimize the number of orphan guns in circulation, which will make it less likely that criminals or aspiring criminals can get them, keep them, and use them illegally.

3. It can prevent disqualified individuals from buying guns by legal means and also prevent them from acquiring guns illegally. Disqualified individuals include convicted felons, parolees, and those under court restraining orders or special monitoring, such as those with mental disorders and those who have demonstrated a propensity toward violent behavior.

4. It can hold gun owners accountable for misuse, unjustified discharge, or negligent practices that allow their guns to fall into the hands of criminals, children, or persons in distress who might use them for suicide.

A national solution, as I view it, will involve five major initiatives, all done on a very large scale:

1. A *gun buyback program*, funded by the federal government, with the goal of reducing the number of guns in America by one-third, or about 100 million guns, possibly spanning a period of about 3 years. Critics may protest the cost and the logistical challenge of collecting so many guns, but we can do it. Estimating an average payment of about $100 per gun, the bill might amount to about $10 billion, a very manageable figure for a government with an annual budget of nearly $4 trillion.

2. A *universal gun registration system*, with the goal of associating at least 95 percent of the guns in the country with legitimate, qualified owners. The registration system will isolate the supply of orphan guns, making it possible for law enforcement officers to confiscate them when they encounter them.

   Critics may also protest the costs and the scale of registering virtually all of the guns in the country. However, we register over 270 million automobiles every year and their owners have become quite accustomed to the annual ritual. The process hardly seems like an infringement on any basic rights that car owners might have. The same priorities for safety and security should apply to guns as to cars. If we can do it with cars, we can do it with guns.

   The National ID Card system, described previously, will simplify and streamline the registration process and the background check process significantly.

3. A *system of universal background checks* for all new gun purchases, without exception, with sales denied to felons and persons with significant history of arrests, people under court orders of restraint, and those deemed by competent examination to pose threats to their own wellbeing or the safety of others.

   Retail outlets will register guns for their new owners, setting up the chain of custody that ensures that every legitimate firearm has a legitimate custodian.

   The law will prohibit the direct sale or transfer of guns between individuals and will require that such transactions go through commercial retail businesses or other authorized agencies, with the appropriate background checks. Just as we require people to reregister cars when they sell them to other people, we can do the same with guns.

4. *Special restrictions on assault rifles and other highly lethal weapons.* A new law will restrict the storage and

handling of AR-15s and similar rapid-fire weapons, to federally licensed commercial gun ranges or armories. Under this law, people will have the right to own a variety of highly lethal weapons, but can never remove them from the custody of a secure facility.

Buying and selling a restricted weapon will require a transaction managed by the gun range, with background checks, documentation, and national registration. The weapon will either remain at the secure facility and simply change registered owners, or the seller can have it transferred to another facility, on behalf of the buyer, using a secure method of transport such as those used for moving cash or other valuable items around.

Once implemented, the law will authorize law enforcement personnel to confiscate unregistered or restricted weapons whenever they encounter them, without compensation to the person in possession.

5. *An aggressive local law enforcement program*, augmented by federal funding, that pulls orphan guns out of high-crime areas, such as the inner cities. Periodic unannounced checkpoints, analogous to sobriety checkpoints that stop drivers and check for alcohol abuse, will enable law enforcement officers to confiscate unregistered or orphaned guns. New laws will impose severe penalties for carrying unregistered guns, transferring them illegally, or using them in the commission of any crime.

THE ULTIMATE FORCE FOR CHANGE: SOCIAL PRESSURE

None of the initiatives just described would limit or infringe on the rights of law-abiding gun owners in any meaningful way.

Registering a gun will involve no more effort or inconvenience than registering a car—certainly less. And even the most vocal gun rights advocates generally agree that laws should prevent dangerous or unqualified people from buying, owning, or carrying them.

We still have a small, highly vocal, and relentless band of gun advocates, aroused and stimulated by the NRA, who bully lawmakers and work hard to scare as many other gun owners as possible. They fervently repeat the fear mantra: *"They want to take away your Second Amendment rights."*

In public health terms, we can find interesting parallels between the current issue of guns in the US and the issue of smoking as it evolved during the past several decades. Up until about the 1980s, smoking in public places stood as an assumed basic right, tolerated by non-smokers. In the face of years of research evidence attesting to the lethal effects, smokers maintained their franchise.

Cigarette ads filled the public space. Magazines, TV commercials, and advertising jingles popped up everywhere. Doctors—or distinguished looking actors posing as doctors—assured Americans of the health benefits of cigarettes and extolled their virtues in helping them relax, unwind, and enjoy life. The Marlboro Man, a ruggedly handsome cowboy actor, became an American icon.

Then, by about the early 1980s, things began to change. Nonsmokers, now aware that they numbered over 70 percent of the populace, began to rebel. As it became increasingly unfashionable to smoke, and after the US government banned cigarette ads in the print media, the news departments of those same media firms began to join the attack on tobacco companies, highlighting the health menace of smoking. And it didn't help when the Marlboro Man died of throat cancer.

Once the tipping point came, legislators began to find their backbones. They passed stricter laws, banning smoking from commercial airplanes, airports, government buildings, and eventually all indoor public spaces. Dire warnings of economic disaster, presumably caused by not allowing smokers to light up in bars and restaurants, didn't materialize. Smokers became the underdogs. As of this writing, about 14 percent of Americans still smoke, but the practice seems headed for eventual extinction.

I believe a similar pattern could play out with gun control as a number of key trends kick in.

For one thing, demand for guns has leveled off over the last decade. The percentage of gun-owning households has declined significantly and so has the percentage of gun owners. A large part of that estimated 300 million gun supply probably includes forgotten guns—firearms stowed away in closets that their owners haven't looked at for a long time.

Gun manufacturers have seen declining sales for a decade or more. Ironically, gun sales have dropped severely when pro-gun presidents have come into office and they've usually spiked when presidents perceived as anti-gun have taken over. That pattern has created a dilemma for gun sellers and gun rights advocates: they don't want an anti-gun president in the White House, but a pro-gun president kills their sales.

In recent years, the legendary arms companies have found themselves burdened with excess inventory and forced to discount their prices heavily. Remington, America's oldest firearms company, went into bankruptcy and has only recently come out. Samuel Colt's legendary Colt Firearms company did the same, leaving creditors holding $500 million in debt. Winchester, the inventor of the iconic "gun that won the West," had already bitten the dust by 1960 and sold itself to another company. The much revered Smith and Wesson—ignominiously renamed American Outdoor Brands —recently posted a 90 percent drop in profits.

The gun culture doesn't seem to have much hereditary potential. Millennials haven't shown much interest in owning or shooting guns, nor has the generation following them. As young people from rural areas and small towns migrate to urban centers, those populations continue to decline.

Indeed, some young people—particularly students from schools that have experienced mass shootings--have taken up the gun violence issue. They bring a new energy and a sense of commitment, as well as a remarkable grasp of advocacy politics and the potential impact of social media.

As if to make matters even worse for the gun extremists, the formidable NRA might well fall on its own sword. As of this writing, it has descended into vicious internal strife; a big red-ink crisis with declining revenues and runaway costs; and accusations of fraud, tax law violations, and misuse of funds for personal use by the key insiders. Some observers and industry old-timers speculate that it might not remain viable, especially if it loses its tax-exempt status. A failed NRA could have a devastating impact on the extremist agenda.

In the long haul—five years or twenty years—America will probably follow the same pattern of other developed societies and guns will become ever more scarce. The faster we move that process along, the more American lives we'll save and the more human suffering we'll prevent.

LET'S CURB POLICE MISCONDUCT

Police misconduct, unfortunately, has become a serious and worrisome problem for America. Every day we see another report of a contentious episode in which citizens or news reports accuse police officers of misconduct, ranging from questionable to outrageously inappropriate.

Recent to this writing, an alarming series of high-profile episodes of police violence, often involving black citizens, has galvanized civil rights activists as never before. Several egregious cases involving deaths during arrest and deaths while in custody have polarized communities across America. Bystanders with cellphones have flooded news organizations with unnerving and incriminating video footage.

Incidents of tampering with police "body-cam" footage have reinforced claims of unethical behavior by officers and departments. Even worse, bureaucratic delays and stonewalling by police chiefs, mayors, and police unions have left many people in minority communities feeling that the police think of them as adversaries, not citizens who deserve security and protection.

Inflammatory news stories can amplify the negative impact of inappropriate police violence, unjustified shootings, general harassment of minorities, or corrupt behavior. People in urban minority communities tend to harbor a deep distrust of their city police. And, they typically consider police management in most departments as prone to ignore officer misconduct, downplay its significance, stonewall inquiries, or even try to cover it up.

The most vocal of the protests have called for abolishing police departments altogether or cutting their funding drastically. Others demand much greater oversight, perhaps by outside agencies; a rethinking of use-of-force policies and practices; and more direct accountability of officers who willfully abuse the rights of those they detain or arrest.

In a broader sense, we may have come to a turning point in our whole conceptualization of law enforcement and the role of tactical police units in preserving the peace and public safety. I suspect that, in the next few years, we'll have to put on our thinking caps and perhaps re-imagine the entire concept of public safety and the role of police forces in it.

Meanwhile, we do have several significant possibilities for restoring some degree of public trust in police organizations, which we'll explore here.

First, let's ground our thinking in the practical realities of police operations.

According to recent estimates, the US has over 17,000 law enforcement operations of various kinds, including a variety of units like city police forces, county sheriffs, state highway patrols, border patrols, customs agents, federal marshals, FBI agents, military police, and school and campus police. Those departments employ about 750,000 sworn peace officers.

From the police perspective, we cannot wish away the basic fact that impoverished and disadvantaged neighborhoods tend to have much higher crime rates—and, obviously, more criminals—than the more affluent ones. When you spend most of your workday dealing with society's misfits and malcontents, it becomes difficult to maintain a charitable perspective toward everyone else you encounter.

Beyond that, we know that police work takes a heavy toll on the body, mind, and emotions of the person who has to perform it every day. Industrial psychologists classify police work, especially for sworn peace officers who carry weapons, as a form of *emotional labor*. They deal with ambiguity on every shift. They never know when a quiet moment might erupt into a violent episode. We want to see the friendly town constable when they walk into the restaurant or coffee shop and yet the threat of violence always lurks just seconds away.

Police work can cause cumulative stress patterns. Unresolved anger, frustration, and the emotional cost of witnessing violence, seeing people with appalling injuries, and seeing death firsthand can add up. Few police departments do an adequate job of supporting the mental health of their officers. In a traditionally male occupation, their cultural conditioning tends to demand a brave front and discounts emotion as weak and unworthy of the warrior.

Police officers rank amongst the occupations with the highest levels of alcohol abuse, marital strife, divorce, domestic violence, and depression. More American police officers die by suicide than by violence in the line of duty.

Currently, we have no real national standards for police procedures, professional conduct, and leadership. Selection and training procedures vary from near-military standards in some cases to minimal or nonexistent in others. Police departments in smaller jurisdictions often don't have the funds necessary to maintain high standards.

Small, underfunded police departments tend to have a higher incidence of incompetent or insufficiently trained officers; dishonesty or corruption; "nomad" officers who get fired from one department and move to another one; and sometimes a complete failure of the collective spirit and attitude of honest and ethical public service.

Here the law enforcement sector can borrow a page from the

playbook of the healthcare sector, in the form of a *national accreditation system* for police departments.

One of the most important institutions in the healthcare sector goes by the nickname JCAHO, (usually pronounced "Jay-Co"), which stands for the Joint Commission on Accreditation of Healthcare Organizations.

JCAHO wields an awesome authority over a wide range of healthcare providers of all kinds—hospitals, clinics, rehab centers, research institutions, and lots of others. By national and state law, they all need JCAHO certification to operate. If an audit finds severe violations of its standards in a hospital, for instance, JCAHO pulls its certification and it closes its doors until management gets the game back up to standard.

The law enforcement sector needs a JCAHO. We need to start thinking of law enforcement agencies as providers of life-critical services, just as hospitals do.

One might ask, "Don't—or can't—police departments police themselves?" No, they don't, for many of the same reasons that healthcare providers fall short: complex organizations; stressful work environments; the ever-present risk of human disasters; pressure to get things done quickly; pressure to cut costs; and the predictable tendency of human beings to try to cover their backsides when things go wrong.

Such an agency for law enforcement could have a big impact on the perceptions of people in minority communities, who tend to believe—rightly or wrongly—that police departments don't want to deal with officer misconduct.

An accreditation system does several useful things. First, it raises the standards of practice across the whole provider community, to a respectably high level. Second, it creates transparency—the audit process tends to expose malfunctions and malpractices that the providers might otherwise overlook or conceal. And third, it provides real sanctions—the prospect of losing the privilege of operating the enterprise occupies the minds of the managers every day.

The law enforcement version of accreditation could involve the creation of an agency analogous to JCAHO, most likely under the jurisdiction of the federal Justice Department. The FBI, with its respected standards of ethical conduct, could serve as the agency with the oversight, inspection, and compliance over every police organization in the country. In the case of a failing local police department, a federal court order could have the FBI step in, assume interim control of the organization, and restore compliance.

We also need a national system for *licensing individual peace officers* and all other security professionals whose regular activity requires carrying firearms. Just as we license doctors, dentists, psychologists—and even hairdressers—we need to set minimum standards for their conduct. This approach would require every armed professional, and especially police officers, to undergo basic background checks; verification of lawful past conduct; firearms proficiency; continuing education; and periodic relicensing.

Considering the costs and risks of not doing it and the serious damage to public trust that can occur as a result of a corrupt or failing police department, the investment would probably yield a very significant return.

SHOULD WE PHASE OUT THE DEATH PENALTY?

As we consider the modern challenges associated with Law and Order, one issue looms large before us: capital punishment, a.k.a. *the death penalty*. The long history of this dark practice that has run through our culture for centuries deserves our thoughtful attention.

Americans have felt conflicted about the death penalty for a very long time. If a person kills another person, shouldn't we require the killer to forfeit his or her own right to live, and somehow even the score, so to speak? But what if the killer acted in defense of his or her own life or the lives of loved ones? Well, maybe that falls into a different category.

What if the killer takes someone's life without intending to, while violating another law, such as during a botched robbery? Do we consider that act less heinous than a premeditated murder? If a woman shoots a violently abusive spouse or partner while he sleeps, has she committed a worse crime than if she had shot him during an attack? What do we mean by "justifiable homicide?"

What shall we do with a serial killer who murders many people? If we rate killing 10 people as 10 times as heinous as killing one, how do we make the punishment proportional to the crime? We can only execute the offender once.

A second big question: how, if at all, does the suffering of the offender relieve or mitigate the suffering of the victim or the co-victims—family members, loved ones, or life partners? Do the loved ones of a murdered person really get "closure" when—or if—the killer gets executed? Or does that event (which typically occurs an average of 15-20 years or more after the offense) just re-victimize them by opening old emotional wounds and renewing their grief and anger?

EXECUTIONS AS ENTERTAINMENT

Our collective experience of state-sponsored executions has definitely evolved over the centuries. In medieval times, crowds would gather in public places to watch the executions of condemned criminals. Those became very festive affairs, with socializing, food and drink, and raucous cheering each time another miscreant met his fate.

In the 1700s, thousands of Londoners would flock to the tiny village of Tyburn, just outside London, to watch the hangings at the "Tyburn Tree," a specially constructed gallows that could hang as many as a dozen people at a time. Officials would transport the convicts from Newgate Prison to the execution site in ox-carts. In those days a person might get a death sentence for a minor crime like stealing.

We modern citizens might find it difficult to fathom the low value attached to human life that formed the substance of those mob events. Onlookers cheered and jostled to get a good look at people "dancing the Tyburn jig." They expected the convicts to wear their finest clothes; put on an "attitude," as we might say in modern terminology; and give the spectators "a good dying." They cheered those who died well and jeered those who showed fear. After they died, the remains of convicts who had no family to claim them went to local cemeteries for mass burial.

The villagers of Tyburn, predictably, opened businesses catering to the spectators. They sold food and ale and even put up a large viewing stand, where people could pay to get a better look at the hangings. Ironically, the stand collapsed on one occasion, killing or injuring over a hundred spectators.

In a bizarre act, Parliament decreed in 1661 that the infamous Oliver Cromwell, who had overthrown and beheaded King Charles I—and who ruled England during the only period in its history when it had no king—should hang for his misdeeds. Cromwell had died three years earlier, however, so they dug him up and hanged his remains.

In 1868, the British government moved the hangings back to the city prison and ended the public spectacle—much to the disappointment of the fans. The decision came, not for humanitarian reasons, but simply because the gatherings had become so rowdy that police couldn't manage them.

TECHNOLOGY BRINGS EFFICIENT KILLING—AND BETTER ENTERTAINMENT

The French, ever keen to outdo their British rivals, had developed their own version of executions as a form of public entertainment with the infamous *guillotine*.

First proposed in 1789 by a physician, Dr. Joseph-Ignace Guillotin, the apparatus would presumably cause instant death, sparing the condemned the painful agony of his final minutes. Hanging didn't bring a quick death, and manual beheading with axes and swords often went horribly wrong, with appalling results. Executions by firing squad didn't always go well either. The "National Razor" would also, presumably, spare the onlookers from the psychic trauma of watching the gruesome final moments.

But before long, the guillotine created for the French what the Tyburn Tree had created for the English—a hugely popular form of public entertainment. The quick and efficient killing machine produced a ghastly death scene, with blood splashing all over the platform and sometimes onto the spectators. Ironically, the blood and gore became part of the entertainment, not a source of horror. Dr. Guillotin's invention—which he never wanted associated with his name —became popular for its drama, not for its humaneness.

The guillotine first performed its macabre service in 1792. The following year, King Louis XVI and his iconic wife Marie Antoinette lost their heads—and their empire—to the fearsome blade. During the short, murderous rule of the fanatical Maximilien Robespierre—the legendary Reign of Terror—an estimated 17,000 "enemies of the French Revolution" lost their heads.

Ironically, Robespierre met his own death on the guillotine after he lost his grip on the revolution.

The guillotine became a hugely popular cultural symbol for the French people. Popular expressions and even songs reflected its influence. Shops sold model guillotines. Some children used toy guillotines to decapitate dolls and even small animals. In some high-society homes, a decorative guillotine would sit on the table, for slicing bread. Guillotine operators became famous for their skills, and whole families took up the occupation of machine-assisted beheading.

By the 1900s, capital punishment had declined in France—as well as England—but the government continued to use the guillotine. The last Frenchman met his death under the blade in 1977. France abolished capital punishment in 1981.

The French had no monopoly over the guillotine. Adolf Hitler liked the method so much that he ordered 20 of them built. Nazi records show that the Third Reich guillotined some 16,500 people by the end of the war in 1945.

THE SEARCH FOR A "CIVILIZED" KILLING TECHNOLOGY

With the modern age, the technology and the psychology of executions have changed. A few countries—notably Saudi Arabia and a few others—still conduct public executions but most now do it in private. Executing people has become a much more clinical sort of process, one we know about but don't want to see. And we want it done professionally, not as a barbaric spectacle.

After the guillotine, the next major technological shift came with *electrocution*, which has also had a gruesome—and peculiar—history. The early story of the electric chair might surprise the modern citizen, because it involves one of America's most revered iconic figures, Thomas Edison.

Historical accounts and Internet sources tend to disagree on Edison's actual role in the use of electricity for executions. Evidence does indicate, however, that he experimented with killing small animals using electric currents.

For all of his inventive genius—over 1,000 patents to his name—Edison felt insecure about competition and he had a long-running rivalry with Nicola Tesla, a brilliant young Serbian immigrant. Tesla had once worked in Edison's lab, but they parted when he began to challenge Edison's ideas.

Tesla concluded that future electrical systems would have to use *alternating current*, created by powerful rotating generators, not the *direct current* produced by storage batteries. He saw "AC" as a more efficient method for producing electricity and especially for transmitting it over long distances. At the time, Edison's storage batteries could only propel electrical currents a few miles at most, which meant that a nationwide electrical system would require many thousands of power stations.

Edison staked his whole reputation on direct current —"DC"—in what newsmakers called the "war of the currents." Tesla left to join forces with George Westinghouse, a wealthy technology investor who agreed with his views.

Historical consensus holds that Edison set out to discredit the AC option in the public's mind, using every means he could think of. As part of his campaign he suggested to law enforcement authorities—who had become curious about using electricity as a means for execution—that alternating current would kill better than direct current. He even referred to the method as "Westinghousing" the offenders.

By 1890, officials of New York State had already tried crude versions of an electric chair several times, including a model built by one of Edison's workers. With typically gruesome and sometimes disastrous results, they managed to kill a few convicts, but didn't have a viable technology for execution.

In a now infamous incident at the Luna Park zoo in New York's Coney Island, in 1903, a crew of keepers and mechanics used AC current to electrocute an elephant. "Topsy," a very old and cantankerous specimen, had become unmanageable and the zoo's managers decided to put her down. It didn't go well. The ghastly photos offended many.

Some reports claim that Edison's mechanics helped them acquire the AC generator. Edison's movie company did film the event. Whether Edison participated directly in the gruesome event remains in dispute, but some biographers assert that he knew about it and encouraged it.

In any case, the public outcry caused by the incident caused a serious blow to Edison's reputation. By that time, AC generation had already won the technological battle. By some reports, Edison later admitted that he had always understood that AC would prove superior to his battery technology.

In prisons, the typical electrocution procedure called for shaving the head and lower legs of the condemned, strapping him into a chair, lowering a metal helmet over his head, and attaching electrodes to his legs. The executioner would throw a switch, which released a current of up to 2,000 volts for about 15 seconds. After a short wait, a coroner would examine the executee to confirm that he had died. If he had not, they would repeat the procedure as necessary.

Through the early decades of the 1900s, horror stories continued to surface about executions by electric chair, telling of prisoners crying out in pain, bodies convulsing in agony, heads and other body parts smoking or catching fire, and blood streaming from ruptured vessels.

DON'T LIKE ELECTROCUTION? TRY THE GAS CHAMBER

The next technology option, the gas chamber, came into use in 1924 when Nevada first tried it. Gas competed to some extent with the electric chair until the late 1990s. With this method, the condemned person sat in a sealed compartment, which the executioners controlled from the outside. Pulling a lever released crystals of sodium cyanide into a container of sulfuric acid, generating a deadly gas known as hydrogen cyanide. When inhaled, the poison gas blocked the body's capacity to absorb oxygen at the cellular level, causing profound *hypoxia*, or whole-body asphyxiation.

The gas chamber presented several practical difficulties not associated with hanging or electrocution. For one, the attending coroner had to verify the death from outside the sealed booth. Typical methods included the use of a stethoscope with a long connecting tube, which passed through the wall of the chamber.

In addition to exercising extreme caution with the deadly chemicals, the attendants had to seal the chamber carefully. They had to pump out the lethal gas afterward and replace it with normal air. They also had to handle the body carefully, as gas could accumulate in the deceased's hair and clothing.

Experts have always considered the gas chamber a gruesome form of execution, both because of the longer time required for the executee to die and the horrifying scene of the person gasping for breath, experiencing convulsions, vomiting, and loss of bowel control. Medical experts agreed that the experience involved panic and agonizing pain. The gas chamber soon lost the race with the electric chair as the preferred technology for execution.

At that point in the evolution of execution technology, all three of the usual methods—hanging, gassing, and electrocuting—seemed equally inhumane, unreliable, and grotesquely unpleasant to watch. Social activists increasingly called for abolishing the death penalty altogether.

The next phase came in with the concept of *lethal injection*. In the mid-1970s, physicians suggested that highly concentrated sedatives and other chemicals, when injected into the condemned person's veins, could render him or her unconscious and then stop all vital functions. This offered the prospect of a peaceful, sleep-like death experience.

The state of Texas became the first to use it in 1982. By about 2000, almost all of the death penalty states had adopted it. As of this writing, lethal injection has largely replaced all other forms of execution, but it hasn't become the ideal solution its advocates had hoped for. What first seemed like a simple, easy, and painless procedure had its own problems.

To recap the typical execution procedure: attendants strap the condemned person to a gurney and insert an intravenous feed line—an "IV" line, in medical parlance—into each arm (one as the primary line and the other as a back-up).

The IV lines and a cable for monitoring heart activity connect to a control center just outside. Once the execution team completes the set-up, they open the curtains on the observation window so witnesses can view the procedure. The condemned can make a final statement, the warden gives the command to proceed, and the process gets underway.

First, the operators introduce a powerful sedative/tranquilizer into the IV line, such as *midazolam, pentobarbital,* or *sodium thiopental.* If all goes as planned, this renders the condemned person unconscious within about 15-30 seconds.

After loss of consciousness they introduce a powerful *paralytic* compound, such as *pancuronium bromide*, which stops the breathing. Medical doctrine holds that irreversible brain death occurs after 4-5 minutes without oxygen.

Then they introduce *potassium chloride*, which disrupts the electrical activity of the heart muscle, causing it to stop beating. The attending coroner announces the moment of death when all cardiac activity stops.

Three problems have plagued execution teams ever since the method became popular. First, the drug combination doesn't always work exactly as expected. In some cases, the executee has cried out or writhed in pain, sometimes for many minutes. Medical experts debate about the actual state of unconsciousness induced by the first drug and whether it might still allow the person to experience pain or anxiety.

Second, the emplacement of the IV needles often presents a problem. Most physicians refuse to participate in executions, considering it a violation of the Hippocratic oath of medicine. In such cases, non-medical prison staff have to set things up. With executions becoming less and less frequent, many of them lack the necessary training or skills to emplace the lines properly. They might fail to locate a suitable vein or might not emplace the needle properly or secure it in place.

Worse, the inmate's veins might have deteriorated due to excessive self-injection of drugs, age, or various disorders. In such a case, the vein could "blow out," causing the chemicals to leak out of the injection site into the surrounding tissue. In one such case, the execution team stopped the procedure, but the inmate died of a heart attack about an hour later.

"Botched Execution" has become a standard news headline, ready for use whenever an execution goes wrong, and rightly so. With the inmate's family or friends observing the final moments through a window in the chamber, along with news reporters, a failed execution or one that goes painfully wrong can become a very distressing emotional experience.

More recently, a third major problem has arisen, caused by difficulty purchasing the lethal compounds from suppliers. A few pharmaceutical companies specialize in making them and the management teams of those firms have become increasingly worried about the social stigma that might affect their brands in the eyes of the public. Several of them have refused to sell the products to State governments without assurance that they won't use them for executions.

Concerns about the results of lethal injection have led some states to allow offenders to request alternative methods. Six states—Arizona, California, Maryland, Mississippi, Missouri and Wyoming—allow the condemned person to choose execution by lethal gas under certain conditions. Nine states still permit the electric chair as an alternative. Oklahoma and Utah allow execution by firing squad under certain conditions. New Hampshire still allows hanging.

THE LAST MEAL: MYTH OR REAL DEAL?

"The condemned man ate his last meal," the news report says. Then, as if to humanize the morbid story of his execution, it itemizes for us the assortment of food items he requested.

This last-meal theme has become a part of the folklore of capital punishment. But does the execution ritual really include this special privilege?

One might think that a person facing a frightful death the next morning would have little appetite for a sumptuous evening meal. Wouldn't the stress of anticipating certain death take away one's appetite?

Well, apparently not—at least, in many cases.

Most states do honor the custom of granting the death-row inmate a special meal a day or two before his or her execution. Historians opine that the custom may have begun in Texas in the 1920s, although Texas no longer allows it. In some cases the inmate just gets the standard meal scheduled for the day. But in many cases prison wardens tend to grant requests they consider reasonable and within the boundaries of reasonable costs and logistical possibilities.

In the state of Louisiana, prison wardens have customarily joined the condemned person for the final meal.

HAVE WE COME TO A TURNING POINT?

We have to ask, will the death penalty eventually become obsolete? Has it outlived its purpose, whatever purpose we might have had in mind?

As of this writing, public support for the death penalty runs at about 50-55 percent, near its historical low. It peaked at 75 percent in the 1990s and has declined steadily ever since.

Political preference makes a big difference in American attitudes about the death penalty, however. People who identify as Republicans typically favor the death penalty much more strongly—recently, at about 75 percent—while Democrats approve at a level of about 35 percent.

Aside from a Republican tilt, the strongest advocates for the death penalty tend to identify as white, male, over 30, Christian, and having less than a college education. Preference for the death penalty typically runs higher in the states of the Old South, the Heartland, and Cowboy Country.

In the most recent year on record, 2018, US State governments executed a total of 25 people and the federal government didn't execute anyone. By comparison, Iran executed over 250 people during that year and Saudi Arabia executed about 150. Experts estimate that China executed several thousand people, although that country keeps its execution statistics a closely guarded secret.

As of this writing, 22 states plus Washington, DC have abolished the death penalty (Wisconsin outlawed it in 1853); 24 still have it; and 4 have a governor-imposed moratorium. But most states haven't executed anyone for so long that they've practically abandoned it, if not formally abolished it.

New York hasn't executed anyone since the Supreme Court lifted the moratorium over 40 years ago. California has executed 13 people in 40 years, the last one in 2006. One state—Texas—has racked up *half of all executions* since 1930, and now does almost *80 percent of the executions* in the US.

As of this writing, the US death row population stands at

about 2,600—a 100-year backlog at current execution rates. Practically speaking, most of them will probably never actually face execution.

The current Pope, Francis, has voiced his unconditional opposition to capital punishment, declaring ". . . it does not render justice to the victims, but rather fosters vengeance."

One last footnote to this conversation: very few discussions of the death penalty ever devote serious attention to a seemingly obvious consideration—*suicide* by the inmate. Suicide rates by prison inmates already run much higher—as much as four times as high—than in the general public, particularly for prisoners with life terms or death sentences.

Can one imagine a greater irony than placing a person scheduled for execution on suicide watch? Presumably, the state has the right to kill the offender, but the offender has no right to end his or her own life. Here, I concede, we skate out onto some very thin ice, morally and philosophically speaking. Americans tend to feel at least as conflicted about suicide—especially managed or facilitated suicide—as they feel about the death penalty itself.

But the question deserves serious consideration. Even if we get rid of the death penalty, should a person sentenced to a miserable state of incarceration for the rest of his or her life have the right to end it voluntarily? Professional executioners might have trouble killing people humanely, but thousands of amateurs in a typical year manage to get it done. We as a society don't seem to want to validate their entitlement, but those views and values have also evolved over time.

R.I.P THE DEATH PENALTY?

A reasonable prediction, after all of our historical review and statistical analysis, seems to come to this:

> *Capital punishment will probably just go out of style in the US—and even Texas—as more and more states abandon it or abolish it. It may reach a point of extinction some time within the next decade or two.*

THE FIX-IT LIST: LAW AND ORDER

So, how can we improve this component of our Republic—Law and Order? Let's start with these actions.

1. *Let's Become a One-Card Society.* As described in detail earlier in this chapter, Congress will pass a law that authorizes the creation of a national Citizen Identification System (NCIDS); allocates funds to set it up; creates or designates the federal agency responsible for managing it; mandates strict safeguards and guidelines to assure that every citizen and legal resident gets included; and assures all of us the right to monitor and control the use of our data.

2. *Let's Rethink Crime and Punishment—Completely.* Congress will pass a comprehensive law that restructures the entire correctional system, as explained in this chapter. This will federalize all high-security prisons and create Remedial Detention Centers (RDCs) to house offenders deemed by local courts as qualified for low-risk confinement.

   Congress will pass a law prohibiting prison sentences for non-violent offenders, except in special cases in which an offender presents a significant risk to public safety. The law will provide for immediate release of non-violent offenders deemed eligible for re-integration into society and will authorize the courts of original jurisdiction to re-sentence offenders.

   The US Department of Justice will develop a set of uniform national crime definitions, with uniform sentencing guidelines that will become binding on local courts. Judges who seek to deviate from those norms in unusual cases will have to provide written justification for alternative sentences.

3. *Gun Violence: Let's Rebalance Rights.* Congress will pass a law and allocate funds to buy up privately owned guns, with the goal of *reducing the number of*

guns in America by one-third, or about 100 million guns. States may set up various administrative mechanisms for turn-in and payment.

Congress will pass a law that establishes a national registration database for all firearms, without exception as to type or purpose of ownership. The law will prohibit individuals from selling or transferring guns directly to one another, but will provide a mechanism for transferring and re-registering them through commercial gun shops or armories.

Congress will pass a law restricting the custody of all highly lethal weapons such as semi-automatic rifles and military-style weapons to commercial armories or shooting ranges. The law will permit individuals to buy, own, store, and shoot those types of weapons, but only at those designated facilities.

4. *Let's License and Accredit Police Departments.* As described this chapter, Congress will pass a law establishing a national system for accrediting law enforcement agencies and for licensing police officers and other security professionals who carry firearms.

   The law will designate a federal agency such as the FBI as the administrative authority for oversight, audit, and compliance. The accrediting body will publish standards of conduct and security practices required of all agencies under its administration.

5. Congress will pass a law that abolishes the death penalty at the federal level and in all states, territories, and military jurisdictions.

Chapter 7.
Let's Rethink Our
Dysfunctional Revenue System:
Taxes

"The winner takes it all,
and the loser takes the fall."
—Lyrics from a hit song by ABBA

The World Economic Forum estimates the total number of billionaires on the planet at just above 2,200. The *wealthiest 26 of them* own more "stuff"—money, stocks, bonds, mansions, cars, yachts, planes, art—than the *3.8 billion people* at the bottom of the economic ladder *combined.*[13]

Currently a typical warehouse worker employed by Amazon gets paid about $10-12 per hour and has a net worth slightly above zero. The man who runs Amazon, according to *Forbes'* estimates, has a net worth of over $200 billion.

A review of the tax returns of 250 large American corporations for the years 2008-2015 discovered that eight of them paid *no taxes during the entire period.* The Institute on Taxation and Economic Policy cited firms like General Electric, International Paper, Priceline.com, and PG&E as leading examples of zero-tax businesses. At least 100 firms in the study—40 percent—paid no tax in at least one of those years. Recent news reports indicate that Amazon, a firm with a stock market capitalization approaching a trillion dollars, paid no tax for the most recent year.[14]

Does it seem like somehow, somewhere along the way, the American economic miracle got hijacked? Did the Founders miss something as they went about designing the economic model for the Republic? How did the "land of opportunity" devolve into the land of "winner takes it all?"

These questions have perplexed political activists for a long time and over the past decade or so they have become ever more acute and more politically urgent. The gap between America's haves and have-nots stands wider than it ever has and it grows wider by the day. Some sociologists predict a looming crisis that could degenerate into class hatred, social unrest, civil disorder, and possibly even violence.

I believe the time has come to *completely rethink the way we pay for the Republic*. The long-running political tug of war between the "soak the rich" faction and the "cut the taxes" faction has gotten us exactly nowhere. So far as I can tell, no significant player in the current national conversation can visualize any option other than trying to push the axis of that conflict toward one extreme or the other.

In this chapter we'll dissect the economic dilemma facing our leaders today, look beyond it to a new and different framing of this critical component of the Republic, and test our intellectual courage in the face of a radically novel approach.

CAPITALISM VS. SOCIALISM: A FALSE CHOICE

If you want a sure-fire way to scare the bejeezus out of most Americans, just say the S-word: *Socialism*. "Socialized Medicine" will usually do it for sure. Tagging a political opponent as a socialist has long had a favored place in the political arsenal.

For decades, America's political leaders have sloganized and emotionalized the national conversation regarding the interplay between politics and economics. The dominant narrative has always framed our choices in terms of class conflict: the presumably irreconcilable difference between the interests of the haves and the have-nots.

For people who like to categorize and villainize competing ideologies, the capitalism vs. socialism dichotomy has become the favorite battleground. They seem to like to position socialism, in its most extreme incarnations—with images of Russian or Chinese communist state-controlled everything—against a virtuous view of capitalism as the natural, benevolent, God-approved way of life.

But any fair-minded comparison of the two ideologies must recognize the toxic extremes of both.

Certainly the colossal failures of the grand Marxist dramas like the cold-war Soviet Union, post-WW2 Communist China, and various Latin American states like Cuba, have shown us the fatal flaws of a mindless state-controlled socialism.

But success stories like the Scandinavian countries have also shown that a share-the-wealth philosophy—which they and many Europeans comfortably refer to as socialism—can co-exist productively and profitably with a democratic free enterprise economic system. Even the Chinese government has adopted "capitalism with Chinese characteristics."

By contrast, we know all too well the history of predatory winner-takes-it-all paleo-capitalism. In the hands of sweat-shop factory owners of the 1800s, and legendary figures like John D. Rockefeller, Andrew Carnegie, and J.P. Morgan, it produced astonishing wealth for some and abject poverty for others. It persists to this day in various incarnations.

Can anyone reasonably dispute that we Americans actually practice and cherish our own brand of socialism, and have for many decades? We just can't bear to call it that.

We have a publicly funded school system throughout the country. We have publicly funded colleges and universities in every state. We have public assistance programs for homeless people; mental health services for the indigent; and unemployment payments for people who lose their jobs.

Military veterans receive a range of government-provided services including medical care, special loans, and educational benefits. The federal government guarantees many kinds of loans for businesses and individuals, including student loans. We even call our retirement system *Social Security*. And, Medicare pays for healthcare services for people who collect Social Security benefits.

THE LEFT VS. RIGHT DOGMA

Old dogs and old dogmas don't change easily. Political doctrines die hard. And few political dichotomies have endured longer and more robustly than the concept of the left vs. right political spectrum.

According to this polarized framing, people who "lean left" in their political views presumably want more government participation in daily life; higher income taxes on the wealthy and corporations; more restrictions on corporate behavior; less economic inequality; more attention to issues of social justice and civil liberties; liberal and progressive policies in law enforcement; and more investment in social welfare.

People who "lean right" supposedly want less government and smaller government; lower taxes on the wealthy and on corporations; fewer restrictions on corporate behavior; economic incentives for corporations to invest and grow; and a hands-off attitude by government toward most of the social problems of the culture, except for law enforcement.

One camp argues that the wealthy and corporations should pay more taxes—their "fair share," supposedly—and those less well off should pay less. Unfortunately, nobody knows how to calculate that fair share.

An opposing camp points out that the wealthy do pay more taxes than the poor. They argue that people who pay no taxes —the "takers"—get a free ride at the expense of those who do—the "makers"—in the lingo of social politics.

The spokespeople for the haves maintain that they use their wealth, voluntarily or involuntarily, to generate more economic activity and consequently more jobs for the less well off. By that noble rationale, taking money from the wealthy will ultimately take money from the working class. History provides very little hard evidence for that claim.

As a frame of reference, this left-right dichotomy inevitably tends to pull the mind into a zero-sum conceptualization of government revenue raising, spending, and investment. Who should pay the most toward the expenses of the Republic? Who should benefit most and least from government spending?

Move the axis point anywhere along the spectrum, left or right, and you presumably give an advantage to one of two competing special interests and you simultaneously disadvantage the other.

What if we could evolve our thinking beyond the zero-sum, left-right spectrum, and find a conceptualization of revenues, expenses, and individual wealth that works for people at all levels of the economic ladder?

I believe we can, but first we'll have to blow up our ancient dogma of win-lose. We'll need to rethink one of the most fundamental concepts of American economic life: *income*. And we'll need to rethink a closely related, taken-for-granted concept that goes with it: the concept of an *income tax*.

LET'S FIND A BETTER WAY

As you read the discussion that follows, I ask, plead, beg, and pray that you can suspend your critical judgment and hold it in check long enough to really grasp the breathtaking significance of a new and radically simple idea: the complete abolition of anything and everything that looks, feels, smells, or works like an income tax.

First, we need to set the groundwork for our thinking. Let's explore an enlightening new perspective for the way humans and corporations relate to the Commons.

LET'S STOP TAXING PEOPLE AND START TAXING TRANSACTIONS

The Internal Revenue Service—our infamous IRS—estimates that the tax gap, or the amount of income tax revenue that goes uncollected each year, averages nearly *$500 billion* on unreported income of about *$2 trillion—every year*. For just the past decade, that astonishing figure adds up to *five trillion* dollars in missing tax revenue.

If we believe those figures, just one year's lost revenue would pay off half of the federal budget deficit or fund the Defense Department's operations for most of a year.[15]

Even with its 76,000 employees, the IRS has not succeeded in closing the tax gap, or even narrowing it by very much. The agency's management *admits that they probably can't.* By recent reports they audit less than one percent of tax returns.

Before we condemn Americans as a bunch of deadbeats and tax cheats, however, let's note that we have one of the highest tax compliance rates in the world, estimated by the Vienna Institute for International Economic Studies at about 83 percent. The UK, Switzerland, France, and Austria clock in at about 75 to 77 percent. The Institute estimates that less than 63 percent of Italians pay their lawful share of income tax.

THE INCOME TAX SYSTEM HAS UTTERLY FAILED

The stark reality of the tax gap makes our long entrenched system of trying to tax income fundamentally and irreparably flawed and unfair. With a one-percent audit rate, people who lie on their tax returns run very little risk of getting found out, so long as they keep their deductions in bounds. Some businesses use questionable or illegal accounting methods to understate income or inflate expenses.

Some people even skip filing altogether and don't get caught. Lots of small business owners who operate on a cash basis justify skimming money from the register by pointing to a tax system they see as unfair to the little guy. Some food service workers justify under-reporting their tips for the same reasons. We have no way of knowing how many workers in the gray economy—housekeepers, gardeners, free-lance construction workers, and others—underpay or fail to pay the taxes dictated by law.

With only 83 percent of the legally mandated income taxes actually coming in, 17 percent of Americans enjoy a free ride at the expense of the rest. As a ratio, five honest taxpayers have to pick up the tab for one dishonest non-payer. As a side issue, consider that nearly 15 percent of the money the IRS takes in goes back out in the form of tax refunds.

But the grotesque unfairness of the practice of taxing an imaginary something called income doesn't stop there. Corporations and wealthy individuals have, for a century or more, bought their way into Congress and state legislatures, offering campaign funds, mysterious "donations," and sometimes outright bribes to get tax laws that favor their interests. While hyper-capitalists complain about the supposedly high tax rates imposed on American corporations, very few corporations actually pay them.

Using creative tax strategies, a person with a net worth of many millions or billions of dollars can appear to have earned no income at all. Their net worth can soar as the corporate stocks and real estate they own appreciate, but unless they collect something called a salary in some form, they have no income tax obligation. If they sell some of their assets for cash, those "capital gains" bear a lower tax rate than the wages of their less affluent fellow citizens.

Financial advisors to the wealthy have a whole toolbox of gimmicks to help them minimize or eliminate their taxes. But Larry and Linda Lunchbucket, the working stiffs who put in their forty hours every week for a paycheck, have no tricks.

Clearly, the income tax system, in any imaginable incarnation, cannot fund the Republic in a fair or equitable way.

A BOGUS ARGUMENT BASED ON A BOGUS CONCEPT

The concept of an income tax doesn't make any sense, it never will make any sense, and it will always handicap our thinking about how to finance a republic. The IRS will always try to argue that you, the wage-earner or the business owner, got more net income or profit than you say you did. And you'll always have to argue that you got less than the amount the IRS claims.

A messy conglomeration of taxes, surtaxes, special levies, and miscellaneous assessments stacks up against an equally messy conglomeration of deductions. Tax credits, depreciation charges, marriage deductions, deductions for dependent children, deductions for education or medical expenses, deductions for home mortgages, home business deductions, charitable donations—the list goes out the door.

Meanwhile, political activists of all stripes keep debating the wrong questions with ever-increasing fervor: who should pay more taxes—the wealthy or the less wealthy? Corporations or individuals?

Inevitably someone will knowingly declare, "Let's have a simple, flat tax system. One tax bracket and one tax rate for everybody. Fifteen percent, maybe." But that makes no more sense than any of the other twists.

Albert Einstein advised,

"There's no right way to do the wrong thing."

The alternative to this unfair and irrational—but blindly accepted—income tax scheme lies in a concept so stunningly new and so elegantly simple that it repels the mind. For that reason it needs a careful explanation. Here goes.

IMAGINE . . .

Of all the innovations proposed in this book, what follows will, I surmise, tax our imaginations (pun intended) more than any other. To paraphrase the Beatles' legendary song,

"Imagine," written by John Lennon, "Imagine there's no income tax; I wonder if you can?"

Let's start by supposing that all income taxes, at all levels, in all sizes, shapes, colors, and incarnations, disappear. All of them, everywhere—gone. No federal income tax, no state income tax. No tax on salaries. No tax on tips. No tax on your retirement pension. No tax on the gain from that rental condo you own when you sell it. No tax on the gain you make when you sell those shares of stock or the bonds or the mutual fund. No tax on the stock dividends you received. No tax on the profit you make with your small business. No taxes on people and no taxes on businesses.

Can you conjure up that alternative reality in your mind? No income tax—none, nada, nichts, zip.

"OK," you say. "I'll hold still while you explain the rest of the theory. But the government has to get the money to run the Republic from somewhere. Who—or what—gets taxed?"

The answer: *we stop taxing people and start taxing transactions.* Our new system for funding the Republic has two key components: 1) a small "goods and services" tax, a.k.a. "value added tax," collected at every step in the value chain, and 2) a small asset transfer tax. Let's see how they work.

LET'S ADOPT A VALUE CHAIN TAX

We already do this to some extent, with what we call sales taxes. Most states have them; currently only five do not.

The only difference—a big one, admittedly—calls for collecting a series of small taxes at all points along the whole value chain—the sequence of hand-offs that runs from the raw material to the finished product the consumer carries out the door.

The big flaw in the ordinary sales tax system lies in the fact that it only kicks in at the last step of the chain, the retail environment. There the end consumer takes possession of something we call a product and has to pay all the tax.

Some might recognize this proposed new method as similar to the value added tax, or VAT, which a number of countries use. Others prefer to call it the goods and services tax, or GST. To the best of my knowledge, however, every country that currently imposes a VAT or GST system also imposes income taxes, so they just layer other taxes on top of an already unworkable income tax system.

This system will only work, I believe—and it could work beautifully—in the complete absence of any semblance of income taxes at any point along the chain. It would make ordinary tax dodging and cheating very difficult and maybe almost nonexistent.

A *vastly simplified tax law* would require each producer to add a percentage—say, ten percent—to the price they charge to the next player along the line. They would each transfer the tax money they take in to the national treasury on some periodic basis, say monthly or quarterly.

All of these little revenue faucets would flow into the common fund and a portion of the revenue would then get distributed back to the various states in proportion to their contributions. At the start of the new system, states might have the option to retain their old income tax systems and consequently give up the payback revenue.

Alternatively, if they preferred to receive the redistribution, they would have to abolish all levies on anything called income. Presumably the new system would make the old system less desirable for states and ultimately not viable.

Imagine yourself as an employee working for some enterprise—a company, a government agency, a military unit —any place that offers a salary. If your employer has agreed to pay you a salary of, say, $1,000 per week, then you get a check for $1,000. No deductions—you get it all.

On the way home from work, if you stop at the convenience store or the supermarket or the coffee shop, you might notice that they charge you a much higher sales tax than the last time you shopped there. But the money your employer previously confiscated from your paycheck and sent to the federal and State governments now gets reallocated to cover the accumulated series of mini-taxes along the way.

You might protest, "Won't all of those individual taxes make the product too expensive to buy at the end of the chain?" No. The free enterprise pricing system and normal competition will see to that. The dynamic political and economic processes that go on all the time will force tax percentages and prices to a level where ordinary people can pay them.

By the way, when you as an employee sell your labor—or the fruits of it—to your employer, you act just like a supplier, not much different from the ones who provide raw materials. Your price becomes the amount of money you and your employer have agreed on. As one of many suppliers along the chain, you'll collect your full price and you'll have to charge a transaction tax. Practically speaking, your employer would handle the payments on your behalf—all employers already have the financial systems set up to do that anyway.

At the end of the year, you can forget about filing that tedious and confusing income tax return. You'll file a one-page document—online, of course—that verifies that you received a certain payment for your labor product and that you or your employer transferred the appropriate amount of tax to the national treasury. Instead of thinking of it as an income tax, just consider it another type of sales tax. You sold your services at a market price, you charged the GST to the buyer —your employer—and the national treasury gets the tax.

So now we've replaced the complicated, confusing, and unfair income tax with a simple transaction tax. Two-thirds of the IRS' employees can move on to more satisfying occupations.

Later in this discussion we'll see how another key tax, applied to stock market transactions, will create a large flow of wealth into the national treasury. More about that shortly.

To make this simple but possibly mind-bending concept clearer, let's just follow the chain of events by which a farmer's wheat ends up in a loaf of bread leaving the supermarket in a consumer's shopping bag. See if you can follow the flow of products and money—and taxes—through the process illustrated in Figure 7-1, as explained below.

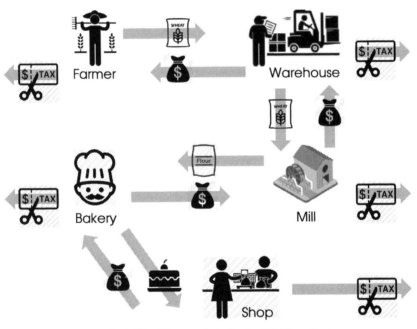

Figure 7-1. The Value Chain & GST Tax System

At each stage of the process, you can see how the product, in whatever form it takes, flows to the next buyer. The little sack of money goes back to the supplier and a little chunk of tax money goes up to the national treasury.

Step 1. The farmer sells the wheat, usually to a firm that stores grains in huge volumes and sells it on to distributors from their warehouse. They agree on a price: so many dollars per bushel or per ton or whatever measure they prefer. The firm pays the farmer the agreed price, plus a small transaction tax. The farmer banks the payment and at the end of the month or the quarter deposits the amount of the tax transactions collected for that period in a special government account. The farmer has *added value* at his or her stage by providing the land, acquiring the seeds, planting them, raising the wheat, and harvesting it.

Step 2. The warehouse firm that buys the wheat probably transports it to a mass storage facility, safeguards it, keeps it from spoiling, and sells various quantities of it to other producers such as millers or bakery firms. This middle-man provider adds more value than one might first think. The mass storage capability relieves the farmers of the need to operate big storage facilities of their own, and it also buffers the flow of wheat along the value chain so that it never piles up or runs short. Each time the storage company sells a quantity of wheat to a customer firm it collects the agreed payment plus a small transaction tax. Just as the farmer did, this company sends the tax on to the government's bank account and keeps the rest.

Step 3. A company that operates a grain mill buys a big supply of wheat—and, usually, other food grains—from the distributor, grinds it into flour, blends various flours into special combinations, and sells them to bakery firms. Each time the mill makes a sale, the same process kicks in: the firm collects the payment plus a small transaction tax, which it dutifully deposits with the government.

Step 4. A large bakery firm, or perhaps a small specialty baker, buys a month's supply of flour from the mill, combines it with various other ingredients—which it buys from other suppliers in similar distribution chains—and turns out delicious breads, cakes, donuts, biscuits, rolls, cookies, crackers, and various other specialty baked goods. It sells them onward, sometimes to wholesale distributors and sometimes directly to retailers. The wholesalers collect and warehouse the baked goods for short periods of time and they sell them on to retailers. Again, these middle-man firms add value by balancing supply and demand so that suppliers always have a steady stream of products going out and consumers always see shelves stocked with the products they want. The familiar standard financial routine plays out (mostly managed by computers): the buyer pays the agreed price plus a small transaction tax. The seller passes the tax on to the government and keeps the rest.

Step 5. In this example, the last step in the chain has a consumer choosing some of the many baked products offered by the market. The cashier collects the amount of the marked price, plus a small transaction tax that the accounting department will pass on to the national treasury. At this point, a multitude of other value chains probably flow into one another, as the consumer might walk out of the store with bread for a sandwich; peanut butter and jelly for the filling; milk for a beverage; a banana or a cookie for dessert; and any number of other items he or she might want to buy during the visit to the store.

At no stage along this improved value chain or value network, does anybody—individuals, small businesses, or corporations—ever pay anything called an income tax, either during the transaction or later. No one files a tax return. No one waits for a refund. Governments won't need to know or care how much income or profit anyone received. The concept of income, from the perspective of tax policy, becomes meaningless.

The players in this story don't have to hire financial advisors or tax lawyers to figure out how to game the tax system. The old system has disappeared and no one can easily game the new one. In fact, very few of them probably even want to. The company tax department only needs a few people—maybe one—to tidy up the paperwork on an annual basis.

This GST concept can apply to just about every buy-and-sell transaction we can think of. Restaurant checks, taxi rides, movie tickets, the popcorn and soda, fuel for cars, and haircuts—everywhere that people exchange value for money. A tax of about one percent or so won't affect the sale very much, but billions of transactions every day will generate a strong and steady flow of revenue to the national treasury.

LET'S ADOPT AN ASSET TRANSFER TAX

The second key part of our new system involves a small—and selective—tax applied to various kinds of asset transfers. These would include, for example, taxes on stock market transactions; taxing real estate and other property transfers; and taxing parts of estates when transferred. In all cases, the tax rate would take only a small percentage of the value of the assets involved, for two reasons: 1) to spread the tax bite widely so that no person or type of asset gets hit too hard; and 2) to keep the rate low enough to avoid tax cheating and political opposition on the part of wealthy people.

LET'S TAX STOCK MARKET TRADES

Every time someone sells shares of stock in any publicly held corporation, the brokerage firm will collect a small tax, based on the selling price, and pass it on to the national treasury. We might consider taxing both the buying end and the selling end of the transaction, which would generate twice the revenue, or we might want to exempt the buyer. A careful analysis by qualified experts would inform that decision.

The same taxation scheme would apply to the whole range of Wall Street investment products—stocks, options, futures, derivatives, swaps, straddles, hedges, short sales, currency trades, precious metals, and investment trusts.

Stock market investors will probably rejoice when they learn that the capital gains tax has disappeared. They'll have the freedom to buy and sell any time they like and they'll never have to give up part of their gains to governments. Those who own bonds will also rejoice. On the other hand, they get no deduction if they lose money on the trade.

The thirteen major stock exchanges in the US—the New York Exchange, NASDAQ, and others—manage the enormous flow of buy and sell transactions every day. Estimates place the number of shares traded daily on the major exchanges at more than six billion, with values of over $200 billion. A tax of one percent, for example, on every sale could accumulate over two billion dollars per day. If we tax both the buyer and the seller at one percent, the revenue jumps to 4 billion.

One side effect of this new taxation system would make some economists happy and it would probably make some super-investors very unhappy. A tax on each transaction will make a lot of the rampant speculation in the Wall Street markets less profitable.

Speculators who use high volume computerized trading to accumulate big profits from many small transactions will probably face big challenges. Similarly, short selling might become much less attractive if the speculators faced taxes on both ends of the operation.

Philosophically, some economists argue that the tax system should favor investors but not speculators. Investors use their own assets in hopes of gaining value by the natural economic processes that play out every day. Speculators, on the other hand, don't add value for anyone else; they merely manipulate the financial markets for selfish gain. Some argue that reducing the massive amount of speculation and market manipulation could make the stock markets more stable.

The issue of taxing transactions in the bond market presents some questions, however. Whereas shares of a corporation have a natural tendency to increase in value over time, as the corporation accumulates profits and its net worth grows, bonds have no such advantage. A corporate or government bond serves as a store of value, with a fixed rate of return. Therefore, taxing bond sales might disadvantage investors more than taxing stock transfers would.

LET'S TAX REAL ESTATE TRADES

Currently, many states charge some form of sales tax when one person buys a piece of property from another. Under the new system, all real estate transfers would incur a small tax and local taxes would disappear. The same rationale for taxing one or both sides of the transaction, as for stock trades, would apply to real estate.

Again, part of the tax revenue collected by the national treasury would go back to the states in proportion to their sales activity.

Hard assets like gold, silver, and other precious metals, as well as investment grade diamonds and other specialized assets would incur the same tax treatment as stocks and real estate when sold. Most of those trades take place through well established brokerages or market systems, so existing computer systems could collect the taxes very easily.

SHOULD WE TAX ESTATES, INHERITANCES, AND GIFTS?

Few topics cause the adrenalin to flow in debates about taxation more than the estate tax, or the death tax, as some factions like to call it. While some opponents consider it immoral and un-American, others just see it as unfair.

Emotional reactions tend to run high but in truth the estate tax rate, as currently set, only affects a small number of very rich people who bequeath their assets to their heirs. As of this writing, the estate tax only applies to about 2,000 estates in the whole country, which works out to about .0006 percent of the population.

However, in order to keep all transfer taxes relatively low and to distribute their effects as evenly as possible, it would make sense to tax those assets of the estate easily denominated in dollars. That would include real estate (at assessed value), plus financial instruments such as bank accounts, stocks, and bonds. Other personal assets not denominated in dollars, such as furniture and personal belongings, collectible items, heirlooms, artwork, patents and copyrights, and the like would not incur taxes.

As with the other transfer taxes, a levy on those kinds of assets of one percent or so during estate transfers would have a very small impact on the value received by the heirs.

THE ONE-PERCENT SOLUTION?

In the transfer tax examples we've considered so far, I've used a tax percentage of "about one percent" as a hypothetical figure. Actually, that figure has a lot going for it. Let's see why.

First, we've designed a system of multiple small taxes, applied at a number of points in our economic system. Instead of requiring the national treasury to rely heavily on income taxes, as we currently do, we can reduce the impact of the tax hit on any one person or company at any one point.

Considering the huge number of shares traded on the stock exchanges every day, a painless one-percent tax assessment would deliver a strong and steady flow of revenue to the national treasury. We could think of the one-percent trading assessment as a kind of dividend paid to the Republic as a figurative shareholder.

We might even apply this concept of the Republic as a shareholder in a literal way, for example, by requiring that every initial public offering of shares in a corporation—the IPO—allocate one percent of the value to the national treasury. That would serve as the initial license fee, so to speak, for the corporation's future entitlement to the resources of the Commons.

Over time, this process would shift enormous resources from the corporate sector to the Commons, without impairing the ability of the firms to generate profits. Long term, this would reduce the infamous wealth gap at a steady pace. The number of billionaires might decline somewhat.

Clearly, a huge advantage of this new system lies in restoring fairness to the collection of taxes. With the income tax dead and gone, no one can cheat on his or her taxes because no one needs to. The transaction taxes get collected by computers all along the value chain. The taxes on stock trades get collected by the systems that already exist in the brokerage firms.

Perhaps an even bigger potential advantage of the one-percent system lies in its resistance to tampering by the wealthy. For years, a privileged group of well-connected billionaires has used their influence in Congress to create loopholes and dodges favorable to themselves. But one can hardly complain about unfair treatment of a particular type of economic interest when the tax hit amounts to only one percent of the proceeds.

Currently, the largest American corporations keep huge stocks of money out of the country in tax havens—locations that offer low tax rates, or none at all. Some American companies have even relocated their headquarters to other countries, preferring to operate in the US as foreign corporations. The abolition of the income tax and the use of the one-percent scheme could eliminate most of the incentives to play those kinds of games.

Provided the corporation honors its responsibilities toward the Commons and contributes ethically and responsibly to the life of the Republic, then all stakeholders should presumably want to see it operate efficiently and generate high profits. With part of the ever-growing share value going back to the Republic in the form of stock exchange taxes, the Republic will benefit as the corporation profits.

YES, VIRGINIA, THE RICH WILL PAY MORE

This new system will probably mean that the wealthiest of the wealthy will become less wealthy over time. Every change in tax policy will advantage some category of people and disadvantage some other. But, considering the enormous gap that currently exists between the wealthy class and the middle class, popular opinion certainly seems to favor such a realignment.

How big an impact would this new revenue system have on funding the Republic? Huge. A reliable answer to that question awaits a more sophisticated economic analysis. However, we might expect that the federal government could pay off a large part of its debt, and operate with a revenue surplus, or at least avoid running a deficit.

Consider the mind-boggling total capital value of all the corporations in the US. We might well see an enormous supply of funds available for the benefit of all citizens. And as we also wind down our profligate spending on unnecessary military programs, we might well have the means to implement universal healthcare and universal education, while also tackling the long delayed upgrades of the national infrastructure.

THE FIX-IT LIST: REVENUE

So, how can we improve this component of our Republic— Revenue? Let's start with these actions.

1. *Let's Dump the Income Tax.* Congress will pass, and the states will ratify, a Constitutional amendment that repeals the Sixteenth Amendment, abolishes all income taxes for individuals and corporations, and prohibits both the federal government and all state and local governments from imposing an income tax. The amendment will authorize Congress to create a single, integrated, national tax system that combines a goods and services tax (GST) and an asset transfer tax.

2. *Let's Reform the IRS.* Congress will pass a law creating a National Revenue Commission, charged with setting key tax rates and eligibility criteria for special exemptions for people in particular circumstances.

   The head of the commission and its members, once appointed by the president and confirmed by the Senate, will have political immunity from removal, in a fashion similar to that of the Chairman of the Federal Reserve and members of its Board. Neither the president nor the Congress will have the power to interfere with its operation.

The law will eliminate the role of the IRS in determining tax liabilities. IRS will have the sole responsibility of collecting revenues and monitoring tax compliance.

3. *Let's Define Corporate Accountability to the Commons.* Congress will pass, and the states will ratify, a Constitutional amendment that formally recognizes the role of the public corporation as an economic entity permitted to operate with the permission, and under the jurisdiction, of the federal government. It will formally declare the responsibility of all public corporations to comply with national and local laws regarding access to the resources of the Commons and their responsibility for preserving the natural environment. The amendment will give Congress the authority to define and implement the shared-value relationship between the corporation and the Republic as described in this and previous chapters.

4. *Let's Require Corporations to Share Their Good Fortune With the Commons.* Congress will pass a law mandating a one percent tax assessment on all stock trades executed in public exchanges through the agency of registered trading firms. Further analysis will determine whether the assessment will apply to proceeds received by both seller and of the shares, or only to the seller's side of the transaction.

5. *Let's Collect the Two Centuries of Overdue License Fees Owed by Corporations to the Commons.* Congress will pass a law mandating a one-time tax assessment of one percent on all common stock portfolios held for investors by brokerage firms, as of a designated date.

The assessment will not apply to accounts opened after the designated date.

6. *Let's Give the Commons a Slice of the IPO Cake.* Congress will pass a law mandating an assignment of one percent of the shares created during all IPOs to the national treasury, or a payment of one percent of the monetary value of the initial offering.

Chapter 8.
Let's Rethink Commerce:
Survival of the Fittest
or Shared Fate?

*"When everyone is out digging for gold,
the business to be in is selling shovels."*
—Mark Twain

According to Milton Friedman, professor of economics at the University of Chicago business school:

"There is one and only one social responsibility of business —to use its resources and engage in activities designed to increase its profits, so long as it stays within the rules of the game, which is to say, engages in open and free competition without deception or fraud."

The billionaire capitalist Malcolm Forbes, founder of the *Forbes Magazine* publishing empire, agreed with Friedman. Forbes put it even more simply:

"The only sin in business is not making a profit."

A century earlier, the legendary robber baron John D. Rockefeller had shown the way to fabulous riches in the oil business by amassing capacity and exterminating his smaller rivals. He expressed his philosophy in equally blunt terms:

"The day of combination [monopolies, mergers, acquisitions, and trusts] is here to stay. Individualism has gone, never to return. Competition is a sin. The American Beauty Rose can be produced in the splendor and fragrance which bring cheer to its beholder only by sacrificing the early buds which grow up around it. This is not an evil tendency in business. It is merely the working-out of a law of nature and a law of God."

Before we take up the question of whether, how, and how much to rein in corporate expansionism, let's pause to acknowledge a very big truth:

The corporation, as an economic entity, probably surpasses all other human inventions in terms of the benefits it has brought to modern societies.

For all of our ambivalence toward corporate influence and our concerns about overreaching corporate power, we must acknowledge the enormous capacity of this remarkable mechanism for getting big things done.

Doing big things in a big way—building a fleet of modern passenger airplanes, sending a spacecraft to Mars, creating a shopping mall, or assembling an aircraft carrier—requires pooling resources, including money, physical equipment and facilities, and human talent. Even if the government pays for it all, nothing happens without well-organized capital, and lots of it. No band of individuals or small business owners, however well motivated, could have built the national railway system, created giant oceangoing cargo ships, or produced enough war materiel to defeat the Nazi empire. Corporations did it, and did it well.

Rockefeller had it wrong, of course. The great benefit of the corporation as an economic mechanism and a strategy for development lies in its capacity to *concentrate resources,* not in its capacity to *concentrate wealth.* That distinction makes all the difference. Any workable policy for oversight will have to support the capacity of corporations to concentrate resources, while limiting their tendency to concentrate wealth in the hands of a few insiders. We need to treat the corporation as a basic component of our modern Republic.

PALEO-CAPITALISM: A DYING IDEOLOGY?

Rockefeller, Carnegie, J. P. Morgan, Henry Ford, Milton Friedman, Malcolm Forbes, and a long line of wealthy older male capitalists—or *paleo-capitalists*, we should say—represent the most extreme ideology of dog-eat-dog commerce. They have long ignored or disavowed the disastrous impacts of unbridled corporate activity on the Commons and have typically rejected any social or moral responsibility to anyone other than their shareholders and creditors.

Ironically, most of the robber barons turned to philanthropy in their twilight years, setting up charitable foundations bearing their names. Presumably, they hoped to imprint a more humanitarian image in the public mind after they'd gone—and perhaps hoped for what my religious friends call "celestial fire insurance."

In the modern era, mega-corporations still rule the land, perhaps more powerfully than ever. As of this writing, the 10 biggest companies in the US, with combined annual sales of over 2 trillion dollars, ranked as follows:[16]

1. Walmart—mega-stores, $514 bn.
2. ExxonMobil—energy company, $290 bn.
3. Apple—consumer electronics, $265 bn.
4. Berkshire Hathaway—holding company, $248 bn.
5. Amazon—online retailer, $233 bn.
6. UnitedHealth Group—health insurance, $226 bn.
7. McKesson—health products, $214 bn.
8. CVS/Health—pharmacies, clinics, $195 bn.
9. AT&T—telecom, $170 bn.
10. AmerisourceBergen—healthcare, $168 bn.

The concern many social activists have with the mega-corporation goes to the simple fact of *self-reinforcing advantage*. Bigger companies can compete in ways that smaller ones can't. Walmart probably stands as the most famous example of this effect.

Typically, when Walmart opens one of its big-box mega-stores in a mid-sized community, it attracts so much of the consumer demand that many of the smaller retailers just can't survive. Because of its enormous size and buying power, the company can cut prices so low that the small fry can't possibly match them.

This *price dominance* advantage, as economists call it, lies at the heart of the paleo-capitalist theology. As both John Rockefeller and Milton Friedman would advise, the devout capitalist pursues *growth* above all. The rewards of growth—the competitive advantage and marketing power that come with accumulating cash—include the satisfaction of exterminating one's competitors.

If Walmart stands as the big success story of brick-and-mortar capitalism, we'd have to nominate Amazon as its counterpart in cyberspace. In all fairness, we have to acknowledge the ingenuity, foresight, and determination of the founders of both of those enterprises. Both Sam Walton and Jeff Bezos stand as remarkable examples of entrepreneurs who saw the power of "scaling," as the popular term goes. They built financial empires by taking advantage of the realities of the American business environment.

Amazon, for its part, went over to the dark side after it became the dominant Internet retailer in the book business, and later moved on to an unlimited range of products. Using brutally competitive purchasing and pricing methods, the company brought the book publishing industry to heel, as it took control of half of the distribution of books in the US.

Amazon became the alpha player, partly by taking losses for the first four years of its existence, racking up over $2 billion in red ink before the turn. It offered big price discounts to customers on one end and squeezed the publishers for lower and lower wholesale prices on the other.

While business experts questioned the need for such deep discounting—Amazon had already become extremely popular for its near-infinite inventory of titles and convenient customer experience—the company persisted, devastating the profit structure of the publishing industry.

The same practices that made Amazon a hit with book buyers also made it the most despised company in the publishing business. Mainline publishers, small independent publishing houses, bookstores both large and small, and even authors have all felt the squeeze of the Amazon monopoly.

In one provocative episode, CEO Jeff Bezos demanded quarterly rebates from the large publishers, on top of discounts off list prices of 55-60 percent. When one of the "Big Seven" rebelled, Amazon's programmers removed the "buy" buttons from all of that firm's titles, bringing their online sales to a halt. A group of the biggest publishers took him to court and he backed off. But during the few weeks of the episode, he made his monopoly power brazenly clear.

For their part, those who run the mega-firms, as well as economists and media cheerleaders who encourage them, offer a formidable defense of the monopoly: *customers get more for their money*. Even the anti-monopoly activists have to concede that a big-box store of the Walmart species can offer a breathtaking selection of products, which the mom and pop players couldn't possibly stock. In practical terms, why would a consumer seek out a small appliance retailer, with a narrow selection of appliances and pay more for their purchase than they know they'd pay at the big-box store?

To counter, advocates for a kinder, gentler form of capitalism point out that, while the mega-firm offers benefits for customers, it harms other participants in the commercial ecosystem, including authors, smaller entrepreneurs, and small suppliers. They question the morality—and, perhaps, the economic logic—of sacrificing the interests of one part of the ecosystem to favor another. The dog-eat-dog model leaves a lot of dead dogs.

In recent years, courts have often ruled in favor of dominant firms accused by their rivals of *predatory pricing*—selling products below cost to exterminate their competitors—on the sole premise that the customers pay less.

CYBER-CAPITALISM: FEUDALISM REINCARNATED?

Some prognosticators say we've moved into a new phase in business—*cyber-capitalism*—which they believe will radically change the economic and social landscape. The rapid spread and acceptance of the digital experience has almost no parallel in our history, with the possible exception of television. Our lives now revolve comfortably around *knowledge at a distance*—fingertip access to worlds of information, online shopping, and management of our personal affairs. In half a generation, the vast majority of the world's affluent people have become digital citizens.

Looking back, however, it seems that some of the grandest fantasies promoted by the early philosophers of the digital age haven't really caught fire. Some have misfired and some even backfired. We didn't get some of what they promised us, and some of what we got we hadn't expected.

The digital pundits declared that the Internet would create a "new economy," somehow vastly different that the one we'd always known. In the red-hot Nineties, before the historic "dot-com" crash, that phrase became the defining mantra of the Internet priesthood. A wider, flatter, democratized, many-to-many marketplace would mean that every entrepreneur with a dream and a computer might get rich. "Old economy" companies would go the way of the dinosaur. The slogan became "e-business or out of business."

But it didn't work out that way. The Internet actually destroyed more fortunes than it created.

Ironically, a new set of monopoly firms now dominates the vast online marketplace: Amazon, Apple, eBay, Facebook,

Google, LinkedIn, Twitter, Yahoo, Youtube, and a few others. Microsoft still dominates the office software market.

We see more monopolization now than has ever existed in "real space." Predictably, the big fish have devoured the small fish. Google acquired Youtube, Microsoft acquired LinkedIn, and Facebook acquired Instagram and WhatsApp, two of the most popular social media companies.

The supposed new economy of the Internet looks a lot like the old economy, only more so. And the mega-firms that had always dominated the physical marketplace, like Walmart, General Motors, Ford, and ExxonMobil, simply extended their operations into cyberspace and kept growing.

So, the feudal model of commerce—the wealthy landowner made richer every day by a horde of toiling peasant farmers —never went away. It just got reincarnated in modern clothes. The much-touted "gig economy," for example, based on supposedly democratic models of cyber-commerce such as Uber, just became a hipper version of the plantation-and-sharecropper system.

As of this writing, Uber claims almost 5 million free-lance cab drivers all over the world, providing their own vehicles and mostly earning something in the neighborhood of a minimum wage. Ironically, Uber and its nearest competitor Lyft have racked up over $10 billion dollars in red ink so far, and neither firm has a clear path to profitability.

It also became painfully evident to many business operators that the Internet wouldn't become the magical fountain of profits they hoped it would. In reality, it turned into a profit grinder. Price transparency, dynamic pricing, and hyper-competition, driven by price-comparison Web sites, put tremendous pressure on retail prices across the board. If the people running airline companies, for example, held any hope of escaping from their decades-long price wars, they saw those hopes dashed by a flock of fare-shopping sites.

The Internet business has become a boundaryless battlefield. The surviving giants increasingly try to invade one another's turf, offering the same or similar products and steadily commoditizing the online experience.

Entrepreneurs with ideas and energy will still get their turns at bat, but the days of garage to global have mostly gone. Small businesses will become increasingly dependent on cheap and accessible cloud-based software services controlled by the digital giants.

Just as the US Congress considered breaking up John Rockefeller's prized Standard Oil Company—and they finally did, in 1911—the same hue and cry has arisen about the mega-firms of the digital age. More and more economists, activists, and politicians have called for the break-up of the cyber-monopolies, especially Facebook and Google.

This time around, though, they've gotten worked up about the issues of digital privacy, illegal manipulation of social media platforms, and foreign interference in public elections. They've mostly given up on free competition in cyber-space.

NEO-CAPITALISM: A NEW MODEL FOR A DEMOCRATIC REPUBLIC?

In recent years a new and more enlightened approach to commerce has emerged, which we might call *neo-capitalism*. In its most advanced form, it recognizes a number of key principles, as suggested in Chapter 3 (The Commons):

1. The corporation survives and thrives by means of its relationship to the Commons. It benefits from the resources of the *natural environment* and makes use of the infrastructure of the *built environment*. In a sense, the corporation holds a license, so to speak, for access to the Commons, and it should pay for that license by returning value to the Commons.

2. The primary purpose of the corporation remains to return a profit to its owners. By law, the board members and the executive team serve as stewards of the shareholders' interests. But they must reconcile the interests of the shareholders with their

responsibility to the Commons and to the society, in terms of the three figurative bottom lines: People, Profits, and Planet. The corporation owes fair and reasonable treatment to its employees, customers, and suppliers; responsible use of the assets of its shareholders and creditors; and ecologically responsible business practices that preserve natural resources and sustain the built environment.

3. The federal, state, and local governments serve as stewards or custodians of the Commons, on behalf of the society. The role and responsibility of government in the commercial dimension of the Republic calls for ensuring that all enterprises, of all types and sizes, carry out their obligations to protect and preserve the Commons; to return value to society and the Commons; and to act ethically and responsibly in their dealings with members of the society.

4. Governments have a legitimate role in promoting *free and fair competition*, which includes preventing the mega-firms and deep-pocket capitalists from running roughshod over the small fry. That implies a proactive role in reining in big-company excess, and includes creating advantages for small businesses that offset the disadvantages of their size.

5. Arguments abound over the means, methods, and limits of this oversight. Considering that governments at all levels serve as custodians of the Commons, it follows that they should have the authority, the means, and the methods to steer all enterprises toward responsible, sustainable development.

TAMING THE CORPORATION: INTELLIGENT OVERSIGHT, NOT SOCIAL ENGINEERING

Most of the Founders of the American Republic already felt a bit uneasy about the potential for commercial corporations to influence society and gain power over governments. They never dealt directly with the problem, however, although the new Constitution decreed that, "Congress shall have power to regulate Commerce with foreign Nations, and among the several States, and with the Indian Tribes."

Thomas Jefferson, more than any of his peers, warned emphatically about corporate power from the very beginning. Aside from standing armies, which he considered very dangerous to a democracy, he opposed corporate monopolies and banks in particular.

He reportedly said,

> *"I hope we shall crush in its birth the aristocracy of our monied corporations which dare already to challenge our government to a trial by strength and bid defiance to the laws of our country."*

And,

> *"I believe that banking institutions are more dangerous to our liberties than standing armies."*

Jefferson reportedly wanted the Bill of Rights to guarantee "freedom from monopolies in commerce," and the prohibition of a standing national army. He got all the other rights he pushed for, but couldn't sell those two.

In modern times, Democrats and Republicans have played political football with the issue of corporate regulation for decades. One faction decries "big business." The other condemns "big government."

One can hardly dispute that federal regulations have multiplied over the years, and a ponderous bureaucracy has indeed formed. And we could easily understand the claim that the bewildering multitude of regulations can sometimes do more harm than good. State government bureaucracies compound the problem even further.

Yet, a long history of greed, dishonesty, fraud, and outright disregard for social responsibility on the part of many corporations has taught us that *laissez faire* capitalism can inflict disastrous costs on the Commons and on the common people. We've seen clearly that they generally don't police themselves if left entirely on their own.

When I hear paleo-capitalists questioning the patriotism of those who advocate limits on corporate freedom, I usually say, "Count me as a big fan of Capitalism, but I have my doubts about capitalists."

In short, we have to live with the necessity and the reality of regulation, but we need to balance it intelligently with the commercial processes that make us a prosperous society.

So, how can we rethink the regulation of commerce? Can we make it more streamlined, more fair, more cost-efficient, and more adaptable to reality?

SOCIAL ENGINEERING DOESN'T WORK VERY WELL

When you visit the charming and picturesque old city of Amsterdam, with its vast network of canals, you'll notice the remarkably narrow houses that line the waterways. Why would so many people in the old days make their houses so narrow, with multiple floors and lots of little windows?

The answer: to avoid taxes. During the Dutch Golden Age in the 1800s, with vast amounts of money pouring in from trade, wealthy merchants started building houses along the canals. Many of them used the attic and rooms in the back to store their merchandise. As they clamored for canal property, the Dutch government set high tax rates, based on the number of meters of canal frontage each house occupied.

Predictably, new houses shrank to a few meters in width, with four or five floors, and extending far back from the street. The stairways between floors became awkwardly narrow, making it very difficult to lug furniture up and down. To get around that handicap, builders installed beams protruding outward from the roof, with pulleys used to raise and lower furniture by ropes.

Can we find a lesson in this charming historical case study? Does it teach us anything about how tax policy affects the behavior of people who operate businesses?

Let's look at another case for a more recent perspective. Some years ago, the State government of Hawaii passed a measure that required all businesses, including small ones, to offer healthcare plans to their full-time employees. Their law defined a full-time employee as one who worked 20 hours per week or more, on a regular basis.

What happened? Hundreds of small and mid-size businesses cut their employees' work week to 19 hours. That required them to have twice as many employees as before, and it forced the employees to find second jobs. Immediately, the public buses filled up as people commuted all over Honolulu between their two jobs. They lost two hours of paid work time and incurred the costs of commuting on top of that.

Several lessons emerge from these case examples. For one: *you can't outsmart the ant army.*

Trying to impose a solution on a large number of independent actors—individuals, businesses, organizations, children—that demands that they behave in ways they see as counter to their interests, will usually cause them to find ways around it.

Second, we confuse means and ends when we try to force people to take actions that we associate with moral responsibility. Motivation works better by offering someone what they want than by threatening them with something they don't want.

In the Hawaiian incident, the experiment in social engineering produced some unanticipated consequences. The architects of the social solution presumably hoped to make things better for all workers, but they managed to make things worse for everybody.

WE NEED A THIRD WAY

Too many political officeholders and activists have promoted brute force measures they hoped would correct perceived injustices in society, marketplaces, or workplaces. For example, demands that all corporate boards of directors include a certain number of women; demands that colleges and universities admit a certain quota of minority students; demands for net-worth taxes imposed on ultra-wealthy people; and demands that schools exclude certain subject from their curricula, all cause defensive and evasive reactions on the part of those targeted. National price control schemes typically create black markets. City rent controls typically cause a decay in the quality of housing, as landlords can't justify investing in upgrades.

The social responsibility trade-off in particular remains a very difficult challenge across a wide range of public issues. Somewhere between an irresponsible hands-off approach and misguided social engineering campaigns lies a thought process for designing solutions that favors the carrot over the stick. We need an approach to guiding and regulating businesses that pulls them in the direction of their own best interests, while inducing them to behave in ways that contribute to the national sense of justice and fair play.

We'll still need the stick—reasonable laws, strongly enforced. But, as Abraham Lincoln reportedly advised,

"A drop of honey catches more flies than a gallon of gall."

LET'S RETHINK OUR REGULATION STRATEGY

Let's introduce a radical alternative into the regulatory bureaucracy: *let's separate the authority to make regulations from the authority to enforce them.* When we give a federal agency the power to create regulations and then allow that agency to enforce the same regulations it created, we set up a conflict of interest. The same problems exist at state levels as well. We have no meaningful way to regulate the regulators.

With literally hundreds of regulating bodies all operating more or less independently of one another, we make it nearly impossible for anyone to get a reliable understanding of all the regulations that affect a particular activity.

The radical improvement for this dimension of our remodeled Republic calls for creating a single federal regulatory agency—call it the Federal Regulatory Commission. We can bring the vast collection of disparate—and often conflicting—regulations and regulatory processes together into one integrated system.

We already have a big head start on a national regulatory system, known as the *US Code of Federal Regulations* (CFR). It brings together a vast collection of federal regulations and organizes them into some 50 categories, referred to as *titles*. Each title has various chapters and subdivisions, usually associated with the various agencies that "own" particular jurisdictions. The Office of the Federal Register puts out an updated version of the CFR once a year.

This approach of separating the issuing body from the enforcing body would leave intact the authority of the various specialized agencies to enforce the regulations within their areas of responsibility. Let's consider the big advantages of this new way of regulating.

▸ All new federal regulations, down to the most specialized or microscopic, would come from the new FRC. Consolidating all regulations could save enormous amounts of money for those who have to comply and it probably would save money for the compliance agencies as well.

▸ Every new regulation would get close scrutiny and a careful evaluation of its impacts and benefits. We could develop a cadre of professionally qualified regulatory analysts, skillful at analyzing the issues, crafting elegant solutions, reconciling new regulations with existing ones, and writing documents that make the regulations clear, concise, unambiguous, and actionable.

LET'S PROMOTE A NEW BUSINESS MODEL: THE ETHICAL CORPORATION

The modern corporation, as an economic entity, has become one of the most effective mechanisms we have for getting big things done. The concept of the corporation forms a basic foundation stone, so to speak, of the entire structure of a capitalist, free-enterprise society. As a society, we have used it for great benefit and we've also misused it in some ways.

Over the last several decades, more and more corporations in America have fallen prey to greedy insiders—a few executives and boards of directors who place their own financial and political interests above those of the shareholders, employees, and the society at large.

This progressive infection reached a crisis point with the mother of all financial disasters—the Wall Street meltdown of 2008.

An unprecedented number of Americans now view banks and most other large corporations as generally corrupt; controlled by dishonest, self-serving insiders; and guided by cynical values that benefit the few at the expense of the society at large.

LET'S ACTIVATE THE ACTIVISTS

Unfortunately, many of the activists seeking to change corporate behavior have two big handicaps: 1) they keep trying to think of the corporation as some kind of living entity, with a heart, a soul, and a conscience; and 2) they have trouble articulating their concerns.

For the first part, they need to remind themselves that a corporation exists only on paper, as an abstract concept—a legal and economic fiction. It does not and cannot have a heart, a soul, or a conscience. It has no value system, no moral code.

All of the creature-like traits we would like to associate with a company and its identity come from the relative handful of people who own and operate it. Their collective value system, their culture, and their motivations make the corporation whatever we experience.

It makes less sense to talk in terms of greedy corporations, and more sense to talk about greedy corporate executives. But if we don't get beyond generalities like honesty, openness, fairness, social responsibility, and sustainability, we won't accomplish very much. I believe we need a concrete agenda—a set of specific reforms that people can see, touch, and verify.

LET'S ADOPT NEW RULES

Based on three decades of experience in studying, working with, and consulting to corporations of many kinds, I've evolved a radical but readily do-able solution for eliminating insider corruption and many of the corporate crimes it makes inevitable. This solution goes to a key leverage point for inducing change: the *corporate charter*. Every registered corporation has one, and the executives who run the corporation must, by law, follow its provisions.

My proposed solution to the current corporate problem calls for a new, "standard model" corporate charter. Some executives will welcome and embrace this new model corporation concept as a way to do business. Many, however, will probably resist until they have it forced upon them by skillful social activists. The following outline of the new rules might provide activists with a tool for change.

The basic rules of the new model corporation's standard charter call for:

1. *A clamp on executive compensation*: the ratio of the highest salary received by anyone in the corporation to the lowest salary may not exceed 50:1.

2. *A clamp on incentive compensation*: bonuses, commissions, and other performance-based compensation paid to anyone in the corporation may not exceed 100 percent of that person's salary.

Severance packages paid to departing CEOs or other executives also may not exceed 100 percent of salary.

3. *A limit to non-monetary compensation*: the board of directors and corporate officers may not approve unusually luxurious or expensive perquisites for corporate officers as a means of evading the first two restrictions.

4. *A limit on the size of the board*: the total number of board members may not exceed 25.

5. *Term limits for board members*: each board member will serve a five-year term, with expirations of terms staggered evenly at one-year intervals. Board members may serve multiple non-consecutive terms.

6. *Board independence.* Neither the chief executive officer, nor any member of the executive staff, may occupy a board position. The title of Chairman of the Board and CEO will not exist.

7. *Employee representation on the board:* board membership must include at least one full-time, non-managerial, non-union employee of the company.

8. *Union representation on the board*: if more than 50% of the company's workers belong to a union, board membership must include at least one full-time, non-managerial union member.

9. *Restrictions on political spending*: no company funds may go to political contributions to any person or political party, or to any person or organization that would use them for that purpose.

10. *Commitment to Social & Ecological Responsibility*: the company will adopt a formal statement of values and principles, acknowledging its responsibility to the society and the Commons. It will report, on an annual basis, its performance compared to established benchmarks for social and ecological standards.

If the shareholders approved the new model charter, the board would have to fully implement the changes within three years.

In general, of course, we should prefer to see corporate leaders and key shareholders adopt this new model voluntarily. Quite a few already have some version of it, if not all of the parts. For those who don't want any part of it, we have two options: 1) government can impose it on them as a matter of law and regulation; or 2) activists can impose it on them by the typical campaign methods of visibility, public pressure, and shareholder petitions.

With regard to the federal option: over the past two decades, federal regulatory agencies have shown remarkably little interest in preventing already huge companies from merging or acquiring one another. This issue calls for much stronger leadership and advocacy from the presidential level.

LET'S REVITALIZE THE HEARTLAND: DE-URBANIZING AND MINIATURIZING COMMERCE

Now, *let's start thinking big* about the dimension of Commerce. Really big. I mean really, really big. I propose an economic power shift from mega-corporations to micro-enterprises that can get us back in tune with the Founders' purposes: a democratic, egalitarian society that works for everyone. If I haven't stretched your gray matter in some of the big ideas we've explored so far, this one will do it for sure.

We begin with a question: have we come to the end of an era in the economic history of our Republic? Have we reached a high water mark, or a turning point, in the dominance by the corporate elephants over the commercial ecosystem? Signals from the American culture and from government indicate a growing sense of injustice with the enormous concentration of wealth in mega-corporations, and the unprecedented concentration of that wealth in the hands of a remarkably few ultra-wealthy people.

Aside from this mind-boggling wealth imbalance, political commentators and social activists increasingly warn of threats to the democratic process by corporations that exert a powerful influence on governments at all levels. Thomas Jefferson still speaks to us from beyond the grave.

People who study generational values and politics tell us that the much-acclaimed *millennial* generation, and probably the "generation-Z" cohort born after it, increasingly reject the traditional hyper-competitive, winner-takes-it-all priorities of the business world. Less motivated by the fruits of conspicuous consumption and the pursuit of status, they question the materialistic agenda of the current ruling class. They declare a greater interest in experiences, quality of life, and shared social values than in things.

They also have serious questions and profound doubts about the quality of life they themselves might have as they live into their middle years and even bigger concerns about the world they might pass on to the next generation. Many of them see a big list of unfinished business challenges and many don't seem to feel that our current crop of leaders understands the urgency of dealing with them.

Many of them, and the political figures they respect, have called for the break-up of the mega-corporations and the use of tax policy to "make the rich pay their fair share." The choices we make for this issue may shape our culture, our economy, and our Republic for decades to come.

HOW WE GOT HERE

To figure out where we go from here, we need to understand how we got here, and what keeps us here. I need to borrow your gray matter for a quick historical lesson on the rise of the mega-corp.

To summarize where the following discussion will take us: To rethink the mega-corporation for the future, we'll have to rethink the *mega-city* at the same time.

Big corporations have co-evolved with big cities. One could never have developed without the other. Why? Because both depend on *population density*—the number of human beings per square mile, or kilometer. We'll see the profound impact of this simple truth later in our discussion.

To flash back just a bit: before the Industrial Revolution kicked into high gear in the 1800s, most "big" cities in Europe looked more like oversized villages. The population of London in 1800 stood at about a million. Paris, Rome, and the German cities had fewer than that. People from the economically depressed countryside flooded into the cities looking for jobs, but when the people outnumbered the jobs, the migration inevitably slowed down.

Then came the fabled steam engine, which supplied energy to run machines on a big scale. And that led to the invention of the *factory*, a concept so revolutionary that it changed all developing societies around the world.

A shoe factory, for example, could turn out 100 times as many pairs of shoes per day as a small shop of shoemakers could. "Productivity" became the new watchword for the owners of growing businesses. How many units can we produce per worker? How much revenue can we get per hour of labor?

Many workers in England reacted with alarm at the prospect that factories would put them out of jobs and somehow tank the economy. In 1811, the infamous Luddite uprisings, led by a weaver named Ned Ludd, saw textile workers attacking mills and smashing mechanized looms. The British government outlawed their activities and hanged a few dozen of them, but life went on.

Paradoxically, for every job the mega-factory eliminated, it created lots more of them due to *economies of scale*, as historians put it.

Here again we see an example of a *combination of trends* that changed things in a big way. The building of the railroads in the early 1800s made it possible to move raw materials to the factories in London quickly and cheaply, and to ship out finished products to all corners of the country. The coal used to power the machinery also became cheap and abundant, as mine owners in Wales and the north of England could ship it cheaply to the factories. At the same time, cheap cotton from America made fashionable clothes available to the growing middle class. The newly emerging banking industry supplied funds for the owners to build bigger and more productive factories. And the revolutionary steamship radically cut the time and cost of trans-Atlantic shipping.

The mega-factory needed a mega-workforce. Poor living conditions in the countryside, plus the promise of good wages in the city, caused a huge migration into town. As the corporations grew, the city grew, and vice versa.

But the revolution didn't bring the economic utopia that many observers predicted. Mobs of hopeful workers soon outnumbered the available jobs. The government of London knew almost nothing about urban planning (the city didn't have a sewer system until 1866). By mid-century, London had become the overcrowded, foul-smelling, soot-covered, disease-ridden crime scene Charles Dickens wrote about in his novels. By 1900, its population had passed the 6 million mark.

Thus began the long—and still ongoing—tectonic shift from cottage industry to mega-industry; from micro-business to mega-business; and from village to metropolis.

The Industrial Revolution reached the shores of America, inevitably, around the early 1800s. Using machine designs pirated from England's best mills, entrepreneurs began building a native textile industry. Other primary industries soon followed.

The American shift happened more slowly and a bit less painfully, partly because the vast supply of fertile farmland supported a rural economy and the development of livable small towns, so the mass migration to the cities became less acute. During the 1800s and into the 1900s, however, immigration from Europe grew the population significantly, with the inevitable growth and hyper-crowding of cities like New York, Boston, and Chicago.

The urban-corporate love affair became self-reinforcing for very simple reasons. First, obviously, capitalists hoping to launch a new business wanted to locate where they could find lots of cheap labor, existing infrastructure, and banks willing to lend them money. And workers, especially immigrants, knew they had a better chance of finding jobs in big urban centers where companies had their factories.

Concentration became the key principle of capitalism. Some cities even became monopolies in their own way. Detroit, Michigan, for example, became the center of the automobile industry, as Ford, General Motors, and Chrysler settled there. Chicago became the center of the meat-packing industry. New York attracted the giant banks, stock exchanges, and financial firms. The oil industry became concentrated in Texas cities like Dallas and Houston. By 1910, Hollywood had become the center of gravity of the film-making industry.

For a century and a half, corporations dominated America's urban landscape. While the farming sector stumbled along and small towns enjoyed a modest prosperity, the corporate giants made the rules. And the main rule decreed that wages should stay as low as possible. Company owners reminded workers that they could always find others willing to work for their wages, or less.

Owners of textile mills in New England, for example, periodically tested the labor market by cutting the wages of their existing workers—typically young women who had migrated from the countryside—and then measuring the number who quit. If very few of them quit, or if they could find replacements at the same lower wages, they concluded that they'd had the wage scale set too high.

Attempts to organize the workers brought quick and brutal retaliation by hired thugs, and often by the local police. Indeed, the legendary Pinkerton Detective Agency got its start when the biggest railroad companies hired Allan

Pinkerton to bring in agents armed with clubs to beat up the striking workers.

Not until 1935, when President Franklin D. Roosevelt signed the landmark Wagner Act, did the government guarantee the rights of workers to organize and bargain for wages and conditions of work. Acute labor shortages during the Second World War, followed by a booming post-war economy and the legal protection of collective bargaining, changed the balance of power between companies and their workers.

By mid-century, the worst excesses of predatory capitalism had mostly given way to a more polite form of economic etiquette, but the big corporations still held most of the chips.

Outright political bribery had mostly gone underground, or had become respectable—now known as lobbying. The American Chamber of Commerce got started in 1912. President William Howard Taft promoted it as a mechanism to counter the rising influence of the labor movement. It now has over 300,000 member firms. Almost all major US cities have a local CoC, and the organization has over 100 "Amcham" affiliates around the world.

Traditionally considered a right-wing organization, the Chamber usually supports candidates run by the Republican party. It spends about $70–100 million on lobbying and advertising in a typical year, more than any other lobbying organization.

Tellingly, the Chamber's 98-year-old headquarters sits on the corner of Lafayette Square in Washington, DC, facing the White House.

CAN THE PENDULUM SWING THE OTHER WAY?

Now, let's indulge in a utopian fantasy—*the re-emergence of the vibrant small-town community*. Let's visualize a new success model that might work in the modern age, taking advantage of new technologies to make new things possible.

A New Kind of Community: How It Could Work

Let's visit Newtown, in the state of Somewhere, USA and ask the people there how it grew from either a ghost town or a green-field development, into a thriving, self-sustaining community. The typical story, admittedly imaginary so far, goes as follows.

1. The US government has created a number of "enterprise zones"—tracts of federal land set aside for economic development, with the goal of allowing small business enterprises to create the conditions necessary for communities to form or revitalize. Newtown will become a special place, with a special model, and a special way of growing up. Federal rules, oversight, and guidance will shape the way Newtown develops.

2. First, the government grants a charter to a nonprofit development agency or consortium, which will go out of business once the town becomes self-sustaining. The governing body will operate somewhat like a homeowners association in a planned community. The appointed leaders, and later their elected successors, will require special training. We don't want clueless hayseed mayors or ignorant bumpkins running the town council. This model requires experienced, level headed leadership.

3. The consortium will have custody of all of the land at first, and will map it into functional zones. These will include a *public zone* that will form the center of a classical small-town structure, with a town square, town hall, parks, public services, and small main-street businesses; a *neighborhood zone* with parcels that provide reasonable living space; and a *commercial zone*, which will extend outward to the countryside and provide space for a "best known for" industry or commercial operation that will fuel its micro-economy. The extended zone might include

land designated for farming and food production if the charter calls for that kind of operation.

4. The consortium will advertise and promote the Newtown development, and will invite prospective citizens to apply for a share of the development. Individuals or families—but not corporations—will buy into the development for a standard, modest, one-time membership fee. Their membership fee entitles them to a parcel of land in the residential zone, which they can develop in accordance with prescribed standards for economical construction and appearance. Each owner becomes a voting member of the consortium.

5. The principles of the charter will make it unfeasible or unprofitable for wealthy invaders to move in and gentrify the place. No absentee owners, no mansions, no ghettos, no rich or poor sides of town, and no skyrocketing real estate prices. When a person or family decides to move away, the consortium will buy back their parcel at a pre-determined price. The consortium will resell the property at a standard price, choosing the next owner by lottery if a number of people want to move there. In choosing new residents, the governing body would maintain a balance of ages, with enough children and young adults to ensure that the community didn't evolve into a retirement community.

6. The consortium will divide the commercial sector, the farmland, or both, into individual units, which business operators can lease for their use. All business owners will have to reside in the community. The charter will specify acceptable types of businesses, appropriate to the "personality" of the community, e.g. vegetable farming, wine production, craft factories, tourism, publishing, online services, or operating a data center for outside firms. Depending on variations in local policies, the community might or might not

allow commercial franchise businesses such as mini-markets, fast food restaurants, or chain coffee shops.

7. Each business will pay an annual fee for use of the property, including utilities and other public services supplied by the consortium. As with residential parcels, business owners who leave will sell their leases back to the consortium at established prices, and they may take with them any capital equipment they've added to the operation.

8. Annual fees from residential parcels and commercial operations—typically much lower than the equivalent urban property taxes—will go into the common fund. The consortium will use the funds to cover the costs of utilities, fire protection, law enforcement, basic medical services, education, and general maintenance, plus investment costs to build out the community.

9. Federal funds will augment expenses for up to three years, as the community becomes self-sustaining. At some point, the start-up consortium will transition to collective ownership by the members of the community.

The Advantages of a New Kind of Community

We'll leave the further details of this social and economic model as an exercise for the student, and just note some of the big advantages the inhabitants of these micro-communities can enjoy by capitalizing on modern technologies.

▸ For one thing, they'll benefit from a typically lower cost of living than their big-urban counterparts will experience. The costs of everyday purchased items will probably run about 30 percent less.

▸ A volatile real estate market, in the conventional sense of the term, won't exist. The closely controlled housing stock won't fall prey to external market forces. Prospective residents won't see prices spiraling out of reach as the community becomes popular; nor will they reap big profits when they cash in their properties if they leave. Sorry, no flipping.

▸ With a small-ish population, demographically balanced, the community can provide basic public services rather cheaply. For example, a small clinic and pharmacy, managed by a nurse practitioner, a registered pharmacist, and a few support staff, can provide the most-needed medical treatments.

▸ The developing technology of *telemedicine* will allow specialists at other locations to consult with local practitioners by video and guide them through special procedures. Circuit-riding medical specialists from urban centers can visit periodically for special procedures. And med-evac services can fly emergency patients to urban centers for treatment.

▸ A small police department, co-located with the fire department, with a one-cell jail—sort of like the ones in the old Western movies—can manage public safety. The community can outsource the handling of more serious offenses to larger cities nearby, and can export dangerous offenders to those jurisdictions.

▸ With gasoline powered cars banned from the community, a combination of locally generated electricity, low-energy housing designs, and an all-electric automobile fleet will minimize energy costs and hold down the carbon footprint at the same time. A community solar farm, plus individual solar units on all dwellings, will power the homes and businesses, and feed excess power into a central grid. During the times when cars sit idle—most of the time—energy will flow back and forth, with the car batteries serving as a collective energy storage system, and returning energy during hours of darkness or low sunlight.

▸ A completely wireless satellite Internet system will eliminate the need for commercial cable systems or fiber optic lines. All homes and businesses will have free access to the community network. Everyone can stream entertainment and do business online— banking, paying fees and taxes, and ordering deliveries.

▸ The educational system can look a bit like the old-time schoolhouse, with a combination of classroom activity, online access to educational resources, and at-home access to lessons. A small number of teachers can manage the educational experience of a large number of students without having to endure crowded classrooms. The school will offer special evening courses for adults, based on popular preferences.

▸ As online learning technology continues its rapid growth, colleges and universities, as well as educational suppliers like The Great Courses company, can offer a comprehensive, flexible, and customized distance education experience. As online testing and credentialing come of age, people in Newtown might well get college degrees online, or through an adjunct program of occasional visits to campuses in larger cities, or even extension programs offered locally by those institutions.

▸ The local library can double as a modern museum, with interactive displays and virtual reality technology helping to extend the learning experience to the outside world.

▸ The local theater can double as a playhouse for live performances, and the locals can pay a small fee to watch movies and educational lectures from a huge community collection of archived resources.

▸ The consortium can own and operate its own bank. Without the need to generate a profit, the bank can make loans to members of the community, and to businesses, at below-market rates.

The list of other advantages and benefits of this new micro-model for planned communities stretches out the door.

Does This Look Familiar?

Maybe this new micro-model doesn't seem so utopian after all. Most of the features would seem like fairly obvious choices to planners and developers today. And history does provide us with some precedents for this model.

The ancient monasteries of Europe, for example, operated more or less like the planned communities discussed here. Communes and co-ops have grown and developed over many years.

The well-known *kibbutz*, for example, widely operated in Israel, includes many of the same features. With a population of just over 8 million, the country hosts over 270 *kibbutzim*, or variations known as *moshavim*. On a proportional basis, the US, with about 325 million people, might host as many as 10,000 micro-communities.

Most of the collective communities we've studied throughout history have one thing in common: they sprouted and grew more or less organically—or haphazardly, we might say—with the collective activities and preferences of their inhabitants shaping their development. In the modern age, with sophisticated planning approaches and enabling technologies that never existed before—including a deeper understanding of the dynamics of human communities—we have the possibility of bringing the small-town culture back to life.

We won't reverse the long-wave pattern of urban-corporate co-evolution, but we can create attractive alternatives for those who still crave the elegance and simplicity of doing things on the small scale.

LET'S DE-MONOPOLIZE, BUT NOT DESTROY THE CORPORATION

Now we can return to the question that has tinted our thought process throughout this chapter: What to do with the corporate giants?

Shall we break up the mega-firms? Shall we forbid them to merge with one another? Or, should we leave them alone, knowing they'll always do the right thing for the benefit of the Republic and its people?

To answer those questions thoughtfully and fairly, we need to agree on the meaning of "too big." How shall we measure size? By annual sales? Total profits? Market share? Stock market capitalization? Number of employees? At what point, if any, in the growth of a corporation shall we declare that it has become too big?

Let's consider the strengths and limitations of MegaCorp, the giant Wall Street operation. Defenders of corporate bigness usually offer several key benefits of super size:

▸ MegaCorp can amass huge resources—factories, facilities, and specialized equipment—to do big things, by borrowing vast sums of money, selling its shares, or issuing bonds. MicroCorp has to make do with owner-supplied capital.

▸ MegaCorp can deliver large-scale customer experiences that MicroCorp cannot, such as airline flights, shopping malls, theme parks, and ocean cruises.

▸ MegaCorp can create lots of jobs, and can sometimes invigorate declining communities.

▸ MegaCorp can foot the bill for research and development of new products and services, which MicroCorp can't afford.

▸ MegaCorp can reach mass audiences through advertising and promotion, so as to build awareness, acceptance, and demand for new kinds of products and services. MicroCorp can benefit from that.

Critics of MegaCorp, however, point to some undesirable side effects:

▸ After MegaCorp grows beyond a certain threshold point, further increases in its size don't bring further benefits to its customers, its suppliers, or its community. Economies of scale always level off somewhere.

▸ Mergers between MegaCorps, according to a number of B-school studies, typically don't benefit the shareholders of the merging companies very much. Fully half of big mergers don't increase shareholder value for either side, although they typically enrich the big shareholders and executive insiders.

▸ If MegaCorp becomes the dominant, or only, major employer in a city, it can foster an economic dependence that can turn into hardship later if its fortunes decline or it decides to pull out and move its operations elsewhere.

▸ MegaCorp's entry into a mid-sized urban market can put lots of small business operators out of business, by absorbing a large share of the demand. A modern neo-capitalist view advocates that the small fry should have a fair shot at success, and that *pragmatic inefficiency* can benefit the overall society more than the localized efficiency that only provides MegaCorp's customers with lower prices.

▸ Reducing the number of key suppliers in any marketplace, either by mergers or competitive extermination, can sometimes limit the diversity of products, services, and choices available to customers. People can become so conditioned by brand names, advertising slogans, and media stereotypes that their critical thinking processes get rusty.

▸ In politics, money talks. MegaCorp and others of its size can use pressure, promises, and payments to legislators to buy laws that favor their interests. MicroCorp has no such advantage; few people ever get elected to public office on the small business vote.

As noted previously, we need to take advantage of the corporation's special capability for concentrating resources, while limiting the runaway tendency to concentrate wealth in the hands of a few insiders.

The current national mood seems to favor significant curbs on corporate growth and power. However, only a few ill-informed zealots could argue for getting rid of corporations and capitalism completely, even if we could. But if we seek a middle road, it might involve changes in the rules for corporate behavior like these:

▸ *Breaking up the oversized conglomerates.* Congressional hearings, followed up by targeted legislative actions, would result in the break-up of oversized companies that dominate their industries. The law would require them to divest themselves of major subsidiaries, and in some cases split the firms into separate businesses, with each one focused on a different segment of the market.

▸ *De-merging and preventing mergers by oversized firms.* Congress will pass a law that prohibits mergers and acquisitions by the largest firms in any market sector where 5 firms or fewer control 80 percent of the market share. No one firm, in any case, could control more than 40 percent. The law would roll back recent mergers that have violated the restrictions.

▸ *Separating shareholder interests.* A break-up or divestiture would create several completely independent business entities, with separate shares, executive teams, and boards of directors. No individual could serve as an officer or board member of more than one of the new businesses. None of the executives or major shareholders of the original firm could own shares of more than one of the new businesses.

▸ *Exclusion of foreign mega-firms with monopolistic influence.* Oversized foreign firms wouldn't have permission to operate in the US, unless they spun off American counterparts that met the competitive standards.

‣ *Targeted regulation of Internet and social media companies.* Continuing irresponsible conduct by the leaders of Internet, telecom, and social media monopolies justifies their break-up, and the imposition of stringent controls on internal practices that safeguard privacy and prevent foreign agents from interfering in internal American affairs.

The most extreme paleo-capitalists might rage against this "anti-business" doctrine, and declare it Un-American, socialistic, and morally flawed. But considering the kinds of extreme measures some of the current actors on the political stage have proposed, the standards just specified seem relatively moderate and fair.

Corporations, of even moderate size, will always have some advantages over the mom and pop species, but these kinds of measures can go a long way toward minimizing the David and Goliath imbalance.

THE FIX-IT LIST: COMMERCE

So, how can we improve this component of our Republic— Commerce? Let's start with these actions.

1. *Let's Limit Cancerous Corporate Growth.* Congress will modernize corporate anti-monopoly laws as described in this chapter, restricting mergers and acquisitions based on limits to collective market share within commercial sectors, and requiring the break-up or divestiture of oversized firms as defined above.

2. *Let's Track Corporate Respect for the Commons.* Congress will pass a law that requires every registered corporation to publish, annually, a report on its "social performance," which will include ecological measures like carbon production, consumption of energy, water, and land use; executive salary ratios and employee benefits as discussed above; workforce mix—headcount and compensation

by gender and ethnic category; and employee perceptions of the quality of work life.

3. *Let's Streamline Federal Regulations.* Congress will pass a law that creates a Federal Regulatory Commission, as described in this chapter, and moves control of all federal regulations to that organization. The law will reaffirm the responsibility of the various Cabinet agencies to enforce regulations in their areas of responsibility. The kick-off for that change will involve a year-long review of all federal regulations, with the goal of eliminating unnecessary ones, rewriting the conflicting or confusing ones, and streamlining the process for creating new ones.

4. *Let's Promote Small Community Development.* Congress will pass a law that creates a Community Development Administration, with the responsibility for developing local enterprise communities, as described in this chapter. Congress will allocate funds on an ongoing basis to support at least 1,000 communities per year.

Chapter 9.
Let's Rethink Public Services: the Rights and Entitlements of the People

*"A candle loses none of its light
when it lights another candle."*
—Rumi (13th Century Arab Philosopher)

S hould the government provide health care for everyone? What about a free college education? Should we force businesses to pay a minimum wage? Should people living in ghettos get money, without having to work for it? Do we want cradle-to-grave services like the Scandinavian countries have, and the high taxes that come with them?

Over the many years of the Republic's life, Americans and their governments have opted for a bewildering inventory of public services. In addition to military protection, homeland security, law enforcement, and public works, we've created a national postal system, an interstate highway system, a national park system, state colleges and universities, and a vast program of scientific and medical research.

When Americans consider the matter of public services— assistance of various kinds provided to citizens by government agencies—the national conversation tends to polarize around two contrasting views. One holds that government should provide a wide range of services for its citizens, especially those facing financial hardship and the effects of disadvantaged environments. The other holds that government should stay out of people's lives and let them fend for themselves.

On one side of the debate, the eternal bogeyman quickly raises its head: "Socialism." The "nanny state." "Do we want the government to do everything for us?" And, "Who pays for all those services?"

Some advocates and activists, who self-identify as Libertarians or quasi-Libertarians, go so far as to insist that we limit government activities to a very narrow range of crucially important requirements, such as defense, criminal justice, and the control of national borders.

On the other side, the traditional American values of compassion and concern for those who, for various reasons cannot help themselves, weigh heavily on the conversation. Many social activists argue that unbridled capitalism has given us an economic landscape where a very few people and corporations own and control an enormous percentage of the wealth in today's society.

We've never taken a real systems view of this vast range of public services provided by governments all across the Republic.

In many ways, the treatment of public services in the national conversation reflects the polarization we've considered a number of times in this writing—that of the Shared-Fate Society vs. the Zero-Sum Society. Maybe we can set aside our convictions for a short while, put our opinions on probation, and take a fresh look at this critical component of our Republic.

THE PUBLIC-PRIVATE TRADE-OFF

Socialism comes in degrees. So does capitalism. Both have their fans and their detractors. Both have their ideological high priests, who preach their respective gospels.

SOCIALISM: FEAR AND LOATHING IN THE HEARTLAND

Ever since the start of the Cold War in the 1950s, US presidents and their political operatives have relentlessly conditioned Americans to react to the term socialism with fear and alarm. It has become an emotionally loaded word, with evil connotations.

But not all post-war cultures give the same emotional loading to the term that Americans have. The term socialism fits very comfortably into the national conversations in countries like the UK, Germany, France, Italy, Spain, the Netherlands, and the Scandinavians. In those societies, it typically refers to *collective economic solutions*, implemented by governments on behalf of the people, and not any Marxian notion that the government owns and controls everything.

SOCIALISM, AMERICAN STYLE

In the US, we've had a quasi-socialistic society and economy for a long time—a sort of "socialism lite."

Consider: in the US, we have a free public education system that offers a basic educational experience to everyone who wants it. We have a national retirement system, which we call *Social Security*. We have national, state, and local systems that provide *social services* and financial assistance for people in dire need. We have a government administered system for healthcare insurance, available to Social Security recipients, called Medicare. We have a vast collection of hospitals and other treatment centers for eligible veterans of the armed forces.

On the other hand, we don't have government owned corporations running our primary industries—no national airline, no national oil company, no national steel company, no national bank. We have a government-operated postal system like many European countries do, but no government operated telecom system as many of them do.

LET'S DUMP THE DICHOTOMY

When we argue about socialism vs. capitalism, we fall into a false dichotomy. We don't have to take either choice to extremes. It makes less sense to think of them in *either-or* terms—we must choose one or the other—and more in *both-and* terms—we use a combination of both practices.

In today's kindler, gentler America, we might think of them more constructively as *neo-capitalism* and *neo-socialism*, as we've discussed before.

CAN EVERYONE HAVE A PIECE OF THE AMERICAN PIE?

Let's begin our investigation of Public Services with a grand question: in a society and an economy like America, can every single person—ideally, at least—have a decent material standard of living? Or, will some people lose out because we just don't have enough to go around? Can we all make it somehow, or do we have to face a harsh Darwinian truth?

At a basic minimum, such a standard of living would include:

‣ Physical security and personal safety.

‣ A place to live, however modest.

‣ Food, clothing, and other necessities of ordinary living.

‣ Access to a basic level of medical care.

‣ Protection from catastrophic loss—injury, a health disaster, or economic ruin.

‣ The basic necessities of life in old age or infirmity.

‣ A basic sense of dignity.

MYTHS AND TRUTHS ABOUT PUBLIC ASSISTANCE, A.K.A. "WELFARE"

Opposition to government programs intended to help people at the bottom of the economic scale tend to rest on three particular claims, which hold that:

1. We just can't afford to support all the people who don't make enough money to have a basic standard of living, as described above.

2. Many—perhaps most—of the "people on welfare," who receive regular financial assistance from government entitlement programs, could actually work but don't want to. They lack the character, conscience, and work ethic to pull themselves up by their bootstraps, so they content themselves with a survival level of existence that demands little of them.

3. Giving handouts to people, especially over long periods of time, tends to destroy their motivation to help themselves, and renders them chronically dependent on the society.

Proponents of all three claims tend to make their case with broad generalizations, sometimes punctuated by some newsworthy case example. Advocates of a much more extensive public service operation tend to invoke what they consider the higher American values of cooperation and compassion.

But seldom does the debate about Public Services benefit from a grounding in basic facts and evidence, so I propose to illuminate the discussion by paying attention to some mega-facts—a few useful and important truths.

LET'S FACE THE FACTS AND FIGMENTS

▸ *We have a service economy and a service culture.* Services of all kinds now form the basic structure of the American economy. Government-provided services, as well as commercially marketed and provided services, make up the lion's share of the economy.

Back in 1800, 90 percent of Americans lived on farms. By 1900, that number had dwindled to 40 percent. Today, about 2-3 percent of the US population manages to produce enough food for themselves, all the rest of us, and a fair part of the rest of the world.

Meanwhile, manufacturing jobs in the US declined from a peak of 31 percent in 1900, to the present level of about 9 percent.

That means that the third component, the service sector, has grown to nearly 80 percent of the economy. One service industry alone—healthcare—contributes 17 percent of our GDP.

▸ *Workers' wages, for the most part, haven't kept up with economic growth.* While paychecks today show much higher dollar amounts than they did in the 1960s, when economists adjust the payroll figures to remove the effects of inflation they find that *real wages*—based on actual buying power—have barely changed over the past 30-40 years. Studies suggest that, if the federal minimum wage—most recently standing at $7.25 per hour—had risen in step with corporate profits, it would stand somewhere near $25 per hour today.

As we'll see, *that one fact alone almost tells the whole story of the "welfare problem."*

▸ Phenomenal gains in corporate efficiency and productivity over the years have led to steadily rising profits. One would expect that workers would have shared in that prosperity, and that an hour of work today would buy a lot more at the supermarket than it did decades ago. Instead, most of the gains have gone to the shareholders and the executives who run the companies, in the form of higher stock prices.

▸ Not surprisingly, corporate managers have taken advantage of every conceivable method for holding down wages. Outsourcing production processes to countries with very low labor costs; the declining bargaining power of trade unions; and the replacement or down-skilling of many jobs by information technology have all combined to keep real wages low. Growing service industries like fast food, retailing, and much of healthcare have produced lots of new jobs, but mostly low-paying ones.

All of these factors have combined to cause the much-discussed massive, long-term economic tilt, or wealth imbalance, as profits have flowed disproportionately to the owners—the shareholders, the highly paid executives who run them, and the Wall Street investors who trade them—and far less to the workers themselves.

THE WELFARE STATE?

Public assistance programs, a.k.a "welfare" payments, have grown steadily over the years, both in the numbers of people receiving support and the amounts paid. During the Depression years, government organizations like the Works Progress Administration created jobs for millions of Americans who suffered from the Great Crash of 1929. Public assistance became a big national priority with the creation of the Social Security Administration, under President Franklin Roosevelt, in 1935.

Federal and state programs now include cash income supplements, food assistance (mostly food stamps), healthcare services, unemployment insurance, housing subsidies, education subsidies, and childcare subsidies.

Recent figures show total state and federal welfare spending (not including Social Security), at about *$850 billion per year*, more than we spend for Defense. The Veterans Administration, which provides medical services for America's 21 million vets, as well as the well-known GI Bill program for educational support, spent a further $200 billion in the most recent year.

DO WE SPEND TOO MUCH ON ENTITLEMENTS?

The federal government's annual budget of $4 trillion amounts to about 20 percent of GDP, and entitlement spending takes about one-fourth of that amount, or 5 percent of GDP.

Consider the food stamp program—known as the Supplemental Nutritional Assistance Program, or SNAP, operated by the Department of Agriculture. Let's check to see how many people actually receive food stamps, compared to the number we might expect based on typical unemployment rates.

Using an unemployment rate of about 5 percent of the civilian workforce, which currently numbers about 158 million people, we might expect to see about 7 to 8 million people receiving food stamps, assuming every unemployed person signed up for those benefits.

Recent figures indicate, however, that *42 million people receive food stamps under the SNAP program—six times as many as the total unemployed population.* Food stamp expenditures average about $4 per day per person— probably enough to survive in most cases, but not enough to dine out often.

What happened? Why, or how, has the "welfare population" exploded? Could we have that many people ripping off the system? We'll always have some level of cheating and fraud, but—42 million people?

A B.F.O.—BLINDING FLASH OF THE OBVIOUS

The basic evidence we've just reviewed points to one big, stark conclusion:

> *Four decades of steadily rising living costs, combined with stagnant real wages, have pushed more than 10 percent of America's people into insolvency and dependence on government financial support.*

> *During the same period, corporate stock prices—a barometer of accumulating profits—have risen at an average rate of 11 percent, compounded, year on year.*

Lately, economists tend to refer to these below-the-line people as the *working poor.* They have jobs but don't earn enough money to fully support themselves or their families independently. Costs of living vary widely across the country, but federal planners estimate that about 13 percent of full-time workers fall below the poverty line, as they call it.

Back to the original question: can we afford to support so many people? Can we sustain such large entitlement programs and such large numbers of dependent people?

Actually, we can and obviously we have. We don't have mass starvation in America, and however loudly some political figures might complain, we've managed to provide for the vast majority of people in need. We certainly don't have a perfect system, an efficient one, or even a fair one, but the one we have has basically worked.

Going forward, however, we'll need different economic solutions—a new logic of public services and public assistance, as we'll see shortly. As we'll see in the following discussion, we can't sustain the rising costs of government programs with our antiquated system of income taxes. Chapter 7 (Revenue) outlined a revolutionary new concept of public finance, which promises to generate significantly more revenue that the current obsolete system of income taxes.

HOW DID WE GET HERE?

A quick historical flashback can help us understand how we got to this lop-sided economic structure and the possible path back to a more sane and equitable arrangement. We've always had poor people and wealthy people, but the presence of this "nouveau poor," or working poor population, presents a new and disconcerting reality. How did we get such an extreme economic tilt that so many activists and political leaders complain about?

The basic engine of the US economy has changed—slowly, but fundamentally—over many years. In the early days of the Republic, the family farm formed the core of our economic system. Typically, a working person who became ill, disabled, or elderly could expect the family to take care of them. People seldom became separated or disconnected from the micro-economy of the family. The family, the village, and the church formed the social and economic support system.

The onrushing Industrial Revolution caused those local economic systems to disintegrate. The mass migration of workers to urban areas under the magnetic attraction of better-paying factory jobs, coupled with the use of fertilizers and factory farms, spelled the decline and near-extinction of rural patterns of society.

And finally, the Roaring Twenties saw the rise of massive corporations dominating the primary sectors like car manufacturing, mining, iron and steel production, railroads, and construction. This relentless deconstruction of the family, the village, and the local community has created a population of free agent workers who must survive without the support of family systems.

Corporations, meanwhile, gradually gained the upper hand in the long-running economic struggle with organized labor. The Great Depression, a series of recessions, and the steady shrinkage of the manufacturing sector weakened the once-powerful trade unions like the United Auto Workers, Teamsters, and the super-unions like the AFL-CIO.

During the 1980s, corporate executives discovered off-shoring—hiring firms in China and other developing countries to manufacture their products at a fraction of the wages they formerly paid to American workers.

During that same period, the 1980s through to about 2000, a major revolution in ocean shipping took place. The monster container ship, capable of carrying 20,000 standard cargo modules, drove shipping costs so low that shipping a TV set from Shanghai to Los Angeles cost less than shipping it there from New York.

The combination of cheap labor and cheap shipping, plus government protections and subsidies, drove the Chinese economic miracle, which ran for several decades with compounded growth in exports. The American economy kept growing, with occasional recessions, but most of the higher-paying manufacturing jobs had disappeared, never to return.

Many of today's young people—possibly most of them—doubt they'll ever attain the good life. A deep disappointment in American institutions, governments, corporations, and political leaders seems to pervade the Millennial culture, and much of the younger cohort that comes after it.

Many of them reject the traditional materialistic values of the Wall Street culture, and yearn for jobs with meaningful opportunities to contribute and make a difference. Many of them now question the investment value of a college education, pointing to the slow growth in the high-paying, high-tech jobs and the progressive automation of mid-skill occupations. And the get-rich fantasy of the Internet start-up business has also begun to fade.

The economic tilt—the wealth imbalance, or the one-percent vs. 99-percent, whatever we prefer to call it—will almost certainly not correct itself. Without some major change in national policy and tax laws, we'll probably have more dependent citizens, not fewer.

We can't create high-paying jobs out of thin air. Much as we'd like for everyone to have a satisfying job with good pay and great benefits, the structure of jobs and wages depends on the self-interested actions of business leaders, and not on government decrees or the demands of well-intended activists. We can expect them to continue automating, down-skilling, and eliminating the most costly jobs in their operations. Indeed, they bear a legal obligation to their shareholders to do just that.

The competition for the best jobs, like a game of musical chairs, will inevitably leave a substantial number of people with sub-survival incomes. Working two jobs might become a new norm—if the jobs exist.

Our current system of government revenue, based primarily on the mechanism of the income tax imposed on individuals as well as corporations, cannot generate enough funds to pay for a huge military establishment; increased entitlements like universal healthcare; neglected infrastructure management; and other critical needs.

The US government has drifted deeply into red ink, with a debt load of over $20 trillion—the highest in our history—currently equal to more than a year's GDP. In recent years the federal budget deficit—the red ink, or the amount by which the government overspends its tax income—has soared to $1 trillion per year, or one-fourth of its annual budget. We can't sustain those levels of debt and red ink for long.

Any attempt to raise tax rates high enough to pay off the debt and operate in the black would certainly encounter overwhelming political opposition. Consequently, one presidential administration after another has continued to kick the can down the road, running deficits and taking on debt that we cannot sustain over the long run. We need a new concept for national revenue, as explained in Chapter 7.

LIVING BELOW THE LINE

To understand the case for offering more services and not fewer, let's consider the day-to-day experience of living below the line.

- ▸ Every dollar, every dime, and every penny counts. You have no discretionary income. You probably know exactly how much money you have in your pocket or your purse, down to the penny.

- ▸ Housing, if you have it, eats up most of your money. Whereas a well-off person might spend 20-25 percent of his or her income for rent or a mortgage, for you it probably looks like 50 percent or more.

- ▸ Kids cost a lot of money. Even without the inevitable medical expenses, you have to feed them, get clothes for them as they keep growing, and provide lunches and miscellaneous expenses for school or pre-school. You have to budget carefully for toys and recreational options that well-off people don't even think about.

- Health insurance? *Fuggeddaboutit.* You just have to hope you and your family members don't get severely ill or injured. You can't afford to miss a day of work because of illness or injury.

- Transportation eats up money. If you can even afford to have a car, the payments, insurance, and upkeep devour another big chunk of your monthly revenue. If you use public transportation, the $20-30 a week still has to come from somewhere.

- Depending on your job, you might have to buy presentable clothes or meet certain dress or grooming requirements.

- Addictions can cost you dearly. Struggles with alcohol, tobacco, or food addictions not only undermine your physical and mental health, they can take a big bite out of your income. According to recent figures, a pack-a-day smoker typically spends at least $50-60 per week for cigarettes—$3,000 in a year and easily 10 percent of gross income for below-the-line workers.

- It takes more than willpower and determination to climb out of the hole. When the daily logistics of living on the cheap, taking care of kids—especially for a single parent—and working a full-time job use up your time and energy, it takes a heroic effort to mobilize yourself to take courses or look for better jobs. Living below the line can wear you down over time.

Indisputably, education makes a difference. People with more education—and those who've made good use of their opportunities—tend to get better jobs, move further up the ladder, and get paid better.

And yet, the cherished American mantra, "To get ahead, improve your head" doesn't seem quite so inspiring these days. The customary narrative that says today's workers don't have the skills and knowledge needed to compete for high-level jobs, and that we just have to educate them so they can move up to those jobs, seems less and less credible.

We'll simply have to face the fact that not all Americans will have high-paying jobs. As in the game of musical chairs, somebody ends up without a place to sit.

A NEW REALITY NEEDS NEW SOLUTIONS

Warning: here comes a conceptual curveball. In the following analysis, I propose a set of solutions for the public services challenge that may seem unfamiliar, counterintuitive, and maybe even outrageous. In the spirit of open-minded investigation of all parts of the Republic, I ask only that you suspend judgment until you see how this reconceptualization might work.

I propose a strategy, a course of action, and a set of programs which we can't feasibly implement as things now stand, but which can become very practical if we make big changes in our economic structure. Let's consider a very new philosophy for managing public services and see how we might make it work.

We'll do more, not less. We'll expand, centralize, and streamline the range of services available to all citizens, especially those in need, and radically rearrange the cost structure to pay for them.

Some people might react with consternation to the idea of having government, especially at the national level, increase its involvement in services across the board. But let's consider one key role for government agencies that doesn't typically get much recognition. Government can function in the role of *catalyst* and *coordinator*, bringing together people, organizations, and resources that might not otherwise combine their efforts. *Centralization* and *standardization* of many services and government functions can sometimes reduce complexity, save costs, and contribute to fairness and equity in the way things get done.

LET'S TAP THE AWESOME POWER OF VOLUNTEERISM

When we think about Public Services—social welfare, healthcare, education, housing, and mental health, for example—we might automatically imagine government or quasi-government agencies applying taxpayer resources to meet various needs. But when it comes to human energy, talent, and motivation, we've mostly overlooked an enormous resource that costs very little: *volunteer labor.*

So, before we delve into some new ideas about public services, let's get an idea of the size, scope, and potential of volunteerism as a phenomenal resource.

We have a huge number of organizations in the US that devote their energies to volunteer service. The big name service clubs such as Lions Clubs, Rotary, Kiwanis, Masons, Optimists, Soroptimists, Shriners, Boy Scouts and Girl Scouts, and Boys and Girls Clubs of America come to mind immediately.

Lions Clubs—the largest of them—has nearly 50,000 clubs worldwide, with 1.4 million members. Over 1 million of them operate in the US. Many other lesser-known groups organize volunteer efforts in their own specialized ways. Thousands of church groups, mosques, and synagogues have outreach programs that help people in need in a variety of ways.

Unfortunately, almost all major volunteer service clubs have seen their memberships declining steadily over the past 30 years. Some organizations have lost almost 50 percent of their members during that time. Very few have managed to grow in recent years. Almost all of them have found it difficult to attract younger members to replace those who retire and pass away.

As far back as the early 1900s, the sense of duty to "give something back" played a part in the lives of successful people. For urban men, the life pattern of arriving at financial security by late middle-age, either by means of a profession or a successful business, brought with it the prospect of joining the local service club and doing something to help others. Partly a ritual of prosperous manhood, perhaps, it nevertheless did make volunteerism a norm all across small-town and big-city America.

With the deconstruction of American society caused by television, and later the Internet and social media, as well as the fading of the small-town culture, the service club model went into a long-term decline. Most American kids no longer consider it cool to become a Boy Scout or Girl Scout. Military service lost its appeal for a generation made cynical by the disastrous war in Vietnam. And in recent years, a foreboding sense of economic uncertainty seems to weigh heavily on the minds of those under the age of 30.

If we could find a way to reawaken and revitalize that community service ethic, all across America, how might it benefit the society and the Republic?

As we ponder that question, let's first consider the enormous potential supply of volunteer labor at our disposal. How many people, out of a population of 325 million, could conceivably contribute their time, energy, and talents?

If we exempt the very young and very old, and those disqualified by circumstances—disabled, serving in the military overseas, homeless or otherwise economically disadvantaged, for example—we'll still have a huge number of prospective volunteers. In the age range of 18 to 65, for example, we'll have over *200 million* able-bodied candidates.

Imagine each of those 200 million people spending just *one hour per month* of their time and energy to help others and serve the community. Two-hundred million hours of useful work per month; *2.4 billion hours in a year's time.* The possible impacts of that much energy, well applied, boggle the mind.

But, of course, with volunteerism on a long-term downward slope, we couldn't possibly get more than a small fraction of them doing productive things. Or, could we?

Let's put on our thinking caps again and think big. Really big. Like, really, really big. We can do two big—and fairly simple —things we've never done before in America, mostly because we didn't have the "technology" to pull it off. Both of them have become very do-able in our electronic society.

First, we'll require, by national legislation, that every able-bodied citizen between the ages of 18 and 65—with certain justified exemptions—must contribute a specified number of hours per year in service to the society. Considering that the typical citizen spends about 6 hours every day gazing at TV and cell-phone screens and quite a few other hours doing mostly nothing, an obligation such as an hour per month, or 12 hours per year, seems like a very small sacrifice for any one person, in comparison to the enormous collective impact.

The fatal flaw in this concept, one would think, lies in the daunting logistical problem. If thousands of volunteer service clubs and other community organizations can't keep the energy level up, what hope do we have of mobilizing so many people? They can do a lot of good within the limitations they experience, but how could we expect them to expand their operations to a macro-scale?

Now we come to the second big-think component of the solution: *an online platform*—a kind of Uber for voluntarism —that will organize and mobilize their efforts on a grand scale. Just as the Uber ride-hailing platform scaled up taxi service to a national and international level, we can scale up volunteer services in very much the same way.

A national coordinating body—let's call it the National Volunteer Service—operated by or sponsored by the federal government, can operate an online platform that connects volunteer service providers with those in need.

Briefly described: each citizen volunteer will have an online identity, specifying the geographical area he or she can cover and the particular kinds of services he or she prefers to offer.

Designated coordinating agencies—lots of them—can organize volunteers at local levels and deploy them to provide services to people and groups who request it.

A convalescent hospital, for example, can ask for volunteers to help with the needs of the patients and families. Schools could ask for tutors, and possibly substitute teachers. Agencies serving the homeless can ask for logistical help in operating shelters and other service facilities. Prisons can request help with tutoring and other educational services. Disabled persons can get free rides to and from treatment locations. The platform will serve a vast range of needs.

The platform will match requests for services with the interest profiles of the volunteers, and will offer various missions, or service tasks, which they can bid for. The system will track the number of service hours contributed against the required minimum, and provide verification that each person has hit his or her target. Of course, people who want to offer more than the required minimum can continue to participate as much as they like.

If we can scale volunteer services up to this kind of level, and coordinate them carefully with the overall portfolio of general public services, we can radically improve the quality of life for almost everyone in America at a very low cost. And we can—if we have the will and the imagination.

LET'S BUILD A REAL NATIONAL HEALTHCARE SYSTEM

As of this writing, the US stands alone as the only major country without a national healthcare system.

Healthcare reform has become a controversial topic in the US and a thorough analysis of the issues and options goes beyond the scope of these discussions. However, a few key considerations do deserve attention.

› The healthcare industry accounts for about 17 percent of the US economy—the largest ratio of any major country. Most of the industry operates on an insurance-based economic model: the customer or employer pays for insurance and the insurance company pays the providers—sometimes.

▸ We have the most expensive system, on average, of all modern countries. Reform advocates claim that, by adopting the Medicare pricing and payment model under a single-payer system (the US government), we could reduce overall costs by as much as 15 percent. That would save up to $500 billion per year with a simultaneous improvement in levels of service.

▸ Although American medical technology ranks near the top by world standards, reform advocates rate our delivery system as one of the most wasteful. They describe it as an industry with a very inefficient administrative structure; afflicted with archaic billing and collection practices; virtually no price transparency or oversight; restricted consumer choices and buying power; susceptibility to fraud and mismanagement; price-rigging by hospitals and various other providers; self-dealing and conflicts of interest by some physicians; unnecessary treatments and overuse of questionable procedures; and denial of insurance coverage for high-risk customers.

▸ In a recent survey, American physicians identified as much as 20 percent of medical care overall as unnecessary and unwarranted—an estimated $200 billion annual outlay. The American Medical Association has reported that 100,000 people die in a typical year from errors in treatments and medications.

In my view, no one in a country as wealthy as the US should have to live without basic medical services.

For a long time, various special interest groups have reflexively opposed the idea of a national system for America, calling on scare stories about socialized medicine and supposedly bureaucratic healthcare systems in nations like England, Ireland, Scotland, Canada, Australia, New Zealand, and the Scandinavian countries. They cite episodes—many of them false or exaggerated—about impersonal care, long waits for service, and inferior medical technology and procedures.

While citizens of those countries often grumble about their national systems, most of them recoil in horror at the idea of abolishing them and adopting anything like the chaotic American free market system. They see the prospect of any citizen of limited means having to go without basic medical care and hoping to avoid getting sick as wholly unacceptable, inhumane, and politically backward.

Recent to this writing, interest in a new approach to healthcare in the US has grown significantly. The frightening outbreak of the infamous coronavirus, or COVID-19 as medical people refer to it, has highlighted the vulnerability of people who don't have health coverage. The nationwide lockdown, with businesses of all kinds forced to close during the pandemic, threw millions of people out of their jobs. Those who had health coverage through their employer plans suddenly lost it and faced the prospect of paying for their own care, at potentially catastrophic costs.

That one factor alone has dramatized the inhumanity of forcing people to gamble with their health.

Nothing stands in the way of the US moving to a national system of universal healthcare for all citizens—except the insurance industry and a population of enablers embedded in Congress. The Medicare system, currently only available to people who draw Social Security pensions, would work just as well as a system of service for all Americans. Extending it to the whole society would involve careful planning, persistence, and political will, but we can certainly do it.

LET'S RETHINK THE ARCHITECTURE OF PUBLIC ASSISTANCE

Remodeling the Public Assistance component of our Republic calls for two kinds of improvements: 1) reducing the cost of living for those below the subsistence line; and 2) increasing the disposable income available for those in need, by means of cash, credits, and exemptions. Let's put on our thinking caps and see what we can do.

FIRST, THE SERMON . . .

Right-wing demagogues who try to pander to the fear, intolerance, and bigotry of white-majority voters routinely trot out an old standard zero-sum lament: "We spend far too much money on 'entitlements'—a.k.a. 'welfare programs'— and most of it goes to waste."

The unspoken subtext hints that most of "those people on welfare" could shift for themselves if they really wanted to. According to this narrative, government handout programs condition people for dependence and indolence. We can't afford to keep supporting these people. We have to get them off the dole and make them work, the recitation goes.

That political narrative calls for 1) cutting taxes for corporations and their wealthy owners—which supposedly creates more jobs for those who have to work for their money; 2) keeping interest rates low so corporations can borrow cheaply to fuel their growth; and 3) cutting wasteful payments to the undeserving poor, to keep the federal deficit and the debt to a minimum and have a healthy economy.

Let's invoke some good old-fashioned common sense here— and some perspective.

The American economy dwarfs all others on the planet. Our closest competitor, China, generates a nominal gross domestic product—GDP—less than 60 percent of ours. Our standard of living—GDP per person—currently runs *six times higher* than China's, at $60,000. We spend more on military operations than all of the other modern countries *combined*. The IRS reports that more than $400 billion in potential income tax revenue goes uncollected in a typical year. And yet we can't afford to care for those who can't help themselves? What a disgraceful ideology.

No one in America should ever have to die alone and abandoned, on the street or in a filthy hovel.

A nation that can spend *100 million dollars* for one fighter airplane—an F-35—or *12 billion dollars* for a single ship—the latest nuclear-powered carrier—can surely afford to care for those who can't help themselves.

No child should ever suffer from malnutrition in a country that throws away 100,000 tons of food every day.

Mohandas Gandhi reportedly told the peoples of India and Great Britain,

> *"A nation's greatness is measured by how it treats its weakest members."*

We don't have a resource problem. *We have a system problem.* But before we can tackle the system problem we have to deal with an *attitude problem.*

Many years ago I heard a comment about the "welfare system" that has stuck in my mind. As I interviewed a line supervisor in a county social services department as part of my consulting activities with that organization, she made a very simple but compelling observation.

> *"The poor and the bewildered are always going to be there,"* she said. *"And we're always going to bear the cost of their existence. We can pay at the 'front end,' by helping them survive and by trying to help their kids escape from the failure cycle."*

> *"Or,"* she continued, *"we can pay more at the other end of the pipeline, with the costs of drug abuse, homelessness, unwanted pregnancies, crime, domestic violence, and more prisons."*

> *"The people who make the rules don't seem to understand that we're always making that trade-off. If we don't want to do it for compassionate reasons, at least we should do it to save money."*

SOME OF THE OPTIONS

We have several options for reducing the cost of living for below-the-line people and we can implement most of those fairly easily. In all cases, the National Citizen Identification System (NCIDS) will play a key role in managing eligibility, and in preventing or policing fraud. Let's consider these possibilities:

> ▸ *Let's exempt people in need from having to pay for various ordinary services.* For example, a National ID Card, presented at the point of sale in supermarkets and other retail stores, would exempt them from sales taxes —a small but significant benefit.
>
> We could easily extend these exemptions to other services, such as gas and electricity charges, telephone service, and online access. This would go a long way toward making the whole American society digitally enabled, as countries like Estonia, South Korea, and Singapore have become.
>
> ▸ Let's make public transport of all kinds—buses, trains, and metro transit systems—*free for all Americans.* Nearly all transit systems in the US already depend on government subsidies; very few of them cover more than half of their operating costs out of the fare box.
>
> A free public transport system would also contribute to the national ecological agenda for reducing urban congestion by reducing the number of cars on the streets as well as reducing emissions.
>
> With a bit of creative thinking, we can make our public transport systems much more useful and appealing to those who wouldn't normally use them. Many elderly people, those with physical limitations, and even many able-bodied people, find the bus and metro systems inconvenient because they have to walk long distances from their homes and workplaces to get to the bus stops or metro stations. Many able-bodied people insist

on the convenience of having their own wheels, even though they may sit idle most of the time.

How can we make public transport so easy and attractive that more people will adopt it as a regular choice? One answer: we borrow a low-tech concept used in developing countries—the "wandering taxi." Known in Istanbul as the *dolmuş* ("dole-mush"), for example, it has free-lance vehicles zipping around the main streets, picking up and discharging passengers *ad lib.* You don't get your own exclusive taxi—you share it with others riding at the moment. You pay the driver a small amount for your part of the ride and the distance. When I first visited Istanbul many years ago I found out where the Chevrolet Impalas from the 1950s had gone to retire—there, and to Cuba.

How could we use the *dolmuş* concept for city neighborhoods in the US? Imagine a fleet of small, low-cost vehicles—electrically powered, of course—zipping around between neighborhoods and the bus lines and metro stations, picking up riders and depositing them, *all for free.* Now we add a booking and scheduling scheme similar to the Uber or Lyft model and we have a system that could attract lots more people than we currently get. The National Volunteer Service, explained above, would provide plenty of drivers.

▸ *Let's have public schools provide day care for children.* The public school system provides one huge benefit that we seldom acknowledge specifically in the national conversation: it offers a safe place to put children while their parents work their jobs. Think for a moment about the impact and limitations imposed on a typical married couple who have children between the ages of 5 and 15. Without some kind of child care, only one of them could earn an income. Single parents would find it nearly impossible to work.

The obvious solution: extend the opening hours of elementary and middle schools and have qualified child care providers to look after the kids before and after school hours. Children of needy families can receive breakfast in the morning and healthy snacks after the school day ends. Again, we have a simple but effective example of shifting costs to solve social problems.

▸ By the way, as we improve the services that schools provide, *let's just make school lunches free for all the kids.* The cost per student won't break the bank. Of course, kids from well-off families can bring their own specially prepared food if they prefer. A number of studies suggest that children from disadvantaged communities tend to miss school much more often than those from more affluent communities, and that the possibility of a free breakfast can motivate some mothers to send their kids to school.

▸ *Let's fund more development programs for vulnerable and at-risk kids in low-income environments.* The Head Start program offers a good example of a program that child development experts believe has produced significant benefits. Created in 1965 by the Johnson administration, it serves pre-school children both in home and pre-school environments, with the goal of enhancing their cognitive skills and narrowing the developmental gap in later years. The Early Head Start program extends the reach of these services to 1 million kids at the "pre-K" level.

People who operate these programs refer to the "cycle of failure," or the "failure pipeline." They recognize that young children, conditioned by their experience in disadvantaged environments, face significant risks with regard to developing cognitive skills, social skills, educational readiness, and self-management skills. These deficits can increase the probability that they may veer into anti-social or self-defeating behaviors as they move into their roles in society. At the extreme, developmental specialists refer to highly dysfunctional home environments as *criminalizing* in their effect.

▸ *Let's Make Sense of the Minimum Wage.* Many social activists have called for increasing the federal minimum wage. Opponents argue that it drives up the prices of goods and services for the very people who can't afford them and that it can eliminate jobs if employers cut their staffs to keep labor costs down. Set too high, it puts people out of work; set too low, it has no impact. As of this writing, the federal minimum wage stands at $7.25 per hour and hasn't changed in quite a few years.

The main difficulty in setting a national standard for the minimum wage involves finding a single "right" level in the face of wide variations in the cost of living for various areas of the country. An hourly wage that can buy a lot of food in a small town or rural area, for example, doesn't go far in a big city like New York, Dallas, or San Francisco.

It would make some sense, however, to set a single national figure as a reference point and then index state and local minimum values to it according to local economic conditions.

I tend to agree with critics who say a minimum wage works rather like a blunt instrument, and can cause as many difficulties as it relieves. Still, I believe it deserves a place in our solution set, albeit perhaps a limited one.

WHAT ABOUT WASTE AND FRAUD?

Opponents of social service programs often cite the supposed high number of incidents of waste and fraud, presumably to argue that we don't get our money's worth from cost-of-living subsidies or income subsidies. Do those problems and costs loom so large as to contradict the basic purpose of public service programs or do they basically come with the territory?

News flash: virtually every government program that involves spending money—defense, education, law enforcement, Medicare, highway construction, name them all—can involve waste and fraud, and sometimes even corruption. Public assistance, like all the others, will have its own share.

To put the issue into perspective: Department of Defense investigators simply couldn't account for at least 15 percent of the $61 billion in reconstruction funds allocated to Iraq after the 2003 US invasion. They wrote off another 15 percent—over $8 billion—as simply "wasted."

The DoD's Inspector General flagged at least $15 billion of reconstruction funds for Afghanistan as waste, fraud, and mismanagement. Over a span of 17 years, the DoD poured nearly *2 trillion dollars* into one of the world's most impoverished areas, with amazingly little economic impact.

So, when we realize that federal assistance programs for Americans can also involve waste, fraud, and corruption, let's think about it realistically. We should never tolerate it, but at the same time we have to consider each investment on its overall merits.

LET'S RETHINK HOMELESSNESS

Social activists, urban planners, and elected political leaders have struggled with the problem of homelessness in America for a long time, and solutions still seem few and far between. Let's review the mega-facts and look for some kind of defining logic that might shed light on possible solutions.[17]

  ‣ Current estimates put the homeless population in the US at about 500,000 people, or about 0.15 percent of the total population.

  ‣ Homelessness occurs very unevenly across the US. A few states account for most of it. California, the state with the largest overall population, also has the largest number of homeless people, over 150,000 of them. New York City comes a close second, followed by San Francisco, Seattle, and the state of Hawaii.

- Current estimates indicate that about 25 percent of homeless people live in cars, which seems to suggest that a large percentage of them may have fallen on hard times, and might still have prospects for regaining financial stability.

- Two-thirds of homeless people live alone; the other one-third belong to couples or family groups.

- Seven percent of homeless people have served in the military.

- At least 20 percent of homeless people have severe impairments, such as disabilities or psychiatric disorders, and cannot adequately manage their lives.

These variations suggest a view of homelessness as a mixture of several distinct problems, none just one. We need targeted solutions, not a one-size-fits-all approach.

Looking more closely at the homeless population, we can readily identify four categories of people, facing four distinctly different kinds of problems that have put them in their respective situations. We have:

1. *The Able-Bodied Nomad.* Probably a small percentage—maybe 5 percent or so—mostly young males, and basically able to cope with life's challenges, they've chosen to detach from society and live the life of a vagabond. They typically can take care of themselves and don't really need public assistance.

2. *The Employable Unemployed.* This person or family has the capacity to earn a living but may have encountered some financial catastrophe or reversal of fortune that has landed them in a hole. Losing a job, a health disaster, a home foreclosure, or a bankruptcy, for example, can put a person or a family behind the eight ball for a period of time. Some experts estimate that this category might include as many as 30 percent of homeless people. Financial experts suggest that as many as half of all personal bankruptcies

result from catastrophic illness or injury, imposing astronomical medical costs.

3. *The Walking Wounded.* This category includes people with impaired coping skills who have lost their connections to families, communities, or other support systems. Most of them manage to survive in the homeless environment but can't seem to get past the subsistence level in meeting their basic needs. Some have developmental disabilities such as retardation or other cognitive impairment. Some have untreated psychological or psychiatric disorders. Many suffer from malnutrition or infectious diseases.

Some experts estimate that as many as 40 percent or more of chronically homeless people may suffer from severe autism, a disorder that prevents them from establishing and maintaining empathic relationships with others who might have the means to help them. And, of course, people in the Walking Wounded category may have fallen into addictions to drugs or alcohol, which compound their difficulties.

4. *The Severely Disabled.* This category includes the extremes of the kinds of disorders that afflict the Walking Wounded and also includes severe psychiatric disorders; extremes of substance addiction; serious illnesses; and severe physical disabilities such as blindness or inability to walk.

Obviously, people facing these various kinds of difficulties need solutions that match their individual conditions. One drawback in most of the current homeless mitigation programs lies in their tendency to treat homeless people as a single undifferentiated population. Police officers tend to focus on dealing with the public nuisance effect of homeless camps, rather than on the needs of the people themselves.

Business operators and affluent citizens understandably feel entitled to go about their comfortable lives without having to interact with homeless people, and often insist that the government or police departments don't get rid of them somehow.

Tourists who visit cities with major homelessness problems find the unpleasant truths hitting them directly in the face. One can walk or drive along a busy street in downtown Los Angeles and see dozens of tents, lean-tos, and other makeshift shelters in a homeless camp that has grown up on some very expensive public property. San Francisco has lost its charming image as a center of offbeat culture. At every turn the visitor encounters squalor; derelict human beings surviving in filthy conditions; open drug abuse and dealing; panhandling; prostitution; and threats to personal safety.

Public libraries in urban centers commonly get overrun by homeless people who use the toilets, wash themselves or their clothes in restrooms, and even park themselves in reading areas to escape bad weather. Library managers often don't know what to do and often fear the possibility of violence if they try to herd them out. They see the numbers of legitimate visitors decline as patrons find interacting with dirty, smelly, and ill-behaved derelicts very unpleasant.

LET'S CREATE MEGA-SOLUTIONS AND SERVICES

The National Citizen Identification System (NCIDS), with its universal Citizen ID Card, can play an important part in tailoring solutions to the various challenges of homelessness.

With the NCIDS in operation, everyone would get an ID card, including homeless people. Social workers, police officers, and others who come into contact with homeless people on a regular basis can help to ensure that each one has an ID card or gets one, and in the process can evaluate that person's needs in terms of the four categories just described. Once a person's national record shows a marker for the kind of assistance deemed appropriate to his or her circumstances, that person could access a specific set of services.

Housing Comes First, Obviously

While people in the Employable Unemployed category presumably want to escape from the homeless experience, get good jobs, and become self-supporting again, things get a lot more difficult with the third and fourth categories, the Walking Wounded and the Severely Disabled. Social services professionals often find them difficult to connect with, socially and therapeutically.

Despite their obvious desperate circumstances, many of them refuse help. They might go to a shelter or eat at a soup kitchen, but constantly gravitate back to the street. Those with psychological problems, addictions, or social adjustment disorders might not have the capacity to think clearly about their problems or communicate in a lucid way with social service professionals.

Legislators and law enforcement leaders have long grappled with the issues associated with forcibly removing people from the street, breaking up homeless camps, and moving homeless people out of city centers and business districts, often with unsatisfying results.

We'll need to create an infrastructure for housing and caring for the Walking Wounded and the Severely Disabled, for several reasons: 1) civil liberties considerations make it unfeasible to just round them up and institutionalize them, except in extreme cases of severe disability; 2) affluent people and commercial businesses feel quite justified in demanding that city governments prevent homeless people from harassing them, their customers, and their employees; and 3) building dormitory style ultra-low-cost housing probably offers the most cost-effective option.

This line of action calls for governments in areas of critical homelessness to construct housing facilities similar to military barracks, where each person can have a bunk, a foot locker, and a larger storage locker for his or her belongings. To get a place, each person would have to give up the shopping cart full of accumulated possessions and reduce his or her holdings to the level typical of a soldier in a training camp. They can live comfortably, if not luxuriously. Those with at least the primary skills of self-management would have assigned duties like cleaning and minor maintenance.

Some of these residential centers will require new construction in carefully chosen areas, and some can make use of abandoned or repurposed facilities such as old schools, decommissioned military bases, vacant hotels, and unused industrial buildings.

People experiencing temporary homelessness could make use of the facilities until they got back on their feet. Those with coping issues would stay longer, possibly transitioning out with the help of social service professionals. Those with severe disorders, who cannot cope with the environment or who might risk harming themselves or others, might progress to higher-level mental health facilities.

Let's Activate the Volunteer Force

The National Volunteer Service described earlier in this chapter would play a key role in dealing with the homelessness issue. Well-trained and motivated volunteers can step in to provide assistance of various kinds, relieving police officers of non-enforcement activities that divert their attention from their primary mission. Volunteers can also support and amplify the contributions of social service and mental health professionals.

LET'S RETHINK THE EDUCATION SYSTEM: SCHOOLS AND COLLEGES

As our methods for educating Americans evolve over the next decade or two—whether voluntarily and deliberately, or under coercion by the forces of economic and social change—we'll witness a collision between tradition and reality. Big *demographic changes* and new *technological options* will take center stage as this evolution unfolds.

Primary and secondary education (K-12) will have to change because 1) we'll have fewer kids to educate; 2) our long-cherished methods of teaching have become painfully obsolete; and 3) digital technology will offer possibilities too good to pass up.

Post-secondary education (we need a better term for it) will have to change because 1) we'll have fewer high school graduates to educate; 2) the costs of getting a college degree have gone crazy; 3) prospective students now question the value of the investment, in time as well as money; 4) the massive shift of educational content to digital media will drive down costs and make much cheaper options available; and 5) we have too many colleges, especially small private ones, for the level of demand we'll see, and many of them won't survive.

We might summarize this coming state of turbulence as a *crisis in relevance*. Like it or not, we'll see the whole concept of a college education, and indeed the whole span of the educational system from prekindergarten through college, and even post-graduate stages, come into question.

Educators have long preached about lifelong learning, and rightly so. Now, we might actually have to take that notion seriously and evolve a more logical set of options that can make sense to a new generation of educable citizens. We'll need to start thinking of the whole collection of resources and options as a system with an overall defining logic.

LET'S RETHINK THE PUBLIC SCHOOL EXPERIENCE

Americans seem to enjoy complaining about the school system but don't seem to agree about its actual flaws. Nor do we agree on very many approaches to fixing it. We seem to enjoy the complaining more than the fixing.

Advocates of school reform have mostly tribalized around three competing ideologies, all of which seem rather questionable.

- Some activists campaign for *privatizing* public schools —a view I tended to favor many years ago but have set aside. They argue that competitive pressures in the marketplace will quickly force the people who operate our schools to lift their game. But so far, our experiences with privatization ventures like commercially operated prisons and private convalescent care services haven't provided much encouragement for that brute-force-economics approach.

- A second contingent, mostly including teachers' unions, predictably presses for radically *increased funding* of schools, higher salaries for teachers, and smaller class sizes. While they certainly have the right to advocate their own interests, considerable analysis shows that the academic performance of kids, pretty much at all levels, correlates more closely to the financial status and educational levels of their parents, more than to the characteristics of the school or the activities of the teachers.

- The third advocacy group recommends *shaking up the educational experience* and revising the traditional classroom process. We've had no shortage of novel educational solutions. The "new math" of the 1960s; phonics training; charter and magnet schools; academic performance standards; terminal behavioral objectives; and whiz-bang programs like George Bush's "No Child Left Behind" and Barack Obama's "Race to the Top"; and, of course, computerizing the school room, have all had their moments on the stage. Yet, we seem to have the sense that we haven't really solved a problem that we haven't really defined.

So, I suppose, I get a turn at bat, hoping to reframe the issue and perhaps identify some alternative solution concepts.

Let's Face the Facts and Figments: Public Schools

Following our preferred investigative strategy, let's begin with a quick review of the mega-facts, and get a better grasp of the presenting issues.[18]

▸ The National Center for Educational Statistics counts well over 100,000 schools in the US, as of this writing. Two-thirds of those serve elementary grades; one-fourth provide secondary education; and the rest operate as combined schools.

▸ The average school serves about 500 students; that number varies between rural and urban communities.

▸ NCES reports a total student population of about 56 million, which amounts to almost 20 percent of the total population. About 10 percent of kids attend private schools and 90 percent go to public schools. About 2 percent of kids attend prekindergarten ("pre-K") schools and about 7 percent go to kindergarten. That puts almost 10 percent of the kids in pre-schools of various kinds.

▸ NCES puts the count of PK-12 (pre-K through 12th grade) teachers at 3.7 million. About 14 percent of those teach in private schools.

▸ *The student population continues to decline* as birth rates drop. By comparison: in 1970, people in California under the age of 18 accounted for 30 percent of the population. As of this writing, the figure looks more like 20 percent. The teachers' demands for smaller class sizes might come naturally.

▸ Recent government figures put the total spending on public schools—with both federal and state funds—at about $680 billion, which works out to about $13,000 per student per year, and about 3 percent of GDP.

Why Twelve Years?

If we want to shake up our thinking about public education, let's ask ourselves some unusual and provocative questions. The science philosopher Alfred North Whitehead advised, "It takes a very unusual mind to make an analysis of the obvious." So, let's question an obvious, long-accepted fact of life. Why does the public school experience, pretty much all over America, and in many other societies, span exactly 12 years? Why not 10? Why not longer?

Did a group of educational masterminds sit down, decades ago, analyze the lives and learning needs of citizens, and decide that exactly 12 years of education would impart the right amount of life knowledge?

Nowadays the most plausible explanation holds that we've organized the school calendar, and our daily schedules, to keep the kids in a safe place while their working parents can earn their livings. That free service has enormous economic value, especially for working couples.

And, by the way, why do we break the school year in the middle, for a two-month summer vacation?

The answer comes from our history. In an earlier time, when most Americans lived and worked on farms, they had to have summer days free to harvest the crops, take care of maintenance, and get ready for winter. Given that most employed Americans now tend to take their vacation time during the summer months, it would make sense for the kids to have that time free as well.

Those simple economic factors might serve as the best reason for continuing the policy. Maybe we had best accept that practical reality and build out the rest of the educational system around it.

Let's Dump the "Container Theory" of Education

We've tinkered with the schools for so many decades that we've just about run out of tricks. None of the revolutionary concepts we've tried seem to have revolutionized anything. We still have essentially the same warehouse style of schooling we had in the 1950s. With the exception of a few innovative and imaginative departures—mostly special concepts developed by a few creative educators—the little red schoolhouse just sort of got bigger. Sure, the school library has computers, and a lot of kids carry around laptops and tablet computers. But, innovation? Not really.

Maybe the time has come for a true revolution in educational thinking. Instead of changing the schools, we need to change the teachers, and change what—and how—they teach.

According to the late professor of education Neil Postman, who taught for many years at New York University, the American philosophy and doctrine for public education has always rested upon what he called the "container theory" of education. In his landmark book, *Teaching as a Subversive Activity*,[19] Postman argues that educators have long viewed students as miniature receptacles, waiting to receive measured amounts of standardized information, or "content."

By specifying the content of each "subject," like English, math, or history, a.k.a. the "curriculum," administrators can operate the school much like a little factory. Each subject-matter class operates like a production line, filling each of the little containers with a particular product.

The container model of education has lots of appeal for those who operate the schools:

> ▸ It makes things *normative* and *measurable*. A group of curriculum experts decides what content goes with each subject—dates, kings, and wars; the anatomical parts of a frog; or the way to diagram an English sentence. Textbook publishers do the heavy lifting and school boards approve their books. Then the school and the teachers can all prove they delivered the content.

> ▸ It makes testing simple, easy, and—presumably— objective. Numerical test scores can eliminate the need

for subjective judgments about a student's knowledge and competence.

▸ It places responsibility for the quality of the educational outcome on the students and not on the educators or the schools. The variations in test scores show, presumably, that some students have more talent or they work harder than the others.

▸ It tends to compensate mediocre teachers at almost the same level as the outstanding ones. In most unionized school systems, seniority—the number of years spent working in the job—determines compensation and special privileges. Rarely does student performance have a big effect on compensation.

Professor Postman has pointed to several important limitations of the traditional method of schooling:

▸ It limits the speed and amount of learning to the rate at which the book and the teacher spoon in the content. No student can learn more, or faster, than the speed of the production line.

▸ It offers few opportunities or motivations for students to develop non-rote skills such as critical thinking, abstract conceptual thinking, hypothesis testing, and creative idea production, or an appreciation for subjective experiences such as art, literature, and music. For example, Postman and other progressive educators make the case for helping kids learn how to *think historically*, rather than just handing them a batch of decontextualized historical "facts." Content rules.

▸ It places very little emphasis on *divergent thinking skills*, such as option thinking, creative idea production, and consideration of alternative solutions. It devotes most of the time and attention to *convergent thinking processes*, which call for finding the "correct answer."

For over a century, the design of both the high school and college experience has relied on the concept of *contact hours*

—the number of fifty-minute sessions that students spend interacting with teachers. School administrators measure teaching time in so-called *Carnegie Units*, or standardized numbers of hours of "seat time." Indeed, the late Peter F. Drucker, a college professor and renowned consultant to corporate leaders, wisecracked,

> *"The people who run schools are convinced that the ass is the principal organ of learning."*

Do We Have the Right Teachers?

Further, Postman makes the provocative claim that a large majority of teachers—in America, at least—have gravitated toward public education jobs because the highly controlled, normative environment fits with their temperament and their *preferred cognitive orientations*. Cognitive assessment profiles suggest that school teachers, on average, tend to have preferred thinking patterns oriented to right-brained and concrete processes, commonly known as *sensory* and *intuitive* modes. They show somewhat less preference for detailed logical analysis or highly abstract conceptualization.

That general characteristic of the teacher population, Postman argued, could partially explain why not enough high school students aim for STEM careers—science, technology, engineering, and mathematics. Teachers who don't have an appetite for STEM thinking or STEM studies may not feel inclined to model or promote them to students. More and more educators now recommend giving every junior high school student a chance to learn software coding, not only for its potential career value, but to give kids a strong sense of logical, systematic thinking.

More broadly, Postman claimed that the cookie cutter experience of the public school tended to send students into the adult world, lacking two key capabilities: 1) critical thinking; and 2) curiosity, especially about science and its implications for American life.

This second deficit, some climate activists claim, might help to explain why many Americans don't engage with the critical urgency of climate change. They survived science class, but most of them never learned to *think scientifically*. Surveys and studies repeatedly find that many Americans like to believe myths and magic, and may reject scientific evidence that disturbs their sense of comfort and conviction.

For example, a recent study published by *Science* magazine indicated that over half of adult Americans reject the basic scientific concept of evolution, in favor of some version of a divine creation story. Outright rejection of evolution correlates closely with educational level, religious affiliation, and political party affiliation.

According to the study, citizens of Iceland, Denmark, Sweden, France, and Japan affirmed the concept of evolution at or above the 80 percent level. US citizens ranked next to lowest, out of 32 modern countries, at 40 percent—just ahead of Turks, who affirmed it at the 25 percent level.

Interestingly, 79 percent of the people of Kazakhstan, a strongly Muslim developing country, accept the theory. Over 80 percent of high school students in Indonesia accept it. Citizens of India, mostly Hindus, accept it nearly 70 percent. Among Israelis, 60 percent accept it; 40 percent reject it.

According to another poll, 26 percent of Americans say they believe in astrology; 23 percent believe in witches; 32 percent believe in UFOs; 40 percent believe in Creationism; and 42 percent believe in ghosts. Some six percent of Americans don't believe that astronauts landed on the moon —they think the US government faked all six landings.[20]

Obviously, science class hasn't worked very well. Indeed, the American society generally remains in a pre-scientific phase, notwithstanding the media attention to the marvels of science. Americans love the technological gadgets that scientists and engineers invent for them, but relatively few understand much about them except which buttons to click.

Let's Adopt the Inquiry Method

In Professor Postman's worldview, kids could learn much more, understand more, think more clearly, and become much more effective citizens, if we would shift the focus from *content* to *competence*. Instead of trying to teach kids *what* to think, he declared, we should focus on teaching them *how* to think. The content, in his view, simply provides the raw material for their thinking.

Postman argued, and again I agree, that young people need to learn two absolutely fundamental and crucial competencies to become effective adults: 1) the skill of *investigation, or inquiry*; and 2) the skill of *critical thinking*. All of the other primary skills of an educated high school graduate revolve around or connect to those two primary capabilities.

Postman took a rather aggressive stance toward teachers he viewed as prisoners of the spoonful-of-knowledge ideology, and who learn just enough of the content to stay ahead of a room full of sixteen-year-olds. With regard to the critical thinking skill especially, he quoted novelist Ernest Hemingway, who said,

> *"Every writer must have a good, built-in, shockproof bullshit detector."*

Critical thinking, in other words, enables one to see the primal truths of the culture. Postman rephrased Hemingway a bit and christened the critical thinking skill "crap detecting," arguing that part of the mission of teaching as a subversive activity included helping kids learn to use their crap detectors.

Postman named this new approach to education the *inquiry method*. The argument for this method holds that simply requiring kids to memorize static, factual information, regurgitate it on tests (and later forget it), does very little to promote comprehension, understanding, or the ability to extend one's knowledge by conceptualization and reflection.

The alternative approach presents a student, or a team of students working together, with a provocative question of some sort, having to do with a scientific principle, a piece of history, or a question about society, for example. They first need to find the information needed to solve it. Then they have to put the information together to create some kind of context for understanding and interpreting the presenting question. Finally, they need to put their conceptual abilities to work, to produce their result.

To state the case fairly, quite a few teachers—and schools— do use the inquiry method, or variations of it. Unfortunately, we have a long way to go before the methods get widely adopted in the public school sector. At most, we could hope to phase it in over time, perhaps over a decade or more, and hope that a new generation of progressive and talented teachers will take it up.

LET'S RETHINK THE COLLEGE DEGREE

As previously cited, a number of trends will come together to make life more challenging for almost all colleges and universities over the next decade or two, and especially the smaller ones. Now seems like a good time to begin rethinking our strategies and structures to capitalize on these trends rather than suffer from them.

Fewer Students Will Mean Fewer Dollars

The incoming student population will decline steadily for some time to come. If you'd like to shock yourself, refer to the "Coke bottle" graph of the US population pyramid at Figure 11-2 in Chapter 11 (Immigration). We'll look at some interesting population trends when we get there and see how they will shape our options for economic development.

Fewer students will obviously spell less revenue coming in from tuition and fees and less government funding.

Except for the ultra-wealthy big name Ivy League schools, competition for students has already forced most institutions to offer scholarships and reduced tuitions to stay competitive. On average, US colleges and universities collect less than 50 percent of the amounts they would otherwise get if they charged their "rack rates" for all students.

Institutions without significant endowment funds also face a disadvantage in competing with the large, well-endowed ones. The same holds true for those without significant government funding for research or grant projects.

Digital Media Will Make Cheaper Alternatives Possible

Recent to this writing, the American Association of Community Colleges reports the average yearly cost of tuition and fees for community college students in the US as $3,347, compared to an average cost of $9,139 at four-year institutions. The cost of tuition alone at a big name Ivy League university can run as high as $40,000 to $50,000.[21]

Student loans haven't necessarily made things better. As of this writing, about 44 million Americans collectively owe $1.56 trillion in student loans.

The case for a cheaper college education has become ever more acute as many people looking at their careers and futures want better options.

Meanwhile, course content has migrated steadily to digital media of all kinds. CDs, phone apps, podcasts, streaming audio and video lectures, and web-based resources all offer cheap and easy access to information that formerly resided only in the pages of expensive textbooks and lecturers' notes. Most institutions have had little choice but to put much of their content online. One day the fifty-dollar textbook might become an endangered species.

Conceptually, at least, a diligent and aspiring student could learn much of the subject matter for a particular course through cheap—often free—online sources. For the moment, the only real asset the college has to sell remains the credential—the degree.

Two Missing Parts of a New System Will Soon Appear

The do-it-yourself-online education experience might conceivably become the preferred model sometime in the future, but it currently suffers from one fatal flaw: *credibility*. How does such a self-educated person persuade a prospective employer that his or her qualifications match or exceed those of a competitor who holds a degree from a brand-name college or university? The accredited college degree has served for so long as the badge of achievement in various content areas that few people think about the basic question: what, exactly, does it prove?

Two big developments, technologically feasible and potentially attractive, can solve the credibility problem:

1. A *cheat-proof online testing system* that confirms mastery of any given academic subject. National corporations, such as Educational Testing Service or others, can operate walk-in retail locations with terminals connected to a central repository of standardized, accredited tests. Service staff would ensure that no one taking a test had access to any reference materials, or help from anyone else.

2. A *national credentialing agency* that would maintain a lifetime dossier for each enrolled individual, recording documented proof of knowledge, competence, and qualifications acquired by a variety of methods including online testing. With authorization from an individual registrant, prospective employers could access that person's qualification package and make decisions appropriately. This agency could award credentials at various levels, such as high school completion; a junior college level associate's degree; a four-year degree; master's and doctoral degrees; and various special qualifications such as medical specialties or trade skills.

Multiple Solutions Will Co-Exist

The standard four-year college degree has served as the gold standard in our society more than two centuries. Now we have to wonder whether it deserves to remain the only definition of a "real" higher education.

Consider, for example, that almost 70 percent of US high school students enroll in college, but a third of them drop out by the end of the first year. And most of the ones who graduate take more than four years to do it—typically six. Recent figures indicate that 36 percent of private-school students graduate in four years, and only 19 percent of those attending public institutions do so. A six-year graduation period has become the norm for educational policymakers.

At the community college level, only five percent complete an associate's degree in the customary two years.

Clearly, our system of higher education costs too much, takes too long and delivers too few graduates.

Let's Make Better Use of Micro-Credentials

Let's consider some possibilities for dicing up the educational experience into smaller products, and credentialing them individually:

▸ Giving the two-year degree a lot more respect could make the junior college experience more attractive to more people. Currently, the academic bigwigs seem to look upon the associate's credential as a "poor man's degree" and not a "real" college degree. Maybe we can have a two-year bachelor's degree and a four-year bachelor's degree.

▸ Every four-year college can grant two degrees—one at the two-year mark and one on completing the full four years. Currently, a person who drops out after one year has nothing to show for it, even if he or she passed the exams, met all the requirements, and earned high grades. Instead of the all-or-nothing approach that leaves people high and without the four-year credential, a respectable two-year degree could become an attractive choice for many people.

▸ Going further, every four-year college can grant a separate certificate for each year completed. A micro-credential proving even one year of successful college work could have real value in the job market. Junior colleges can use the same approach, offering a one-year credential and a two-year degree.

▸ The one-year option might also attract more people to the college experience later in life. They'd have the option of taking their education in one-year bites, with something to show for it after each year.

What About Brain Surgery?

Many educational experts remind us, and rightly so, that learning some kinds of subjects and skillsets calls for direct experience and personal interaction of some kind. Many specialties like surgery, music, graphic arts, welding, and acting require direct experience and skill building. Each institution has to develop its own processes for imparting those kinds of skills in an experiential learning environment.

HR departments might rejoice at the prospect of a central, searchable database of verified qualifications for job applicants. Instead of having to conduct their own background checks, verifying prior employment, or confirming the educational achievements, they could—with authorization from the candidate—access his or her complete history. That capability could cut recruiting costs significantly, and also reduce mistakes, fraud, and misrepresentation.

THE FIX-IT LIST: PUBLIC SERVICES

So, how can we improve this component of our Republic—Public Services? Let's start with these actions.

1. *Let's Centralize the Design and Individualize the Delivery of an integrated System of Public Services.* The combination of a National Citizen Identification System (NCIDS) and a revolutionary system of revenue that eliminates income taxes and replaces them with transaction taxes will enable the funding of a reinvented system of Public Services.

2. *Let's Mobilize Our Collective Talent.* Congress will pass a law creating a National Volunteer Service, with implementing statutes that require all able-bodied people between certain ages, such as 18 through 65, to donate a small number of hours of their labor each year to public service.

3. *Let's Finally Adopt Universal Healthcare for All Americans.* Congress will pass a law creating a National Healthcare System with a structure and pricing arrangement based on the highly successful Medicare model. The system will assure free basic medical services for all citizens and people with proper legal standing for prospective citizenship.

4. *Let's Use Targeted Subsidies for Cost Relief.* Using the NCIDS to establish levels of need and eligibility, federal and State governments will sponsor a series of cost-relief measures for below-the-line individuals and families in need of financial assistance. A unified program of subsidies will allow for exemption of those in need from costs such as local sales taxes; fees for public services such as driver licenses and car registration; public transit fares; and continued use of food stamps.

5. *Let's Have a Single, National Solution for Homelessness.* The US government's Health and Human Services Agency will launch a national program for homelessness mitigation, providing funds to local areas with high incidence. As explained in this chapter, State governments will build or adapt

military-style group housing in selected inter-urban areas, and invite all homeless people, according to their circumstances, to make use of those facilities. Only when we have an adequate supply of shelters, can we make camping in public areas illegal.

6. *Let's Modernize Teaching Practices.* The US Department of Education will launch a major initiative to enable school systems to begin the conversion from teaching kids *what* to think, to teaching them *how* to think. This program will keep the traditional model from Pre-K through fifth grade and begin reinventing the educational experience onward through grade twelve. This will involve designating various transition schools to implement and refine approaches such as the inquiry method, and allocating funds to recruit and train—or retrain—a cadre of master teachers who can train other teachers.

7. *Let's Standardize Online Testing.* The US Department of Education will set up, or encourage the commercial development of, a universal online testing system consisting of walk-in centers where college students and others can take proctored exams associated with the credentials they hope to acquire.

8. *Let's Build a National Credentialing System.* The US Department of Education will set up, or encourage the commercial development of, a national-level credentialing body for educational achievement and skills development. It will create a master database, coordinated with the National Citizen Identification System described in Chapter 6. The agency will receive credentialing updates from its registrants, and will update their records to show the total range of education and training certifications they've received.

Chapter 10.
Let's Rethink Civil Liberties:
Balancing Freedom
With Responsibility

"No man is an island, entire of itself;

. . .

Any man's death diminishes me,
because I am involved in mankind;
and therefore never send to know
for whom the bell tolls;
it tolls for thee."

—John Donne
English poet, 1630

As we learned in Chapter 1, the Founders gave a lot of thought and debate to safeguarding individual rights. They knew well the violent history of the oppressive European monarchies, including their own ancestral homeland of England. They understood the risks of unbridled power in the hands of unaccountable heads of state.

The Federalists, led by Alexander Hamilton, John Adams, and John Jay, seemed confident that a strong central government would rule humanely. But the Anti-Federalists, led by Thomas Jefferson, James Madison, and Patrick Henry, had their doubts. Indeed, they first opposed the new constitution entirely, because they saw it as shifting too much power from the states and local communities to a central government.

The Anti-Federalists blocked the new constitution until the Federalists agreed to add specific amendments that would guarantee individual rights and limit the powers of the central government. Once they made that deal, both sides agreed to approve the constitution in 1788 to get the new Republic started. They went ahead with the understanding that immediately thereafter they would add a series of amendments that would finish the job.

Both sides kept their word. Shortly after ratification the new Congress, created by the new Constitution, adopted the first ten amendments that have become the legendary American Bill of Rights.

The original proposal actually included a dozen amendments, but two of them didn't survive the debates.

By the way, when it comes to amending the Constitution, you might like to know that the President has no role in the process. Under Article II, he or she has no authority to initiate, approve, or veto a constitutional amendment.

THE BILL OF RIGHTS: LIMITING THE POWERS OF GOVERNMENT

Anyone can easily look up the text of these ten big principles, but I've chosen to include them here word for word, so we can consider their impact on the history of our Republic and the ways they illuminate the issues we face.

Brief, concise, elegantly simple, and powerful in their impact, they've stayed with us for over 200 years. Let's consider them one by one.

First Amendment:
Freedom of Religion, Speech,
the Press, and Assembly

"Congress shall make no law respecting an establishment of religion or prohibiting the free exercise thereof, or

abridging the freedom of speech or of the press, or the right of the people peaceably to assemble and to petition the government for a redress of grievances."

Comment: short and sweet. This stands as one of the most powerful statements of human rights in any political system.

Second Amendment:
The Right to Bear Arms

"A well-regulated Militia being necessary to the security of a free State, the right of the people to keep and bear Arms shall not be infringed."

Comment: this one has evolved, over time, into one of the few really controversial provisions of the Constitution. Debates rage and tempers flare over the question of how to interpret it in a modern age, when the noble citizen-soldier no longer exists.

Third Amendment:
The Housing of Soldiers

"No soldier shall, in time of peace, be quartered in any house without the consent of the owner, nor in time of war but in a manner to be prescribed by law."

Comment: this one has become pretty much obsolete. It stands as a reminder of the militant history of the early Republic.

Fourth Amendment:
Immunity from Unreasonable Searches and Seizures

"The right of the people to be secure in their persons, houses, papers, and effects against unreasonable searches and seizures shall not be violated, and no warrants shall issue but upon probable cause, supported by oath or affirmation, and particularly describing the place to be searched and the persons or things to be seized."

Comment: another blockbuster foundation concept. It guarantees, as Supreme Court Justice Louis Brandeis put it, "The right to be left alone." Note the ancient history of the term, "probable cause," which we often hear in TV police dramas.

Fifth Amendment:
Due Process of Law

"No person shall be held to answer for a capital or otherwise infamous crime unless on a presentment or indictment of a grand jury, except in cases arising in the land or naval forces, or in the militia, when in actual service in time of war or public danger; nor shall any person be subject for the same offense to be twice put in jeopardy of life or limb; nor shall be compelled in any criminal case to be a witness against himself, nor be deprived of life, liberty, or property without due process of law; nor shall private property be taken for public use without just compensation."

Comment: that covers a lot of ground. This one gave us the famous "Fifth Amendment" defense, as well as the concept of *double jeopardy*, or immunity from retrial after acquittal. It also prohibits the government from confiscating private property, such as land, without compensating the owner.

Sixth Amendment:
The Right to Trial by Jury

"In all criminal prosecutions, the accused shall enjoy the right to a speedy and public trial by an impartial jury of the state and district wherein the crime shall have been committed, which district shall have been previously ascertained by law, and to be informed of the nature and cause of the accusation; to be confronted with the witnesses against him; to have compulsory process for obtaining witnesses in his favor; and to have the assistance of counsel for his defense."

Comment: we tend to take this right for granted, but consider the many countries in which the government can jail or execute someone without trial, or after a sham trial that doesn't meet the standards specified here: a speedy trial, an impartial jury, an adequate defense, and legal counsel.

Seventh Amendment:
Rights in Civil Suits

"In suits at common law, where the value in controversy shall exceed twenty dollars, the right of trial by jury shall be preserved, and no fact tried by a jury shall be otherwise reexamined in any court of the United States than according to the rules of the common law."

Comment: this one seems a bit peculiar, like an item tossed in at the last minute. Setting a threshold of twenty bucks seems a bit mundane for a grand document like the Constitution, and the grammar of the last part of the sentence seems rather muddy. We won't dissect it here; we can understand the basic intent, and the rest doesn't really cause any problems.

Eighth Amendment:
Excessive Bail, Fines, and Punishments

"Excessive bail shall not be required, nor excessive fines imposed, nor cruel and unusual punishments inflicted."

Comment: without some guideline or criterion for defining "excessive," courts throughout the US have free rein, and some judges send people to jail who cannot afford to pay the bail they set. This remains a problem area with respect to the rights of minorities and people from disadvantaged environments. This amendment also gave us the concept of "cruel and unusual punishments," which has played a part in debates about capital punishment that continue to this day.

Ninth Amendment:
Other Rights Retained by the People

"The enumeration in the Constitution of certain rights shall not be construed to deny or disparage others retained by the people."

Comment: worded a bit peculiarly, this one warns the central government that other civil rights, not spelled out here, still exist, and that just because the Constitution doesn't specify a particular right, that doesn't mean the government can override it.

Tenth Amendment: Powers Not Given to Government Remain with the States and the People

"The powers not delegated to the United States by the Constitution, nor prohibited by it to the states, are reserved to the states respectively, or to the people."

Comment: this one seems to overlap with Amendment 9. It spells out a firm doctrine, commonly referred to as the "states' rights" principle, which means that the federal government only has those powers specifically given by the Constitution; all other powers remain with the states.

Interestingly, although the founders feared that the presidency—a rather novel concept in political systems at the time—might evolve into a quasi-monarchy, none of the ten amendments they attached to the Constitution specifically mentions the President. Most of the provisions seem to focus on the law-making and law-enforcing process.

Nonetheless, the basic Bill of Rights did establish a solid foundation for protecting individual liberties. For more than two centuries, courts throughout the land have used it as a yardstick for evaluating laws passed at the federal, state, and local levels, and deciding lawsuits challenging them.

Over the next two hundred years or so, Congress added 17 other amendments, for a current total of 27. Several of them, enumerated here, deal specifically with civil liberties.

Abraham Lincoln pushed through the Thirteenth Amendment, abolishing slavery, even before the Civil War ended, although he died before the states ratified it.

The Fourteenth Amendment, ratified in 1868, confirmed the right of citizenship for anyone born in the US, including former slaves. And the Fifteenth Amendment, ratified in 1870, granted voting rights to former slaves, but strangely, didn't say that women—of any color—could vote. Women had to wait for another 60 years to get the right to vote when the Nineteenth Amendment became law in 1920.

The Twenty-fourth Amendment, ratified in 1964, specifically prohibited the states from imposing poll taxes, which had the effect of discouraging poor people, especially black people in the Old South, from voting.

The Twenty-sixth Amendment, ratified in 1971, lowered the voting age from 21 years to 18. The time from approval to ratification, 107 days, set a record for the fastest amendment.

In this chapter, we'll highlight several key issues for the Civil Liberties component of the Republic, recognizing that they represent only a portion of the full range of challenges we face, both immediately and in the long run.

Later in this discussion, we'll consider extending the enumeration of the personal rights of every American, with a proposed *Universal Declaration of American Rights*.

The Supreme Court has the last word on questions of constitutionality. It has faced some difficult challenges in applying the guidance of the Bill of Rights to a number of contentious issues over the years. Social activists and constitutional scholars have argued that the institution of slavery itself violated basic human rights guaranteed by the Fourth Amendment. The forcible relocation of Indians to reservations came into question for the same reasons. The incarceration of over 100,000 Americans of Japanese descent during WW2 and the seizure of their property certainly seemed to violate the Fourth Amendment.

Sometimes a law or a government action clearly oversteps one of the ten basic rights, but more often the dispute requires a careful interpretation of the guidance. Landmark cases, known by the names of the two contending parties— such as "Marbury v. Madison," "Roe v. Wade," or "Griggs v.

Duke Power," establish all-important *precedents*, which the Court uses to decide similar cases coming afterward.

CIVIL RIGHTS: WHO GETS TO RIDE THE BUS?

The Bill of Rights *promises* key civil liberties but it does nothing to *guarantee* them. The Founders left it to Congress and the states to figure out how to protect them with laws.

As of this writing, the historical report card for American lawmakers on the civil rights front shows a barely passing grade. The last two centuries have seen an appalling series of abuses of the civil liberties of various categories of people by presidents, congresses, state legislatures, and political leaders at national and state levels. A few notable examples illustrate the point:

▸ Federal laws and presidential orders deprived tens of thousands of Native Americans—the "Indians"—of their land and forcibly relocated them thousands of miles to designated reservations.

▸ All across the Old South local Jim Crow laws severely restricted the civil liberties and economic opportunities open to black people. The Union may have won the Civil War, but the Confederacy won the peace. Things didn't change much until the 1960s when Presidents Eisenhower, Kennedy, and Johnson enforced court orders that outlawed segregation.

▸ President William McKinley "annexed" the Hawaiian Islands in 1898, partly because of the strategic significance of the US Naval base at Pearl Harbor, and partly to satisfy the economic aspirations of Methodist missionaries who had overthrown the islands' last queen, Lili'uo'kalani. Hawaii became a designated territory in 1900 but its people had no rights of citizenship until 1959 when it became the 50th state.

▸ Women in America couldn't vote before 1920. Eminent political figures like President Grover Cleveland resisted female suffrage vigorously. "Sensible and responsible women do not want to vote," he declared. "The relative positions to be assumed by man and woman in the working out of our civilization were assigned long ago by a higher intelligence than ours."

▸ Labor unions, on the railroads especially, faced brutal repression from company thugs and local police until the Wagner Act of 1935 imposed collective bargaining.

▸ President Franklin D. Roosevelt issued the infamous Executive Order 9066 in 1942, which directed the mass rounding up and internment of 120,000 Americans of Japanese descent in detention camps. He did so with full concurrence by senior government and military leaders and little protest from the American public or the media. War hysteria and press advocacy fed the fear that they might somehow sabotage the American war effort or assist the Japanese war effort in some way. FDR rescinded the order in 1944 and the last of the 10 camps closed after the Japanese surrender in 1945.

▸ The US Army had assigned black soldiers to segregated units for decades. The superior performance of many all-black units, and particularly the Tuskegee Airmen, who earned their remarkable reputation for protecting Allied bombers flying over Germany, overthrew stereotypes of blacks as inferior soldiers. President Harry S. Truman bucked the mainstream of public opinion when he desegregated all military units by executive order in 1948.

And through it all, for more than a century, the two major political parties—the Democrats and the Republicans—have fought for control of the lawmaking process all across America and at all levels, from the Congress to local school boards. The history of civil rights in the US reads like the history of the two-party system.

Over those many years the two parties have become ever more polarized and mutually antagonistic in their ideologies, goals, and tactics. No third party has ever gained enough influence to seriously threaten the top two.

The 60 percent of Americans who vote have aligned themselves more and more with one or the other of the parties, so much so that they typically vote for any candidate their party puts up. Truly independent voters number perhaps 20 percent of those who actually turn out, with independent candidates scarcer than that.

At the state level, about 7,500 legislators battle for control of some 99 chambers, or lawmaking bodies (Nebraska, known as a *unicameral* legislature, only has one chamber).

As of this writing, Republicans control two-thirds of the state legislatures but they only have full control of 21 State governments—the governor's office plus both chambers. Democrats have full control of 18. Overall, that means that almost 80 percent of State governments operate under one-party monopoly control.

Republican governors currently outnumber Democrats slightly, by 27 to 23. By contrast, two-thirds of the 50 big-city mayors identify as Democrats. So while Republicans tend to control State governments, Democrats control the big cities.

CIVIL RIGHTS AND THE GREAT POLITICAL INVERSION

For the past 50 years, the states of the Old South, the Heartland, and the Cowboy States have leaned heavily toward the Republican party as their favored political machine.

But for many decades before that, up through the early 1960s, the Democrats had enjoyed the status of their preferred party.

What happened?

Before the civil rights movement of the 1960s, the Democrats had positioned themselves as the party of the common man —working people, labor unions, farmers, and small-town folk. They tended to steer clear of divisive issues like social injustice, segregation, and women's rights.

By contrast, the Republicans sold themselves as the party of the white upper class, representing moneyed people and so-called "conservative" values. Some historians have referred to the political players of that era as "Eisenhower Republicans" or "Reagan Republicans."

The civil rights movement hit the political scene of the 1960s like a thunderbolt. Martin Luther King and his followers had brought the issue of racial injustice to the center of American attention. The legendary marches through the South, like the one in Selma; the year-long bus boycott in Montgomery, Alabama; and the legendary sit-in at the Woolworth lunch counter in Greensboro, North Carolina animated TV screens all over the country. They also ignited conversations among a newly politicized population of college students.

President John Kennedy had faced down the blatantly racist Alabama governor, George Wallace, and forced him to allow the desegregation of schools and colleges in that state. Two landmark laws, the Civil Rights Act of 1964 and the Voting Rights Act of 1965, deeply offended the white political class of the Old South.

After he signed the Civil Rights Act into law, Lyndon Johnson —a native Texan—reportedly commented to his associates, "We've probably handed the South to the Republicans for a generation, at least." His prophesy came true.

Johnson decided not to stand for re-election in 1968, and Richard Nixon, a hard-core Republican, won the presidency. Nixon understood the "between the lines" messaging of white supremacy and signaled to southern political leaders that he might slow down the civil rights train if they elected him.

Ever since that remarkable political inversion the Republican party has projected a populist ideology, becoming the advocate for the "little guy." Perversely, they succeeded in painting Democrats as the party of the snobbish "Eastern elites" and Democrat party leaders to this day haven't figured out how to shake that image.

LET'S CREATE A UNIVERSAL DECLARATION OF AMERICAN RIGHTS

While the Bill of Rights has stood the test of time as a basic control on the powers of government, we Americans have come to expect a much wider range of civil liberties, and we expect our governments to support and protect them. Some of them have laws to protect and enforce them; others we accept as part of custom and common understanding.

For example, each of us has the right to practice the customs of our ethnic sub-culture; we have the right to vote; we can run for public office; we can engage in contracts and operate businesses; we can travel freely throughout the country; and we have lots of other rights.

So far, however, we haven't codified this broad inventory of rights into a single written manifesto. Perhaps we should.

We might consider, as a model for our mega-bill of rights, the United Nations' *Universal Declaration of Human Rights* (UDHR). In 1948 the UN commissioned a group of distinguished scholars from a variety of disciplines and asked them to produce such a model. They came up with a specification of fundamental rights that all nations and governments should acknowledge, respect, and preserve. The General Assembly approved it in Paris on 10 December 1948 and ultimately translated it into over 500 languages.

As a matter of policy, the UN expects all member states to respect and preserve the 30 basic human rights the UDHR lays out, and to bring to justice those who violate it.

For citizens of a stable and peaceful democracy like the US, some of the UDHR's provisions seem jarringly basic; so basic that one might not even think to itemize them. In the interests of brevity, I won't list all of the provisions here, but I strongly recommend that every American read the full document.

I propose that we develop, publish, and promote a *Universal Declaration of American Rights* (UDAR), in a format similar to the UN's UDHR. We can specify a full range of civil rights and privileges, all in one place. As a start, we can consider the following provisions.

Proposed Universal Declaration of American Rights

1. The right to physical safety; freedom from assault or fear of bodily harm.

2. The right to modesty and privacy of one's physical person; the right to remain clothed.

3. The right to privacy in the experience of intimacy or sexual activity.

4. For women, the right of reproductive choice, which includes the right to prevent, initiate, or terminate a pregnancy.

5. The right to basic medical care.

6. The right to make fundamental end-of-life decisions, if medically and legally competent, including the right to refuse unwanted medical procedures, and to end one's life voluntarily.

7. The right to security and privacy of one's domicile and possessions.

8. The right to a nationality, and the right to change it by choice.

9. The right to practice the activities and customs of one's subculture.

10. Freedom from persecution, intimidation, humiliation, or bullying, whether social, psychological, or physical.

11. Freedom of—and from—religion; the right to practice one's own religion without interference and the right to live free from the imposition of religious doctrines by others.

12. Freedom from social or economic discrimination or unfair treatment on the basis of age, sex or gender orientation, racial or ethnic orientation, religion, national origin, physical or developmental disability, or marital status.

13. Freedom to move about within the country, and to visit other countries and return.

14. The right to marry or form a legal domestic partnership with a consenting partner. Also, the right to terminate such a relationship with or without the consent of the partner.

15. The right to own, buy, or inherit property, and the freedom to sell or bequeath it to others.

16. The right to enter into contracts and to require the counter-parties to abide by the terms.

17. Freedom from arbitrary arrest, detention, or harassment by police or government authorities.

18. Freedom from arbitrary search or seizure of personal possessions.

19. The right of peaceful assembly.

20. The right to own a firearm and use it subject to the restrictions of applicable laws.

21. The right to vote.

22. The right to compete for, and serve in, public office.

23. The right to file suit in civil court to secure or protect these enumerated rights.

24. Freedom of self-expression: verbal, literary, and electronic.

25. The right to protect one's reputation or social image from libelous or slanderous actions by others.

26. Freedom from theft, fraud or economic exploitation.

27. The right to a basic education.

28. The right to participate fairly in the job market.

29. The right to a fair wage.

30. The right to safe and humane working conditions.

31. The right to engage in commercial or profitable activity.

32. Freedom from intrusive surveillance, either by government or commercial entities.

33. The right of information privacy—to limit or control the use of one's personal information for commercial or political purposes. This includes the right to know which entities have possession of one's personal data and their intentions for using it.

If well crafted and wisely applied, this universal declaration could have the moral force of law. A person disadvantaged on any of the enumerated rights, if able to prove the violation, would have a strong case for action against a government agency, an employer, or a commercial establishment.

Of course, we have to recognize that all rights, including those spelled out in the Constitution, have their boundaries. For example, the right to freedom of expression does not permit a person to libel or slander someone else. When two rights come into play, a trade-off becomes necessary.

I hope this preliminary round-up of critical rights and freedoms can stimulate further discussion and that other thoughtful contributors can extend and refine it.

PELVIC POLITICS: ROE V. WADE AND THE WAR BETWEEN RELIGION AND SECULARISM

Three major cataclysmic events have shaped gender politics in America in a very big way, beginning early in the 1900s:

1. The belated *Eighteenth Amendment*, ratified in 1920, gave women the right to vote, one of the most fundamental defining rights of citizenship.

2. The medical breakthrough in 1960 that made *female contraceptives* widely available—"The Pill"—enabled American women to take control of their reproductive experience. With the so-called sexual revolution, young women began to think about their sexuality in new ways, and began to assert new freedoms and set new social norms for sexual behavior. The Pill also enabled millions of women to think about jobs and careers in new ways and contributed to a radical increase in the number of two-income households.

3. *Roe v. Wade*, the momentous Supreme Court decision in 1973 that struck down state laws that criminalized abortion, gave women new alternatives to traditional marriage and the right to terminate their pregnancies without facing criminal penalties or serious risks to health and life.

These and other developments fueled a rebirth of feminist ideology, politics, and activism that continues to this day.

WHEN ROE MET WADE

The term "Roe v. Wade," the Supreme Court's case-handle for one of its most important rulings, has become emblematic of a struggle between two diametrically opposed ideologies. On one hand, a faction composed mostly of white, Christian, older males with less than a college education—the "WCOM" cohort—wanted to severely curtail abortion practices and possibly outlaw them in all forms.

The other faction, understandably spearheaded by female activists, wanted to keep reproductive choices off-limits from the law. They wanted to establish a woman's right to prevent, initiate, or terminate a pregnancy as an entirely private matter, not subject to interference by legislators or law enforcement agencies.

Roe v. Wade would become the figurative Gettysburg battlefield of that war.

Abortion laws in America go far back in our history. Some states gradually relaxed them over time, but by the late 1960s terminating pregnancy remained illegal in most states.

Texas had a law prohibiting abortion in all cases except for a direct risk to the life of the pregnant woman.

In 1971 a woman named Norma McCorvey filed suit against the district attorney of Dallas County, a man named Henry Wade, who had vigorously prosecuted women under Texas' strict abortion law. McCorvey claimed the right to terminate her pregnancy. She requested anonymity in the court documents, which identified her as Jane Roe, a commonly used moniker in legal proceedings. The case became known to legal beagles as Roe Versus Wade, or as commonly abbreviated, Roe v. Wade.

The case dragged on for several years. McCorvey, a person of limited means, gave birth to her baby and gave her up to adoption. It ended with a decision by the Supreme Court on January 22, 1973.

The Supremes declared the Texas law unconstitutional, ruling by a vote of 7 to 2 that it violated the right to privacy implied by the Fourteenth Amendment. That one ruling shot down laws in 46 states and launched a new era of women's rights. Termination of pregnancy became a recognized medical specialty, with the inevitable development of methods, instruments, and medications.

As a curious footnote to the case: McCorvey later became a high profile anti-abortion activist, speaking publicly and campaigning for stricter laws. Several decades later, in 2017, she admitted that she had received more than $400,000 from Christian evangelical groups for her services as a media spokesperson calling for laws to criminalize abortion.

In any case, the movement she ignited swept across the whole of America.

For the white-Christian-older-male faction, (WCOM), Roe v. Wade didn't settle anything. For them, it signaled a ratcheting up of the "liberal assault" on traditional American values—as they defined them.

They saw the Supreme Court's decision as a call to war. For nearly a half-century after the ruling, they constantly pushed for its reversal, chipping away at its boundaries in just about every way they could think of.

Although Roe v. Wade has stood as "settled law" for almost 50 years, the WCOM cohort has recently managed to open up a new battleground in the war. This time they hope to re-engineer the Supreme Court itself.

In recent years, an ideological split has gradually widened amongst the nine justices, mirroring the increasing polarization between Democrats and Republicans. Whenever a vacancy opens up, the party in control of the White House tries to fill the slot with a candidate who leans ideologically in their direction. Each new appointee comes under intense scrutiny for his or her perceived ideological bias.

Because the Senate has the power to confirm or reject the president's nominees, the ideological fate of the Court depends on a combination of two factors: which party controls the White House and which one controls the Senate.

As of this writing, Republicans control both the White House and the Senate, so the last two appointees have caused a socially conservative slant.

But just as important, hundreds of federal judges across the country also get their jobs by presidential appointment and Senate confirmation. Opponents of Roe v. Wade hope to engineer a collective judicial bias that could cause the Court to overturn the 1973 decision.

The pathological animosity between Democrats and Republicans in Congress reached its historical extreme in early 2016, during the last year of President Barack Obama's second term.

When a Court vacancy opened up, Obama nominated his preferred candidate for the seat, but the powerful Senate Majority Leader refused even to present the nomination to the Senate. He argued that a lame duck president should not have the privilege of filling such a crucially important position. As a result, he kept the seat vacant for over a year, leaving only eight sitting justices, until Obama's successor came into office and appointed a Republican-leaning judge to fill the vacancy.

In at least a dozen states, mostly those of the Old South and parts of the Heartland, WCOM activists have succeeded in pushing through anti-abortion laws so strict as to obviously violate the Roe v. Wade ruling. A number of them have openly admitted that they've made the laws so extreme—"trigger" laws, they call them—as to provoke court challenges by reproductive rights activists. They want to get another landmark case up to the Supreme Court, where they hope a more conservative majority will overturn Roe v. Wade or at least allow some state-law restrictions to stand.

OTHER SUPPORT FOR REPRODUCTIVE RIGHTS

This new wave of political conservatism, however, does not necessarily doom Roe v. Wade as a foundation for reproductive rights. The Court's decision cited the Fourteenth Amendment as its basis for protecting a woman's reproductive experience as a right of privacy, but that provision has some good company.

Although the Constitution does not specifically refer to privacy as a civil right, scholars have long treated it as strongly implied.

In fact, the Fourth Amendment seems to offer a much stronger basis for privacy than the Fourteenth. It declares, in part:

The right of the people to be secure in their persons, houses, papers, and effects, against unreasonable searches and seizures, shall not be violated . . .

One might plausibly interpret a government agency's investigation into a woman's reproductive status as a violation of her right to the security of her person.

Yet another argument for reproductive rights, perhaps an even stronger one, comes from the First Amendment. As the logic goes: almost all anti-abortion activists invoke religious beliefs—either directly, or by implication—in declaring abortion a sin. Some of them declare abortion an act of murder, in that it supposedly deprives a human being of its life. That premise inevitably frames any attempt to outlaw abortion as a form of *religious activism*—specifically Christian activism, in the case of the American culture.

The First Amendment's freedom of religion clause gave rise to the long-standing doctrine of *separation of church and state*. That means that the Republic can never have an official state religion, nor can it outlaw any particular religious denomination. That doctrine certainly seems to imply freedom *from* religion as well as freedom *of* religion—a person's right not to have someone else's religious beliefs and practices imposed on them.

Many orthodox Christians declare that life begins at the instant of conception—when a female egg cell, referred to as an *ovum*, and a male sperm cell unite to form a *zygote*. The zygote, they imply, does not belong to the woman whose uterus formed it, and after it forms she has no right to remove it from her body.

Reproductive rights activists, on the other hand, and a majority of reproductive scientists, consider the zygote—which initially develops as a vaguely defined cluster of cells attached to the wall of the uterus—simply a part of the woman's anatomy. They consider life to begin much later, at a subjectively defined point of *viability*, the point at which the fetus has developed into a fully formed human and could hypothetically survive outside the womb. Many healthcare practitioners consider the end of the second trimester—six months after fertilization—as the onset of viability. As it happens, very few abortions take place that late in the gestation period.

Having begun my education and my professional career as a scientist—a degreed physicist and later an engineer—whenever I see religion colliding with science, I tend to side with science.

Yet another development that might ease the anxiety of reproductive rights advocates, and frustrate the efforts of those who don't believe in abortion, involves the medical do-it-yourself option—the so-called abortion pill. A medication known as *mifepristone*, also known as RU-486, typically used in combination with *misoprostol,* can terminate a pregnancy with little risk or complication. This combination works with about 95% effectiveness during the first 7 or 8 weeks of pregnancy, the most common period for voluntary termination.

In this part of our investigation, we've focused mostly on the aspect of reproductive rights as a key element of the civil liberties question for women. Obviously, however, this component of the Republic includes a whole range of other concerns, such as fair employment, pay, and benefits; non-discrimination in education; nondiscrimination in housing; nondiscriminatory access to medical care; freedom from sexual exploitation, harassment, or assault; and humane treatment of rape victims; and quite a few others.

Space doesn't permit a thoughtful treatment of each of those components, so we've necessarily focused on a few of the most challenging issues for a start.

LET'S RESUSCITATE THE EQUAL RIGHTS AMENDMENT

Nearly 50 years have gone by since we last changed our Constitution. Many civil rights leaders contend that we have unfinished business with regard to various forms of discrimination, and that the Equal Rights Amendment—as one specific update—deserves immediate attention. The case for the ERA actually dates back to 1923, with the Suffragettes led by Alice Paul and others.

In its original—and still current—incarnation, the ERA dictates that:

"Equality of rights under the law shall not be denied or abridged by the United States or by any state on account of sex."

Congress passed the ERA in 1972, but it gathered dust for nearly 50 years because the required three-quarters of the states had not ratified it. Until recently, thirteen states held out—not surprisingly, the states of the Old South and parts of the Heartland, as illustrated by Figure 10-1.

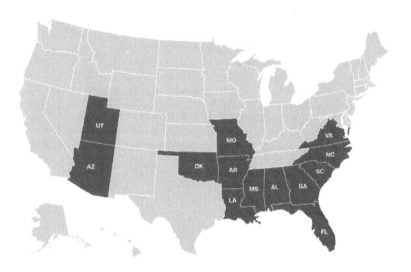

Figure 10-1. States Not Ratifying the Equal Rights Amendment

Recent to this writing, Democrats captured the governorship and both legislative chambers of the state of Virginia and immediately moved to ratify the ERA, bringing the approvals to the tipping point of 38. Procedural questions remain about whether too much time has elapsed since the original passage and whether it would need reauthorization.

In the forty-plus years since the passage of the ERA, however, we've seen increasing civil rights problems for people in other categories, such as those with non-traditional gender orientations; immigrants from certain cultures and religions such as Muslims; racial or ethnic minorities; older people; and people with disabilities.

An updated expression of these universal safeguards in modern language might read something like:

> *"Equality of rights under the law shall not be denied or abridged by the United States or by any State based on age, sex or gender orientation, racial or ethnic orientation, religion, national origin, physical or developmental disability, or marital status."*

While getting a whole new amendment through Congress and getting it ratified by the states would pose a tougher challenge than getting ratification of the existing ERA, I believe the much stronger range of protections would justify the extra effort. And these days, political parties might embrace them somewhat more readily than they did then.

LET'S CONSIDER RESTITUTION FOR DISENFRANCHISED PEOPLES

In 1988, President Ronald Reagan signed the *Civil Liberties Act*, a landmark piece of legislation that formally acknowledged and apologized for the mass incarceration, without due process of law, of 120,000 Americans of Japanese descent—the *nisei*—during WW2.

THE JAPANESE AMERICAN EXPERIENCE

The legislation declared the decision to round them up, force them to abandon their homes and businesses, and relocate them to 10 internment camps in various western states, "a grave injustice" that arose from "race prejudice, war hysteria, and a failure of political leadership," not from any well conceived analysis of strategic risks.

The law allocated funds to grant each surviving internee a reparation payment of about $20,000. Some 82,219 people received checks.

The bill passed with the support of the majority of Democrats in Congress, but the majority of Republicans voted against it.

The Act that Reagan signed into law seemed like it might set a new standard, a landmark for the treatment of people disenfranchised by federal actions. Many advocates began to hope that similar reparations might become possible for other populations: American Indians; enslaved blacks; Native Hawaiians; and Alaskan groups like the Inuit, Aleut, Iñupiat, and Yupik—generally referred to as "Eskimos."

But the reparations train never really left the station. No equivalent law, program, or policy followed on from that landmark decision. US government efforts at reparations for various other groups have involved a variety of half-way measures, political gestures, spotty legislation, and little or no centralized attention to the issues.

THE AMERICAN INDIAN EXPERIENCE

Earlier, in 1946, President Harry S. Truman signed a law that created the Indian Claims Commission, a body designed to hear historic grievances and compensate tribes for lost territories. The program awarded some $1.3 billion to 176 tribes and bands. The various groups used the money in various ways, sometimes distributing some of it to their members, and sometimes spending it on developmental projects. On average, the reparations amounted to about $1,000 per person of Native American ancestry.

The apology, however, didn't come along until 60 years later. In 2009, a Congressional committee included language in a defense spending bill that apologized for "many instances of violence, maltreatment, and neglect inflicted on Native Peoples by citizens of the United States."

Native Hawaiians didn't fare much better. The invasion of the island kingdom in the late 1800s by white merchants and Methodist missionaries from the mainland largely pushed them aside. The influx created crowded living conditions that exposed the natives to diseases for which they had no immunity. By 1920, only 22,600 Native Hawaiians remained, having declined from an estimated population of 700,000 in 1778, when Europeans first arrived.

A coalition of merchants led by one Samuel Dole (founder of the Dole commercial enterprise) overthrew the Hawaiian queen, Lili'uo'kalani, in 1893, with the support of a US Navy force sent by President Benjamin Harrison. Immediately after the overthrow, the new "government" petitioned the US government for acquisition. The next president in line, Grover Cleveland, opposed the plan, so Dole declared Hawaii an independent republic with himself as head of state.

Cleveland's successor William McKinley took up the mission again. With nationalistic fervor running high just after the wildly successful Spanish-American war, the US government "annexed" Hawaii (a euphemism for a bloodless take-over) in 1900 and declared it a territory with Dole as its governor.

Hawaii remained a US possession for nearly 60 years, housing a strategic military base at Pearl Harbor; providing an abundant supply of sugar cane and tropical fruits for export to the mainland; and serving as an exotic vacation paradise for wealthy Americans.

By the time Congress moved to make Hawaii a full-fledged state, in 1959—along with Alaska, which Andrew Johnson's government had bought from Russia in 1867 for $7.2 million —native Hawaiians had experienced the near-destruction of their culture and their way of life.

Over the years, a variety of federal programs aimed at offsetting poverty amongst Native Hawaiians and providing preferential treatment in leasing property from the government. No real reparations program ever materialized, however.

The apology came in 1993, 100 years after the overthrow of Queen Lili. As apologies go, however, it does deserve a bit of praise. It took the form of a joint resolution of Congress, passed on the anniversary of the overthrow. In four rather glorious pages, it detailed the disreputable history of the annexation, offered no excuses, and validated the grievances of the Hawaiian people.

TERRITORIAL PEOPLES

As mentioned earlier, in Chapter 1, we still have a large number of "semi-Americans"—people of the territories whose citizenship status, voting rights, and other rights remain somewhat vaguely defined. These include people of American Samoa, Guam, Northern Mariana Islands, Puerto Rico, and US Virgin Islands. All of them deserve to have their status clarified, upgraded if appropriate, and accounted for in federal funding for development.

VICTIMS OF MISCARRIAGE OF JUSTICE

Another category that certainly deserves attention, and possibly a national standard for restitution, includes people who got the short end of the stick from the criminal justice system. We regularly see news reports detailing the appalling experiences of people improperly imprisoned as a result of police misconduct, incompetent or biased treatment by prosecutors, conviction by dysfunctional juries, or inappropriate sentences by corrupt or misguided judges.

A person who spends 20 years or more in prison, and then gets exonerated by new evidence or a new trial, certainly deserves some sort of compensation for his or her suffering. Again, a national law would appropriately dictate remedies, such as cash reparation payments, in those cases. Some advocates have recommended a payment of $100,000 for each year of unjustified incarceration.

As of this writing, Americans seem very conflicted about the idea of reparations for disenfranchised peoples. While many of them, including many white people, tend to support some kind of acknowledgement of past cultural offenses, most of them don't seem to favor cash reparations.

A recent survey found that, while 73 percent of black Americans—understandably—favor cash payments to the living descendants of slaves, over 67 percent of non-black citizens oppose that option.

As with many such issues, party affiliation correlates with opinions. Over 90 percent of people who identify as Republicans oppose cash reparations, two-thirds of Independents oppose, and Democrats split almost evenly on the issue. Regional preferences also show clearly: in the Old South and the Heartland, nearly 70 percent oppose cash reparations.

Part of the citizen ambivalence seems to revolve around the question of compensating the *descendants* of those who suffered. In the case of the Japanese-American internees, all of the ones who received payments had actually endured the relocation and incarceration. Many Americans consider direct cash payments fully justified in those cases.

Presumably, the suffering of the Japanese interned in the camps had follow-on effects for their descendants. Some third-generation Japanese-Americans—the *sansei*—confide that they still feel uncertain about their lives and roles as Americans. Some have tended to underplay their heritage, declining to decorate their homes with Asian designs, for example. Some say they feel instinctively reluctant to call attention to themselves in social situations, possibly as a hold-over of the cultural memory of the unpleasant past and lingering race prejudices in the post-war years.

A parallel argument arises for the living descendants of enslaved black people. The effects of those atrocities have clearly cascaded down through many generations of black people. Many sociologists would assert that the disproportionate levels of poverty, limited education, and crime in black communities reflects cultural and psychosocial wounds from past centuries.

Apparently, however, most Americans—particularly whites—don't consider the cultural hand-me-down impact severe enough to justify direct reparations, either to Japanese-Americans, nor to the descendants of enslaved blacks, nor to present-day American Indians. Native Hawaiians seem to come somewhere in the middle of the calculation, partly perhaps due to the erosion of their culture and their cohesive ethnic identity.

Clearly, the Republic has unfinished business with the descendants of disenfranchised peoples. Congress should create a permanent *National Commission for Social Justice* (NCSJ), tasked with the advocacy and implementation of a comprehensive program for restitution and ensuring the rights of living descendants of the identified groups.

LET'S TAME THE DIGITAL ECOSYSTEM: THE GREAT PRIVACY PUSH-BACK

Big revolutions usually start with big hopes, big dreams, big visions, and big promises. Of all the big revolutions in our history—from agriculture and industrialization to the automobile and television—the internet and all things digital have raised heart rates and hormone levels more than perhaps any other.

The "Third Wave," as futurist Alvin Toffler christened the emerging age of information, became a tidal wave with the arrival of the microchip and digital information technology. Those made possible the internet and ubiquitous information—*knowledge at a distance.* And between 1990 and 1995, the commercial tidal wave of digital products and experiences began to rise exponentially. Today, about 25 years into the revolution, perhaps we need to wake up from our infatuated trance with the electronic experience and see what the revolution has done for, with, and to us.

THE INFORMATION REVOLUTION'S BROKEN PROMISES

The rapid spread and acceptance of digital products, services, and experiences has few parallels in history, with the possible exception of television. Our lives now revolve comfortably around instant communication, with fingertip access to worlds of information, online shopping, and management of our personal affairs. The vast majority of the world's affluent people have become cyber-citizens.

Looking back, however, it seems that some of the grandest fantasies promoted by the early self-nominated philosophers of the Internet age haven't really caught fire, or have misfired, or even backfired. We didn't get some of what they promised, and some of what we got we hadn't expected. At least four of their grand promises didn't come true:

1. *The Internet Would Become a World Community.* The cyber-prophets told us the Internet would bring us all together, reduce ethnic and tribal strife, and foster understanding and cooperation among all peoples.

   The sober reality: not so much. The term "community" has taken on a new and somewhat warped connotation in the Internet age. Now, it just means any collection of people who can contact one another electronically. Immersion in the information environment has given us a multitude of relationships, but we experience them as much more shallow, socially and emotionally. Some experts counter that these technologies have actually *atomized* the human experience, rather than collectivizing it.

2. *The Internet Would Spread Democracy.* A New Age would dawn, the digital philosophers told us, in which oppressed peoples would have a new and powerful voice, and dictators could no longer rule by fear.

The sober reality: it hasn't happened yet. *Swarm advocacy*—the use of social media to mobilize people and get them out into the streets—has helped to bring dictators down in some cases, but has proven mostly useless in organizing democratic alternatives. The social media have done far more to promote tribalism, intolerance, and factional conflict than democratic cooperation.

3. *Digital Technologies Would Narrow the Wealth Gap.* The cyber-pundits assured us that access to the wonders of the digital world would give everyone a shot at the good life. Free and abundant information, including education, would raise the poor out of their imprisoning circumstances and create more jobs, better educated workers, and a fairer distribution of wealth. And e-commerce would turn vast numbers of online entrepreneurs into millionaires.

The sober reality: mostly, the opposite happened. Paradoxically, digital technologies appear to have done more to *widen the wealth gap* than almost any other phenomenon—social, political, or economic.

The vast digital marketplace soon fell under the control of just a handful of huge monopoly firms: Apple, Amazon, Google, Facebook, Instagram, LinkedIn, Microsoft, Twitter, Uber, Yahoo, YouTube, and a few others.

4. *The Digital Generation Would Save Us.* Digital information technologies, they told us, would produce a new generation of "tech-savvy" kids, smarter than their parents, who would run the world more intelligently than the generation that spawned them.

The sober reality: not so's you could notice it. Today's kids haven't really become tech-savvy; they've just become button-savvy.

Very few of them know or care what goes on inside their smartphones, laptops, video games, or tablet computers. Cell phones and a host of other digital products only became wildly popular after engineers figured out how to design them so that even a monkey could use one. The kids haven't gotten any smarter—they've just become enthusiastic consumers, hyper-attentive to an engaging experience they love. Most adults could learn everything a tech-savvy teen knows about media products in a few hours.

Regardless of the admiring attention given to them by some social observers, we've seen little evidence that today's high-school grads have become smarter, better informed, or more socially aware than any previous generation.

As to whether today's young digital natives will grow up to become better (or worse) leaders than their parents, we have little evidence to go on.

HOW THE DIGITAL ECOSYSTEM THREATENS OUR DEMOCRACY AND OUR CIVIL LIBERTIES

In less than a decade, most Americans completely and willingly surrendered one of the most cherished of all personal privileges—*the right to privacy*. They voluntarily and enthusiastically provided commercial corporations with the kinds of data they'd have had to spend billions of dollars collecting—all for free.

A company like Facebook, for example, has used free online experiences to herd together a target population of *several billion people*, each one identified and catalogued in detail. These "useful idiots" contribute commercial value in countless ways, all the while soaking in an addictive social media experience. Lately, George Orwell's dystopian *1984* scenario seems less far-fetched than it has in the past.

Ironically, many gun-rights activists still push the government take-over scenario, which has the jack-booted federal agents descending on ordinary citizens and confiscating their firearms. They like to think of gun ownership as the citizens's ultimate defense against an oppressive central authority. Most of them probably haven't thought about the prospect of a digital take-over. A government that can control their personal information and eliminate all forms of privacy needn't bother with their guns.

LET'S GETS SOME PERSPECTIVE ON THE PRIVACY ISSUE

For our purposes in this chapter, we need to narrow the focus and get down to some specific solutions, knowing that the global issues will get argued out for years to come. Let's look at an actual regulatory model—a set of conditions we can impose on companies that operate in the human information industry.

As of this writing, the big questions of information privacy and security play prominently in the national conversation, but Americans seem confused, concerned, conflicted, and divided about how to settle them or even how to frame them.

Three distinct ideologies have emerged, each with its advocates and its preferred narrative:

1. *The Benevolent Big Brother View.* Promoted, understandably, by the founders and leaders of the social media companies, and by ideological advocates who assure us that the benefits to society, and to us as individuals, far outweigh the inconveniences that come with digital citizenship. They acknowledge the dark side of the digital ecosystem, but placidly remind us that some rain always comes with the sunshine.

2. *The Lost Cause View.* Many techno-futurists, and a rather large swath of the general public, seem to take it for granted that the pace of digital technology will continue to outrun the political processes that might try to rein it in. They tend to invoke a kind of mantra of inevitability and fatigue, and, although they might lament the passing of the age of the private citizen, they recommend that we accept our unavoidable future and try to make the most of it.

3. *The "Hell No, We Won't Go" View.* Social and political activists, across the spectrum, refuse to accept the premise of inevitability, and believe that a concerted effort, with strong government leadership, can turn the ship around. They point to policies of a number of European governments and societies, which refuse to acknowledge the right of corporations to act like shadow governments. They call for a massive, energetic push-back, and express very little sympathy for the painful and costly adjustments the social media companies will have to endure under such a counter-revolution.

For the record, I side with the "Hell-No" contingent. I advocate an all-out, energetic, comprehensive campaign to push back the boundary lines and re-take the flag. If it ultimately doesn't succeed fully, and we get the default state of the world, then at least we might avoid the worst human impacts of the Big-Brother state.

The Hell-No cause has a lot going for it already. A recent poll showed that two-thirds of Americans want big technology companies regulated and, if necessary, broken up. At the policy level, 47 out of 50 state Attorneys General have opened investigations of Facebook, which harvests the data of hundreds of millions of Americans without their consent.

REGULATION: WHO, WHAT, AND HOW?

Given the practical limitations on space, we can only highlight here some key ideas and examples, realizing that this enormous and important issue will deserve attention from very high-level experts and agencies.

Let's consider the possibility of a single, all-encompassing, modern national law that specifies the requirements commercial operators—and governments—must meet in order to make use of our personal information.

Let's Adopt a New Vocabulary for Information Privacy and Security

One of the challenges we face in selling Americans on the possibilities for digital regulation comes from the abstract, dehumanized, mechanistic terminology imposed on us by the techno-geeks. Lifeless terms like digital media, platforms, data privacy and security, digital footprints, cyber-security, and cloud storage fit the minds and mental habits of people who make their living doing digital things.

But for the typical guy or gal in the street, they signal a vague, abstract reality, far removed from their personal, sensory, everyday experience. We "users" have only adopted the geek terminology out of necessity, not because we find meaning or enlightenment in it. This factor, I believe, lies at the very heart of the problem of getting J.Q. Citizen to actively engage with the issue. We need a real-life vocabulary they can understand, relate to, and use to express themselves.

I propose we adopt some familiar human-language terms to frame these issues, and use them in place of the geek-speak terminology that we've had forced on us. We can also invent a few useful terms of our own. Let's consider these 10 options:

1. *Personal information*: not "digital data," not "digital footprint," and not "online identity." Personal information means any and all information, in any form or format—audio, video, photographic, text, facts, statistics, DNA—name it—that describes, defines, or refers to an individual human being.

2. *Personal Information Package*: a collection of interrelated information items, in any form or combination of forms, that describes, defines, or refers to an individual human being. Examples might include one's online search history, email conversations, credit status, medical history, investment portfolio, or musical preferences.

3. *Information Owner*: the individual human being

described, defined, or referred to by an information package; all others have no rights in ownership except those explicitly granted to them by the owner.

4. *Information Custodians*: those entities, whether individuals, commercial enterprises, local governments, or law enforcement organizations, that have specific authorization to store and use someone's personal information, for specified purposes and specified periods of time.

5. *Privacy*: the right to decide who gets access to our personal information and what we will allow them do with it, not only generically but on an individual, case-by-case basis.

6. *Security*: the assurance that no entity—an individual, a commercial operation, a public agency, a law enforcement organization, or a malicious actor—can use our personal information without our permission and knowledge, or without due process of law.

7. *Allowed Lifetime of Information*, a.k.a. "perishability": the defined and allowed period of time during which authorized custodians or temporary users of a person's information package may keep and use it, after which they must destroy all traces of it from all media under their control.

8. *Surveillance*: any action or process on the part of a public agency that involves observing the behavior of an individual and collecting information about his or her activities. In the case of a law enforcement organization, this requires that they demonstrate probable cause for suspecting a crime, and that they exercise due process of law in acquiring the information. It could involve visual observation by a human agent, electronic recording, or electronic break-ins to gain access to digitally stored information.

9. *Defined-Purpose Surveillance*: the process of observing

the behavior of individuals in a designated location, and temporarily retaining the information, for the purpose of detecting problematic behavior. This could include security monitoring, traffic monitoring, illegal transactions such as drug sales, or legally authorized sting operations. The custodian of the surveillance information should preserve the privacy of non-involved people observed during such an episode, by destroying all information not relevant to the questionable behavior in a timely manner.

10. *"Vacuum-Cleaner" Surveillance*: mass, non-selective harvesting and recording of information about large numbers of individuals, with no specific cause or justification. It includes photographic and video surveillance of large numbers of people in public places, "just in case," with the generic prospect of discovering someone behaving inappropriately. Other examples include fishing through the commercial records of large numbers of people—such as telephone activity records or credit card purchases—on the prospect of discovering or tracing illegal behavior.

Let's Pass a Universal Personal Information Privacy and Security Law

The current state of laws, lawmaking, standards, and enforcement needs a radical rethinking. We have a patchwork of laws, some quite ancient and out of date; federal and state laws that don't match up; and haphazard enforcement practices. We need a single, comprehensive, national solution to a national—and global—problem.

The most effective course of action, I believe, calls for Congress to pass a *Personal Information Privacy and Security Act* (PIPSA), which sets up a broad legal framework for regulation and enforcement. The Act will create a single, national *Information Privacy and Security Agency* (IPSA), which will have the authority to set specific regulations that will govern the activities of all information custodians, without exception.

Let's Move the Boundary Line Back—Way Back

Whatever regulatory approach we commit to will probably make some people happy and others unhappy. Accepting that probability, I suggest we favor the interests of information owners over those of information custodians.

The executives of the big, highly profitable companies that operate in the personal information industry will understandably protest any movement to regulate them, break them up, or otherwise limit the free rein (or reign) they've enjoyed since the early days. And they'll probably fight back hard, using money and political pressure. But no corporation has the right to profit without regard to its impact on the Republic and its people.

Let's Regulate Information Products and Services

So, how shall we actually regulate the use of personal information? What shall we require the custodians to do, and what shall we forbid them to do? We might find that challenge much less daunting and more readily do-able if we approach it from a particular angle, as we'll soon see.

I propose a somewhat off-beat and possibly counter-intuitive starting point for regulation. Instead of trying to dwell on the vaguely defined behavior of a huge number of custodians all messing with our information, *let's focus on the products they provide.* Let's adopt a Consumer Product Safety approach.

Let's recognize something obvious: every consumer experience that involves the interchange of personal information between its owner and a custodian of any type *requires some kind of an electronic device.* The features, functions, and operations of that information device become the points of control, quality assurance, privacy, and security.

Think of the control over the information package as determined at three levels of an overall system, which manages the interaction between owner and custodian:

1. *The Device Level.* A computer, a laptop, a tablet, a smartphone, a dumbphone, a Wi-Fi network router, a TV that streams, a navigation system in a car, a voice-actuated control device, a doorbell video—all of these provide the first link in your relationship with the custodian. And, if we have the will to do so, we can impose controls on those devices and their functions.

2. *The Local Software Level.* Every consumer information device has installed software that allows it to perform its functions. Some of this code forms the built-in processing capacity of the device—usually referred to as the *operating system.* Other packages of code—typically referred to as *applications*, or "apps"—provide specific services, such as making phone calls, playing music or video, browsing websites, or creating documents. Some of these software units come pre-installed on the device, and some devices also allow the user to download or install apps for special tasks.

   Just as we require truth-in-lending practices of banks and mortgage companies, we can require truth-in-software practices that enable a novice user to fully understand what the device does with his or her information and observe its activity.

3. *The Platform Level.* Almost every kind of online activity that a person might engage in involves a pathway between the user's device and a *server* somewhere. A server, typically one computer unit in a rack of hundreds of them, receives the user's information, runs various procedures—which might include exchanging information with other servers—and returns information to the user's device.

For the record, I advocate a drastic push-back against the uncontrolled confiscation and use of personal information by commercial entities. A true commitment by regulators to transparency, privacy, and security would require giving the user the right to deny custodians the right to use their information for any purposes unrelated to the specific transactions requested.

Let's Outlaw Vacuum Surveillance

Above and beyond the misdeeds and infractions of commercial operators, we face another potential misuse of personal information, and an invasion of privacy that potentially outweighs all others in its gravity and severity. That misuse of personal information, as previously defined, comes with the grand scale operations we've referred to as vacuum surveillance.

This issue will surely heat up our national conversation, and it deserves a place there. It could well become the signature question of the entire information privacy issue. We've already moved part-way down that road, with local governments and law enforcement agencies outfitting public spaces with video surveillance systems. In most cases, they don't inform the citizenry about the use and lifetime of the information, and citizens typically don't ask.

What makes vacuum surveillance a defining issue of information privacy, and possibly the most crucial question of all for the Civil Liberties dimension of our Republic? Let's call it the Big Brother Proposition.

The Big Brother Scenario

Let's imagine an extreme scenario, in which a central government and its various agencies throughout a country monitor all online activity by all citizens, all the time, 24/7. Let's further imagine that the head of state, backed by an all-powerful mono-party, controls the primary sources of power in that government and pretty much runs things his way.

In this hyper-vigilant society, the government owns, operates, and controls the Internet, which stands alone, not plugged into the World Wide Web. Any citizen or business seeking to operate a website, a blog, a social media platform, or an email system must get permission and a license from the central government.

In this dystopian scenario, government employees numbering in the thousands continually scan and monitor the network, searching for any information, conversations, or activity deemed inappropriate by the State. Using special software tools to detect offending content, they shut down websites, delete conversations, and remove unauthorized images by the thousands every day with no warning or explanation.

The government censors also identify and catalog misbehaving individuals and businesses in the press, in academic institutions, and in the social media environment, and they report them to their superiors.

This government has also installed millions of video cameras that record human activity at every conceivable location—main streets and intersections, shopping malls, parking lots, train stations and train cars, airports, hotels, government buildings, hospitals and clinics, schools and colleges, sport stadiums, gymnasiums, movie theaters, apartment complexes, and public parks.

Other government employees, also in the thousands, sit and monitor the video feeds from the many observation points, watching for "problem" behavior or tracking individuals assigned to them for surveillance. People who misbehave, either in public or online, get their faces and names tagged in an all-encompassing database that includes virtually every person in the society.

Each person gets a social responsibility score, which measures his or her value to the society. Those with high scores—meaning they don't spit on the street or throw litter, they pay their taxes on time, they don't miss payments on their loans or credit card accounts, they don't get traffic tickets, they don't dispute with their neighbors, they get to work on time, they don't have too many children, and they don't belong to the wrong groups or hang out with banned people—get preference for various benefits that the State provides. They or their children might go to the top of the list when they apply to elite high schools or colleges. They might get first dibs for scholarships or financial assistance. They might become eligible for certain kinds of government jobs.

Those who get low citizenship scores face an experience of reduced social status, fewer privileges, and fewer opportunities. They might find themselves ineligible for passports and not allowed to travel outside the country. The government might decide to limit their movements within the country, restricting where they can live and the kinds of jobs they might get. They might wait longer for government services such as various permits or driving licenses, waiting lines in airports, and even healthcare services.

We can imagine lots of other ways in which such a government could use a system of universal surveillance to intimidate, control, and motivate citizens. With modern digital technology, a determined dictator could control a society in ways the legendary tyrants like Josef Stalin and his contemporaries could never have imagined.

But surely, one might protest: such an extreme scenario could never really come true? Or, could it? Would any government go so far in its attempts to control a society?

Welcome to China.

The People's Republic of China, a one-party autocracy with a sham constitution, no real democratic representation, no meaningful civil rights laws, and obedient citizens who haven't voted for a government in 4,000 years, seems like the ideal model for the digital surveillance state.

Recent to this writing, the Chinese government, under the iron hand of a powerful autocrat, has embarked on a long-term program of surveillance and control very much like the version we just imagined. It has passed well beyond the stage of imagination, and it becomes more and more real every day.

With complete control over all public media, his propaganda machine paints him as immensely popular, revered, loved, and respected by everyone. He has become the "Dear Leader" they all crave and worship.

Could this dark scenario play out in our Republic—the America we love, cherish, and believe in? Maybe not; probably not. But, clearly, it could. Do we want to make that gamble? At the moment, we have no safeguards to prevent it.

If that sacred covenant fails, the destruction of the democracy and the death of the Republic does indeed become possible.

We can look to China as a live prototype of the kind of dystopian society we might become, if we continue to sleep through this very dangerous phase in the life of our Republic.

We began this chapter with a thoughtful consideration of the Bill of Rights, which the Founders considered absolutely fundamental in limiting the powers of government. We close with a whole new set of existential questions about rights and freedoms. What would the Founders do?

Yes, Let's Break Up the Cyber-Monopolies

After we pass the master law governing privacy and security of personal information, we'll move to create a much more competitive commercial environment, in which newer and smaller enterprises can sprout, survive and grow. We need to have lots more players in the information services sector.

The first step would involve *de-mergers*—rolling back or undoing acquisitions by the monopoly firms that have had no public benefit, but have only served to control markets and limit competition. In cases where the acquired company has disappeared into the acquiring monopoly, the process would separate the monopoly into distinct lines of business, and require it to spin off all components but the main one.

The next step would involve laws to prevent more mergers, in cases where they would limit or reduce the number of competing enterprises in a particular business sector.

We might not need a new law to force the break-up of the cyber-monopolies. Laws already on the books will allow agencies like the Justice Department, the Federal Trade Commission, and the Commerce Department to negotiate or impose break-up plans on the major cyber-monopolies.

We do need a national policy arm, such as the Information Privacy and Security Agency (IPSA), and we do need the Personal Information Privacy and Security Act (PIPSA), both recommended previously.

As with many of the forward-thinking solutions we've explored in this book, we'll need strong leadership from the White House and the Congress, as well as from activist groups, to turn them into reality.

We've had a long journey through this controversial territory of Civil Liberties, and yet we've only dealt with a few of the biggest questions. I hope the topics we've covered can contribute meaningfully to the national conversation, and I do acknowledge the need for a much richer and more extensive process of reflection.

THE FIX-IT LIST: CIVIL LIBERTIES

So, how can we improve this component of our Republic—Civil Liberties? Let's start with these actions.

1. *Let's Adopt a Universal Declaration of American Rights.* Congress will pass a joint resolution of both houses, adopting the *Universal Declaration of American Rights* as proposed in this chapter and the President will sign it. It will require all federal agencies to support and enforce those rights in all of their activities.

   Let's extend citizenship status, including the right to vote in national elections, to all territorial peoples: American Samoa, Puerto Rico, Guam, US Virgin Islands, and Northern Mariana Islands.

2. *Let's Finish Ratifying and Activating the Equal Rights Amendment.* Congress will pass any required measure

needed to complete the process of ratifying the ERA, and will formally declare it the 28th Amendment to the Constitution. According to constitutional provisions, the action will not require or involve the participation or signature of the President.

3. *Then, Let's Supersede the Equal Rights Amendment with a Much More Comprehensive Amendment.* Congress will pass an updated version of the Equal Rights Amendment, with language such as recommended in this chapter, and send it to the states for ratification. When ratified, the amendment will supersede the original version.

4. *Let's Honor the Rights of Descendants of Disenfranchised Peoples.* Congress will create a permanent *National Commission for Social Justice,* tasked with advocacy and implementation of a comprehensive program for ensuring the rights of living descendants of the identified groups.

5. *Let's Push Back the Boundary on Personal Privacy and Information Security.* Congress will pass, and the President will sign, the Personal Information Privacy and Security Act (PIPSA), which will create the Information Privacy and Security Agency (IPSA), which will have the responsibility and authority to enforce the provisions of the act.

6. *Let's Break Up the Cyber-Monopolies.* Congress will create a *Commission on Anti-Competitive Practices in the Digital Information Industry.* The commission will carry out an intensive review of all major commercial enterprises operating in the digital information industry and recommend, as necessary and appropriate, the deconstruction of those enterprises engaging in predatory or monopolistic practices.

Chapter 11.
Let's Rethink Immigration:
Managing the "Coke Bottle"

"Keep, ancient lands, your storied pomp!"cries she
With silent lips. "Give me your tired, your poor,
Your huddled masses yearning to breathe free;
The wretched refuse of your teeming shore.
Send these, the homeless, tempest-tos't to me,
I lift my lamp beside the golden door!"

—Emma Lazarus
Inscription on the Statue of Liberty, 1903
(Excerpt from "The New Colossus," 1883)

Let's consider a simple case study that illustrates our insanely dysfunctional immigration process—I hesitate to call it a system.

A decade ago a young man from one of the Latin American countries managed to slip across the southern US border. He met some American citizens of Hispanic origin who sheltered him and helped him get a start. He kept his nose clean, found a job, learned a trade, saved some money, bought a car, and married a young Hispanic woman.

She came in on a student visa. She completed her education but overstayed her eligibility period. She applied for citizenship and now waits with a long list of other applicants for a court hearing. She launched a successful retail business. They make a comfortable living and both pay income taxes.

They had two children together. The kids attend school regularly and have done well in their studies. They've always spoken English and only understand a smattering of Spanish. She has become pregnant again and they expect their third child within a month.

Here we have a mixed, partly illegal family. Under the Constitution, the two children automatically became US citizens at birth, but both parents remain illegal for various reasons. Technically, they've violated US laws.

One day, the ICE agents—Immigration and Customs Enforcement—show up at their door. The question: which ones should they arrest? Whom do they deport?

Should they arrest both parents? If so, what do they do with the kids? Can they deport the kids—American citizens by birth—along with the parents? Do they deport the parents and send the kids into foster care? What will they do with a newborn baby—also a "birthright" citizen?

Do we as a society want them to tear a family apart to punish the parents for long-ago infractions of laws we've never diligently enforced?

Now multiply that fairly simple case example by about 100,000 and you can see the near-comical insanity of our so-called immigration "system."

IN SEARCH OF SANITY

Let's begin our investigation of the Immigration component of the Republic by acknowledging the daunting complexity of the issue.

We Americans have a tendency to look for—or hope for—big, simple answers to our big questions. And when we can't find them we demand them anyway. We want our leaders to fix things. We don't like situations with too many moving parts. So whenever we face a dauntingly complex problem or issue, we often fall for the temptation to reduce it to a two-sided battle of emotional slogans.

The noted scientist and intellectual philosopher Albert Einstein liked to say,

"Everything should be made as simple as possible, but not simpler."

Let's make it as simple as possible, but not simpler.

I'll state my premise out front: *we haven't solved the immigration problem because we never defined it intelligently.*

We've misunderstood it, misdiagnosed it, and mis-framed it as an emotionally charged stalemate between two incompatible mindsets. Regardless of which side gets its way, we won't have solved it. Until we reframe our understanding of the problem and begin to apply some systems thinking, we'll keep repeating the same old slogans and fighting the same old battles.

Let's make things Einstein-simple. Let's define only two categories of people who might stand on American soil at any moment: 1) citizens, and 2) visitors. If we set aside the various emotionally charged labels, we can recognize immigration as just one part of a bigger system. Let's call that bigger system *population management. Solving the population management issue will solve the immigration issue.*

The category of *visitors* has various sub-categories: short-stay guests; people visiting families and friends who live here; people attending conferences or special events; day shoppers; airline crews making turn-arounds; people here to do business with Americans; foreign students; and lots of others.

Then we get to the collection of people who want to live here for a long time or indefinitely. That breaks down as refugees and people seeking asylum; people who want to work here for some period, and possibly send money back home; people who want to live here without changing citizenship; and people who aspire to become US citizens.

And finally, we have the problem cases—people with various stories who didn't get permission to come here or stay. That includes people who arrived on approved visas but overstayed their deadlines—possibly the largest majority—and people who made their way across unsecured borders and dissolved into the general population.

Pro-immigrant activists call this last group "undocumented migrants." Anti-immigrant activists call them "illegal aliens." As a society, we can't seem to decide how we feel about them.

HOW DID WE GET HERE?

To understand how we've mis-framed the issue and to see how we can re-frame it more intelligently, we'll take our usual quick historical flashback for perspective.

About three years prior to this writing, the immigration issue exploded into an emotionalized war between the two dominant political parties, the Democrats and the Republicans. It had simmered at a sub-critical level for decades, but the arrival of a new political actor on the scene, one Donald J. Trump, turned it into a near death struggle between the two parties, and between the activist factions that have tribalized around the controversy.

Politics and social conflict have always contaminated American immigration policy, so the current storm seems rather familiar from the historical perspective.

In the early days of the Republic, no one paid much attention to borders or citizenship. The vast continental territory seemed almost limitless. Anyone could head west and claim a bit of land as his piece of the New World. Most of the colonists held British citizenship and the status of the "miscellaneous" people like Indians, slaves, and wanderers of all sorts didn't seem to matter much.

The new Constitution provided for citizenship through *naturalization*, which Congress defined in a 1790 law as open to "free white persons."

One could fairly say that the Republic had no coherent immigration policy and no rational system for managing it for at least the first 100 years since the Founding. Congress didn't get around to creating the Immigration and Naturalization Service, or INS, until 1933. By some unfathomable act of wisdom the legislators placed it under the US Department of Labor. In 1940 they moved it to the Department of Justice, where it stayed for another 60 years.

After the devastating terrorist attacks of 9-11, the Homeland Security Act of 2002 disbanded the old INS and moved its operations to three new federal agencies, under a new mega-bureaucracy known as the Department of Homeland Security (DHS).

The current scheme for handling people coming into the country has four sub-bureaucracies:

▸ The *Customs and Border Protection* agency (CBP), better known as the "Border Patrol," polices the land borders and operates the 328 official points of entry, or POEs— land border crossings, airports, and seaports. They prevent the entry of illegal persons, weapons, drugs, and commercial goods. As of this writing, CBP has about 20,000 agents.

▸ The *Immigration and Customs Enforcement* agency (ICE) has jurisdiction inside the country, and agents arrest violators of laws that govern border crossing, customs and trade, and immigration. ICE operates 500 detention centers throughout the United States that hold about 34,000 people on any given day. As of this writing, ICE has about 6,000 agents.

▸ The *US Citizenship and Immigration Services* agency (USCIS) handles the processes for legal immigration and naturalization. That includes issuing "green cards," which confer formal residency; holding eligibility hearings for citizenship; and naturalization procedures.

▸ The collection of *58 Immigration Courts*, originally part of the old INS, falls under the Department of Justice.

Currently, some 400 overworked immigration judges hear cases for asylum, citizenship, and deportation.

The American Bar Association has declared the immigration court system as "on the brink of collapse." The ABA and many other legal experts have called for moving the Immigration Courts out from under the Department of Justice and putting them under the Supreme Court. Placing the courts under the DOJ, they claim, has politicized their role, and subjects judges to arbitrary pressures from the Executive Branch.

You Can't Get There From Here

As of this writing, the situation at the southern US border has become acute, intense, and intolerable. It makes the case for completely rethinking the whole process painfully obvious.

An unprecedented influx of migrants from Central and Latin America, beginning about 2018, overwhelmed the processing capacity of the Border Patrol and ICE. A rising number of legal applicants, plus a tide of people caught crossing illegally, swamped the whole operation.

SHOTGUN SOLUTIONS

In a breathtaking demonstration of system blindness, the President and his advisors announced a "crack-down on illegal aliens." Calling it a "zero tolerance" policy of border control, he ordered CBP units to detain all illegal crossers and hold them for trial. That order abolished the older "catch and release" policy of the past, under which CBP agents simply booked them and released them to await court hearings.

Critics of the catch-and-release policy held that it rewarded people who crossed illegally and made suckers of those who came in at the official points of entry. Indeed, in the absence of a functioning visitor management system, it certainly did. But the medicine soon became worse than the disease.

After the President's "catch and keep" order, there followed a ghastly example of unintended consequences. The aspiring migrant population had lately mushroomed into a mixture of families, single mothers with children, pregnant women, and even unaccompanied children. Even worse, their numbers had increased radically.

Predictably, the rising tide of detainees quickly maxed out CBP's detention capabilities. In the past they had detained only lawbreakers—typically young, able-bodied males trying to run drugs, smuggle weapons, or commit other crimes. Now their jammed-up system couldn't process people out as fast as new ones came in. And just as predictably, the quasi-military CBP agents had no idea how to deal with a large population of children, ranging from infants to teen-agers, many of them unaccompanied.

In their defense, as a quasi-military force they had no training, no special facilities, no assistance from qualified social service professionals, and mostly no sensitivity to the unique needs of children and families. No one had prepared them for that mission.

CBP agents had little choice but to just keep stuffing more and more people into holding pens designed only for short-term detention, without adequate food, water, basic sanitation or personal hygiene, or medical care.

Overwhelmed, confused and desperate, the CBP's local commanders figured out how to make the worst of a bad situation. Faced with a federal statute that prohibited keeping children in detention for more than 20 days, and still required to detain the adults, they began separating the children from their families and transferring them to other holding facilities, sometimes in out-of-state locations.

The situation quickly exploded into a humanitarian catastrophe, widely observed and widely denounced around the world. Investigative journalists and members of Congress descended on several detention centers and reacted with outrage. They condemned both the appalling lack of sanitation and overcrowded housing conditions and the thoughtless treatment of vulnerable children like cattle.

Congressional hearings predictably ensued. CBP agents had

separated more than 3,000 children from their families before court rulings put a stop to the practice.

Mental health experts spoke out, condemning the operation of the detention centers as tantamount to officially sanctioned child abuse. The American Academy of Pediatrics formally condemned the practice of separating emotionally fragile children from their families. Their experts cited the likelihood of extreme psychological trauma, phobias of abandonment, fear of strangers and unfamiliar environments, impaired child-parent bonding on reunification, and long-term mental health problems.

DOING THE SAME WRONG THING—HARDER

The President, however, apparently not understanding the drama created by the first decision, decided to double down on the campaign. He announced that he had ordered ICE to "arrest and deport millions of illegal aliens." He implied that they would leave the country in very short order.

After the President's announcement, news stories circulated like wildfire, detailing Gestapo-like raids and round-ups by ICE agents, further polarizing Americans around the "illegal alien problem." Many people conjured up images of midnight arrests with ICE agents hauling truckloads of fugitives to the border and dumping them back into Mexico. Some incident reports seemed to justify those perceptions, and immigration advocates predictably began to call for the abolition of ICE.

But the practical reality didn't match the scare stories. In most cases the person accused of unauthorized entry or presence has the right of due process, which usually means a court hearing in front of a judge.

At most, ICE agents could simply arrest people, detain them for a matter of days, and then deliver them to courthouses for a first hearing. In most cases, that brief pre-trial hearing just starts a long process in motion. Once booked into the legal calendar, the detainee goes free, with the instruction to return on an assigned date for the real hearing.

But with a current backlog of over 900,000 cases and less than 400 immigration judges to try them, an individual typically faces a waiting period of many months up to 2 or 3 years or longer. Meanwhile, they go on with life, with the distant threat of deportation hanging over their heads. So much for rounding up and deporting millions of them.

As the scare stories multiplied in the aftermath of the President's declarations, mayors of a number of "sanctuary" cities instructed their law enforcement agencies not to comply with ICE requests to detain and hand over undocumented residents living in their communities. Officials in Los Angeles, San Francisco, Seattle, Denver, Chicago, New Orleans, Boston, Baltimore, New York, and Philadelphia, as well as various local jurisdictions also refused to give ICE agents access to people arrested for domestic crimes or to share key law enforcement data.

The President's call to add 5,000 more officers to both CBP and ICE soon collided with the simple reality of time and logistics. It typically takes nearly a year to add a patrol officer to such an organization. The training phase takes six months or more. Aside from that, candidates for law enforcement jobs typically consider CBP and ICE as some of the least desirable agencies to join. They perceive border work as hot, dirty, mostly outdoors, often solitary, often stressful, unrewarding, low-paid, and low in status.

CBP especially has a general image in the law enforcement community as somewhat lacking in professionalism and susceptible to corruption. Described by some organizational psychologists as having a culture of toxic masculinity, the agency has had more than its share of incidents of mistreatment of migrants, including extortion, sexual abuse, and violence. Agents also encounter the temptation to accept bribes from desperate migrants, or from the *coyotes* who try to smuggle them across the border.

THE ANCHOR BABY COMPLICATION

Abraham Lincoln and his Congress inadvertently bequeathed us a hot potato, politically and socially speaking, in the form of a simple phrase in the 14th Amendment, which granted citizenship to former slaves. That one phrase has confused, confounded, and enraged anti-immigration activists.

Section 1 of the Fourteenth said,

> *"All persons born or naturalized in the United States, and subject to the jurisdiction thereof, are citizens of the United States and of the State wherein they reside."*

Abe and his advisers couldn't foresee a situation where the US population—about 30 million in 1860—would grow to over 300 million humans. The coast-to-coast build-out that made modern America possible has forced us to decide who becomes a citizen, and under what circumstances.

The birthright citizenship provision, just quoted, has evolved into a big-time loophole for foreigners who hope to outflank the Byzantine American immigration process.

A foreign woman who has entered the US, with or without permission, can give birth to an "instant citizen." That event instantly anchors her to a US citizen, making it much more difficult and complicated to deport her or the child. Some pro-immigration activists object to the term "anchor baby" as somehow demeaning, but the metaphor applies. Someone has decided to use a child as a tool to game the system.

With a long-term view, even if the mother had to leave the country, she could place the child with someone else, or if she took the child with her, the child's re-entry rights—those of a citizen—would presumably extend to her. An anchor baby grown to adulthood would presumably have the option to return to the US and sponsor his or her parents and possibly siblings, for expedited immigration status.

Further to the extreme, a cottage industry has recently emerged, particularly in California, for "birth tourism." Wealthy and pregnant Chinese women, in particular, pay phony travel agents huge sums of money to arrange tourist visas, timed for arrival ahead of their expected delivery dates.

The expectant mothers live in furnished condos kept and serviced especially for that purpose. When they deliver their babies, typically at local hospitals, the children get birth certificates and Social Security numbers, making them full-fledged Americans. After a few months, or when their visas expire, they take their American babies back to China.

The dual-citizenship child becomes a family asset and an insurance policy for the future. At college age, the son or daughter could choose to live in the US unrestricted and attend college with the same privileges as all other Americans. He or she could stay in the US after graduating and start a career or return to work in China. Both options would continue indefinitely.

Many wealthy Chinese, like the wealthy in other totalitarian countries, look for ways to reposition their assets in safe havens like the US. Many of them buy houses in affluent neighborhoods, just in case the political environment might turn against them and they would decide to flee their home country. They would hope to use their American family member to facilitate their exit if necessary.

From the systems point of view, closing the anchor-birth loophole deserves a very high priority. A constitutional amendment, redefining the criteria for citizenship by birth, could bring a great deal of sanity to a crazy non-system.

DO WE STILL WANT THE TIRED AND POOR? FACTS AND FIGMENTS

America has welcomed foreigners for all of its history.

- For the past several decades we've minted an average of about 700,000 new citizens a year—almost 2,000 a day.

- As of this writing, naturalized citizens number about 22 million, or roughly 7 percent of a total population of about 325 million.

- About 13 million people have green cards, which give them permanent resident status. About 9 million of those qualify for eventual citizenship. About 65,000 serve in the armed forces, although they can't vote.

- Government figures estimate the number of people in the country without permission—"undocumented residents"—at about 11 million, or roughly 4 percent of the total population. Most of them have partly assimilated.

Decades of neglecting the southern border, plus lax law enforcement by the federal government, have allowed a steady accumulation of undocumented people, most with uncertain or ambiguous status.

MYTHS ABOUT MIGRANTS

Myth: the menacing threat-image of millions of alien fugitives roaming the country and hiding in the woods, promoted by anti-immigrant activists, misstates the situation.

Reality: experts estimate that a large majority of undocumented people have already assimilated to various degrees, working at jobs, paying taxes, paying rent, driving cars, going to schools, and raising families. Not surprisingly, most new arrivals begin to assimilate as soon as they get here, for the obvious reasons of self-interest.

Leaders of the sanctuary cities assert that the federal government has tolerated, and implicitly condoned, this below-the-radar "gray citizenship" status for many years. In many cities, governments and community groups openly acknowledge their presence and consider them semi-citizens with nearly a full set of rights. Some advocates refer to them as "PAMs," or Partly Assimilated Migrants. They reject the characterization of undocumented but highly assimilated people as common criminals.

Myth: some anti-immigration advocates contend that the US can't absorb more immigrants than the current stream.

Reality: that narrative, largely inflamed by the traffic jam at the southern border, and compounded by the ignorance of the American public, conflicts entirely with the facts on the ground. America has a relatively low population density—the number of people divided by the area of habitable land. Drive through vast stretches of the beautiful countryside in Montana, Wyoming, Idaho, and the Dakotas and you'll see nothing but wildlife and farm animals for miles.

In fact, many small towns and local communities in the US have begun to see *declining populations* and painful worker shortages, as birth rates drop and young people move away to the cities—domestic migration, as some analysts call it.

Enterprising individuals can't start new businesses or grow existing ones without workers. Farmers who depend on foreign workers worry about threats of ICE round-ups and deportations, which could put them out of business. We'll see more and more small communities becoming ghost towns.

Myth: the current US President has described Latin American immigrants, both legal and illegal, as a highly criminalized population. He campaigned for his office by describing them as "rapists, murderers, gang members, and drug smugglers."

Reality: the federal government's own statistics indicate that immigrants commit proportionately *fewer* crimes than US citizens. Researchers surmise the simple reason that they have more to lose by getting caught, so they tend to keep their heads down and their noses clean.

Myth: several news commentators have claimed, without evidence, that most immigrants in the pipeline—those having applied for legal status—don't show up for their scheduled court hearings. One such talking hair-do surmised that "Only three percent of them show up for their hearings."

Reality: the federal government pegs the appearance rate at over 75 percent for most applicants and over 90 percent for asylum seekers. Some analysts estimate that processing errors such as mistakes in assigning trial dates; incorrect addresses on notifications; and erroneous instructions might account for five percent or more of the no-show rates.

THE "COKE BOTTLE" EFFECT

In the face of so much confusion, misinformation and demagoguery, let's approach the immigration issue from a completely new angle. To do that we need to start with a clean sheet of paper—and a very interesting chart known to experts as a *population pyramid*. It shows, graphically, the relative numbers of people living in a country, grouped by age range—typically in 5-year bands.

First, let's look at a chart for a typical developing country, like Nigeria, as in Figure 11-1. It shows the arrangement of people in the various age bands as percentages of the total population.[22]

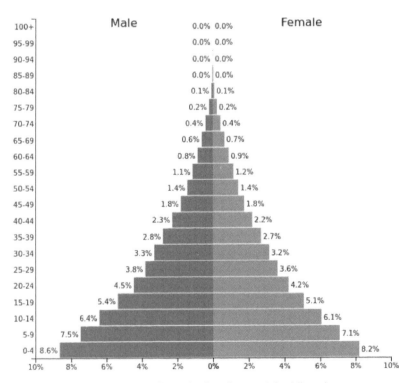

Figure 11-1. Population Pyramid – Nigeria

Note the very high number of infants, on the bottom row, and note how rapidly the numbers drop off going up the age scale. This indicates very high birth rates, low survival rates for children, and a very short life expectancy for most of the 190 million people living there.

Note that the age band of birth-to-age-5 for this country includes 8.6 percent of males and 8.2 percent of females. Almost 30 percent of this country's people fall below age 10. Over half fall below the 20-year mark, or the *median age*, as statisticians call it.

For a poor country with a weak economic structure and low productivity, this pyramid pattern spells doom—or at least hardship for many years to come. With 40 percent of the people too young to work and dependent on the rapidly dwindling numbers of workers in the prime productive years, no one eats well. Even worse, this population will likely continue to grow rapidly because of the high birth rates, making the economic challenge worse, not better.

This country has two obvious policy challenges: 1) reducing the birth rate; and 2) improving the survival rates of people in their productive years. Nigeria needs far fewer dependents and lots more workers—as well as a modern economy.

The population pyramid can offer us a lot of insight as we decipher the story concealed in those percentages. Space limitations prevent a more revealing exploration, but we can apply a similar reasoning process to the chart for the US.

Figure 11-2 shows the pyramid for the United States, which telegraphs a stunningly different story. This unique shape, nicknamed by demographers as the "Coke bottle" chart, has a very different meaning for the future of the American Republic, in contrast to that of a third-world state like Nigeria.

Note the remarkable drop-off in the numbers of people at the bottom of the chart, which hardly resembles a pyramid. The slight bulge just above the center represents the well-known post-war baby boom, caused by a surge in birth rates as the country returned to stability and prosperity after WW2. A small secondary bulge comes along about 20 years later.

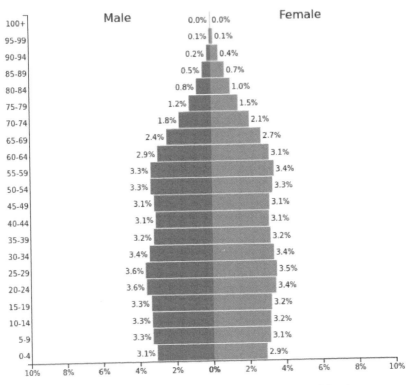

Figure 11-2. Population Pyramid – United States

After the baby boom, birth rates took a radical dive beginning in the 1960s, with the arrival of The Pill. Other factors, such as increasing educational levels and higher career aspirations amongst young women, have also driven down fertility rates.

Statisticians tell us that, for any country's population to grow, the average lifetime birth rate per female must exceed a factor of about 2.1, referred to as the *replacement rate*. That means that each woman has to replace herself and one man, plus a little extra to offset early mortality rates. For every woman who does not reproduce, some other woman—or combination of women—will have to deliver an extra 2.1 babies to make up the shortfall.

As we can see from the chart, American couples in the primary childbearing years—20 to 40—haven't replaced themselves. As birth rates have declined, America has passed the point of "ZPG," or zero population growth, and the total population has begun to shrink. Recent to this writing, demographers estimate the US fertility rate at about 1.77.

The bottom line: *if we don't increase our birth rates or change our immigration system, we'll see a steadily growing shortage of workers—and taxpayers—for several decades at least.*

We'll have fewer people in the primary productive age range at the same time that the boomers and post-boomers move into retirement and expect the younger generations to keep them comfortable. At some point, this shortage will become acute and politically significant. As of this writing, we have about 2.8 full time workers for every person receiving Social Security payments. Government analysts expect that ratio to drop to 2.2 by 2035.

How do these discoveries relate to the immigration issue? We'll soon see.

But first, let's not feel too sorry for the American society, because a number of other countries have an even tougher demographic problem on their hands. Consider the case of China, for example, as shown in Figure 11-3.

The top of the Chinese pyramid shows the typical pattern of a population that grew rapidly in the distant past, but then something put on the brakes. In the 1980s, the Chinese government, worried about a population that had shot past the 1 billion mark, imposed the strict one-child policy, which mandated that couples couldn't have more than one child without special permission. Those who violated the restriction faced public shaming, economic sanctions, and loss of social privileges.

The policy worked well—perhaps too well. Experts estimate that the restriction probably prevented as many as 400 million births during the 35 years it remained in force. The government dropped the policy in 2015. But by then many young Chinese had become accustomed to a one-child lifestyle. They liked the economic freedom of a two-income household and easy access to the pleasures of the rapidly developing consumer economy.

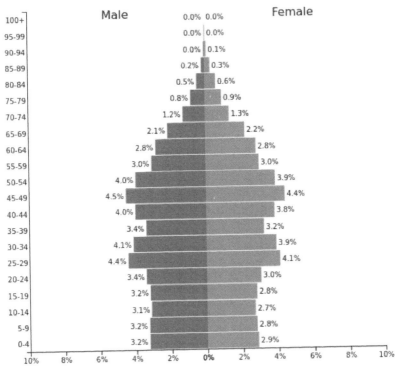

Figure 11-3. Population Pyramid – China

China's problem now: a similar one to the US's problem, in spades. They have plenty of people—perhaps too many—but they have the wrong age mix. They have a huge elderly population with a long life expectancy, riding on the backs of a shrinking population of workers and taxpayers. China has also joined the club of ZPG nations. Its planners will have to figure out some creative solutions.

Japan and Russia also face similar demographic challenges. Russia, with an alarming drop in birth rates, ZPG status, and population curves even more distorted than those of the US and China, probably faces the biggest challenge. Taiwan, according to the CIA's *World Factbook*, currently has the lowest fertility rate, at 1.13 children per woman.

A number of other countries, particularly in Europe, have recently moved into or toward ZPG territory and their leaders have cast around for strategies to refill their Coke bottles. Ironically, a number of European countries, including the ZPG candidates, have adopted anti-immigrant policies in the throes of a recently contagious neo-nationalistic fever.

What do these charts tell us about the immigration issue now facing our Republic? They tell us that, if we want to maintain economic stability, *we'll need at least 20 million new citizens —mostly young ones—over the next decade or so.* Otherwise, we'll have to start shooting the old ones.

Even with computers and robots taking over lots of work processes, the workforce will shrink and the need for imported workers will become a critical part of our economy. In fact, we might even have trouble importing enough new citizens to fill the bottom of the American Coke bottle.

So here we have two very contradictory ways of thinking about immigration. One view, a highly emotionalized one, sees immigrants as threatening to our society. Some political advocates have even called for building a huge wall across the 2,400 miles of the southern border to keep them out.

Another view, more attentive to the evidence, holds that America can, and should, actively invite more new citizens, so long as we can assimilate them effectively.

If we look to the future, beyond the current "border crisis"— a politically manufactured crisis, some would say—most of the evidence and common-sense logic point to the more progressive option. We can replace the current insane immigration process with a comprehensive, logically designed, and effectively operated system.

LET'S REFRAME "IN-MIGRATION:" LAWS, LOGISTICS, AND ASSIMILATION

Creating 20 million new citizens over the next 10 years, or 2 million per year, would require us to triple the usual rate of naturalization. Clearly, the federal government's administrative system for immigration and naturalization couldn't possibly handle that load. We'll have to rethink the whole process from end to end and design a viable system that can handle the challenge. Building an effective *visitor management system* will require a massive commitment, something on the scale of the Apollo moon program.

LET'S DO SOME SYSTEM THINKING

Let's pause for a one-paragraph short course on system thinking. By a *system*, we mean a combination of *parts*, or *components*—things, people, organisms, organizations—that go together in some special *relationship* to serve some desired *purpose*. A viable system needs an *organizing principle*—a value proposition that makes it more than just a bunch of parts. Think of the water supply system in your house; the system for registering the new car you bought with the Department of Motor Vehicles; or the exquisitely designed entertainment system known as a Disneyland park. The parts all work together to serve a clear purpose.

In the strictest sense (okay, two paragraphs), a haphazard conglomeration of people and activities doesn't qualify as a system, or certainly not an intelligently designed one. And when it comes to government operations, the system usually extends beyond the boundaries of any one agency or department. Every system—and every problem—intertwines with other systems and problems. What we do with one system usually affects the other systems intertwined with it. We need to keep that in mind as we work out the logic for a new way of dealing with immigration.

We need to start thinking of immigration management as part of a larger system—our *visitor management system*. We need a comprehensive concept, policy, and system for managing the status and entitlements of all human beings within our borders. As we noted in Chapter 6 (Law & Order), we can start by recognizing only two categories of people: citizens and visitors. We can use modern information technology and management methods to identify every such person, track his or her status continuously, and support the transition from visitor to citizen when appropriate.

A smart visitor management system, I believe, will need four main components, or subsystems, as described below. We currently have bits and pieces of each of them, but few of our national leaders, advocates, or activists understand them as a comprehensive system. Some of the key components don't exist at this time and some exist in fragmented form, not really integrated with the rest. Each component includes a variety of organizations, both government and private, and they must all interact effectively. Let's briefly review how each of these four systems, or subsystems, would work:

1. *Visitor Outreach System.* This component includes agencies like the State Department's foreign consulates and visitor services centers; visitor information centers at points of entry (POE)s such as airports, seaports, and land border stations; joint operations with neighboring countries, especially Mexico; tourist service agencies; and community social services groups. All can contribute to inform, educate, and counsel prospective entrants about the importance of entering legally.

2. *Identification and Intake System.* At every POE, every single person who steps onto American soil, *without exception,* will first get photographed, fingerprinted, and recorded in a National Visitor Identification System (NVIDS)—a parallel system to the National

Citizen Identification Database (NCIDS) described in Chapter 6 and elsewhere. POE screening units will assign each person a status, which can include immediate return (at the entrant's expense); detention if charged with a serious crime (other than simply crossing a border illegally); acceptance for entry as a casual visitor (e.g., a tourist or a day shopper); or acceptance for applicant status and entitled to enter and move about, subject to status management.

3. *Status Management System.* Once the authorized entrant leaves the POE jurisdiction and moves into the general territory of the US, various other agencies—which must coordinate their efforts closely—will track his or her status, keep the NVIDS updated, and intervene as appropriate at key points during the duration of his or her stay. Violation-of-status events, such as arrests for serious crimes or engaging in certain unauthorized activities, will trigger detention, expedited hearings, and deportation. Authorized changes of status, such as completion of required waiting periods, eligibility for green cards, completion of university studies, marriage, birth of children, approval of asylum status, and others will come to the attention of case management officers. This part of the overall system also includes various social services agencies, both government and private (such as church groups or charitable agencies), which offer support and advocacy to visitors in need of assistance.

4. *Assimilation and Naturalization System.* Case Management Officers will maintain ongoing contact and status management with all authorized long-term immigrants, as they move toward permanent resident status or seek to become naturalized citizens. *Managed assimilation*, almost completely missing in the current immigration process, can supply the country with productive workers and taxpayers, and

can significantly minimize the social service costs associated with impaired assimilation. English as a second language training (ESL) for example, will have a high priority in this system. Free and widely available ESL programs, through a variety of providers, can make the single biggest difference in the immigrant's capacity to participate in the American society. Job training, job readiness, and job placement will have an equally high priority. Early eligibility for employment, subject to effective status management, will also reduce social support costs.

BUT FIRST: THREE BIG PILLS TO SWALLOW

But even with a more rational system in place, we won't have a real solution to the immigration problem until we come to peace with three critical truths, which we can do.

All three of those realities will require changes, not only in our policies and laws, but also in our mindset. Let's start thinking about them in a serious way:

1. We'll have to normalize the status of millions of undocumented people in the US who have already assimilated, leaving a smaller and more manageable number of true candidates for deportation.

2. We'll have to radically reduce the number of migrants who choose to sneak across borders rather than go to one of the official points of entry. Arresting and imprisoning illegal entrants and separating kids from their parents doesn't seem to have changed their motivations. Instead, *we have to make the legal option more attractive than the illegal one.*

3. We'll have to reduce and simplify the onerous red tape and waiting periods imposed on people eligible for residency and citizenship. We'll need to *help* people become Americans, not make it difficult for them. We could clear a huge percentage of the cases backlogged in the immigration courts by authorizing well-

qualified Case Management Officers to make determinations, instead of requiring every immigrant to appear before one of the scarce and overloaded judges.

Let's consider each of these realities—these psychological pills—on its own merits.

Big Pill #1: Let's Normalize the Status of Assimilated Migrants

In 1984, President Ronald Reagan led a campaign to bring undocumented immigrants who had assimilated into communities out of the shadows and line them up for citizenship. He declared,

> "I believe in the idea of amnesty for those who have put down roots and lived here, even though sometime back they may have entered illegally."

The Immigration Reform and Control Act, piloted through the Congress by Wyoming's Republican Senator Alan Simpson, made all immigrants who'd arrived before 1982 eligible for citizenship. The bill won approval in both houses and Reagan signed it into law in 1986.

The term "amnesty" had taken on a very negative significance during the debates, so the sponsors chose to tout it as a process of "legalization." In fact, they promoted the overall bill as a crackdown on illegal immigration and a cleaning up of the messy immigration non-system. That law-and-order narrative soothed the conservative factions who looked with suspicion at any effort to dilute the country's traditionally white population with foreigners. Amnesty came along as the hidden prize in the Cracker Jacks box.

Political activists still argue about the law's benefits, and some critics still view it as a failure, but many of its supporters consider the benefits of the amnesty process its best selling point. According to Senator Simpson, "It's not perfect, but 2.9 million people came forward. If you can bring one person out of an exploited relationship, that's good enough for me."

Of the 2.9 million people who acquired permanent resident status under the Reagan-Simpson program, 1.1 million went on to become naturalized citizens. The American society didn't collapse, and the Republic moved on.

Now, three decades down the road, the situation looks strangely familiar. The federal government's continued neglect of the southern border and haphazard application of the immigration laws has allowed the undocumented population to grow again, this time to much larger numbers.

No surprise: a comprehensive amnesty program must once again become the centerpiece of the reformation. Considering that the term still carries negative emotional loading for many people involved in the reform, let's give it a new handle. Let's call it *normalization*.

We can choose to take a realistic approach and forgive ancient misdeeds. Once we come to peace with the idea of *pragmatic forgiveness*, we can move on to *pragmatic solutions*.

Big Pill #2: Let's Make Legal Entry the Preferred Choice

To reduce the "dash and dare" incentives, we first need to scale up the processing system for legal entry with a large number of *Case Management Officers* and *Immigration Status Adjudicators* who have the authority to grant eligibility status directly, without overloading the courts.

Then we can strive to change the motivations of many people who might consider crossing illegally, by adopting a procedure called "return with prejudice."

Under this procedure, CBP agents will take illegal crossers they've apprehended to the nearest point of entry, where processing personnel will photograph and fingerprint them and record their identities into the National Visitor Identification System (NVIDS).

Now comes the part that some readers might find hard to live with: CBP agents then simply *take the illegal crossers to the entry point and send them back across the border.*

"Wait a minute," some will protest. "They violated our laws by coming in illegally, and we just send them back, with no punishment?" But let's think about it in a more practical way.

CBP agents face a dilemma. With the old catch-and-release policy, people who entered illegally could stay in-country and get a shot at immigrant status—a long shot, maybe, but still a shot. That policy would probably encourage, rather than discourage illegal crossings.

On the other hand, the catch-and-keep policy, as we've seen, overloads CBP detention resources and causes appalling humanitarian consequences. That approach would also do little to discourage illegal crossings.

The return-with-prejudice policy would save enormous amounts of money and staff time, compared to detention. I for one would consider the moral trade-off a slam-dunk.

But wait: the illegal crossers would indeed have to pay for their offenses—with their futures. When apprehended, they'll learn that, if they ever hope to enter legally thereafter, they'll have to pay a substantial retroactive fine, plus a security fee as assurance that they'll obey the conditions of their entry. The visitor database system has a long memory.

We would work to make the return-with-prejudice policy commonly known throughout the aspiring migrant population. Word usually gets around fast in that kind of a situation. With a joint program of extensive publicity, in cooperation with Mexican and other Latin American governments, we could sell the benefits of legal entry.

Big Pill #3: Let's Make Citizenship Quicker and Easier

Should a person who aspires to become an American citizen —a law-abiding, diligent person with the best of intentions— have to wait five years, or even ten years, to get there? Should an able-bodied person who wants to make a living in America have to wait and hope for years to get a special type of visa or a work permit?

Somewhere in our ancient past, I presume, political leaders decided to make the process of becoming a citizen, or even a permanent resident, a difficult climb. Now, if we really want to fill in the bottom of the American Coke bottle, and we need to mint new citizens three times faster than our typical rate, we need to rethink the barriers.

Our current policies probably overplay the element of risk— the likelihood that a person might become, as the early framers put it, "a ward of the state." Maybe we've misplaced the emphasis. Maybe we should emphasize *assimilation* rather than insurance.

Going back to our system model, let's get serious about the fourth subsystem, *Assimilation and Naturalization*. If we can build pathways and channels into the many support systems we already have, can we ensure that almost every able-bodied and well-meaning person we let in will try—and probably succeed—to make a go of it?

Let's remind ourselves that not all native-born Americans have succeeded to the fullest. We still have homeless people, people whose lives have collapsed, and people who've gotten on the wrong side of the law. An immigrant population will surely have a certain percentage of them also, but probably no more than the native population.

So, let's adopt a saner set of rules for work permission, residency, and eligibility for citizenship. We can map out a streamlined process of movement from temporary resident status to permanent residency, and naturalization if desired.

I see no reason why we can't progress a qualified person from the status of visitor to the status of full-fledged citizen in less than three years.

THE FIX-IT LIST: IMMIGRATION

So, how can we improve this component of our Republic—

Immigration? Let's start with these actions.

1. *Let's Normalize All Assimilated Undocumented People currently in the US.* Congress will pass the Immigrant Status Normalization Act, which will provide for undisputed eligibility for permanent resident status and expedited transition to citizenship, for the undocumented people who come forward. They will receive guaranteed immunity from prosecution, deportation, or other punishments, provided they have no record of charges for specified crimes. Those who can demonstrate a record of law-abiding participation in their communities, with character references, will become eligible for expedited naturalization.

2. *Let's Change the Rules for Birthright Citizenship.* Congress will pass, and the states will ratify, a Constitutional amendment that defines the conditions under which a person born in the US becomes a citizen. The language will read something like:

   "A child born in the United States acquires the most favorable status of residency or citizenship of the two biological parents as of the time of birth. If either of the child's biological parents holds citizenship at the time of birth, or has resided legally and continuously in the United States for at least two years as of the time of birth, the child becomes a citizen at birth.

   "A child whose foreign-born biological parent, foster parent, or legal guardian becomes a naturalized citizen before the child's 18th birthday becomes a citizen at the time of naturalization.

   "A child born without automatic rights to citizenship becomes eligible for expedited naturalization if taken into the legal custody of a foster parent or guardian who holds US citizenship.

"Citizenship by naturalization becomes a permanent right, not subject to revocation or invalidation by any law or public agency.

"Congress shall have the power to enact legislation to enforce the provisions of this amendment."

3. *Let's Re-engineer the Immigration Court System.* Congress will pass a law that restructures the immigration court system, moving the courts out from under the Justice Department and under a new component of the Supreme Court (described in Chapter 4 [Governance]) which will oversee the entire federal court system.

   The law will provide for an adequate number of Case Management Officers—trained professionals who oversee each candidate's eligibility and progress toward defined legal status. Some of them will serve as Immigration Status Adjudicators, acting as officers of the court, who can decide the status of any candidate. Only cases involving misconduct or appeals from the Adjudicators' rulings will go to the courts.

4. *Let's Make it Easier to Come in Legally than Illegally.* CBP will adopt a new set of policies and practices for managing migrants apprehended trying to cross a border outside of established points of entry. This will include provisions for "return with prejudice," as described above.

   An energetic promotional program, in cooperation Latin American governments, will spread the word that America does indeed accept migrants, even the tired and the poor, but only when they come in by the official golden door.

5. *Let's Make the Path to Citizenship Easier and Faster.* We can debate the details, but some scheme like the following would seem to make sense.

   a. Any person who passes a primary screening

process, either at a border or as part of a foreign visa application process, will have permission to enter the country and take employment from the time he or she arrives. The accepted visitor will receive a mini-green card, conferring eligibility to work for 6 months, pending application for extended status. The employer must pay at least the prevailing local minimum wage, and must withhold a percentage of the payment as a non-refundable immigration tax, such as 15 percent.

b. After the first probation period, the well-behaved newcomer will become eligible for an official green card, allowing a one-year period of residence. During that period, he or she can take regular employment, will receive a Social Security number, and will become a regular taxpayer.

c. At all stages of the process, a Case Management Officer working as part of the Status Management System will monitor the progress of the visitor who aspires to join the American enterprise. Any violation of the terms of eligibility or criminal behavior could subject the visitor to deportation.

d. After the trial period, if the candidate has demonstrated full compliance with the terms of eligibility, the Case Management Officer and the Adjudicator will confirm his or her eligibility for citizenship. The candidate will attend an orientation course, pass an exam, and receive a certificate confirming readiness for naturalization.

e. Candidates in final status will participate in naturalization ceremonies and become permanent US citizens.

Chapter 12.
Let's Rethink Foreign Relations: America's Deal With Our Neighbors

"America is the only nation
that has gone directly
from barbarism to decadence
without the usual interval of civilization."
—George Bernard Shaw

The Foreign Relations component of our Republic, more than most of the others, seems to involve the greatest sense of uncertainty, ambiguity, and unease in the minds of Americans.

Throughout our history our leaders, big thinkers, activists, and citizens have struggled with two conflicting streams of thought. The national conversation has almost always involved some version of the same argument: should we engage actively with the other nations of the world or should we mind our own business and stay out of their affairs?

GLOBALISM VS. TRIBALISM: THE BASIC CHOICE

The preferred answer to that question has shifted back and forth many times as presidents have come and gone; wars have flared up and burned out; alliances have formed and collapsed; economic conditions have improved and gone sour; and foreign governments have become more and less antagonistic to American's existence and role in the world.

"AVOID ENTANGLING ALLIANCES"

As George Washington stepped down from his second four-year term as America's first president and retired from public life in 1796, he offered a memorable warning to his successors:

> *"It is our true policy to steer clear of permanent alliances with any portion of the foreign world."*

Thomas Jefferson affirmed that doctrine in his inaugural speech in 1801 as:

> *"Peace, commerce, and honest friendship with all nations— entangling alliances with none."*

Various presidents since that time have tried to apply their advice, with mixed results. In the modern era, for example, Franklin Roosevelt saw his dream of a "New Deal for the American people" derailed by the outbreak of WW2.

After the war, Dwight Eisenhower hoped to preside over an enduring *pax Americana* but saw the country swept into a long Cold War defined by a costly arms race and a terrifying nuclear stand-off with the Soviet Union. America's participation in the United Nations and the NATO military alliance entangled the country as never before.

Ike's successor, John F. Kennedy, saw his "New Frontier" domestic agenda pushed aside by the Armageddon scenario of the Cuban missile crisis in 1962, which followed the botched Bay of Pigs invasion six months earlier. The precarious stand-off with Nikita Khrushchev's Soviet Union preoccupied him and his advisers for the rest of his term.

Lyndon Johnson, who succeeded Kennedy after the assassination in 1963, had staked his political fortunes on his concept of the "Great Society," which he promised would eliminate poverty and racial injustice. He saw it thwarted at every turn by the ruinous costs and political distractions of the Vietnam conflict. He decided not to run for re-election.

George Bush, Jr., won the election of 2000 and came into office hoping for a quiet watch, unaffected by the faraway strife in Europe and the Middle East. His world turned upside down with the infamous 9-11 terrorist attacks on New York and the Pentagon in 2001.

Through all of these episodes, adventures, and misadventures, the American people have struggled to find a sense of perspective, meaning, and purpose in the often misguided foreign policy expeditions of their governments.

REPUBLICS GROW UP IN PHASES, JUST AS PEOPLE DO

The history of America's interactions with the rest of the world, while seemingly haphazard, actually shows an intriguing pattern. If we rewind the movie all the way back to the founding and play it in slow motion, we can see a kind of cyclic progression of distinct phases, each spanning about 25 years or so. Let's do a bit of historical detective work and explore these quarter-century periods:

1. *Surviving (1650-1775).* From the founding of the 13 original English colonies up through the RevWar, just staying alive kept everyone busy. The colonists, still British subjects and under the control of the Crown, focused on economic stability and tried to assert basic civil rights without antagonizing their military minders.

2. *Building a Republic (1775-1800).* The Declaration of Independence, the painful RevWar with England, and the building of a democratic republic dominated the lives of the newly minted American citizens. Washington, Jefferson, and other key leaders tried to keep us from getting drawn into the age-old conflicts between England, France, and Spain.

3. *Proving Ourselves (1800-1825).* The RevWar didn't really settle animosities between the US and British

governments. While the British had their hands full in a life-and-death struggle with Napoleon's *Grande Armée* across the whole of Europe, President James Madison took the opportunity to declare war. Britain's seizure and impressment of American sailors on the high seas gave him the provocation he needed. Madison also launched a series of attacks into Canada, hoping to drive the thinly stretched British empire out of North America and make Canada part of the US.

The British landed a modest invasion force of ships and soldiers near Baltimore, attacked Washington, and set fire to the White House. After a series of indecisive battles, Andrew Jackson's forces defeated the British at the Battle of New Orleans in 1815, a few months before the Brits defeated Napoleon at Waterloo.

The Crown gave up all hope of a reconquest, the two countries signed a peace treaty, and the new Republic had truly arrived as a full-fledged nation.

4. *Flexing Our Muscles (1825-1850)*. This period saw the aggressive expansion of American territory by a series of presidents and the rise of the concept of "Manifest Destiny." That idea held that God intended for the new Republic to spread democracy and capitalism across the whole North American continent, and that its leaders had the moral authority to do it by almost any means necessary.

A whole new set of forces, trends, and events came into play—a rapid rise in birth rates and immigration; the western movement of millions of settlers looking for new land and new opportunities; completion of the awesome 363 mile-long Erie Canal, which connected the Great Lakes to the Atlantic Ocean; Mexico's independence from Spain in 1830; the break-away of Texas, then a part of Mexico (led in 1836 by American settlers Davy Crockett, Jim Bowie, and

William Travis of Alamo fame); the annexation and statehood of Texas in 1846; the War with Mexico and the treaty in 1846, which ceded Arizona, California, Colorado, Nevada, New Mexico, Utah, and Wyoming to the US; and the relocation of thousands of American Indians from their lands in the east to reservations in the west.

By the time the Civil War broke out, the American Republic stretched from coast to coast and from the Canadian border to the Caribbean.

5. *Coming Unglued (1850-1875).* The rapid territorial expansion of the early half-century had big side-effects. For one, it fueled a fierce conflict over the issue of slavery. It raised the very divisive question of whether new states joining the Union could allow slavery.

The slavery question split the national conversation and the political process completely in two. Practically speaking, no political actor could get away with claiming neutrality; one had to take a side. Like a speeding train with no brakes, the Republic barreled on toward partition.

When Abraham Lincoln ran for president in 1860 he vowed to end slavery completely. His campaign speeches provoked a blind rage amongst a group of southern political leaders and activists, who threatened to pull their states out of the Union if he won. By the time of his inauguration they had formed a coalition of 13 states, which they named the Confederate States of America. They formed an interim government under the leadership of a wealthy but inexperienced slave-owner named Jefferson Davis.

Southern forces fired on Fort Sumter in Charleston, South Carolina, setting off a violent 4-year conflict that cost the lives of more than 600,000 citizen soldiers on both sides. After a long, bloody, and exhausting conflict, the Union forces finally prevailed.

For Northerners, the Civil War settled the question of slavery once and for all. The Republic could now heal its wounds and go about the task of reconstruction. But for Southerners, it didn't settle anything.

As one of the conditions for readmission to the Union —and access to desperately needed funds to pay for reconstruction—Congress required the legislative houses of each of the rebelling states to swallow a bitter pill. They first had to ratify Lincoln's 13th Amendment, which abolished slavery forever.

The adolescent Republic had grown to full size, it had nearly come unglued, and now its protectors tried to glue the parts back together. But the divisions never healed. Racism, both institutional and cultural, remained the dividing factor separating the Old South from the rest of the American culture for a long time.

6. *Getting Back to Business (1875-1900)*. After the Civil War, a series of presidents set about finishing the build-out of the nation-state. An authoritarian ideology seemed to descend upon the political conversation and it guided a process of social realignment. Asserting the power of government became a guiding principle of politics. We could also justifiably refer to this phase as "Going White."

As southern governments went about immobilizing the black population, departments in Washington finished the job of forcibly relocating Indians to reservations in the West and the Interior. A federal agency, the Bureau of Indian Affairs, emerged as a mechanism for negotiating treaties and agreements with some 600 recognized Indian groups.

This phase included a long running effort to indoctrinate native groups with the values and norms of the white culture, using such practices as separating young children from their families and putting them in boarding schools. Their minders forbid them to speak their native languages; required them to wear European-style clothes and hairstyles; and encouraged them to abandon their native religions in favor of Christianity.

Through the last decades of the century, Washington politicians argued and made deals about the numbers of immigrants the Republic might admit from various countries. Chinese immigrants, previously used as laborers during the build-out of the great railway lines, became an unwelcome nuisance. The unapologetically named *Chinese Exclusion Act* of 1882 stopped all Chinese from entering the country.

During this period, American leaders also dabbled in colonialism, although on a small scale. They acquired American Samoa and the Northern Mariana Islands, which remain US protectorates to this day. The purchase of Alaska from Russia in 1867 had already put a new group of native peoples under supervision of the federal government, a number of tribes referred to collectively as Eskimos.

Perhaps the most impressive new jewel in the American imperial crown came with the annexation of Hawaii in 1898.

While blacks, Indians, Hawaiians, Eskimos, immigrants, and the working stiffs grappled with their own survival issues, a new social class began to materialize: the *nouveau riche*. The booming economy, fueled by the new factories of the industrial age, produced a growing subculture of millionaires, some known as the "robber barons."

They spent their money lavishly, building luxurious mansions, entertaining ostentatiously, and vacationing abroad in the new style of luxury steamship travel. Mark Twain referred to this new period in American life as the Gilded Age, meaning that the vulgar display of wealth concealed a lack of aesthetic sensibility and respect for subtlety.

7. *Becoming a Real Country (1900-1925)*. During the last few years of the 1800s and well into the new century, Theodore ("Teddy") Roosevelt influenced the developing Republic in a number of ways. A dramatic personality gifted with a keen intellect, TR projected a hyper-masculine style of leadership. He had made it his personal mission, even before his accession to the presidency, to position the US as a first-tier country worthy of respect among the great nations.

Teddy saw his ambition fulfilled in three big adventures: 1) starring in the Spanish-American war, which kicked the tottering Spanish empire out of the western hemisphere after a slam-dunk little war in Cuba; 2) building a world class deep-water navy; and 3) coercing the government of Colombia to give up land for the construction of the Panama Canal, which the US operated profitably under a 100-year lease agreement. Teddy often expressed his personal philosophy of foreign relations as, "Speak softly and carry a big stick."

The First World War, a.k.a. the "Great War," a.k.a. the "Unnecessary War," broke out during Woodrow Wilson's first term in 1914, when a catastrophic series of political aberrations triggered an interlocking set of war alliances. At the time, neither Wilson nor the American public wanted any part of a European war and Wilson limited the country's role to selling weapons and ammunition to Britain and France.

By 1917, however, German atrocities had moved Wilson's thinking and public opinion toward war. Two big provocations tipped opinion against Germany and in favor of war. First, a German submarine sank the passenger liner Lusitania in 1915 with 123 Americans onboard, setting off a humanitarian outrage.

Second, in 1917 a bizarre incident referred to as the Zimmerman Telegram caper pretty well forced the issue. British cryptographers deciphered a telegram from German Foreign Minister Arthur Zimmermann to his counterpart in Mexico, proposing to offer a deal to the Mexican government. If Mexico would join with Germany and help defeat the United States, Mexico would get back the western states lost during the old territorial wars.

The US declared war in early 1917 and by the time of the Armistice in late 1918 had participated for less than two years. The country's full commitment, however, and the strong performance of American troops, signaled to the other nations that the US had indeed arrived as a world power.

The planning for post-war operations included a new and provocative concept: a League of Nations that would bring together the allied countries into an association that could ensure cooperation and a coordinated defense against possible future threats from Germany or other belligerent countries.

Wilson staked his political future on this venture and promoted it vigorously. Ironically, although he received the Nobel Peace Prize for his efforts, his own Senate stabbed him in the back and voted not to ratify the treaty. Without the US, the League staggered on in a weakened state and died during WW2.

8. *Learning to Suffer (1925-1950)*. Following the relatively painless recovery from WW1, the period known as the Roaring Twenties brought a short-lived phase of prosperity, self-indulgent consumption, and an optimistic sense of limitless possibilities. Then it all came crashing down with the Great Depression. A massive economic collapse, triggered by greed and reckless gambling in New York's powerful new

financial industry; the astonishing crash of the Wall Street stock exchanges in 1929; and unforgivable bumbling by government overseers, plunged the economy and the society into chaos.

A massive slowdown in the economic machinery caused an unprecedented number of bankruptcies and drove unemployment to levels never before seen. Many people lost their jobs, homes, cars, and savings. Caught flat-footed, President Herbert Hoover and his administration fumbled the ball for almost two years.

Unemployment continued to soar, prices and profits collapsed along with falling consumer demand, and banks closed their doors, unable to meet the demands of panicked depositors who wanted their cash. Poverty, homelessness, bread lines, and long lines of men hoping for work became a familiar sight. Thousands of homeless encampments, dubbed "Hoovervilles," sprang up under bridges, along rivers, in public parks, and in back streets and alleys.

The crisis soon spread to other countries, especially those with financial systems closely linked to the Wall Street empire. What began as an American catastrophe soon metastasized into a world-wide downturn.

Franklin Delano Roosevelt won the presidency in 1932 and set about trying to revive an economy that many perceived as near death. He launched a massive program of public assistance aimed at creating jobs, putting money in Americans' pockets, and restoring the economic tempo. His New Deal for the American people spanned across two consecutive presidential terms, from 1933 through 1939. His reforms began to take hold, economic activity began to recover, and more and more people started going back to work.

Historians generally credit FDR's emergency measures with helping the country climb out of the

Depression, but some also assert that the coming of the Second World War clinched the revival. Hitler's great adventure began in 1939 with the Nazi invasion of Poland, but the US sat out the early phase of the war until December 7, 1941. On that day the Japanese bombing of the Pearl Harbor naval base in Hawaii forced Roosevelt's hand.

Until the Japanese attack, FDR had resisted getting the US involved in what many political leaders, journalists, and citizens saw as another round of the never-ending European wars. He did, however, authorize American firms to sell military weapons and war materiel to the Allies. That decision led to a rapid and far-reaching industrial mobilization that brought the country back to full employment.

Americans still got a good education in enduring hardship, however. The immense commitment to exporting weapons, supplies, and food to the Allies— and later providing them to American troops fighting in Europe and Asia—led to chronic shortages.

The US government rationed everyday necessities like milk, eggs, bacon, butter, coffee, chocolate, and gasoline as well as basic materials like paper, rubber, aluminum, and steel. Ration books and coupons became a familiar part of everyday life. Spam, a cheap canned-meat product, became a familiar part of life.

After the German surrender in April of 1945 and the Japanese surrender in August of the same year, the phenomenal post-war recovery got fully underway.

The destructive impact of the war had never reached the American mainland, so our infrastructure remained mostly intact. Industrial capacity also remained strong. The US lost far fewer soldiers in the war than any of the major Allied countries, so the medical and human costs never added up to the appalling levels the others experienced. Those factors gave the US a big head start and an economic advantage that endured for decades.

9. *Amplifying Everything (1950-1975).* The arrival of television in American homes in the early 1950s touched off an explosive phase of cultural change that continues to this day. America began its transition to an electronic culture. That one phenomenon caused or catalyzed many of the big changes that made this the most turbulent period in the life of the Republic. TV became the great amplifier, detecting and exaggerating differences in all parts of society.

The list of social, economic, and political changes that came with the new frenetic culture runs long:

▸ Rock 'n Roll music captured the energies of the teen generation. Music and movies became part of the cultural language and collective awareness.

▸ Flamboyant entertainers like Elvis Presley and the Beatles galvanized the popular culture. American music and Hollywood films became one of our most significant exports, extending a kind of cultural colonialism into many other countries.

▸ The ever-present Cold War and the frightening nuclear stand-off with the Soviet Union weighed heavily on the minds of Americans and eroded their sense of security.

▸ The invention of a reliable female contraceptive, "The Pill," in 1960 changed reproductive rights and attitudes for a generation of women. A powerful feminist movement began to find its voice.

▸ The Cuban revolution in 1960, led by Fidel Castro, and his alliance with the Soviet Union, precipitated the infamous Cuban Missile Crisis in 1962, which brought the two Cold War powers nose to nose with nuclear disaster.

▸ The assassination of President John F. Kennedy in

1963 devastated the nation and brought Lyndon Johnson to the White House just as the Vietnam conflict began to spiral out of control. The war ultimately sank his plans for the Great Society.

▸ An unprecedented anti-war movement, especially among young people, opposed the Vietnam presence and called for the end of the draft. College campuses became hotbeds of student activism. Sit-ins and campus riots made hot news stories.

▸ Civil rights activism, led by charismatic figures like Martin Luther King, convulsed the cultures of the Old South and made Northerners uncomfortably aware of the lingering injustices.

▸ Environmental activists began to warn about the accumulating effects on the Earth's ecosystem due to mass industrialization and unsustainable practices of resource extraction. Books like *Silent Spring* by Rachel Carson in 1962; *The Population Bomb* by Paul and Anne Ehrlich in 1968; and *Future Shock* by Alvin Toffler in 1970 captured public attention and gave impetus to a gradually developing consciousness of the finiteness of the planet's resources.

▸ A hedonistic subculture of drugs and sexual self-indulgence, whose disciples rejected traditional American values and priorities, found voice in mob scenes like the Woodstock music festival in 1969.

▸ The Space Race with the Soviet Union and the American triumph with the Apollo 11 moon landing in 1969 boosted national pride.

▸ The disastrous failure of the Vietnam adventure and the ignominious pull-out of US forces in 1973 shattered the cherished illusion of America's military invincibility.

▸ China became a recognized player on the world

stage when the UN General Assembly voted to expel Taiwan in 1971 and give the membership to mainland China. President Richard Nixon stunned western leaders the following year when he went to China to meet with Mao Tze-Tung. That meeting and visits by later presidents led to reduced tensions and a new trade relationship between the countries.

> A series of scandals and episodes of corruption, especially the Watergate scandal that drove President Richard Nixon from office in 1975, dominated the national conversation and caused many Americans to lose their faith in government and public institutions.

> The intense drama of TV news, played out every evening in living rooms across the country, made Americans hyper-sensitive to a whole range of social, political, and economic issues around the world. TV coverage of the Vietnam conflict brought the disturbing reality of war into their homes.

10. *Losing Our Best Enemy (1975-2000).* In the post-Vietnam era, a series of presidents wrestled with the question of America's role on the world stage. The Cold War; membership in the UN and NATO; and international commerce all pulled Americans deeper into the global drama. The country became ever more entangled economically, politically, and socially, to a degree the Founders could never have imagined.

Ronald Reagan won the presidency in 1980 and immediately confronted the Soviet Union's leaders in a very public and dramatic exchange of threats. By 1985, however, a new and unusual Soviet leader emerged. Mikhail Gorbachev, a self-declared reformer, offered a dialogue with Reagan that evolved into a respectful relationship. A long and difficult series of negotiations eventually led to the end of the Cold War and the ungluing of the Soviet empire.

Gorbachev's quasi-democratic vision, unfortunately, didn't survive the unwinding of the empire. The Soviet Union crashed out in 1991. All of the satellite states broke free from its orbit, leaving Russia as the only surviving relic of the old order and in a crippled state, militarily and economically.

11. *Seeking the Elusive "New World Order" (2000-Now).* The astonishing fall of the USSR set the Washington policymaking industry into a frenzy of speculation, argument, and advocacy. The bipolar power struggle that had pitted the US and its allies against the USSR for four decades had collapsed. What arrangement might replace it and how could America's leaders get the one they wanted?

Think tanks, university professors, and free-lance policy wonks all rushed to offer their recipes for a "new world order." Three main theories emerged:

▸ A *unipolar* situation with the US at the center, overshadowing all other countries and regions, militarily and economically.

▸ A *bipolar* situation with the US in head-to-head economic competition with the newly powerful European Union.

▸ A *tripolar* situation with a three-way power dance involving the US, the European Union, and a potential Asian power bloc that some predicted would emerge, probably dominated by China.

A highly vocal clan of Washington policy merchants, referred to by political scholars as neo-conservatives, or "neo-cons," aggressively preached the notion of a window of opportunity for the unipolar option— unchallenged US world leadership. They adopted the concept of "American exceptionalism" as their rallying cry and mantra, sounding a not-so-faint echo of the old doctrine of Manifest Destiny. President Bush paid little attention to the neo-con pitch at first, but circumstances soon turned his head around.

Less than a year into his presidency, the surprise terrorist attacks of September 11, 2001, a.k.a. the 9-11 tragedy, forced him and his advisors to think about another sphere of power and influence—the Middle East. He began to listen to the policy hawks, especially his VP Dick Cheney, and finally bought into the unipolar doctrine.

US military units, aided by British forces, immediately invaded Afghanistan, where intelligence sources had reported that the 9-11 mastermind Osama bin Laden had his base of operations. The mission to find and capture him never panned out but it turned into a long, fruitless, and mind-bogglingly expensive military operation in that wasteland, one that has stretched on for more than 19 years as of this writing.

A second venture, even more catastrophic, mounted a "regime change" invasion to remove Saddam Hussein from power in Iraq. Bush and Cheney used questionable intelligence data to support the claim that Saddam has sponsored the 9-11 attacks. They assured the American public of a quick and easy operation. Iraq's oppressed people, longing for liberation from his brutal regime, would welcome US forces—a Christian army invading an Islamic country —as heroes and friends.

It didn't work out that way. Having destroyed the Iraqi army—and overseen Saddam's hanging by an interim Iraqi leadership—US forces drifted into the unenviable role of trying to reconstruct a failed state. As of this writing, US forces still operate in various parts of Iraq, trying to quell sporadic uprisings against a weak and ineffectual puppet government.

So much for the New World Order.

Bush's successor Barack Obama showed little interest in world dominance. Meanwhile, the EU nations had become more organized, more self-assertive, and less likely to look to the US for leadership. With the rapid rise of the Asian tiger economies—China, Taiwan, Hong Kong, South Korea, Japan, and Singapore—the tripolar model won out.

12. *Facing the Midlife Crisis (2020-Onward).* Americans and their leaders seem more confused, conflicted, and uncertain about the role of their Republic in world affairs than perhaps ever before in their history.

We've grown up. We began as a little cluster of colonies struggling to survive on a patch of land on the coast of a huge unexplored continent. We grew and developed through a difficult adolescence into a fledgling empire; we took our place in the community of nations; we endured wars, economic strife, and internal turmoil just as the other great nations had; and we advanced to adulthood, finally achieving the status of a primary center of power and influence. And now we seem to have arrived at middle age.

Just as we humans tend to come to a point of self-awareness and self-questioning somewhere along our personal roads, nations come to a point of self-identity. We've arrived as a Republic; where do we go from here?

THE TOUGHEST KID ON THE PLAYGROUND

Considering the series of historical phases we've just reviewed, our foreign relations program—if we might call it that—seems to have consisted of a long succession of idiosyncratic reactions to unforeseen events.

We can, however, perceive a few common themes that seem to have shaped the general patterns of foreign engagement.

Militarism, a.k.a. "gunboat diplomacy," certainly ranks as one of the strongest. As early as 1854, Admiral Matthew Perry led a massive naval expedition that forced the government of Japan to open its markets to US merchants. Ever since the

Spanish-American War, US presidents have tended to wave the Big Stick, reminding other heads of state of our superior military capacity.

Economic interest—opening up commercial opportunities for American corporations—ranks a close second. New territories have always provided new sources of raw materials like oil, gold, and industrial commodities, and sometimes new markets for domestic goods. Much of the foreign aid currently offered to developing countries takes the form of economic credits, which they have to spend with American companies, buying agricultural products and equipment, technological resources, or military weapons.

A third and somewhat more troubling component of our behavior toward other nations involves *covert operations*—secret activities carried out to disadvantage particular national governments that someone in our political hierarchy considers a threat to our safety and security.

A kind of cynical pragmatism, often promoted by key presidential advisers, has sponsored espionage; bribery; channeling funds secretly to shadow groups trying to overthrow heads of state; sponsoring acts of sabotage by anti-government factions; secretly supplying weapons or training to insurrectionist groups; and direct or sponsored attempts to assassinate unfriendly heads of state.

We do seem to have a common philosophy of foreign engagement—the same one we've had for over a century: plain and simple, we want the starring role on the world stage. We've claimed our place as the toughest kid on the playground.

THE KISSINGER DOCTRINE

If any one thinker or political personality stands out, whose ideas have propelled US foreign policy more than any other, the prize would go to Dr. Henry A. Kissinger. A German-born refugee from Hitler's Nazism, brilliant, articulate, Harvard educated, a respected political scholar, and a Nobel laureate,

Kissinger served as National Security Adviser and Secretary of State to President Richard Nixon.

Kissinger preached an approach to diplomacy known to political scholars as *realpolitik* (a German term, by the way), meaning a focus on specific goals related to a certain situation rather than general philosophical beliefs, doctrines, ethical standards, or morals. He expressed what some have called the Kissinger Doctrine as, "America has no permanent friends or enemies, only interests." The term "interest" decodes to "Whatever we want to get from this situation."

Kissinger declared, in a sense, that he and the leaders he served didn't need to declare any kind of theory or general concept of diplomacy. They would approach each situation, not in terms of any presumed relationships or promises, but solely in terms of America's specific interests at that time and in that part of the world. He felt little or no obligation to explain or justify America's behavior to anyone and didn't want constraints on his freedom of action in any situation.

Many of the actors on the political scene, particularly those in the right wing of the Republican party, found satisfaction in Kissinger's guidance. For many, he bluntly articulated an ideology they already held to some extent. His doctrine echoes to this day in the public statements and actions of most foreign policy hawks—a.k.a. the American exceptionalism narrative. It also emboldened those who advocated building an awesome military machine as part of America's message to the other kids on the playground.

The *realpolitik* approach seemed to satisfy Kissinger and his sponsors but it had a crazy-making effect on almost everybody else. It kept other heads of state, diplomats, and political observers constantly guessing about what the US might do next or what it might do in some other world situation similar to the one at hand. Some saw America's behavior abroad as erratic and uncoordinated; some saw it as selfish, cynical, and shortsighted.

HOW DO PEOPLE AND LEADERS IN OTHER COUNTRIES SEE AMERICA—AND AMERICANS?

Just as Americans hold mixed feelings, perceptions, and conceptions about the role of their Republic in the world, so do people in many other countries.

A PERSONAL PERSPECTIVE

I've traveled to more than 30 countries in the past few decades, and to half of those in just the past 5 years. I've made it a regular practice to try to get into conversations with people wherever I go—cab drivers, waiters, students, shopkeepers, hotel managers, tour guides, veteran travelers, college professors, executives, and clients I've worked with professionally in years past. I've tried to gain an impression of their attitudes toward America and Americans, and possibly learn what kinds of actions and practices on the part of our leaders have shaped their feelings.

In countless conversations, I've heard variations on the same theme. "America is a great country, but—," or "We like Americans, but—." I seem to hear a conflicted narrative that mixes a feeling of grudging admiration with a feeling of affection and good will, but tainted perhaps by concerns about the ethical behavior and motivations of our leaders.

Admiration still ranks high in the attitudes of many foreigners toward America—with some exceptions. Many of them freely concede or volunteer that individual freedoms in America, as well as economic opportunities; educational opportunities; consumer products; popular music; films; literature; scientific and technological advancements; and business practices all deserve high regard.

Many foreigners consider Americans likable. They tend to view us as mostly friendly, accommodating, and generous. Those who visit the US typically comment on the friendly and attentive customer service they experience in commercial establishments.

Before the 9-11 attacks, the US usually ranked as the first or second most popular tourist destination. After that, partly because of severe travel requirements imposed on foreigners by the State Department, tourism dropped off radically and didn't recover for over a decade. As of this writing, the US ranks third in tourist arrivals, just behind France and Spain and just ahead of China and Italy.

That general sense of respect and admiration on the part of many foreigners and political leaders often comes mixed with a feeling of concern, frustration, and even resentment. Many foreign leaders and political observers have tended to view the US as somewhat like that oversized kid on the playground—big enough to push the other kids around but immature, self-absorbed, and lacking in social sophistication.

I believe many, many people in other countries see America as a phenomenal example of national success, and yet they also see us as not living up to our potential for doing good in the world. Many of them don't believe we've accepted our responsibility as a superpower to provide moral leadership and compassionate action across that global playground.

THE END OF THE KISSINGER LEGACY

The Kissinger Doctrine worked well for its intended purpose —keeping political leaders of other countries guessing. Unfortunately, it has kept our citizen counterparts in those countries guessing as well, and wondering about the consistency our values and motives.

Should it surprise us, for example, that many people and political leaders throughout Latin America see the US as a regional economic bully, doing deals with corrupt and disreputable heads of state while trying to topple others? Do they judge us unfairly for strangling a small, struggling country like Cuba with brutal economic sanctions; or because we maintain a military base—Guantanamo—with troops stationed on their sovereign soil against their wishes? Why has our government normalized relations with Vietnam, a diehard communist regime, but not with the one in Cuba?

Should it surprise us that many people and political leaders in the Middle East feel bullied and cheated when the US intervenes in conflicts there, destabilizes the situation even further, and then walks away? Do they judge us unfairly as seeking political and economic control over their single most valuable asset—oil?

Should it surprise us that many people and political leaders across Africa see the US as playing out the last historical echoes of a colonial tradition, and believe that we have little interest in the struggles of nations and peoples who don't have anything we want?

Should it surprise us that many people and political leaders in developing countries consider our leaders hypocritical or cynical when they confront some regimes on their egregious human rights records, while giving a free pass to others with whom we have profitable trading agreements or military alliances?

Should it surprise us that many people and political leaders in developing countries hesitate to commit to costly climate programs when the current US government has repudiated the scientific consensus for action?

I believe the time has come to clean up our act.

WELCOME TO THE *REAL* NEW WORLD ORDER

If we compare the world as we see it today with the old world of the Cold War, we see big differences—lots of them. Socially, politically, economically, technologically, militarily, and ecologically—we face a very different global reality from the Kissinger world of 50 years ago. As the world around us evolves ever more rapidly and radically, we must evolve with it. We need to think deeply and creatively about what this new reality will require of us.

We've become grotesquely over-militarized; burdened with colossally expensive weapon systems we've never used and never will use; hostages to an obsolete but still frighteningly dangerous nuclear arsenal; spending vast sums of tax money on outdated weapons technologies that will have no tactical value by the time they go into operation; and addicted to a game of one-upmanship with Russia and China, chasing ever more lethal and destabilizing new weapons technologies.

Let's face it: we won the arms race a long time ago. We can outgun everybody. We can outspend everybody. And we've acquired more power and influence on the world stage than even Teddy Roosevelt might have dreamed of. Now, what?

THE THREATS HAVE CHANGED

For most of our history as a republic, our leaders have defined our existential challenges for us in terms of competition, conflict, and compromise with the other nations. Going forward from here, however, it looks more and more like our challenges—and the threats to our survival—will arise from our troubled relationship with the planet, not our troubled relationships with other regimes. Let's consider some of the major planetary threats:

1. *Epidemics and Pandemics* will become more frequent and more deadly. As of this writing, leaders of all major countries face a deadly virus outbreak known as *SARS-CoV-2* (or, informally, as the coronavirus or COVID-19). The infection has gone pandemic—it affects virtually all modern countries. The US government's response to the outbreak deserves a failing grade for foresight, organization, and follow-through. We've experienced a number of other global health crises in the past and in every case our response capacity has fallen short. To deal with the next ones coming at us we'll need far more cooperation within governments and between nations, including those typically antagonistic to one another.

2. *Long-term climate change* looms ever larger as a

national issue and a planetary concern, and the US has lost precious time in dealing with it. That challenge above all others calls for a massive, aggressive, coordinated program of planned change, one nearly unprecedented in world history. Practically speaking, we haven't even started.

3. *Extreme variations in weather* have become an undeniable part of long-term climate change. We've already seen more frequent and more devastating natural events such as hurricanes, earthquakes, mega-fires, floods, droughts, and heatwaves. We currently have a very primitive transnational process for coordinated responses to planetary catastrophes.

4. *Humanitarian catastrophes* associated with natural disasters, warfare, political upheaval, and state-level persecution of minorities have made millions of people into refugees. Volunteer agencies can't possibly cope with those numbers, and as of this writing, the international mechanisms for managing those disasters barely exist. We have the elements of transnational coordinating mechanisms, but nothing on a par with what we'll really need.

5. *Worldwide infrastructure development*—the Global Commons—begs for our attention. Almost all modern nations have underinvested in their domestic infrastructure. We and they have big challenges ahead, to repair, rebuild, and modernize the built environment that plays a critical role in our ongoing economic survival. Indeed, all modern nations have a shared responsibility to support infrastructure developments across Africa and in other disadvantaged regions.

All of those planetary threats and challenges have one thing in common: no country can solve or eliminate them single-handedly. They will all require a level of international cooperation beyond anything we've developed so far.

Can we do it? Can we, collectively, as a family of nations, set aside—or mitigate—our ancient feuds and frustrations and rise to the challenges? I believe we can. Do I believe we will? I still struggle with that question.

DO WE HAVE THE COURAGE TO SEEK PEACE?

Rethinking the Foreign Relations component of our Republic will require one of the most difficult changes of all: *changing mindsets.* We'll somehow have to bring about a fundamental shift in the long-held ideologies, deeply held convictions, and habits of thought of our senior military leaders, the policy architects who advise them, and the leaders of our diplomatic establishment.

A NEW MINDSET FOR A NEW WORLD

Let me declare emphatically that *I have the highest respect for the senior officers who guide our military establishment.* I served as an Army intelligence officer and I know that the caliber of our leaders today—mostly men, but increasingly including women—would impress any thoughtful citizen. Those who want to see them as mindless warmongers misunderstand them completely. Any admiral or general officer one might meet would very likely hold a Ph.D. and would have acquired a very broad background of experience, to include joint-service assignments and policy-level experience in contact with foreign governments.

But old mindsets don't die out easily. The Cold War ended thirty years ago. No nation has ever fired a nuclear weapon in the 75 years since Hiroshima and Nagasaki, and none ever will. The last significant land war—Vietnam—ended 45 years ago. Russia, the only remnant of the extinct Soviet Union, struggles to maintain an aging and decrepit military machine, with a desperate economy smaller than that of the state of Texas. China, the only other presumed adversary, shows little appetite for a hot war with its trading partners.

Yet our political, legislative, and military leaders keep spending our resources on ever more destructive weapon systems. With the support of a comatose Congress, a timid press establishment, and a compliant population conditioned by years of war propaganda, Eisenhower's dreaded military-industrial complex just keeps rolling.

Some students and advocates of social and political change speak of an emerging new global consciousness that wants to see the powerful nations redeploy their energies, assets, and collective brainpower to move us from the constant threat of conflict, toward global cooperation that raises the quality of life for all planetary citizens. Maybe they have a case.

Maybe Americans, Russians, Chinese, Cubans, Israelis and Palestinians, Iranians and Iraqis, North and South Koreans, and their counterparts elsewhere have had enough of living with the threat of war. Maybe they just want to live peaceful lives, feed their families, raise their kids, give the kids an education, and maybe save a few yams for a rainy day.

Maybe they want a new crop of leaders who get that.

FOUR BIG GEOPOLITICAL CHALLENGES: HOW SHALL WE MEET THEM?

As of this writing, American leaders face highly problematic relationships with four particular nation-states: Russia, China, North Korea, and Iran. Those four stand out from other geopolitical relationships in that they pose bigger and more immediate threats to our interests. Their ruling autocrats have their own unique intentions and behavior patterns. Each requires a unique relationship strategy.

A NEW PARADIGM FOR CO-EXISTENCE: THE "DIFFICULT MARRIAGE" MODEL

How shall we frame a new ideology for foreign relations—a rationale for action both optimistic and cooperative on one hand, and fully realistic on the other? How do we cope with foreign leaders still committed to the win-lose psychology of hardball power politics?

For a long time, the most ardent advocates of rethinking

America's role in the world have tribalized around two opposing ideologies. One, which we might call the "Big Stick" proposition, holds that our safety and security can come only from our strength in arms—a mighty military machine that could surely crush any opponent in an all-out war.

The opposing tribe, in some cases expressing views just as extreme, promotes the "peace, love, and understanding" approach—the "kum-ba-yah" ideology, as some might call it, or perhaps the "Big Carrot."

One ideological extreme, unfortunately, can pull us into a desperate win-lose race to nowhere. The other can get us taken for a ride by cynical foreign leaders who see it as symptomatic of a weakness they can exploit.

In Chapter 5 (Defense), we considered ways to avoid or reduce the ruinous costs of the massive kinetic warfare machine, and ways in which a more carefully considered investment in military operations could actually strengthen our hand in dealing with antagonistic foreign governments. Here, we explore that potential synergy further.

An alternative to both extremes, I believe, would not consist of some proportional mixture of the two, but actually a very different conceptualization—a third way.

We can think of this pragmatic approach to managing our relationships with the "Sore Four," as well as other less than friendly governments, as somewhat like living in a difficult marriage. When two people face the prospect of a troubled relationship without any prospect of a peaceful divorce, they can choose to make each other miserable or they can choose to co-exist—if not amicably, then perhaps with less rancor.

This difficult-marriage model of our relationship with each of the Sore Four governments offers a realistic way of thinking about it as a long running series of episodes that the parties must navigate. We may cooperate in some ways; oppose each other on others; temporarily avoid some conflicts, and patiently work through others. Each sticking point will stand more or less alone, with its resolution not necessarily depending on the resolution of any other.

Let's consider a few key realities that apply more or less equally to all four of our challenging relationships:

> The adversary won't go away. We'll have to accept the fact of their existence and whatever that implies.

> Short of a disastrous all-out military confrontation, we can't realistically expect to defeat them and they can't realistically expect to defeat us. Our military machine can serve to prevent foolish behavior on the part of their leaders, but it can't make them want to cooperate.

> We can concentrate on making their lives miserable and they can do the same to us; or we can adapt to the reality of a long-term difficult relationship.

> We can influence their actions by finding a better balance between the Big Carrot and the Big Stick. But first, we must understand their motivations. What do they want, and what do they seek to avoid?

> The intentions of a nation's leaders might not align with the values, hopes, and aspirations of its people. We can *reach out to the people* with one kind of appeal and simultaneously *confront their leaders* with a more challenging set of choices.

> We have at least four ways to push a nation's leaders toward more cooperative behavior (or, at least, toward realistic compromises): 1) military pressure; 2) diplomatic initiatives; 3) economic consequences; and 4) covert activities such as cyber-operations. We need to do a better job of combining these options to fit the unique geopolitical realities of each of those countries.

> We can also invite the people of another country to lean toward cooperation by various carrot-oriented options like trade, educational outreach, and tourism. Imaginative measures there could serve to drive a wedge (a small one, at least) between antagonistic political leaders and the people who want peaceful

relations with other countries. We'll look more closely at the idea of citizen outreach later in this chapter.

WHAT DO THEY WANT?

In any conflicted relationship, however strong the animosities may have become and however distasteful the interaction seems, it still makes sense to understand the motivations of our counterparts. We might consider their motives misguided, immature, selfish, or disreputable, but it makes sense to recognize them, acknowledge them, and understand how they shape the other party's behavior.

Let's consider briefly what we know and can surmise about the motivations of the political leaders and the citizens (remembering that their motivations might not coincide) of the four key antagonists we currently have to deal with.

What Do the Chinese Want?

Available evidence suggests that China's leaders and its people both want two big things very badly. First, they want *continued economic development* with a constantly rising standard of living. They've become addicted to economic growth and it tends to overshadow almost all everything else. And second, they want their country to enjoy the *respect*— and even envy—of the rest of the world.

The first point hardly calls for dispute. But Americans and their leaders seem nearly oblivious to the second priority, and collectively we've done little to help them achieve it.

Americans and their leaders have enjoyed first-power status for so long that we tend to take its benefits for granted, but consider China's experience of the last hundred years. The fall of the last Manchu emperor in 1912 led to decades of violent unrest and civil war, suspended only by the greater violence of Japanese invasions before and during WW2.

The Chinese people suffered terribly at the hands of the brutal Japanese occupiers They've felt aggrieved ever since that the Western powers did nearly nothing to help them, militarily or economically. People in those cultures have a long memory for those kinds of injustices.

When WW2 ended in 1945, and with it the Japanese occupation, China's unfinished civil war immediately broke out again. After a long and bloody clash between the armies of Mao Tze-Tung and Chiang Kai-Shek in 1949, Mao's forces drove Chiang's army off the mainland. With the assistance of the US Navy, Chiang and his followers fled to the island of Taiwan.

During the 25-year economic and political winter of Mao's Marxist-Communist rule, tens of millions of Chinese people died from the violence of the revolution and massive famines induced by his disastrous "Great Leap" fantasies. Meanwhile, political leaders and the news media of the Western nations conditioned their people to look upon the Chinese as backward, ignorant, and unworthy of trust or respect. The Chinese haven't forgotten that either.

When the UN formed, Taiwan—not China—got the invitation to join. Not until 1971 did China become a UN member, displacing Taiwan in a politically painful turn of events.

This *collective desire for both self-respect and international respect* might explain some of the attention-getting moves by the Chinese government, such as building impressive infrastructure works like bridges, high-speed railways, and dams. It also propels investments in advanced technology such as medical research, computer science, advanced military systems, and space missions. Do the Chinese really need to send a robotic landing craft to the moon? Yes, they do. Do they need to build some aircraft carriers? Yes, they do.

If we think of these developments as coming-of-age ceremonies rather than as threats to American status in these various areas, we might adopt an entirely different viewpoint about helping China take its place as a respected modern nation. If it comes to a choice between the proverbial stick and the carrot, offering the Chinese people our genuine support in their quest for *national maturity* might help to steer them toward peaceful co-existence.

China's political leaders, on the other hand, have set a very aggressive geopolitical agenda for the country, which goes well beyond the people's desire for respect and coming of age. We'll have to develop strong containment strategies to deal with their determined efforts to eclipse the US as the world's pre-eminent economic and political force.

What Do the Russians Want?

Interestingly, Russia's leaders and their people share mostly the same wish-list with the Chinese, at least when it comes to the first item: *respect.* Respect, with a capital "R."

The collapse of the grand Soviet empire in 1991 had a devastating effect on Russian national pride.

Until that time, they had wielded awesome military power around the globe, facing off against the United States and the NATO allies with the most advanced weapons. Russia exercised unchallenged military and economic dominance over a ring of surrounding "client" states, which it had seized in the turbulent aftermath of the fall of Nazi Germany.

Russia's leaders and its people saw themselves as proud agents of a new political and economic order that would eventually span the entire globe.

Russian scientists (with the help of spies inside the US Manhattan Project) had developed their own atomic bomb, stalemating America's formidable nuclear advantage.

Then they one-upped the US by launching the first satellite into Earth orbit—the famed *Sputnik*—in 1957, delivering a stunning blow to American pride. And in another surprise first, Yuri Gagarin, a handsome Russian Air Force colonel, became the first man to orbit the Earth. For a while, it looked like the USSR might permanently lead the new space race.

But gradually, the weaknesses of the Marxist-Communist command economy began to show. A series of bone-headed economic moves, gloriously trumpeted as Five-Year Plans and

Great Leaps Forward, failed disastrously. Stories began to leak out about food shortages, famines, aging and collapsing infrastructure, and corruption infecting the Soviet system.

Meanwhile, a series of US presidents and the heads of the NATO countries kept up the relentless military and economic pressure on the Soviet Union as the terrifying Cold War arms race played itself out.

In a particularly painful blow to the Russian national psyche, the US won the space race with the legendary Apollo moon landing in 1969.

By the late 1980s, the Soviet empire had started to come unglued. Mass confusion reigned and in a final political spasm the empire began to collapse from within.

The infamous Berlin Wall fell in 1989 and East Germany soon became free after fifty years of Soviet rule. By the end of 1991, virtually all of the USSR's client states had gained their independence and within a few years nearly all had applied to join the European Union.

What remained of the legendary Soviet Empire? Just one country—Russia. Having lost the economies of a dozen former satellites, as well as control of their military resources, Russia emerged as a weak shadow of the former empire. The mega-economy of the Cold War days had shrunk to less than one-tenth that of the United States.

Just as WW2 left the Chinese people and their leaders feeling cheated, impotent, unloved, and disrespected in the world, a parallel series of events left the Russian people and their leaders feeling much the same way. After a turbulent struggle for control, leadership of the deeply wounded culture passed to a steely ex-intelligence officer named Vladimir Putin.

Just as Mao Tze-Tung's successors correctly diagnosed the psychic pain of the Chinese people; and just as Hitler understood the deep sense of humiliation and resentment felt by Germans under the harsh conditions imposed by the victorious allies after WW1, so Putin accurately read the sense of loss and aggrieved national pride felt by the Russian people. Just as the others had, he began to sell the narrative of a Russian comeback—a return to the days of past glory.

What Do the North Koreans Want?

Food.

Several decades of the most oppressive, intrusive, dictatorial control imaginable over the lives of North Koreans have made the entire country and its culture a modern basket case. As of this writing, the third-generation dictator of the line sired by the autocratic Kim Il-Sung, a young man known as Kim Jong-Un, rules with an iron hand, a paranoid sense of hyper-control, and an appalling ignorance of economics.

Kim (in Korean cultures, the family name comes first in the title) has bankrupted his country with a wasteful nuclear weapons program and a massive military build-up. His belligerent posturing toward South Korea, Japan, the US, and other allied nations have brought economic sanctions against the regime that have impoverished most of the country.

The only apparent—and contrived—contrast to the desperate poverty and food shortages lies in the capital city of Pyongyang. Kim has siphoned desperately needed funds and resources from the rest of the country in order to make Pyongyang look like a modern city with high-rise buildings, shopping areas, and well-dressed citizens on display.

Journalists and political analysts have found it very difficult to assess the state of the public psyche in North Korea, in the face of the effects of decades of relentless indoctrination with the "Dear Leader" icon-worship of all three men of the Kim dynasty. But by no stretch of the imagination could a reasonable observer judge the culture as either physically or psychologically healthy.

What Do the Iranians Want?

Historical patterns suggest that a large majority of the Iranian people long for a liberal form of *modernity*: a modern society, a modern economy, and a modern government. For forty years they've struggled under a schizophrenic governance structure that combines an ultra-conservative Islamic theocracy with a secular form of administration that tries to establish modern institutions and practices.

The theocrats—*ayatollahs*, in their nomenclature—wield a formidable veto power over most of the administrative establishment, including the authority to decide who gets to run for the elective offices.

Things got that way in 1979, after the violent overthrow of the Western-leaning Shah, Reza Pahlavi, who got his job when the CIA engineered the overthrow of the democratically elected Iranian government in 1953.

During the two decades of the Shah's autocratic rule, he and his administrators began an outward-reaching transition of the Iranian culture to a more liberal, commercial, and Westernized style of operating. Many of today's Iranians—well-educated, relatively secular, politically liberal, and fond of the consumer experience, favor more open relations with Western countries, increased travel and overseas education, and exchange of cultural traditions. This liberal stream of thought running through the Iranian society puts the theocrats in opposition to the people they govern.

THE STRATEGY OF ASSISTED SELF-DEFEAT

As much as the better angels of our nature might incline us to want to treat foreign political leaders in a kindly way and assume that they'll respond to kindness with kindness, history doesn't make a strong case for that policy.

Power-addicted men, when in control of failing or floundering nation-states, tend to have their own specialized logic for dealing with reality. They typically cling to a binary, win-lose model of politics, where not winning means losing. They see gestures of conciliation—by them or others—as evidence of weakness and lack of resolute purpose. And they typically have to devote constant attention to controlling the sociopolitical apparatus that keeps them in power. They rule by fear and propaganda, and they can never rest.

Better angels aside, therefore, common sense dictates that we apply continuous, unrelenting pressure on those kinds of political players, always striving to limit their behavioral options to those less antagonistic to our interests.

We can think of this general strategic approach as helping them to defeat themselves by capitalizing on their unique weaknesses, disadvantages, and internal threats to their control. This might not look and feel like a very powerful method of operation, but considering the realities of the difficult-marriage model we have to live with, it seems like the most realistic approach over the long run.

In the interest of brevity, we won't dwell on the details of this process, except to consider a few clarifying examples.

The first step in this assisted self-defeat strategy will pinpoint the critical weaknesses of each of our four primary prospective adversaries. What essential flaws in their systems of control make them vulnerable to losing it? What makes them most nervous about losing control? We can consider China as just one example.

> ▸ China's monolithic power structure puts the party leaders, paradoxically, in opposition to their own people. Without a mandate to govern from the people (the Chinese have had no experience of democracy in more than 4,000 years), their entire existence depends on maintaining control—political control, economic control, social control, and even mind control.
>
> An increasingly restive social class of better-off, better educated, liberal minded, cyber-sophisticated Chinese —many of them young—poses a perpetual threat to the presumed universal control of the dominant coalition. If we can influence the beliefs and aspirations of that cohort, we can amplify the weaknesses of the totalitarian regime.

▸ The Chinese government has two other major political risk situations on its hands, and they will almost certainly become ever more difficult to manage. Hong Kong, with a fiercely democratic-minded activist population, will keep them busy for some time. Another problem child, Taiwan, defies the long-running imperial claim that it has no right of sovereignty and must eventually become a province of the communist regime. World opinion stacks heavily in favor of full independence for both of those modern, democratically oriented, and economically successful states.

We and our allies can use those political risk factors for leverage over the behavior of the leaders of the regime. For example, the UK has recently offered citizenship to Hong Kongers who want to leave and return to the experience of British governance. The US could offer similar appeals. A coordinated effort to promote a punishing "brain drain," as the most affluent and best educated people move out, could present a significant economic threat to the regime.

Other weak points present themselves. As of this writing, China has some 360,000 students in US colleges and universities. Some political observers frame that policy as simply a matter of outsourcing their higher education needs to the US until they can build out their own system of colleges. The US could handicap the regime's plans for technological superiority by refusing to sell that service or by narrowly restricting eligibility to fewer students.

In all four cases of the antagonistic relationships, the assisted failure strategy operates the same way: 1) focus on a point of vulnerability that jeopardizes their control; 2) find ways to change that situation to make control more difficult; and 3) offer trade-offs—the carrot for the stick—that invite them to behave in ways less antagonistic to our interests. "If you stop doing A, we won't do B." "If you do X, we'll do Y."

By applying this assisted failure strategy creatively, diligently, and calmly, we might have some hope of steering each of the troubled regimes into a less threatening pattern of behavior. If that strategy allows us to dial back from the enormously wasteful military burden, and allows us and our fellow nations to focus on the emerging planetary risks and give less energy to threatening one another, it sounds like a worthwhile option to try.

LET'S PROMOTE CULTURAL OUTREACH: CITIZEN DIPLOMACY

Rick Steves, America's pre-eminent travel adviser, writer, TV personality, and all-purpose guru of tourism, tirelessly promotes the idea of getting Americans out of their comfort zones and into the wider world. He cites two important reasons why they should hit the road: 1) to gain a wider perspective on the world and their place in it; and 2) to serve as ambassadors to other cultures, helping them get to know us better. We can expand on both of those possibilities.

According to Steves:

> *"If Americans traveled more, we'd better understand our place on this complex planet and fit in more comfortably. And eventually, perhaps, we wouldn't need to spend as much as the rest of the world combined on our military to feel safe.*

> *"Those who don't venture out to see or experience the world often cling to stubbornly held world views based on little more than TV news. Travel gives us a firsthand look at the complexity and struggles of the rest of the world, enabling us to digest news coverage more smartly. Travel helps us celebrate—rather than fear—diversity."*

Almost every veteran traveler I've met confirms my own experience: getting outside the American cultural bubble and meeting people in other lands changes their whole perspective on life—and their sense of identity as Americans.

In recent years, Americans have begun traveling abroad in

record numbers. In 1990, less than five percent of them had passports. By 2000, it had tripled, to 15 percent. As of this writing, it stands at nearly 45 percent. While fewer Americans have passports than their counterparts in other modern countries, and not everyone who has a passport has actually traveled abroad, the trends do offer encouragement.

Tourism can build bridges across national boundaries—even between peoples whose governments can't seem to get along. Would a more world-wise population of Americans and their counterparts in other countries begin to react differently to demagogues and nationalists? Would they begin to favor cooperation and a turning away from tribalism?

The Sister Cities program offers another interesting avenue for connecting peoples from many different cultures. Sister Cities International facilitates more than 2,000 alliances between cities and communities in over 140 countries. The organization "strives to build global cooperation at the municipal level, promote cultural understanding, and stimulate economic development."

Imagine an outreach program, strongly supported by the US government, to develop links between American communities and those in countries with antagonistic regimes. Why restrict these kinds of approaches to countries with which we enjoy cordial relationships? With the probable exception of North Korea, we could certainly begin building these kinds of relationships with China, Russia, and Iran.

Perhaps Martin Luther King summed up the proposition most compellingly. He said,

> *"People fail to get along because they fear each other; they fear each other because they don't know each other; they don't know each other because they have not communicated with each other."*

Maybe we have indeed come to a turning point in world history. Maybe a shared global view of our challenges and opportunities will win out. Maybe we can reduce hostilities between governments by building bridges between cultures.

Maybe the human species will finally grow up and fully understand that cooperation, not conflict, must become the model for our survival.

THE FIX-IT LIST: FOREIGN RELATIONS

So, how can we improve this component of our Republic—Foreign Relations? Let's start with these actions.

1. *Let's Declare Peaceful Intent.* By resolution of Congress and presidential signature, we'll disavow the belligerent practices of: 1) running destructive or destabilizing covert operations against sovereign governments with which we have not declared war, and which have not attacked our interests either overtly or covertly; 2) attempting to overthrow such governments, either by force or by covertly engineered coup operations; 3) unilateral attempts to assassinate the heads of such governments; and 4) unilateral military strikes within their territories, without permission, against political figures or leaders of stateless combatant organizations operating inside their boundaries.

   This policy will not otherwise limit ongoing espionage activities by US intelligence services conducted for defensive or national security purposes.

2. *Let's Get Serious About a Post-Nuclear World.* By a resolution of Congress and presidential signature, we'll reaffirm our promise never to launch a first-strike nuclear attack on any nation, and invite the other eight nuclear nations to make the same commitment.

   We'll revalidate the promising nuclear arms reduction treaties with Russia that have worked well, but which both governments have recently pushed aside. Russia's leaders might come back to the table if they see good reasons to do so.

   Through a UN resolution, we'll invite all nuclear

nations to reduce warhead inventories, first to agreed "MAD" thresholds, and then progressively toward zero. We'll invite all participants to agree on a realistic program of on-site inspections by a UN-accredited agency.

3. *Let's Bury the Hatchet with Cuba.* We'll start the process of normalizing political relations with Cuba, subject to commitments on the part of its government to move toward democratic and human rights norms compatible with the status of a modern country. We'll deal with the reality of a Marxist state in the last throes of its transition toward democracy.

   We'll return the base at Guantanamo Bay to Cuba, with no strings attached. Let's consider funding the redevelopment of the base as a modern, "green" Latin American tourist zone with amusement parks, hotels, casinos, and a cultural center.

4. *Let's Take the Lead on the Worsening Climate Crisis.* We'll restart the Paris Process, which invites all nations to commit to strenuous targets for reducing greenhouse gases and other key environmental initiatives.

   Let's practice what we preach. Let's commit our own nation to achieve the agreed-upon goals of the international climate accords. We'll launch a serious initiative to limit energy demands, increase conservation, improve energy efficiency, and shift energy production to sustainable sources by a realistic target date.

5. *Let's Fund and Support the Expansion of the World Health Organization's Mission,* to include an operational system for predicting and planning for international human disasters, collecting, stockpiling, and allocating emergency resources, and coordinating aid.

Chapter 13.
Let's Rethink Our Environment: Caring for the Commons

"Saving our planet, lifting people out of poverty,
advancing economic growth . . .
these are one and the same fight.
We must connect the dots between
climate change, water scarcity,
energy shortages, global health,
food security, and women's empowerment.
Solutions to one problem must be solutions for all."

—Ban Ki-Moon
Former Secretary General, United Nations

In April of 1815, Mount Tambora, on the Indonesian island of Sumbawa, blew its top so violently that it virtually shook the world. The explosion obliterated the top one-third of the 12,000-foot mountain and set off a mind-boggling chain of events. One can only try to grasp the enormous scale of the energy released by the eruption, in terms of its immediate effects and its long-term impacts on global weather patterns.

The great Mt. Vesuvius, which buried the city of Pompeii in the year 79 CE, looked like a firecracker compared to the biggest volcanic eruption ever observed.

Tens of thousands of people lost their lives in the immediate aftermath of the explosion, and the eventual death toll approached 100,000. The shock wave from the eruption created hurricane-force winds that wiped out whole villages on the surrounding islands, uprooted trees by the hundreds, and threw *millions of tons* of ash, dust, and smoke high into the atmosphere. Chunks of pumice rained down for days over a radius of a hundred miles or more. Fifteen-foot tsunami waves crashed down on settlements a thousand miles away.

For months after the explosion, observers all over the Pacific region reported bizarre weather effects—fluctuating temperatures, blackouts of the sun, and strangely colored sunsets caused by the massive amounts of volcanic debris circulating in the upper atmosphere.

By the following year, the atmospheric debris had spread across most of the globe and caused severe weather disturbances as far away as Europe. Through most of 1816, temperatures there stayed abnormally low, causing crop failures, sporadic famines, and even starvation.

Only decades later did scientists begin to fathom the scale of the Tambora eruption, and 1816 became known as "the year without a summer."

LET'S LEARN PLANETARY THINKING

I begin with this story for several reasons. First, I want us to stretch our thinking habits to a grand scale. We need to think *big*. I mean really, really big. Most of us spend our days thinking about the various goings-on in our lives and our immediate bubble of experience. For this particular journey, we need to make a strenuous mental leap to the scale of the entire planet we live on.

Second, I want us to orient our thinking as vividly as possible to the *physical reality* of this component of our cherished Republic—the Environment—and, as we've referred to it, the Commons. I want us to bring distant realities closer to our own personal experience and imagine natural processes as we might actually experience them.

And third, I want us to become ever mindful of the colossal *scale* of what goes on beyond our individual field of view. Before we take up the contentious issue of climate change and the difficult truths of eco-politics, let's educate ourselves for the conversation. The more we learn to think about the Commons as a vast, *complex adaptive system*, the more we can understand about its influence on our future—and our influence on its future.

To warm up our brains for this expedition, let's use Figure 13-1 as a wide-angle snapshot of the relationship between the natural environment and the built environment, highlighting some of the important features of both.

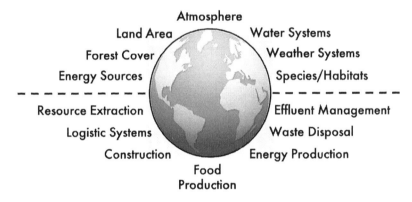

Figure 13-1. The Commons: Natural Environment & Built Environment

THE ILLUSION OF THE INFINITE ENVIRONMENT

Climbing Mount Everest has ranked as one of the most awesome physical challenges for adventurers ever since Britain's Sir Edmund Hillary and his Tibetan guide Tenzing Norgay made it to the top in 1953. For many years, the Everest climb held its place as one of the premier lifetime achievements for extreme performers.

Today, however, trying to climb the 29,029-foot peak has evolved—or devolved—into a boutique tourist experience, for which well-heeled high achievers pay from $50,000 to $100,000. More than 1,000 climbers attempt the summit in a typical year, with Tibetan and Nepalese guides who carry their gear, pitch their tents, and cook their meals.

In a typical year, about 60 percent reach the top. A dozen or so die. Due to the extreme weather conditions at the top and a narrow time window each day for reaching the very peak, those who make it may have to queue for hours waiting for their moment of glory and their photo at the top of the world.

Who Cleans Up the Mess?

The same thing has happened to the summit of Everest that happens with many popular tourist destinations: it has turned into a massive trash dump. Many climbers abandon their gear—tents, ropes, climbing equipment, oxygen bottles, food containers, and human waste—on the way down.

Despite making rules and imposing fines that require climbers to carry down a certain weight of garbage, the mountain's minders still have to haul down tons of garbage of all kinds (typically one-third of it composed of human excrement), including the occasional frozen corpse.

The Everest story, for me, summarizes the concept we began exploring in Chapter 3 (The Commons), namely the *illusion of the infinite environment*. Many of us tend to cling to the unvoiced assumption that, no matter what we cast off, no matter what we burn or bury, no matter where we go or what we do, dear old Mother Nature will always forgive us.

Our collective cultural memory of the legendary Mount Everest has always pictured it as a noble, pristine, unassailable feature of the Earth's geology, an iconic natural wonder we can revere for all time. And yet, we have to acknowledge the current reality: *we've trashed Mount Everest*. No part of the Earth stands immune to the collective behavior of seven billion members of our species.

Who Owns the River?

In Chapter 3 (The Commons) we asked, rhetorically, "Who owns the river?" Now we have to ask the question literally. In recent years, we've begun to see another troubling impact of the human attempt to control the natural environment. The Nile River, the legendary Mother of Africa, has become the center of a political conflict between nations.

The 4,100-mile waterway flows north through Egypt and empties into the Mediterranean. It serves, figuratively, as the life blood of a region largely composed of deserts. In most years, it overflows and floods the upper delta during the summer months. Sometimes it recedes and leaves most of the country in a drought.

Egypt, unfortunately, doesn't control all of the Nile. Further south, the branch known as the Blue Nile arises from Lake Tana in Ethiopia, and a second branch known as the White Nile arises from the vast Lake Victoria that borders three other countries. The two branches meet in Sudan and form one river on its way north.

Recent to this writing, the government of Ethiopia has decided to dam the Blue Nile to divert more water for irrigation and electrical power. That will seriously reduce the already tenuous water supply to Egypt. Now we have a situation that will test the global community's capacity for shared-fate solutions to ecological challenges. Neither Ethiopia nor Egypt "owns" the Nile, yet both countries claim entitlement to its natural gifts for their territories.

The Hip Bone's Connected to the Thigh Bone . . .

A similar eco-political conflict has arisen in recent years with the Amazon River, a waterway so vast that scientists study it as a whole ecological system.

Climate experts at the UN and in other concerned nations have noted the alarmingly high rate of deforestation of the

Amazon ecosystem, particularly in Brazil. Clear cutting by logging firms and other commercial interests, aggravated by thousands of wildcat fires, have significantly reduced the forest cover of the region. Scientists estimate that more than 10,000 square kilometers of the forest disappeared in 2019 —about 10 football fields per minute. As of this writing, the forest cover stands at about 80 percent of its size in 1970.

Brazil's president, responding to offers of assistance by the UN and others, declared that they had no call to interfere in his country's internal affairs. His government, he said, had the right to do whatever they wanted with the Amazon.

Anyone who survived high school science class knows that Nature doesn't recognize national borders. Egypt and Ethiopia; Brazil, America, the European Union—these don't exist in eco-reality. Planetary thinking requires that we become more conscious of connections, interactions, and cause-and-effect chains of relationships that span the globe.

The 3,800-mile Amazon gets its start as rainfall high in the Andes Mountains of Peru. The second longest river on the planet (after the Nile, and just ahead of the Yangtze and the Mississippi), it flows eastward through nine countries. It gathers water from hundreds of tributaries as it goes.

The Amazon delivers about 20 percent of the Earth's total river flow to the oceans. It pours *175,000 cubic meters of water (46 million gallons) per second* into the Atlantic Ocean. It also transports some *1.3 million tons of sediment per day* to the sea. It propels a plume of fresh water 250 miles out to sea, which fans out to 100 miles wide before it blends with the seawater.

The river and the rainforest form an inseparable ecosystem. The rainforest, the largest on the planet, stretches over 2 million square miles. Less than 60 percent of it lies within the imaginary borders of what the Brazilian president considers "his" country.

WHY SHOULD I CARE ABOUT THE AMAZON RAINFOREST? I DON'T LIVE THERE

Actually, you *don't* have to know or care about the Amazon rainforest if you don't mind allowing other people to make certain decisions about your future.

You can think of any environmental issue, such as the fate of the rainforest, in terms of its *psychological proximity* to you—how near to your personal experience it might come, both in space and time. Some of the goings-on in your planetary environment will demand your immediate attention, some can wait, and some you'll never notice in your daily life, at least not in the near term.

What happens in and to the Amazon rainforest probably ranks pretty far away on your proximity scale. You might react to the occasional news article that tells about the deforestation. You might wrinkle your brow and ask, "Why do those people get so worked up about the rainforest?"

That question has a very compelling answer, and I hope you'll keep an open mind during the following brief discussion, to learn the reasons why.

Follow the Carbon

Did you know that *trees breathe*? They certainly do. In fact, all green plants inhale and exhale to the atmosphere. Their cycle of breathing works in exactly the reverse direction to the breathing of humans and other animals.

Whereas we humans breathe in *oxygen* (remember O_2 from science class) and breathe out *carbon dioxide (*CO_2), trees do the reverse: they take in carbon dioxide (through their leaves) and release oxygen back into the atmosphere. Maybe you have an imaginary "partner tree" somewhere on the planet, that shares your breathing process. As you exhale your CO_2, your hypothetical tree-mate breaks it down, uses the carbon, and gives back the O_2.

Eco-scientists call this never-ending exchange the *carbon*

cycle, and it controls all life on the planet. Every living organism contains carbon, usually together with oxygen and other elements. Life, for our planet, depends fundamentally and absolutely on the *circulation of carbon atoms and oxygen atoms*, and various molecules that include them.

The Amazon rainforest exchanges so much O_2 and CO_2 with the Earth's atmosphere that scientists refer to it as the "lungs of the planet." Some of the atoms of oxygen you inhaled a few seconds ago might have come from the Amazon forest canopy. Some might have come from the vast Canadian timber forests. Some might have come from that rosebush or that tomato plant in your garden.

We humans breathe; the trees breathe; *the planet breathes.*

And Brazil doesn't get its own private atmosphere.

Follow the Food

By the way, what do trees do with all that CO_2, and what do humans and animals do with all that O_2? The simple answer: they feed off of each other.

Think about a food plant—an apple tree, a tomato bush, or a grapevine.

The plant breathes in CO_2, sucks up water through its roots, absorbs sunlight, and combines them with a photo-chemical with the familiar name of *chlorophyll* (the compound you learned about in science class, which makes leaves green). Little chemical factories in the plant rearrange the atoms to form *carbo-hydrates* (mainly glucose), which it stores in the leaves and in the fruit that it produces. The process liberates oxygen molecules as a byproduct, which the plant exhales back to the atmosphere. Your science teacher, you might recall, referred to that process as *photosynthesis.*

When you eat the apple, the tomato, the grape, or any other plant-based food, your digestive system combines the oxygen you inhaled with the glucose to generate the standard energy fuel that energizes every cell in your body.

All animals in the food chain depend on carbohydrates and the carbon cycle that creates them. Carnivorous animals may survive solely on the meat of other animals, but their prey animals usually live on vegetation. Consequently, no animal could survive without the carbon cycle that captures CO_2, mobilizes water, produces food, and releases oxygen.

Follow the Water

While the carbon cycle goes on circulating carbon and oxygen around the planet, another crucial natural cycle rolls along with it. Scientists call it the *hydrologic cycle* (or simply the water cycle), and it moves *water* around the planet.

In the case of the Amazon jungle, scientists call it the rainforest for good reasons. The trees along the river soak up enormous amounts of water and release it through their dense forest canopy. In some areas it rains back down almost constantly.

Much of the water evaporates into the atmosphere and drifts freely with the winds (the atmosphere never settles down or stops moving). It travels thousands of miles, unimpeded by the hypothetical borders of countries like Brazil.

That fluffy white cloud you see above the hillside contains water vapor, which makes it visible. Those menacing dark clouds have picked up so much water that they've become overloaded, and a small rise in temperature will cause them to release it as rainfall. We can think of clouds as Nature's water tanks—a remarkably effective design solution, from an engineering point of view. They can pick up water, store it, deliver it anywhere on the planet, and release it as needed.

This never-ending cycle of evaporation, transport by clouds, rainfall, and flow through waterways makes a lot of sense once you get the basic idea. Recall, for example, that the Amazon gets its start from rainfall high up in the Peruvian Andes. It releases part of the flow into the trees and the atmosphere as it goes. And finally, it delivers its payload to the Atlantic Ocean.

The Earth stores its water supply in four main systems: 1) the oceans; 2) surface freshwater, which includes rivers, lakes, and underground aquifers; 3) atmospheric moisture; and 4) frozen deposits such as the polar caps, arctic and antarctic ice sheets, glaciers, icebergs, and mountain snowpacks. All four systems hold enormous volumes of water, and they continually exchange water amongst themselves.

As you think of these intimately connected flows of air and water—both essential for human survival—does that familiar song from the popular movie "The Lion King" come to mind: "The Circle of Life?"

THE TRAGEDY OF THE COMMONS

In the vocabulary of environmental science, the phrase "tragedy of the Commons" has become increasingly accepted as a way to call attention to the global impacts of unregulated human activity.

The germ of the concept surfaced many years ago in an essay written by the British economist William Forster Lloyd in 1833. Lloyd pointed out that allowing farmers to graze their animals on public—or "common"—lands led to over-grazing and eventually made the lands unfit for use.

The concept got its modern name in 1968 when an American biologist, Garrett Hardin, published an essay extending it to the entire ecosystem. Hardin asserted that any shared natural resource—the atmosphere; the oceans; rivers, lakes, streams, and underground aquifers; croplands or grazing lands; roads and highways; aviation airspace—when unregulated, could progressively deteriorate as the human population grew and per-capita consumption increased along with rising standards of living.

Each individual user of the resources of the Commons tends to see him– or herself as having an insignificant impact, but the combined effect of billions of users can overwhelm or exhaust the resource. An old expression, variously attributed, reminds us that, "Every snowflake in an avalanche pleads its innocence."

To summarize the concept more brutally: sooner or later, we'll even trash Mount Everest.

Environmental activists tend to frame the story of the movement partly in terms of long-range trends that signal the deteriorating condition of the Commons, and partly in terms of various landmark disasters, both natural and man-made. Both considerations, they assert, illustrate the general lack of coordinated responses by national governments and international bodies.

Figure 13-2 illustrates some of the most significant threats to a tranquil environment, both natural and man-made.

NATURAL THREATS

| Climate Disasters | Earthquakes | Volcanos | Pandemics |

MAN-MADE THREATS

| Oil Spills | Nuclear Accidents | Water Politics | Displaced Populations (Refugees) |

| Micro-Plastic Pollution | Great Pacific "Garbage Patch" | Species / Habitat Destruction |

Figure 13-2. Planetary Threats, Natural & Man-Made

Let's review some of the most famous—or infamous—man-made disasters, to see what lessons they might teach. Not all environmental scientists or activists would necessarily agree with this particular selection, but each one has its own instructive value.

1. *The Great Plains "Dust Bowl."* Years of haphazard agricultural practices by US farmers on the Great Plains during the 1930s and 40s set the conditions for one of the most disastrous ecological episodes in the nation's history. The combination of depleted farmland and extreme drought conditions displaced vast areas of topsoil—100 million acres of it. Huge dust storms, rising as high as 10,000 feet, blew across the flat tablelands, blocking the sun and depositing layers of fine dust. An estimated 2.5 million people lost their farms and homes. Hordes of them pulled up stakes and migrated to the West Coast, but in the middle of the Great Depression they found conditions there not much better.

2. *The Love Canal Toxic Waste Dump.* First envisioned as a miniature model city in 1890 by the wealthy entrepreneur William T. Love, the project occupied a 36-square block neighborhood in a corner of the city of Niagara Falls, in New York. Love began excavating a canal to bring water from the Niagara River for hydro-power generation.

   The plans fizzled out, however, and the city acquired the site, eventually using it to deposit municipal refuse. The partially-dug canal—about 1 mile long, 50 feet wide, and 40 feet deep—became a huge rainwater pond, used by children for swimming in summer and skating during the winter.

   In the 1940s, the Hooker Chemical Company bought the canal from the city, drained it, and used it to bury tons of chemical byproducts from the manufacture of rubber, synthetic resins, and solvents. In 1953, as concerns about the toxic deposits continued to grow, they ended the practice, filled in the canal, and sealed it. Hooker's management sold the canal and a patch of land around it to the city School Board for $1, subject to the city's agreement to release the company from all future liabilities related to the buried waste.

Construction activities breached the underground storage facilities, releasing toxic chemicals into the soil and groundwater. For over a decade, however, the city government and private builders ignored the growing concerns about the leakage of pollutants and toxins, and continued building public facilities and private homes over the canal.

By the mid-1970s, the canal had become a major biohazard and a political albatross. Eco-activists managed to bring the issue to front-page status, and Love Canal became an iconic case for irresponsible environmental practices. The most tragic consequence came with the health effects of *dioxin*, a powerful agent known to cause multiple, severe birth defects.

President Jimmy Carter announced a federal health emergency and authorized immediate remedial measures. The expensive clean-up operation required the creation of a new national funding mechanism, which became known as the environmental superfund.

3. *The Great Smog of London.* London's use of coal for most of its energy processes peaked in 1952 when freak weather conditions, combined with the massive production of coal smoke and soot, blanketed the city for five days. Medical experts estimated that as many as 12,000 people died immediately or over the next few years as a direct result of the smog. The event forced the British government to enact the Clean Air Act, which began the process of moving away from

coal-fired energy systems.

4. *Japan's Minimata Disease: Mercury Poisoning.* Industrial wastewater discharged into the ocean from the Chisso Corporation's chemical factory in Japan's Minimata city had continued unchecked from 1932 to 1968. A highly toxic compound of mercury, unrecognized until 1956, had accumulated in the ocean water, in fish, and shellfish, to levels that began to cause severe neurological disorders and grotesque birth defects in the surrounding population. The government and the company had both looked the other way for years, ignoring the mounting reports of catastrophic disorders in people and animals. Not until 2001, after more than 2,200 officially diagnosed cases and 1,800 deaths, did the government officially acknowledge the disaster. By 2004, the company had paid $86 million in compensation. Only then did the government issue a decree requiring the company to stop the contamination. An eventual settlement in 2010 created a fund to allow for future compensation of undiagnosed victims.

5. *Agent Orange: Mass Defoliation.* US military planes sprayed nearly 20 million gallons of herbicides over the jungles of Vietnam during the long-running conflict, particularly from 1968 through 1971. As part of an inventory of "rainbow" herbicides, designated variously as White, Purple, Blue, Pink, and Green, Agent Orange accounted for more than half of the compounds used to defoliate vast stretches of forest canopy, denying concealment to the Vietcong forces.

Dioxin, the main active ingredient, degrades slowly—over a period of decades—and large areas of jungle and farmland in Vietnam remain contaminated to this day. As with all chemical and biological weapons, the soldiers who use it face the same health risks as their enemy counterparts. For years after the war, returning GIs presented at VA clinics with a variety of symptoms which US authorities eventually—and reluctantly—acknowledged as caused by exposure to the compound, and particularly its dioxin component.

Military medics eventually associated at least 14 disorders directly or indirectly with Agent Orange exposure. They seem to have paid little attention to the effects of the defoliation on the Vietnamese population, or subsequent death rates compared to the one million who lost their lives during the conflict.

6. *The Bhopal Chemical Spill.* An accident at Union Carbide's chemical plant in Bhopal, India in 1984 released a highly toxic pesticide compound, *methyl isocyanate*, into a densely populated industrial area. The release, estimated at 32 tons of the compound, killed an estimated 15,000 people and afflicted possibly hundreds of thousands more with blindness, organ failure, and birth defects. Much of the city remains contaminated and Bhopal continues to rank as possibly the worst chemical disaster in history.

7. *The Chernobyl Reactor Melt-Down.* An explosion in 1986 at the Chernobyl nuclear power plant in Ukraine, then part of the Soviet Union, spread radiation as far as Europe and left the facility a dangerously reactive waste heap. It remains inaccessible to this day, with a large no-man's land exclusion zone for miles around it. The United Nation's Chernobyl Forum Report estimated the total number of deaths from cancer caused by the radiation exposure at about 4,000.

8. *The Exxon Valdez Oil Spill.* Exxon Corporation's mega-tanker ran aground in Prince William Sound, Alaska, in 1989, spilling over 10 million gallons of crude oil into the environment. The spill contaminated the waters for miles around and washed up on the shore, killing hundreds of thousands of birds and other wildlife along the coastline. The company paid fines of

$125 million to the US government and nearly a billion dollars in civil claims, plus direct costs for the clean-up of more than $2 billion.

9. *The Deepwater Horizon Oil Spill.* In 2010, an oil-rig explosion in British Petroleum's deep sea drilling operation in the Gulf of Mexico, 40 miles off the coast of Louisiana, caused the loss of control of an uncapped wellhead a mile below the surface. For 87 days it continued to vent oil and methane, which rose to the surface and spread for many miles. The gusher released over five million barrels of oil before the company got it capped. Eleven workers lost their lives in the episode. The company paid over $18 billion in penalties and settlements, including fines to the US government.

10. *The Fukushima Reactor Meltdown.* An offshore earthquake caused a wave surge that swamped Japan's coastal nuclear facility in 2011. The flood shorted out its electrical power supply, causing its control systems to fail. The loss of control triggered a melt-down of the reactor's core. The episode destroyed the reactor and leaked a significant amount of radiation into the surrounding area. Japanese authorities evacuated over 125,000 residents, and as of this writing many still cannot return.

This list doesn't include some other, more infamous man-made disasters, like 1) the legendary—and avoidable—Johnstown Flood in Pennsylvania in 1889, which killed over 2,000 people; 2) the Great Boston Molasses Flood in 1919, in which a 40-foot tide of molasses burst from a giant pressurized storage tank and inundated a whole neighborhood in the north of the city; or 3) the grounding and complete destruction, in 2012, of the Costa Concordia, a $600 million luxury cruise ship carrying 4,200 passengers and crew, off the coast of Italy, caused by gross incompetence and negligence on the part of its captain. History books record many other disasters of various kinds and scales, all of which bear testimony that human error can have colossal consequences.

A few simple lessons stand out from these reports:

▸ Any potent resource that can concentrate large amounts of energy—heat; electrical power; explosive force; kinetic energy of moving parts; a great volume of liquid that can flood and flow; a toxic or corrosive chemical; or a massive amount of weight that could collapse—can do an appalling amount of environmental damage if not properly managed.

▸ Executives who control large corporations don't always act wisely or responsibly in safeguarding the natural environment from the impacts of large-scale resource extraction, nor have they always acted honorably in dealing with disasters.

▸ Government bureaucracies don't always meet their oversight responsibilities effectively, nor have they always acted aggressively to protect the public interest from irresponsible corporate activities.

▸ Government bureaucracies typically haven't prepared well for, responded to, or managed ecological disasters very well—whether naturally occurring or man-made.

With 51 governing bureaucracies and a bewildering number of special-purpose administrative agencies, the US has no real integrated national system for preventing, planning for, or managing large-scale disasters. A number of major episodes over the past two decades have clearly demonstrated the need for a national solution.

THE POLLUTION OF OUR BACK YARD

The space available to us here doesn't allow for a full exploration of all the ways in which collective human activity burdens the resources of the natural environment. Certainly, however, the problem of global waste pollution—humanity's garbage output—deserves a central place. Two particular man-made processes deserve special attention for our purposes: 1) micro-plastic pollution and 2) the so-called "Great Pacific Garbage Patch." We'll explore them shortly.

The Other Grand River

As part of what we've called the illusion of the infinite environment, most of us have very little understanding of what happens to the trash we discard after it leaves our custody. We throw our unwanted material into the waste bin and periodically we set the bin out for the garbage collectors. After that, it probably fades out of our consciousness, but it doesn't stop existing just because we don't know where it went.

A vast, never-ending tide of unwanted material, of every conceivable type, flows from individuals, families, and businesses to places all over the planet. Much of it, unfortunately, ends up in the oceans. Just as the majestic Nile, the vast Amazon, the placid Yangtze, the mighty Mississippi, and the holy Ganges carry water from the mountains to the sea, so the waste stream relentlessly moves material all over the planet. Indeed, we might think of it as a counterpart to the world's great rivers, with many branches and tributaries of its own. Maybe it deserves a name. For our purposes, let's just refer to it as the Great Waste River.

Eco-scientists think of the flowing content of the Great Waste River as carrying both *managed* waste and *unmanaged* waste. Managed waste includes material collected and moved about by established methods that keep it under control at all times. Unmanaged—or mismanaged—waste includes material that people, businesses, or governments just discard into the ecosystem with no concern for what happens to it.

In an ideal world, mismanaged waste wouldn't exist. Everybody would deliver their unwanted material to systems that collect it; safeguard it; store, recycle, or process it; and keep it localized. In the world we have, however, many countries have no waste management systems at all. Many governments make no attempt to influence their citizens toward eco-friendly practices.

As governments of developing nations vent their sewage systems into rivers and oceans, and dump garbage into vast unmanaged landfills, those waste products become a permanent part of the marine and land-based ecosystems.

When people flush toxic chemicals down their toilets, along with unwanted medications and small items of debris, they feed the part of the waste stream that flows into sewage channels and eventually out to the sea. As they discard debris in rivers and on public beaches, it also washes out to sea.

As boating fans throw their garbage overboard, it becomes a permanent part of the marine ecosystem. As fishing boat operators toss their damaged or worn-out nets into the ocean, they drift about forever, tangling and killing fish, dolphins, and sea turtles.

As cargo ships from some countries discharge raw sewage into the sea and dump all kinds of waste materials overboard, the oceans become global sewers and junkyards.

As we've discovered, the great rivers of the world all flow from their sources to their destinations as part of a global water cycle, constantly exchanging water resources everywhere. The Great Waste River, however, doesn't exchange or recycle anything. It simply disperses the 2 billion tons of man-made matter produced each year.

That 2 billion tons works out to an average of about 1.5 pounds of garbage per person per day, for all 7 billion inhabitants of the Earth. Obviously, people in the wealthier countries discard much more than those in the poorest countries. The US Environmental Protection Agency estimates Americans' garbage output at about 6 pounds per day, per person. Those estimates peg the US recycling rate at about 20-25 percent, with a net daily delivery of unprocessed waste of about 4.5 pounds to the environment.

The wealthier countries have made considerable progress on recycling and reprocessing waste, particularly metals and plastic. However, the current state of progress remains limited at best, and nearly nonexistent for third-world states.

The Plastic Surprise

To understand the story of plastic pollution, we have to start with oil. About 10-12 percent of the world's oil production goes to the manufacture of plastics of all kinds.

The question: why and how have oil and plastics become so absolutely fundamental to the operation of all modern societies? *The answer*: because they've become extremely useful and extremely cheap. We've become addicted to them as a society and as individuals. Dealing with plastic pollution requires that we understand the depth and breadth of this dependency. Let's consider a brief historical flashback.

The commercial history of oil goes back only about a century or so. The legendary oil baron John D. Rockefeller first made his fortune by extracting kerosene from it, which he sold as a substitute for whale oil and candles. He and his competitors usually dumped the unwanted oil residue into storage ponds or rivers. They burned off the natural gas that came out of the wells, treating it as just a waste product.

By about 1900, however, scientists began to realize how many energy-bearing compounds came along for free in that 42-gallon barrel of oil. The discovery of gasoline, for example, enabled the development of the internal combustion engine and kicked off a whole new economic phenomenon: *motorized transportation*, in all its forms. Diesel powered generators also made electricity abundant, cheap, and universally accessible. Before long, they recognized natural gas as an important energy source in its own right.

Just as Kentucky farmers could make moonshine whiskey by *distilling* it—cooking corn, yeast, and water; steaming off the fermented alcohol; and then condensing it to liquid form again—a refinery could distill crude oil into *fractions*, like kerosene, gasoline, diesel fuel, benzene, liquid natural gas, lubricants, naphtha, paraffin wax, petroleum jelly, and tar.

Even the remaining sludge yielded asphalt, useful for roads and construction. Oil truly became the miracle material.

As the science progressed, researchers also figured out that they could recombine the hundreds of unique *hydrocarbon* molecules (containing various combinations of carbon and hydrogen, plus a few other elements) into specialized giant molecules to make radically new materials never seen before: *plastics.*

Very few other materials or products have taken a permanent place in the human experience faster or more completely than plastics. Brightly colored plastics; transparent plastics; flexible plastics; lightweight plastics; strong and durable plastics; plastics that look like shiny metals; plastics molded into complex shapes; hoses and pipes; cheap plastics used for product packaging, bags, and containers of all kinds; styrofoam cups and package fillers; polyester fabrics— manufacturers and consumers fell in love with all of them.

By the 1950s and 60s, plastics began showing up in everything from children's toys, to automobile parts, to construction materials. Plastics helped accelerate a profound and little understood shift in American cultural patterns, habits, and values: *transience and disposability.*

Now we fast-forward to 2000 and beyond, and face an awful truth: *plastics never go away.* Once released into the natural environment, they endure virtually forever. Plant-based materials like wood, paper, and cloth all eventually deteriorate and decay, returning to the environment in their elemental form. Even the wreckage of the Titanic continues to rust and decay as it sits on the ocean floor. Plastics don't.

Stated more precisely: plastics may physically *disintegrate* over time, but most of them don't *decay* back to their original atomic elements. Their remarkable durability comes from their highly stable molecular structure. The many little sub-molecules—*monomers*, the chemists call them—fit together like Tinker-Toys to make larger complex structures called *polymers.* A polymer consists of a bunch of monomers hooked together. A particular arrangement gives a certain plastic its characteristics—color, texture, flexibility, and resistance to heat, for example. The polymers hook together in long chains, sometimes with thousands of monomers.

You've probably noticed that, when you leave a plastic container outdoors for a long time, the plastic begins to deteriorate from the effects of the sun and the weather. The plastic becomes brittle and discolored, begins to crack, and eventually breaks up into fragments.

The ultraviolet energy in the sunlight shatters the linkages in the polymer chains and causes them to fall apart. As the chains unhook from one another, the plastic bucket disintegrates physically, but not chemically. After you hand it over to the garbage collectors, it continues to disintegrate as it bounces around in the waste stream. It might end up in a landfill, and the pieces just keep getting smaller and smaller.

Over a long time, one big piece of plastic becomes many smaller pieces, each chemically identical to the original. Eco-scientists use the term *micro-plastics* to refer to the smallest of these particles, typically less than a half-centimeter in size. Those, and their microscopic descendants, pose the greatest problem for the natural environment.

By the way, chewing gum—another petroleum-derived product—also stays in the waste stream for a very long time. The US National Institutes of Health estimates worldwide gum consumption at 560,000 tons per year. Chewing gum and cigarette butts make up a significant portion of waste discarded in public areas.

Plastic in the Oceans

The issue of plastic pollution in the world's oceans has set off alarms among environmental scientists, for a number of reasons. Estimates vary from 8 to 12 million tons of plastic waste going into the oceans each year, year after year, mostly through rivers. Scientists expect that volume to increase steadily for the next decade or so.

Ocean plastic waste varies all the way from soft drink bottles, styrofoam containers, plastic bags and plastic straws, to small floating particles that fish and sea birds mistake for food. Some estimates put the number of single-use plastic bags going into the ocean at 1-2 billion per year.

Where does all that plastic waste go? It doesn't disappear, so what happens to it?

As we've learned, once a piece of plastic begins to disintegrate under the influence of the ultraviolet rays of the sun and the physical agitation of the seawater, it doesn't stop. It will contain to disintegrate, day by day, year by year, into ever-smaller pieces, until it gets down to the level of the very molecules that compose it.

Scientists believe that most of the ocean plastic disintegrates almost completely and either disperses into the water or settles down on the ocean floor. Probably only a small portion of it floats at or near the surface—possibly as little as 1 percent. Some estimates put the volume of plastic waste that has settled to the sea floor as high as 70 million tons.

Which countries discharge the most marine plastic waste? In the Pacific Ocean, China contributes the highest share of mismanaged ocean plastic by far, with over 25 percent of the global total. Indonesia accounts for about 10 percent, and another 20 percent comes out of the Philippines, Vietnam, and Sri Lanka. The US contributes less than 1 percent of the total.

At this point, we have no solution for marine plastic pollution. We certainly don't have the technology or the resources to somehow gather up all of the dispersed plastic, or even a small portion of it. Scientists don't know for sure how plastics will affect the ocean as an ecosystem, or how the invasion of plastic compounds into seafood affects humans.

The Great Pacific Garbage Patch

In 1997 the captain of a racing yacht, sailing from Hawaii to California, began to notice items of household trash swirling around his vessel as it passed through a remote area of the northern Pacific Ocean. On a closer look, Charles Moore realized he had sailed into an enormous floating garbage patch. He saw household items like plastic soft drink and water bottles, plastic garbage bags, shoes, chunks of cardboard, styrofoam containers, and countless small chips of plastic, floating in the water around him.

How could all of this man-made debris have moved thousands of miles from land out to the most remote stretches of the ocean? When he arrived in California, Moore reported his experience to responsible government agencies. The investigations that followed produced a surprising and appalling result.

Oceanographers had known for some time that a combination of long-range ocean currents formed a vast Pacific whirlpool of sorts, causing a gradual swirl of water toward a central region. They realized that floating objects of any kind would come under the influence of this vast rotating mass of water, referred to as a *gyre*, and would eventually drift toward a common point of concentration in the middle.

They could associate some of the debris, marked with commercial labels, with several countries of origin. Some of it came from the US West Coast; some came from China; some from Indonesia; and some came from various other Asian countries. Since that time, environmental scientists, government policymakers, and activists have worked to understand the size and scope of the phenomenon, and have looked for ways in which they might reduce or eliminate it.

The sheer volume of plastic debris that has accumulated in the Pacific gyre boggles the mind. Scientists estimate the largest of two distinct patches as at least twice the size of Texas. The slurry of plastic material, ranging from large distinct objects down to microscopic particles, occupies the top several meters of the ocean surface. The relentless effects of the sun and ocean turbulence keeps breaking the particles down to smaller and smaller sizes.

Depending on the tides, two separate garbage patches sometimes form, separated by hundreds of miles. Mostly, however, eco-scientists tend to refer to all or parts of the Pacific collection of plastic waste by its familiar nickname the Great Pacific Gyre, or Great Pacific Garbage Patch.

Does the Atlantic Ocean have its own garbage patch? Unfortunately, it does. Scientists have known about it for at least as long as its Pacific counterpart—which has received considerably more press attention—and have studied it extensively. They find a lot of similarity between the two patches in terms of the types of plastics there, particle size, movements with the currents, and settling to the ocean floor.

CLIMATE CRISIS? WHAT CLIMATE CRISIS?

Overheard:

> *"Global warming and climate change will be the biggest existential threats that human society has ever faced."*

> *"Global warming is a hoax. The climate has always been changing."*

> *"We must eliminate fossil fuels completely."*

> *"We can't destroy whole industries just because a bunch of alarmists claim the sky is falling."*

> *"Apathy is our most dangerous enemy."*

> *"Climate hysteria is our most dangerous enemy."*

Global Warming: that phrase has become an emotionally charged shorthand—a handle for a whole grab-bag of controversies, conflicts, issues, problems, and—for some people—opportunities to bring the American Republic into the modern age.

Few themes in the national conversation have generated so much heat and so little light, and few topics have tribalized Americans so intensely around competing ideologies.

We need to unpack this relatively simple concept, look at its components, and get some sense of its politics—how Americans currently think and feel about it, if they think about it at all.

GLOBAL WARMING DEMYSTIFIED

A commonly accepted definition of global warming has it as:

A gradual, irreversible rise in average local temperatures across the Earth's surface, associated with the build-up of various "greenhouse gases" in the atmosphere such as smog, carbon dioxide, methane, and chlorofluorocarbons, which trap heat and reduce the amount of sunlight energy reflected back to space.

The idea of calculating an "average" temperature for the whole Earth seems like a strange undertaking, because of the obvious differences between hot and cold regions, and the huge variations through the seasons every year. However, scientists have evolved a rather clever way of collecting temperature readings from many scattered locations, and combining data from those local readings over time to determine whether temperatures *in general* have gone up over the years, gone down, or stayed pretty much the same.

Technically speaking, they measure the *average change* in temperatures, not some hypothetical overall temperature.

Since about 1880, scientists have kept records of these temperature readings all over the world on a continuing basis. Over the many decades, they've set up more and more measuring stations, and international researchers have shared and analyzed the data. In recent decades, thousands of sensors, most of them now reporting electronically, have helped to map the local patterns.

These increasing yearly deviations from the long-term average temperatures amount to small fractions of a degree, year by year, but over many decades, they've grown to a cumulative increase of nearly 2 degrees Centigrade.

Two degrees might not seem like much, but consider the

immense amount of heat energy it would take to raise the entire Earth's temperature by even a fraction of a degree. That extra heat drives regional and seasonal temperature extremes, reducing snow cover and sea ice, intensifying heavy rainfall, and changing habitat ranges for plants and animals—expanding some and shrinking others.

With increasing global surface temperatures, the possibility of more droughts and increased intensity of storms will likely increase. As more water vapor evaporates into the atmosphere, it fuels more powerful storms. More heat in the atmosphere and warmer ocean surface temperatures can also cause higher wind speeds in tropical storms.

WHAT DO AMERICANS BELIEVE?

As of this writing, Americans seem concerned, confused, and conflicted about a variety of environmental issues, including climate change. According to studies by the Pew Research Center and others, for example:[23]

> ‣ Two-thirds of Americans say the federal government hasn't done enough to reduce the impacts of climate change. Similar numbers fault the government on protecting air quality, natural water systems, animals and their habitats, and public lands. Those numbers might seem somewhat encouraging, but they put Americans at last place in a comparative survey of attitudes in 21 major countries.

> ‣ Further, those averages conceal big differences in political ideology. Ninety percent of people who identify as Democrats, or as leaning toward that affiliation, believe the government should do more on all five of those dimensions, while less than 40 percent of Republicans say that.

> ‣ Generationally, younger people and millennials express more dissatisfaction with government action than older people. Gender also makes a difference: 46 percent of women disapprove of government performance, while

34 percent of men disapprove.

▸ On the issue of energy, more than three-quarters of Americans say they favor developing alternative energy sources rather than increasing production of fossil fuel sources.

▸ Again, however, political affiliation makes a difference. A breakdown of that average shows 90 percent of Democrats favoring alternative energy sources but only 62 percent of Republicans agreeing. Three-quarters of millennials agree, but barely half of boomers and older Americans agree. Two-thirds of women agree, while 58 percent of males agree.

▸ About 60 percent of the people surveyed say climate change affects their lives or communities in some noticeable way. They believe episodes of severe weather —heat waves, droughts, severe storms and floods, and wildfires—have become more frequent. Over half believe that rising sea levels have begun to affect shoreline communities.

▸ On the central question of *anthropogenic climate change* —the extent to which human activity affects climate— Americans differ radically by party affiliation, probably more than on any other political issue. As a gross average, about half of Americans say they believe human activity has a big influence on climate change. Another 30 percent believe it has some effect. Only 20 percent believe it has very little effect.

▸ Splitting the responses by political affiliation, again, shows that over 80 percent of liberal Democrats rate human influence as very high, while less than 15 percent of conservative Republicans agree. Moderate Democrats and moderate Republicans come somewhat closer, but still divide more than 60/40 on the question.

▸ As we might expect, the opposing argument—that most of the climate changes come from natural forces in the Earth's environment—divides the two camps in a similar way. Ninety percent of conservative Republicans believe that natural forces cause most of the change, while 15 percent of liberal Democrats agree.

▸ As to the second central question, on the role government should play in trying to manage the effects of climate change, the partisan divisions also prevail. Researchers asked the survey participants to rate major government policies on two dimensions: 1) how much they benefit the environment; and 2) how much they help the US economy. On both questions, Democrats and Republicans differed widely.

▸ On average, over half of those surveyed say government environmental polices help the environment rather than harm it. About a third believe they don't make a difference. Fifteen percent believe they do more environmental harm than good.

▸ Again, Democrats and Republicans diverge significantly in their opinions: over 70 percent of Democrats believe the policies help the environment, while a similar number of Republicans believe they either have no impact or that they harm the environment.

WHAT DO THE SCIENTISTS SAY?

The UN's Intergovernmental Panel on Climate Change (IPCC) analyzed a vast collection of peer-reviewed scientific papers, as well as presentations and interviews with thousands of scientists who specialize in climate issues. They reported that:[24]

> *More than 97 percent of practicing climate scientists have concluded that human activity has caused most, if not all, of the global warming and climate change the Earth has experienced, going as far back as 1950.*

Furthermore, closer inspection of the research products of the presumed 3 percent of scientists claiming to contradict the conclusion discovered questionable methodology and investigator bias in most cases. Several of the more provocative contrarian studies didn't survive attempts to replicate them and others failed peer reviews. After adjusting for those questionable sources, some reviewers put the degree of reputable consensus at microscopically close to 100 percent.

Surprisingly, however, surveys by Yale University, George Mason University, and others indicate that fewer than 20 percent of Americans fully realize the overwhelming extent of scientific consensus. The researchers described Americans as ranging from Alarmed, through Concerned, Cautious, Disengaged, Doubtful, and Dismissive.[25]

Confused perceptions on the part of Americans go back to the start of the George W. Bush presidency in 2000. Prior to Bush's accession to the presidency, Bill Clinton and his VP Al Gore had begun to raise the global warming issue to a more prominent place in the national conversation. Gore had written a well-respected book, *Earth in the Balance*, in 1992, just before he joined the White House leadership.[26]

As Clinton and Gore handed the keys to the White House to Bush and his VP Dick Cheney, a new ideology of environmental politics began to set in. With his party in control of both the House and Senate for most of his two terms, Bush and his advisers began to offer a new narrative.

Bush and Cheney both came from the oil industry. Bush descended from a long line of Texas oilmen and Cheney had served as CEO of Halliburton Company, one of the world's largest oilfield service companies. Both men maintained deep ties to the petroleum industry, and their historical loyalties strongly influenced their ideologies about the projection of American influence into the oil-rich and politically conflicted Middle East.

Neither one had much room in his ideological kit bag for vague notions about the far-off effects of global warming or climate change. Energy policy for them meant securing access to strategic sources of oil and assuring the future of the petroleum industry.

THE IDEOLOGICAL STAND-OFF: POLITICAL PARALYSIS

A loose coalition of special interest players began to form, including oil industry executives, members of Congress from oil- and coal-producing states, newly influential talk show hosts, and ultra-conservative news industry personalities.

The new counter-narrative painted Al Gore as the patron of an idealistic subculture of soft-headed, tree-hugging activists who wanted to indulge their New Age aspirations at the expense of the American economy and its business sector.

"Global warming is a hoax!" became the mantra and rallying cry of this anti-ecological coalition. "Just keep an open mind," one right-wing talker advised his loyal listeners, implying that global warming and climate change remained in dispute.

A long-running propaganda campaign tipped a majority of Americans in the direction of doubt and skepticism, and instilled a sort of indefinite wait-and-see attitude. Someday, the narrative went, we'll know for sure whether human activity affects global climate. Until then, we won't know what laws to pass or what changes to make. Let's not rush into this—it will all work out eventually.

As of this writing, *we have a paralyzing ideological deadlock in the American national conversation.* One tribe—identifying mostly as Democrats—declares global warning and climate change a full-fledged emergency and calls for all-out war. The other tribe—identifying mostly as Republicans—declares the whole issue a tempest in a teapot and sees no need for any major expedition to mitigate it.

These compelling truths explain why the US government has made no significant movement on the ecological agenda. We face a simple prognosis:

> *Whether the US launches a grand effort to slow climate change and take on other big environmental issues in the next few years will depend almost entirely on which political party controls the government.*

A DO-ABLE AGENDA: CAN WE FIND A MIDDLE WAY?

Looking at the current state of play, the national conversation seems to involve two very different prospective courses of action, backed by two factions who don't seem inclined to agree or compromise.

The two scenarios currently present as:

1. *Business as Usual.* A modest assortment of token climate initiatives; a few modest changes in laws and enforcement; and perhaps a reluctant drift in the direction of alternative energy developments. Advocates of the Business as Usual scenario see a major national initiative as unnecessary at best and destructive to the economy at worst.

   One wing of this faction actually favors *reducing* budgets for operations such as the Environmental Protection Agency (EPA) and other government entities responsible for the Commons; eliminating regulations on the use of fossil fuels, CO_2 emissions, water quality, and land use; and expanding territories available for oil drilling, pipeline construction, and forest cutting.

2. *All-Out War.* A full mobilization, equivalent to that of WW2, engaging government, the corporate sector, and the general population in an unprecedented program of conservation; environmental clean-up; and greenhouse gas reduction. The US would rejoin the Paris Agreement, which currently includes almost every other nation on the planet. This agenda would have an extremely ambitious set of goals, generally considered necessary to hold the global temperature rise to 2 degrees C, or less, above pre-industrial levels.

In my estimation, neither of these two scenarios has any chance of success.

Why Business as Usual Won't Work

The Business as Usual course of action, according to virtually all reputable scientists, would probably bring on a kind of anaphylactic shock to the natural environment—an irreversible decline in the status of critical Earth resources. This could include a rise in CO_2 levels beyond the temperature-critical threshold; colossal shifts of water from frozen stocks to oceans and surface deposits, with shoreline water levels rising destructively; irreparable loss of forest cover; melting permafrost; loss of species and habitats critical to human co-survival; desertification of arable lands; more frequent mega-fires; and more frequent weather disasters such as hurricanes, floods, and droughts.

These changes, if they occur—and most reputable climate scientists believe they will, without a massive corrective response—will turn millions of people in marginal economic status into refugees; create food shortages and public health crises; increase political instability in regions that already suffer from too much of it; and stall global economic growth.

Why All-Out War Won't Work Either

The All-Out War course of action, on the other hand, seems like the preferred way to go—indeed, perhaps the only acceptable one, considering the seriousness of the challenges.

However, I believe it has virtually no chance of succeeding.

Over the course of a 30-year career as a business consultant, working with corporations, government organizations, and nonprofits; and observing and advising senior leaders of all stripes, I've seen what bureaucracies can—and can't do. I've seen far more big adventures fail than succeed.

The All-Out War option would involve a scale and degree of complexity unlike anything any national government or international coalition of governments has ever undertaken.

The readiness of the American public for such a venture, as

we've seen, doesn't come anywhere close to the level of acceptance, perceived importance, and sense of urgency necessary to declare the war.

And even before we try to figure out how to coordinate the efforts of dozens of major national governments, plus organizations like the United Nations (which has a ponderous bureaucracy of its own), the US itself has not organized well for the mission. We have a national bureaucracy, often at odds with 50 state bureaucracies. At the federal level, we have a loose assortment of uncoordinated agencies like the Department of the Interior; the Environmental Protection Agency; the Department of Agriculture; and the Department of Energy as well as others, all clinging to their own favorite parts of the elephant.

Put all of those factors together and try to imagine a successful undertaking on a par with, say, the Apollo moon landing. I can't.

Let's Go for a Do-Able Agenda

I imagine some readers may condemn me as a pessimist, a defeatist, or a traitor to the ideals of the environmental movement. I accept that possibility. However, to invoke an ancient figure of speech, I'd prefer to go for half a loaf than end up with no bread at all.

In my view, *we humans and our political leaders won't "win" the climate war.* We've passed that point. We'll have to settle for a draw at best.

We've started too late, we've done too little, and we can't mobilize ourselves to the level required for the extremely ambitious goals of the Paris Agreement. As of this writing, most of our political leaders don't want to do it, and a sizable percentage of our fellow citizens don't even consider it necessary. Technologically, we might have a good shot at it, but we certainly don't have the political will for it. No advocate or activist, however passionate or articulate, can manufacture that political will out of nothing.

Once we face that sobering fact, I believe we can mobilize ourselves for a more realistic agenda—still a major war, for certain—and do our utmost to mitigate the changes already in motion. And who knows—maybe we can build upon the half-a-loaf approach to accomplish a lot more than we might have originally hoped for.

APOLLO II: AMERICA'S NEW BIG IDEA

In Chapter 2 we considered the idea of the Big Idea—some grand new adventure, a big commitment, an urgent shared purpose—as a way to mobilize the energies of an entire society. Americans, and citizens of most cultures, tend to rise to meet the big existential challenges of their times, *if and when their leaders call them to it.*

The great wars, the great Depression of the 1930s, health pandemics, the space race, all have united Americans in some common experience. We've coped with economic hardship. We've coped with the fear of nuclear war. We've coped with shortages and rationing of everyday necessities like food, motor fuel, and raw materials. We've lived through them and we've become stronger for it.

Can Americans make the great adjustment to a radically different relationship with the planet? Can we grasp the urgent need for a rethinking of our entire logistical structure and move to—or at least toward—a sustainable long-term relationship with Mother Earth?

Maybe.

With a strong visionary leader in the White House and a Congress activated by enlightened, informed, and progressive legislative leaders, we might succeed in a grand venture reminiscent of the exciting and engaging race to the moon— the historic Apollo space program.

Apollo II, as we might call it, would have to exceed the size and scope of almost every other great historical undertaking, with the possible exception of WW2. It would involve an economic commitment of several trillion dollars over at least a decade, to have any hope of a significant restructuring of our relationship with the Commons.

LET'S MAKE CONSERVATION THE FIRST GREAT BATTLE

As the first phase of the venture, *a massive conservation effort* could buy us some time to get our act together for the rest of the journey.

As of this writing, I know of no prominent figure in America —a political leader, a commentator, a business leader, a media figure, a celebrity, or a spiritual leader—who strongly and consistently advocates conservation on a grand scale. By any reasonable observation, most Americans don't seem to care how much energy, food, water, or manufactured output they use.

Sure, we give lip service to "doing our part." We recite the little mantras of "reduce, reuse, recycle, and repurpose." We separate our household trash for the sanitation department. And maybe we take our own bags to the grocery store. But on a grand scale, we continue to waste the Earth's resources at a phenomenal pace.

Let's consider a few random examples.

▸ Americans buy 7 billion greeting cards every year—a product with a useful lifetime of about 15 seconds. The US Postal Service delivers about 2 billion of them. We've had electronic greeting cards for years, and yet printed cards remain hugely popular.

▸ Over 20 percent of our GDP goes to buy discretionary products no one really needs: fad fashions, fad foods, high-calorie snack foods, bottled water, gag gifts, and toys that go straight into the closet.

▸ The US Department of Agriculture estimates that about 30-40 percent of America's food production goes to waste. Food waste makes up the largest category of material in municipal landfills. This also wastes land, water, labor, energy, and other resources used in producing, processing, transporting, preparing, storing, and disposing of discarded food. Meanwhile, 20 million Americans and nearly a billion of the Earth's people can't get enough food to maintain basic health.

▸ Government estimates rank the US at eighth place in energy efficiency amongst the 23 top energy consuming countries.

▸ As of this writing, we still get 18 percent of our energy supply from coal, undeniably the dirtiest of all sources.

▸ A casual drive along a typical suburban highway after midnight reveals huge car dealerships and shopping centers with bright lights blazing all night and no one there except the occasional security guard.

▸ Thousands of downtown commercial buildings glow from self-illumination all through the night. Many of them have lights burning all night in empty offices.

▸ Gasoline-powered cars burn about 2 billion gallons of fuel per year sitting at traffic lights or crawling in slow- and-go traffic. Electric cars use almost no energy when they sit or idle.

We have lots of opportunities to save energy, save food, and reduce waste production, right at our fingertips. We can make a number of significant changes starting today. Let's consider a few examples:

▸ As we progress toward sustainable non-fossil fuel energy production, we can significantly reduce our current usage along the way, starting with municipal ordinances that restrict the wanton waste of electricity.

▸ We can make significant cuts in gasoline consumption —and traffic deaths—by reinstating the national highway speed limits that worked so well in the 1970s. When the Organization of Petroleum Exporting Countries (OPEC) cut supply and jacked up prices in 1973 (an act of vengeance aimed at nations that supported Israel in the so-called *Yom Kippur* War) the federal government instituted a nationwide limit of 55 miles per hour. Not only did gasoline consumption drop significantly due to increased fuel efficiency, but traffic accidents and deaths dropped significantly as well. Over the years, waning compliance and lax enforcement eroded the benefits, and Congress repealed the restrictions in 1995. Modern technology can make enforcement much more uniform and less expensive.

▸ The Department of Agriculture has launched an intensive campaign aimed at reducing food waste by 50 percent over the next decade. Programs like this, and others, offer possibilities for immediate action and generally don't suffer from the paralysis that afflicts the Congress.

WE'VE ONLY JUST BEGUN

The wide-ranging discussion of this chapter still falls short of dealing with the full scope of our relationship to the Commons. We haven't dealt with a number of major issues, such as water management; species preservation and habitat protection; disaster management, including pandemics and other public health crises; and the massive deterioration of our aging public infrastructure. I hope, however, that readers who take a special interest in any of those issues will appreciate the limits of space imposed by this form of discourse.

THE FIX-IT LIST: ENVIRONMENT

So, how can we improve this component of our Republic— The Environment? Let's start with these actions.

1. *Let's Launch the "Big Idea" for America: the War on Climate Change.* The President, with the endorsement and cooperation of the Congress, will launch a comprehensive ten-year "Apollo II" environmental recovery program, with an intensive focus on resource conservation of all types; accelerated development of sustainable energy sources; waste reprocessing,

especially for plastics; aggressive enforcement of pollution control measures; and infrastructure modernization. We need to rescue the Commons.

The President will issue an executive order, coordinated with a resolution by Congress, that will return the US to membership in the Paris Agreement for mitigating climate change, rejoining over 190 other countries in a commitment to global action.

The US government will apply political and economic pressure on the governments of major polluting countries such as China, India, Indonesia, and others, and will offer technological and economic assistance to help them make the transition to sustainable energy usage and sustainable waste management practices.

2. *Let's Unify Our Forces for the Assault on the Climate Crisis.* Congress will pass a statute that merges the whole collection of cabinet-level agencies that have bits and pieces of responsibility for the environment into a single Department of the Environment (DOE). The new department will have equal status in the Executive Branch with State, Defense, and Homeland Security.

The component agencies will include the Environmental Protection Agency, as well as the Departments of Interior; Agriculture; Energy; Transportation; Housing and Urban Development; and possibly the Federal Emergency Management Agency (FEMA). Every agency that has a primary mission for dealing with the natural environment or the built environment will become part of the new organization.

The Department of the Environment will have central responsibility for environmental research; policy development; resource management; regulation and enforcement; environmental clean-up and damage mitigation; disaster management; and infrastructure modernization.

The statute will mandate that funding for the DOE will not fall below military expenditures in any year.

3. *Let's Make Conservation a Mega-Priority.* By executive order, the President will launch a nationwide program to encourage—and mandate—intensified conservation practices by individuals, businesses, and local governments. Reminiscent of WW2 practices of allocation (and even rationing in some cases), these practices can reduce the waste of food, electricity, fuel, and other materials, and they can reduce the flow of material to the landfills.

4. *Let's Slow Down, Save Lives, and Cut Pollution.* Congress will pass a statute that limits motor vehicle speeds on all highways to 65 miles per hour. The allocation of highway funds to the states will depend on their diligence in enforcing the standard.

5. *Let's Build an Army of Experts.* The President will issue an executive order, coordinated with a resolution by Congress, that will elevate the discipline of *environmental engineering* to a preferred academic status, with the objective of increasing the number of available environmental engineers within one four-year academic cycle. Federal grants and loans will incentivize students entering college to specialize in environmental technologies.

Chapter 14.
Summary, Recap, and
Final Thoughts

"The problem with not knowing
what you're talking about is that
you never know when you're done."

—Tom Smothers
1960s Folk Singer, Comedian

We've covered a lot of territory in this expedition into the history of our Republic and the 10 key systems that make it work. In this final chapter, we step back, take a breath, and let it soak in.

Along the way, I've tried to paint the big picture—the long-wave patterns that have had the greatest influence on the development of our enterprise. And I've proposed some rather bold changes—big-scale, outside-the-box ideas that can energize and enrich the national conversation.

I hope those who read this book will delve into these possibilities more deeply. You might find one of the 10 key components we've studied especially interesting for you. Or, you might decide to actively support and promote a certain idea, change, or innovation.

For a recap, let's refresh our understanding of the high-level trends and developments that will come upon us over the next couple of decades, and summarize the big, far-reaching changes we need to get working on. And just to keep our brains in the creative mode, I'll throw in a few more suggestions for fixes we could easily make.

The ultimate value and contribution of this book will depend on what you and your fellow readers do with these ideas.

SEVEN BIG TRENDS THAT WILL SHAPE OUR FUTURE

The following trends, while not exhaustive by any means, highlight some of our most significant rising concerns, problems, and opportunities. We need to think about them, talk about them, find ways to adapt to them—and possibly even capitalize on them.

1. *The American Twilight.* America's special standing in the world community has eroded steadily over several decades, and more significantly over the most recent decade. A series of questionable military ventures and a haphazard foreign policy have left many world leaders less than impressed with America's leadership, politics, and institutions. Simultaneously, the developed countries of Europe and Asia have progressed dramatically in economic prosperity, technological capacity, and social stability. Our leaders will find it much more difficult to call the shots in the international arena, and more necessary to accept solutions crafted by mutual interest.

2. *The American Search for Meaning.* The American culture seems to have drifted into a mid-life crisis, so to speak. The national conversation has become ever more strident, polarized, and antagonistic. Conflict seems preferable to consensus. Deadlocked political leaders seem more inclined to divide rather than unite. More and more Americans seem to feel anonymous, alienated, and disconnected from the American story. We seem to have lost the story itself, so to speak. Activists in black communities, feminist

organizations, and other civil liberties advocates increasingly feel that America has not progressed very far, and indeed may have regressed in some ways.

We need leaders who understand our deep need for meaning; understand how powerfully it can energize a new agenda; and can figure out how to make it real. In Chapter 2 we considered the notion of a new "big idea" for America—a common cause, a higher purpose, something to sign up for. In Chapter 13 (Environment), we considered a candidate for a new Big Idea—an "Apollo II" program, so to speak, to tackle the *environmental crisis* in a big way.

3. *The Socio-Economic Meltdown.* Decades of mostly steady economic growth have raised the "average" standard of living in the US—defined as the total GDP divided by the number of people. But this rising prosperity curve has not lifted all boats to the same extent, and indeed has not lifted some of them at all. For most middle-class workers, real wages—adjusted for inflation—have remained flat for three decades.

This wealth gap—the increasing concentration of assets in the hands of a small segment of the population—has aggravated the effects of other socio-economic gaps. Social activists have become ever more vocal about the impact of these disparities on women, people of color, and people in rural and small-town communities, in addition to their impacts on workers in general.

These disparities, and the perceived unfairness of the economic system that perpetuates them, now occupy the attention of activists, media commentators, and elected officials more than ever before. We'll almost certainly see an increasing level of populist energy for leveling the economic playing field, through legislation; activist pressures on corporate executives and boards; and possibly even street-level uprisings.

4. *Digital Everything.* Americans have accepted, mostly with blind enthusiasm, the infiltration of digital information media into virtually all aspects of their daily lives. After a decade or two of rejoicing about the wondrous benefits to society of the digital revolution, we've begun to see—and try to understand—the dark side of this brave new world.

Complex and contentious social issues arise from all directions: violations of individual privacy and the theft of personal data; confiscation of personal identities (a.k.a. identify theft); hacking and theft of business data; misuse of personal data by police and governments; the threat of a surveillance state; news stories manipulated by foreign actors, and in some cases, by recognized news agencies; and tampering with election campaigns by foreign actors, including proxy agents used by foreign governments.

Mental health experts now recognize a new category of disorders, known broadly as *digital addictions.* Its victims become obsessively attached to the experience of online social groups, video gaming, and living out imaginary online personas via social media.

Legislators, government leaders, and law enforcement officials in the US haven't kept up with the rapid development of malicious and criminal digital technologies. Governments of European Union nations have passed stringent laws for privacy protection, and cracked down on monopolistic practices by the powerful social media companies like Google, Facebook, and Twitter. We'll almost certainly see a similar rise in concern—and legal action—in the US.

5. *Weaponizing Information.* In Chapter 2, which set forth the concept of the *national conversation,* I declared that, "We've officially entered the Age of Bullshit." Please forgive this rare use of a somewhat vulgar expression, but I believe that now and then we

need to put things bluntly.

With the mind-boggling tide of provocative information that continuously washes over us and swirls around us—24-hour news coverage; non-stop broadcasting of inflammatory opinion shows; right-wing websites, blogs, and streams of propaganda over channels like Twitter, Instagram, and Facebook; and misleading planted stories—information has become a weapon as well as a resource.

Heads of state, political parties, and candidates play fast and loose with the truth, trying to discredit their opponents. Increasingly, we see a new standard of wanton disregard for the practices of truthful discourse. Fact-checking has become a standard occupation in the news industry. We don't know how this new phenomenon of polluted information will shape the national conversation in the long run; how it will affect the news process and the political process; or how it might affect the ethics and values that Americans have always considered sacred.

6. *Life at a Distance*. Near-universal online access to information means that people spend less time in direct personal contact and more time interacting virtually. Email systems, conferencing platforms, and small-meeting systems keep people in contact, but in a less personal way. The webinar has become a popular medium of education and training.

Online ordering and rapid delivery have restructured the brick-and-mortar retail economy, with a dual-mode pattern of shopping. More and more people order fast food online and pick it up at drive-through windows. Teen-agers tweet to one another from their bedrooms rather than meet at the park or the mall.

The unprecedented nationwide lockdown, made necessary as a part of the fight against the infamous COVID-19 virus, made school and college students familiar with home-study experiences, supported by online study materials and online lectures by their teachers and professors.

Many businesses modified their processes to make the best of at-home workforces, quarantined by the virus. Some of them have found remote working and remote managing more effective than the traditional ways, in some cases. Many will retain some of those changes.

7. *The Environmental Bill Comes Due.* As of this writing, more than a third of Americans, and at least that many of their elected representatives, still don't fully grasp or accept the magnitude of the climate crisis that gets more acute every day. Contrary to ultra-conservative messaging and right-wing propaganda, reputable scientists actually agree—almost unanimously—that human activity causes rising planetary temperatures and problematic changes in climate.

Regardless of which party gains control of the White House and the Congress, however, the bill for our neglect of the Commons will come due sooner or later. The later we recognize it and get serious about it, the more limited we'll find our options for dealing with it.

SEVEN BIG SHIFTS WE NEED TO MAKE

To summarize our Blueprint for a New America in terms of the big-wave changes we can make, let's conjure up the mega-to-do list. Let's consider some "de-'s"—things we need to do less of, or eliminate completely—and some "re-'s"— things we need to return to, preserve, or increase.

THE "DE-'S": LET'S DO LESS OF THESE THINGS

1. *De-bureaucratization.* We desperately need to simplify and streamline the organizational structure of the federal government.

2. *De-fossilization.* We must move as rapidly as possible to reduce, and eventually eliminate, the burning of

fossil fuels (oil, coal, and natural gas), which pour millions of tons of CO_2 into the atmosphere, and replace them with renewable and sustainable forms of energy production.

3. *De-consumerization.* Most Americans can significantly reduce their ecological footprint—the amount of discretionary consumption of the earth's resources—without any great suffering. We can become much more thrifty, and even frugal, in order to reduce CO_2 emissions and reduce the global waste stream. Not every kid needs sneakers with lights on them and not every kitchen needs an electric butter knife.

4. *De-carceration.* Let's stop incarcerating people for non-violent crimes, and use prisons for offenders who pose a threat to public safety. We can repurpose many structures such as closed-down schools, military camps, and other underused properties, as remedial detention centers, which truly provide corrective experiences to non-violent offenders.

5. *De-taxation.* Let's radically reform our system of revenue gathering at the national level, as explained in Chapter 7 (Revenue). We can eliminate all forms of the obsolete income tax, and replace it with a new system that taxes transactions instead of people.

6. *De-urbanization.* Let's create financial incentives and opportunities for more people to migrate out of the densely crowded urban areas, to newly developed small communities. See Chapter 8 (Commerce).

7. *De-conglomeration.* Let's rein in the unlimited, cancerous, anti-competitive growth of US corporations by mergers and acquisitions. We can set limits that prevent companies in any particular sector from acquiring one another if the number of players falls below a certain critical limit.

THE "RE-'S": LET'S DO MORE OF THESE THINGS

1. *Re-immigration.* The US population has gotten steadily older, on average, and it has stopped growing. We'll soon see a relative shortage of people in the working age range, and we'll start running low on taxpayers. We need to mint about 20 million new American citizens over the next decade, mostly young people and children, if we hope to rebalance our population. Instead of demonizing immigrants, as some political figures and activists have, we need to completely overhaul our immigration system to assimilate more young and productive workers and families.

2. *Re-volunteerism.* We can make the US economy phenomenally more productive by tapping into an enormous resource that goes to waste every day: the time and energy of our citizens. We can set up systems, as described in Chapter 9 (Services), to mobilize volunteer labor and put it to productive use.

3. *Re-education.* We need to completely rethink our public education system, and make the transition from trying to teach kids *what* to think—the "container" theory of education—to teaching them *how* to think, how to investigate, how to discover, how to reason, how to think critically, and how to use their creative abilities in all aspects of their lives.

A FEW MORE OFF-THE-WALL IDEAS

Here, I offer a few more ideas that I find interesting, which didn't find a home in any of the key chapters. Please add your own favorites to the list.

1. *Let's Have a New National Anthem.* The venerable "Star Spangled Banner" has served as our national patriotic song for over a century. President Woodrow Wilson declared it so in 1916 by executive order, and Congress eventually formalized it in 1931. Over the past few decades, a growing conversation proposes to

replace it with a more appropriate song, or to have an altogether new anthem composed.

Critics of the original song point out that, 1) most people can't sing it decently, because it goes too high on the musical scale for untrained voices; 2) it tells of a single battle in a long-forgotten war—the British bombardment of Fort McHenry in Baltimore during the War of 1812—rather than peace and progress; and 3) it celebrates a symbol—the flag of the Republic, but not the Republic itself. I suggest we hold a competition for a new anthem. Let's give those overpaid musical celebrities something useful to do.

2. *Let's Run a Boot Camp for Bigwigs—Presidents, Governors, and Mayors.* Many, if not most, of the people who get elected to public offices that involve executive responsibilities—presidents, prime ministers, cabinet members, governors, and mayors—have little or no experience in leadership or management when they step into the jobs. Consequently, they typically have to learn on the job, by trial and error, at the public's expense.

No corporate board of directors would even consider hiring a CEO without some leadership experience. Yet, we as a people seem perfectly willing to choose a public sector executive by means of the emotional beauty contest known as an election, and we let that person take the reins with no preparation at all.

The US government can create a special short-course residential learning center, to give newly elected officials and those already in the job an introduction to the basic principles of leadership and management. The format might include a 2-week period of intensive study in residence, with online follow-up over the next 2 weeks, and a final residence program of 1 week.

Such a program would enable public sector leaders in all kinds of roles and in various cultures to learn from each other, sharing experiences, perspectives, and points of view in highly relevant case studies.

Foreign heads of state, cabinet ministers, provincial governors, and mayors could attend for free, as a contribution of the US to international relations.

The components of such a service already exist. For example, the US Federal Executive Institute (FEI) in Charlottesville, Virginia, has provided leadership training for senior government executives—but not elected leaders, so far—for many years. President Lyndon Johnson got it started, and it has trained thousands of senior civil servants in its flagship program, "Leadership in a Democratic Society."

FEI could easily develop a special program for elected officials. Imagine, for a moment, the impact and benefits of having elected heads of government equipped with the knowledge and skills of professional management, rather than simply bumbling along, trying to figure things out as they go.

3. *Let's Abolish Daylight Saving Time.* It makes little sense for most parts of the world today, including the US. DST advocates started to tout moving the clocks forward during summer well over a century ago, mostly to increase the number of daylight hours available for work. They argued that it would also reduce the consumption of coal by getting people into and out of bed sooner. Germany implemented it in 1916, to save energy during WW1. England and other Europeans copied the practice. The US followed suit in 1918, dividing the country up into 4 time zones.

Critics of the practice claim that setting the clocks back in the fall wastes the energy that setting them ahead saved, as darkness comes on earlier and electricity use goes up. Within the US, two states with very high temperatures during summer, Hawaii and Arizona, don't change their clocks either way.

Residents there say they want *less* sunlight later in the day, not more. Some public health experts claim that switching the clocks twice a year tends to increase traffic accidents and aggravate *seasonal affective disorders* (SAD), which afflict some people when weather and daylight patterns change.

The approach that seems to make the most sense: set all clocks to maximize prime time daylight hours during the summer and leave them there.

4. *Let's Abolish the Penny.* Getting rid of the penny could do two things: 1) save a lot of time, labor, and money in the economy; and 2) test Congress' capacity to do something very simple without making a mess of it.

The venerable penny has outlived its usefulness. A century or two ago, a penny would actually buy something—maybe a loaf of bread or a hunk of cheese. Now pennies just clutter up cash register drawers, waste the time of workers who have to restock them, and take up space in pockets and purses. Workers who do armed cash transport risk back and knee injuries carrying heavy sacks of coins. The US Treasury reports that it costs 1.5 cents to make each penny—about $46 million per year.

Eliminating the penny could actually save millions of labor hours in the economy. Prices would vary by 5 cent intervals, not 1 cent. Every entry in an accounting system would have a zero or a five as its last digit. The biggest benefit could come in reducing the costs of accounting procedures, by saving labor and reducing mistakes. Keying errors would decrease, and clerical workers could easily add figures in their minds.

5. *Let's Phase Out Zoos.* The conventional zoo, with animals in cages and enclosures, seems more and more out of date with each passing year. Eco-activists have long complained about the ethics of capturing animals and confining them, even if their keepers

make their best efforts to care for them and give them medical attention.

Very few zoos make a profit or break even. Even the San Diego Zoo, the biggest and most respected zoo in the US, requires government subsidies and charitable donations to operate. The San Diego Zoological Society, the zoo's operator, cares for some 8,000 animals in over 800 species, and has a reputation as one of the world's leading facilities for preserving endangered species. Over 3 million visitors per year come to see the collection, so it certainly deserves appreciation for contributing to the enjoyment and education of Americans and people from all over the world.

Looking ahead, however, one can make a case for phasing out most zoos, and developing other ways to continue the work of the premier scientific institutions. With the state of the art in virtual reality advancing rapidly, and the enormous amount of audiovisual media available, the visitor to tomorrow's eco-museum or eco-park can experience virtually almost any species or environment on the globe.

Combining the immersive experiences of a zoo, an aquarium, an undersea environment, a rainforest, and even a prehistoric ecosystem, a virtual eco-park could supply much of the tactile experience of the traditional zoo, including sounds and smells; plus the usual fast food, entertainment, and souvenir-buying experience. With creative applications of the technology, such an experience could well surpass the traditional zoo in entertainment value, particularly in cities without zoos, or those with very modest ones.

6. *Let's Combine Libraries and Museums—the "Libraseum."* As with zoos, neither libraries nor museums typically cover their operating costs from admission fees. Chronically underfunded, with the

exception of the largest ones in big metro centers, most of them struggle to attract visitors. Very few have the funds to modernize their visitor experiences with high-tech resources like video programs and virtual reality media.

Both types of institutions have similar purposes and ways of operating. Both essentially provide information and educational experiences in a walk-in environment. Both desperately need modernization, making use of new digital technologies. Merging these operations in a particular city or community could make it economically feasible to turn them into immersive, interactive, entertaining, and educational centers that deliver vastly greater cultural value.

The library part of a facility would still maintain and loan physical books and publications (now that we understand that ebooks won't make real books extinct), but the museum side would no longer have to store and manage its own physical collection.

With virtual displays streaming from central locations, on a subscription basis, any visitor to any libraseum could see a famous artifact from anywhere in the world. One wouldn't have to go to London to see the legendary Rosetta Stone in the British Museum. An immersive, virtual reality experience would make it just as available and just as real to the visitor in any small town.

This application of modern technology can revitalize both libraries and museums. It has the potential of creating a whole new entertainment experience, possibly surpassing the conventional movie theater as it becomes ever more obsolescent.

7. *Both Political Parties Should Adopt New Brands and Symbols.* Neither the Democrats' donkey nor the Republicans' elephant has a particularly distinguished history, and neither seems very inspiring in the

modern American brand culture. In 1828, Andrew Jackson's opponents called him a jackass. Rather than take offense, he rather liked the term and began using an image of the animal on his campaign posters. The association stuck for a long time, but the popular political cartoonist Thomas Nast actually made it the *de facto* symbol of the Democratic Party in the 1870s.

Nast also attached the image of an elephant to the Republican Party, as he used his drawings in newspapers to portray the various political candidates as different species of animals. By the 1880s, other cartoonists and commentators began using his symbols, and they eventually became the permanent mascots for the parties.

It seems like both parties could use a bit of modern brand-building technique, to position themselves better in the minds of the public.

8. *Let's Combine Counties.* As of this writing, the 50 states in the US have a total of 3,143 counties, an average of 62 per state. Texas has the most—254 at last count. Delaware has 3. Hawaii and Rhode Island both have 5.

   The concept of the county, and the name, descend to us from British land practices of medieval times. A *county* refers to a landholding ruled by a count or a countess, under permission from the Crown. A *shire* refers to an administrative subdivision owned and managed by the kingdom. For historical accuracy, we should probably refer to our subdivisions as shires, not counties. By the way, our modern term *sheriff* descends from the old English title of *reeve*, the enforcer of the king's authority over the shire. The term *shire-reeve* got smoothed into sheriff.

   American historical tradition has it that, as the first colonies became states, and as the states spread out over the whole continent, local governments took shape and the county became the preferred model.

Custom prescribed that elected officials should live within a day's ride by horse and carriage from the seat of government. They would leave their farms or homes occasionally, travel to the county seat to vote on necessary matters, and return home, presumably within 3 days. That would explain why Texas, the largest heavily populated state (Alaska holds the record for total square miles), should have so many more counties than tiny Delaware.

As with many other features of our Republic, today's reality doesn't match the ancient reality. Except for Alaska and Texas, one can easily travel the whole length of every state by car in a day. Based on travel time alone, we would need far fewer counties than we have. Texas might get by with 25 instead of 254. California might get by with 10 instead of 58.

Habit, inertia, politics, and bureaucracy have maintained the oversupply of counties for a long time. If we took a fresh new look at the art of local government, we would likely divide states up according to the major concentrations of population, rather than land area. It seems incredibly wasteful to have over 3,000 miniature governments, with boards of supervisors, budgets, taxes, sheriff's departments, jails, water departments, local ordinances, rented buildings, and employees.

A better solution, for example, could use the concept of a *metroplex*—a major population center of 100,000 people or more, as the hub of an extended mega-county. It already has a city government, and it would make sense to combine city and county services into a single more efficient unit. As of this writing, the US has 285 centers with six-figure populations. If we divided states up in this way, and made special arrangements for smaller states that don't have large metro centers, we could probably operate with less than 300 subdivisions, providing all of the governance and services now handled by a multitude of counties.

A BLUEPRINT FOR A NEW AMERICAN?

In Chapter 2 we raised the question, do we Americans deserve the Republic we've inherited? Can we just go on comfortably living in this favored land, and not doing our parts as individuals to make the dream more of a reality? If we hope to make it a better Republic, will we need to become better citizens?

PLATO WARNED US

Plato, the Greek philosopher who taught and wrote about the idea of democracy 2400 years ago, offered a warning to all future generations. Democracy, he said, has one fatal flaw. Its greatest benefit, ironically, always becomes its greatest weakness. He had doubts about whether democracy would survive the centuries as a way of running a society.

The big flaw, he declared, lay in the popular vote. In his day, all of the citizens of Athens would come to the *agora*, a big open space where political leaders, activists, and ordinary citizens could tout their solutions to the republic's problems. When everyone had had his say, they (men only, of course) voted to choose the course of action they liked best.

Over the decades and centuries, as the ancient city-states evolved into big empires, a second phase of governance emerged—*representative democracy*. In a modern republic, the people elect representatives to go to the seat of government and vote on their behalf.

Plato considered all versions of democracy dangerously flawed. Anyone with the ability and the intent, he said, who could charm the citizens and get them aroused—angry, afraid, resentful, jealous, vengeful—could sell them on the most perverse or destructive course of action, including war.

Throughout human history, time has proven Plato mostly right. The Founders of our Republic knew this well, and the old philosopher's warnings haunted their deliberations constantly. Alexander Hamilton, for one, cautioned about too much democracy, in a sense. He and others wanted to limit the voting rights to men of property and social station. He warned about the influence of demagogues who could "inflame the passions of the ignorant mob."

PLATO PAYS US A VISIT

In Chapter 3 (The Commons), we climbed aboard our magic time machine and journeyed back to advise the Founders as they went about building the Constitution for our Republic. For the present discussion, let's imagine that Plato himself pays us a visit. He climbed aboard his own time machine and rocketed forward through two millennia to advise us. How might a conversation with him go?

Possibly, something like this:

K.A.: Welcome, and thank you so much for this honor, and for sharing your perspectives with us. May I call you Plato?

Plato: Thank you for inviting me. Actually, my real name is Aristocles. My friends gave me the nickname of Plato. You can call me Plato.

K.A.: OK, thank you, Plato. May I ask you for your first impression of our American democracy? How do we stack up against your ideal society?

Plato: First of all, congratulations—for lasting this long. Your democracy has endured, through some very tough times. As you know, I've had my doubts about whether democracy and the rule of law could survive the constant attacks of clever demagogues, aspiring dictators, and ignorant citizens.

K.A.: Thank you.

Plato: Second, I congratulate you on building a system of government that allows all citizens, regardless of rank, wealth, or social station, to participate. You've eliminated slavery—something my society hasn't yet accomplished.

You've made women full citizens with full voting rights. And you've done all of that on a scale that includes hundreds of millions of people.

You've also elevated the democratic conversation—which in my day we experience as the physical gathering of citizens at the *agora*—to a vast scale. With your modern "electronic technology," you now have a "virtual agora"—a marketplace of ideas that transcends all physical boundaries, and even transcends time. Information and ideas that, in my time, require days or months to move about, now travel instantly over unlimited distances.

K.A.: Thank you for the kind words and the reassurance. And, what about the other part of the report card—the things we need to do better?

Plato: Of course, you still have much to do. You have a democracy, but you don't have equality of opportunity. In an ideal democracy, each person can strive toward his or her own personal aspirations, within the same rules. Unfortunately, the fruits of your democracy don't always come to all in equal measure. The rules don't always apply to everyone in the same way.

You have a multi-cultural society, but the members of some groups don't enjoy the same benefits and opportunities as others. A few of your citizens enjoy vast wealth while many, many others struggle to survive.

K.A.: So, what do we do? How can we solve these problems and have a Republic that benefits everyone?

Plato: First, you must make the rules apply fairly and equally to everyone. Beginning with the laws, and considering the systems and practices of governments at all levels, you must strive for fairness and equal treatment for all people, in all ways. Commerce, public services, law and order, civil liberties—all the domains of a successful republic—must treat people equally. Only then can they truly strive and compete for the lives they want to lead.

K.A.: Yes, indeed. That remains a pressing problem for all of American society. What else?

Plato: Second, you must educate your citizens for a much higher standard of democratic thinking and action. You haven't solved the fundamental problem of democracy that I write and teach about every day—the problem of *human ignorance*, and the vulnerability of ignorant people to manipulation by demagogues and aspiring dictators.

Your educational systems and practices fall far short of producing enlightened, thoughtful citizens worthy of participating in a modern democracy, especially for the difficult times you will surely face in the coming decades. Most of what your educators think of as teaching amounts to little more than the mindless, ritualistic pursuit of useless information.

An *intellectual underclass* has formed over these many years, consisting of people whose educational experiences haven't prepared them for their roles as citizens. Your scientists—*psychologists*, I believe you call them—identify a rather large number of your citizens as "willfully ignorant," stubbornly and emotionally attached to a biased and misinformed view of society, and unable to reconsider their beliefs.

I want you to make a serious commitment to revolutionizing the entire experience of citizen education. You must begin teaching people *how to think*, not merely what to think. You must teach all citizens, from birth and early schooling, to think democratically.

K.A.: What should we do about racial prejudice? Ethnic conflict? Intolerance? Persecution of minorities? We seem to have become more and more polarized between the complacent white majority and various minorities.

Plato: You haven't solved those problems because you haven't understood them.

K.A.: Explain, please?

Plato: You've named the problem "white supremacy." You would better have conceived of it as *male supremacy*. The male biological propensity for violence, conquest, and dominance energizes *all* of your racial, ethnic, social, political, religious, and generational conflicts—*all of them*.

We haven't solved it in my society. The Romans certainly didn't. Nor have the Europeans, the Latin Americans, or the Asians. America could become the first society to find real peace through equality between men and women—a true "partnership" society.

K.A.: But how? That seems very difficult.

Plato: Education and enlightened leadership. With the right leaders—people with intelligence, strength of character, humanitarian values, and the determination to reshape the society—more and more males will understand the prospect and value of true partnership, in place of dominant relationships based on coercive power.

In your modern, civilized, technological world, physical strength and fighting ability no longer count for much, except when needed by soldiers. Males and females have the same mental capacities; the same willingness to work and strive; and the same desire to see the whole society succeed. Building a true partnership society might take you fifty years; or a hundred; or ten. Why not get started?

K.A.: Thank you, thank you indeed. Any final thoughts?

Plato: Yes. I want to see your elected leaders strive to bring people together, not set them against one another. Too many of your political leaders promote disharmony, resentment, jealousy, and animosity between groups of people as the instruments of power.

Now, more than ever in the history of your Republic, you need to create a *spirit of community*, within your society and reaching out to all societies of the wider world.

Your "national conversation," as you call it, has become noisy, strident, antagonistic, rude, and dishonest. Most of your citizens spend far more of their time entertaining themselves, and one another, than they spend on educating themselves.

K.A.: So, what of our future? How do you see our prospects?

Plato: A thousand years from now—or even a hundred—will some enterprise known as America still exist? Will your descendants look back on these times and admire your leaders for what they've done?

You and your fellow Americans now stand at a momentous turning point in history. Will your democracy survive and thrive?

The answer to that question, my friend, and the fate of America, lies in your hands.

K.A.: Thank you so much, Plato. We appreciate your perspectives, and your wise advice and guidance.

Plato: You're welcome, and good luck. I may check in with you again in a hundred years or so.

WHAT YOU CAN DO FOR YOUR COUNTRY

Lets replay President John F. Kennedy's 1961 inaugural speech, in which he famously challenged Americans,

"And so, my fellow Americans, ask not what your country can do for you; ask what you can do for your country."

What, indeed, can we do, as individual citizens—owners and custodians of the world's most admired republic, to become worthy of our inheritance? Let's start with a few basics:

1. *Learn your history*—the history of your country and its culture, and the history of your own heritage.

2. *Join the national conversation.* Talk with friends and acquaintances about the big issues of the day and

about the unfolding news stories.

3. *Get your news from more than one source.* Keep your crap detector turned on and tuned up; learn to separate facts and evidence from opinions and spin.

4. *Don't join any political party.* If you belong to one, resign from it. Think for yourself, not as some ideological meta-mob wants you to think.

5. *Hold fewer opinions and have more questions.* Know your own biases. Form your conclusions and judgments thoughtfully and sparingly, and keep your opinions on probation. You don't have to have a firm "position" on every question. You can suspend judgment on any issue and learn more about it. You have the right to change your mind.

6. *Practice the art of intelligent, thoughtful, and civil conversation.* Show respect for the ideas, views, and values of others. You don't have to make every conversation into a win-lose battle of wits. Talk less and listen more—we don't learn much while talking, and even less when we shout.

7. *Model, demonstrate, and teach these principles* to your friends, your associates, and your children. Help others adopt the practices of enlightened democratic thinking.

ONE FINAL THOUGHT

We'll get the Republic we deserve. Will we deserve the Republic we want?

Chapter Notes

1. Postman, Neil. *Amusing Ourselves to Death: Public Discourse in the Age of Show Business.* New York: Random House, 1985.

2. Historians debate the actual language of the speech given by Chief Seattle in January of 1854.

3. Smith, Adam. *An Inquiry into the Nature and Causes of the Wealth of Nations.* London: W. Strahan and T. Cadell, 1776.

4. Lecture by Bill Moyers at Boston University on October 29, 2010, "Welcome to the Plutocracy." Visit BillMoyers.com.

5. Union of Concerned Scientists: https://www.ucsusa.org/nuclear-weapons/worldwide

6. Stockholm International Peace Research Institute; https://sipri.org

7. "Global arms trade is a $3 trillion business." CNBC website. https://www.cnbc.com/2020/02/04/global-military-expenditure-and-arms-trade-report.html

8. International Campaign to Ban Landmines (ICBL): https://icbl.org

9. "Incarceration in the United States." https://en.wikipedia.org/wiki/Incarceration_in_the_United_States

10. ibid: graph of incarcerated populations, 1920-2014.

11. Figures compiled from various official sources.

12. *The American Journal of Medicine*, Vol 126, No 10, October 2013.

13. "The top 26 billionaires own $1.4 trillion" CNN website. https://www.cnn.com/2019/01/20/business/oxfam-billionaires-davos/index.html

14. "These 91 Companies Paid No Federal Taxes in 2018". https://www.cnbc.com/2019/12/16/these-91-fortune-500-companies-didnt-pay-federal-taxes-in-2018.html

15. "IRS releases new Tax Gap estimates." IRS website. https://www.irs.gov/newsroom/

16. These Are America's Top 10 Largest Companies by Revenue." CEOWorld Magazine, July 26, 2019. https://ceoworld.biz/2019/07/26/these-are-americas-top-10-largest-companies-by-revenue-2019/

17. "Ten Facts About Homelessness," Huffington Post, Dec 6, 2017. https://www.huffpost.com/entry/ten-facts-about-homelessn_b_5977946

18. National Center for Educational Statistics. https://nces.ed.gov/

19. Postman, Neil and Charles Weingartner. *Teaching as a Subversive Activity*. New York: Random House 1971.

20. Compilation of findings from various surveys.

21. American Association of Community Colleges. https://www.aacc.nche.edu/

22. The population pyramid charts used here come from a useful website, populationpyramid.net. Used with permission, Creative Commons licensing.

23. "How Americans see climate change and the environment." Pew Research Institute website. https://.pewresearch.org/fact-tank/2020/04/21/how-americans-see-climate-change-and-the-environment-in-7-charts/

24. "Scientific consensus on climate change." Wikipedia website. https://en.wikipedia.org/wiki/Scientific_consensus_on_climate_change

25. "Climate Change in the American Mind." Yale University. https://climatecommunication.yale.edu/publications/climate-change-in-the-american-mind-april-2020/

26. Gore, Al. *Earth in the Balance*. New York: Earthscan, 1992.

INDEX